STUDIA
POETICA

Poetry in Exile

Czech Poets during the Cold War and the Western Poetic Tradition

JOSEF HRDLIČKA

UNIVERZITA KARLOVA
NAKLADATELSTVÍ KAROLINUM
PRAHA 2020

This publication has been published with the financial support of the grant provided by The Czech Science Foundation, no. 16-00522S, entitled "Poetry in Exile", implemented at the Faculty of Arts of Charles University.

KAROLINUM PRESS is a publishing department of Charles University
Ovocný trh 5/560, 116 36 Prague 1, Czech Republic
www.karolinum.cz

Designed by Filip Blažek (designiq)
Set and printed in the Czech Republic by Karolinum Press
First English edition

Cataloging-in-Publication Data is available from the National Library of the Czech Republic

ISBN 978-80-246-4657-2 (pb)
ISBN 978-80-246-4660-2 (epub)
ISBN 978-80-246-4659-6 (mobi)
ISBN 978-80-246-4658-9 (pdf)

Content

Introduction

This book came into being over several years, during which time I clarified my view of the questions and issues that stood at its inception. These stemmed from two main areas. One was the study of lyrical poetry and the regular lectures I was giving on this topic to comparative literature students at the Charles University Faculty of Arts. From there stemmed questions regarding the writing of poetry outside the boundaries of a linguistic and cultural community. Exile, or so I believed, represents or may represent a context in which the fundamental and not always thematized prerequisites of a poem – especially its linguistic and cultural framework – are disrupted. I have tried to formulate these points in more detail in the opening chapter.

The second area of my interest was the poetry of Czech Exiles after 1948. It has not been thoroughly researched to this day, and no one had in any structured way posed the question how exile influenced the works of numerous Czech poets. Between 1948 and 1989, dozens of Czech writers published their poems abroad. To take just three anthologies *Neviditelný domov* [Invisible Home, 1954], *Čas stavění* [Time for Building, 1956] and *Almanach české zahraniční poezie 1979* [Almanac of Czech Poetry Abroad], these cover the poems of some sixty authors, with many others left out, for various reasons. It has to be said that the poems are often not of exceptional value, which makes exile poetry no different from 'home grown' poetry, but this fact is in a sense more noticeable within the body of works produced purely in exile. In any case, a number of interesting poets appear in the broad field of Czech exile poetry, some of whom have made a substantial contribution to the overall picture of Czech poetry in their time. Regardless of how these poets might be rated, they can be examined together, from the perspective of issues raised by the specificity of exile. This aspect was well captured by Milada Součková, when in a 1956 letter she mentioned Ovid and compared him to the poets of an anthology she herself had contributed to:

'He differs from the fifteen poets of the *Invisible Home* in that his is poetry writ large. But what he felt was identical, and there are a myriad parallels.'[1] We may with some justification doubt that Ovid actually expressed what he felt in his writing, as pointed out by a number of studies; his are rather rhetorical stratagems, which makes the alleged authenticity of his feelings highly questionable. After all, this notion also occurred to Součková herself. Yet the parallels do remain, even as regards the stratagems, albeit they need to be approached in the full recognition of historically quite distinct situations, both political and poetic.

A significant impetus, if not indeed the one that set my whole thought process in motion, was the study by Jean Starobinski, *Mémoire de Troie* [Memory of Troy]. In it he points out the significant motive force in the exile literature of European or Western culture, namely its close link to tradition. I have tried to develop Starobinski's ideas more specifically in my second chapter, *Shaded by Reminiscence*.

Czech exile poetry provides good material to test whether the theoretical questions we started from make any sense at all, and what answers to them individual poems do provide. The concept of exile in Western culture has since the 19th and up to the 21st century covered a broad range of meanings from expulsion to travels abroad, touching on various forms of exile as driven by geopolitical conditions, so it is not realistic to write one definitive book on poetry in exile, and cover particular poems in depth, yet keep the material and conceptual apparatus sufficiently coherent. In this respect, of course, any narrowly defined area of interest also brings its own limitations. In the case of this book, the boundaries are set by the political situation of the period discussed, as well as by how far prior traditions in Czech literature impinge. Boundaries also provide an opportunity to articulate with more exactitude what lies beyond them and to describe more precisely what the given material owes to its historical constellation, and where it retains a more general reach.

Nevertheless, this book is not primarily a historical study and certainly does not try to exhaustively map Czech poetry in exile during the Cold War. There are many poets I have only touched on, given too brief a mention of, or even completely neglected, although they ought to have their place in a chapter contiguously relating to Czech poetry: they include, among others – Antonín

---

1   M. Součková: *Élenty*, p. 199, letter dated 20 January 1956 to Olga and Ladislav Radimský.

Brousek, Karel Brušák, Vladimíra Čerepková, Viktor Fischl, Tomáš Frýbert, Jiří Gruša, Ivan Jelínek, Jan Křesadlo, František Listopad, Milan Nápravník, Rio Preisner (also as an exile theorist), Jiří Volf, whose fate is little known, and more. My intention, which stems from the aforementioned starting points, was to describe the poetics of selected authors, and above all to try to articulate some more general conclusions about poetry in exile conditions.

The opening chapter sets out the vast scope in which exile can be talked about and tries to capture the relationship between exile and poetry. I find it important to consider, on the one hand, exile *de facto*, for which Ovid's elegies can serve as the model, and exile in the absolute sense, the idea that one is exiled by the very life one leads – in modern poetry, this pole is represented by Baudelaire's poem *Le Cygne* [The Swan]. Such polarity does not preclude the two poles being connected, or there being a range of positions between them. One significant element is also the relationship to the prior tradition of exile, which affects the given poetry in different ways. The other three chapters are devoted to comparative studies of topics cardinal to exile, at least as seen from the perspective of this book: the question of Exiles whose fate fades from memory; exile as sheltering and exile associated with the concept of Arcadia and, more generally, the idealized realm of poetry. In that section, prose could not be overlooked. The reason is obvious: exile in the Western world is intrinsically about narrative. I briefly come back to this question, and distinctions between exile poetry and storytelling, in the final chapter.

The second part of the book is devoted to Czech poetry. In the first chapter of this part I deal with the *Invisible Home* anthology, the flagship book about Czech exile in the 1950s. That is followed by three chapters focusing on the work of selected poets: Ivan Blatný, Milada Součková and Ivan Diviš. The last two chapters briefly discuss topics that are on the verges of exile in the narrower sense and point to a clear easing and a shift of emphasis at the end of the Cold War.

For foreign-language poems, and with very few exceptions, I have referenced the original and sometimes its Czech translation, and also present the original for selected prose and theoretical texts. Where no other translator is mentioned, the excerpt translations are by Václav Z J Pinkava, apart from Chapter 3, previously translated by Matthew Sweney.

At this point I would like to thank those who have helped me with advice and assistance. First and foremost, Justin Quinn, with whom I've had the opportunity to discuss the book as I went along and who encouraged me in a new direction many times. Furthermore, Michael Alexa, Peter Demetz, Lukáš Klimeš, Petr Král, Caroline Lederer, Benoît Meunier, Zuzana Nagy, Kristián Suda, Jan Šulc, Antonín Petruželka, Václav Z J Pinkava, Martin Pšenička, Robert Pynsent, Jan Rubeš, Vladimír Svoboda, Matthew Sweney and Jaromír Typlt. Last but not least, Anne Hultsch for numerous comments on the text, Klára Soukupová for many apt remarks and Adéla Petruželková for thoroughly editing the whole book.

My work has been supported by funding from several institutions acknowledged in the opening part of the bibliography. I thank the The Czech Science Foundation (GAČR) for supporting my work on this book.

Some parts of the book were published before it came out as a whole, in all such cases I edited and supplemented the texts for the book publication itself.

The second chapter has been published in French:

À l'ombre du souvenir. Exil, littérature et exclusion du souvenir, *Revue de littérature comparée* 92, no. 1 (2018), pp. 3–17, transl. Benoît Meunier.

The third chapter has been published in earlier form as:

Exile and Shelter in the Work of Egon Hostovský, Vilém Flusser and Ivan Blatný, *Central Europe* (2020), DOI: 10.1080/14790963.2020.1758448, translated by Matthew Sweney.

Parts of the tenth chapter, here substantially reworked, were published as follows:

Emigracja i nomadyzm w czeskiej kulturze XX wieku. In Kiklewicz, Aleksander, Dudziak, Arkadiusz (ed.), *Nomadyzm i nomadologia: rozważania i analizy*. Olsztyn: Centrum Badań Europy Wschodniej, 2018, pp. 113–126, transl. Michael Alexa.

Jazyky v poezii exilu, *Svět literatury* 29, no. 60 (2019), pp. 55–63.

Josef Hrdlička

1. Poetry and Exile

Qui sait encore le lieu de ma naissance ?
Who only knows where I was born?
Saint-John Perse

Does it make sense to define exile poetry as other than just poems written in exile, but otherwise in principle indistinguishable from those written 'back home'? Is there such a thing as exile poetry, or is there no reason to contemplate a category of that kind? The question is often set within the more general framework of exile literature, and a fairly recent summary notes that *"key questions like the difference between exile literature and literature written in exile remain unsolved. Conferences and compendia aimed at defining an aesthetic of exile do not, as a rule, get beyond discussing whether the question is even valid."*[1] Indeed, is the combination of the two concepts – exile and literature, inappropriate, as Marek Pytasz suggests: 'they come from different areas, so we can find them a common denominator in the sociology of literature, in the description of literary life and literary culture, but struggle to do so in the inherent poetics'[2]; or is the experience of exile so exceptional that it is also reflected in the poetics? Underlying such questions seem to be the often varied concepts of exile and home, but also the antithesis between a non-exiled and an exiled author or poet, the first of which is supposed to represent a kind of normative state, while the latter is in a situation both extraordinary and likely to affect their work. If we stay with poetry, is such an influence so significant and can it manifest itself in poems in such a way that it makes sense to talk about exile poetry? On the

---

1   A. Stephan: Introduction, pp. 9–10.
2   M. Pytasz: *Wygnanie, emigracja, diaspora*, p. 17.

other hand, wouldn't it be excessive to say that all poetry written in exile is 'exile poetry' in more than its external-origin sense? Or ultimately – isn't exile, with all the word's meanings, just one of the many themes that have attracted poets and readers? And is exile really some strange, symptomatic situation?

We can find arguments for, and against. In 1953, the publisher, poet and organizer of the post-February[3] exodus to exile, Robert Vlach, wrote to Věra Stárková, best known for her essays in exile magazines:

> Of course, you're not some 'poet of exile', and, I beg to ask, whyever should you be? Why should all poets in exile be exile-poets? Life isn't just about exile. Besides, the wind is turning, Exiles are settling down, regrets fade, and soon the exile-poet will become a pilgrimage curiosity ... Don't even think about aiming for some kind of exile poetics! Be sure to stay true to yourself! There's no need to shy away from one's public, but you cannot chase after it. If you tried to write poetry about 28 October or 7 March or some such, that would be a truly unforgivable lapse – given who you are.[4]

Robert Vlach does, of course, see the poet at one with her life, assumes that her poems express her life or are significantly connected, but at the same time he says that exile is not a situation exceptional enough to completely drive one's life, and one's poetry far less so. Another Czech poet, Karel Zlín, writes in a poem ensemble called *Listy z exilu* [Letters from Exile] dated 1977:

> Zde září květy mimózy. Říkám: zde. Ale kde je to Zde?
> Vždyť mluvím-li rodnou řečí na tomto místě,
> jsem vlastně nepřítomen.
> A tedy nepřítomen Zde i Tam,
> píši svým blízkým.

---

3   The 1948 Czechoslovak coup d'état.

4   The letter is in safekeeping with the estate of Věra Stárková in the Literary Archive of the Museum of Czech Literature (PNP) and part of the typewritten ensemble *Setkání* [Meeting].

Here the mimosa flowers beam. I say: here. But where is this Here?
Why, if I speak my native tongue in this place,
I absent myself from it.
And thus, absent Here and There,
I write to my loved ones.[5]

In this poem, by contrast, exile appears to be a substantial formative element of the poem's speaker – the exiled person is torn away from their language, which fundamentally changes their relationship to the place, as if their very existence was diminished and split by their dislocation. Similar motifs of an existence diminished (even until death) by exile, and the duality of the situational relationship are seen in Ovid's work, referenced by the name of Zlín's poetic cycle. But that takes us onto the field of poetics. Both poets create a certain type of speaker, whom we might call the 'exiled subject', who is expressive in this odd situation, speaking elsewhere (not being at home) and from abroad (writing letters), with their self-identity split between *here* and *there*, while also enabled to speak differently. The question of speech and the speaker or subject tends to be one of the fundamental elements by which poetry is defined in the modern era.

There can be no doubt about the influence of exile on poetics and their interrelationship, but it is certainly not a clear and simple matter, from either side. *Exile* and related phenomena and terms take on different forms and meanings at different times; and *poetry*, inasmuch as it relates to exile, is not just about portraying the harsh conditions of exile, but giving a particular notion of exile some poetic treatment. If we seek to contemplate poetry and exile, we need to consider the notions of exile that poetry portrays and poets work with, without needing to be true Exiles themselves.

I

The word exile appears in many treatises as more or less representing or summarizing a number of similar or related terms, such as banishment, emigration, displacement, exclusion, migration etc, as well as loneliness, withdrawal or

---

5   K. Zlín: *Poesie*, p. 105.

'internal emigration', diaspora and colonization, which have different meanings, and most notably are often associated with very different social and historical contexts. Yet it is not uncommon to see a word being used in such an encompassing or paraphrasal way. To take an example, we find just such an aggregate concept of exile in Paul Tabori's *The Anatomy of Exile*. In the introduction he defines it as follows:

> The dictionaries define exile as forced separation from one's native country, expulsion from home or the state of being expelled, banishment; sometimes voluntary separation from one's native country. The state of banishment can also be one of devastation or alienation. Enforced removal from one's native land, according to an edict or sentence, penal expatriation or banishment, is another version.[6]

He then lists a whole range of synonyms that characterize historically, politically and geographically distinct manifestations of exile. Sara Forsdyke gives a working definition of exile as follows:

> Exile in the broadest terms can denote any separation from a community to which an individual or group formerly belonged. Exile in the strictest sense involves a physical separation from the place where one previously lived. In the modern era, however, we know of many cases of what is called 'internal exile', in which an individual or group is removed from the immediate surroundings but not expelled from the country altogether.[7]

This internal exile, let us add, can also in some of its forms manifest as a voluntary withdrawal from social or political life, without involving any geographical dislocation.[8] Most texts about exile focus on a certain historical period or a specific aspect of the issues, but we do also find attempts at a summarizing

---

6   P. Tabori: *The Anatomy of Exile*, p. 23.
7   S. Forsdyke: *Exile, Ostracism, and Democracy*, p. 7.
8   On the concept of internal emigration cf. E. Doblhofer: *Exil und Emigration*, pp. 221–241; R. Preisner: Na obranu německé „vnitřní emigrace" v letech 1933–45.

approach or at least a broader perspective.[9] The various forms of exile, migration or exclusion are undoubtedly significantly different, but when Paul Tabori
was working on his book and asking various Exiles for their views, he also
noted a generalizing, albeit personally involved attitude, which has its reasons:

> I do not consider it a happy solution to contrast the definition of the
> exile with refugee, emigrant, etc. – and for purely practical reasons.
> Of course, you can only include people who left because of the con-
> ditions dominating their countries – but these can be transpositional.
> That is, political, economic, or religious corruption or backwardness
> affect intellectuals far sooner than others. Moholy-Nagy, Vásárhelyi
> (Vasarely), for instance, did not leave Hungary because of an explicit
> political persecution – it was the country's backwardness, the Phi-
> listinism of the ruling classes that motivated them – and it was from
> this situation that the religious and political persecution to which you
> refer, developed. In other words: I would keep the "exile" expression,
> but would broaden its definition so that everybody could be included
> of whom one must speak in such a book.[10]

The rather simplistic attempt to regard exile in the broadest possible terms is,
not only here, clearly politically motivated: to be mentioned in a publication
about exile means not only some form of recognition, it is also to take one's place
in collective memory and history, in that sense also mitigating one's exclusion.
In poetry, this regard for collective memory manifests itself in a similar way.
Even in the earliest written documents on exile we find testimony mingling
with fiction and myth, and there comes a point when the expelled, the refugees
or Exiles tend to reference or liken themselves to their predecessors, as links
in one chain of history, irrespective of how their standing, legal status or political situations differ. In the Middle Ages, one of the paradigmatic examples is
Ovid,[11] who in his turn compares himself to legendary archetypes, especially to

---

9   The aforementioned book by Tabori; M. Tucker: *Literary Exile* seeks to sum up 20th century
    literary exile; J. Simpson: *The Oxford Book of Exile* presents an anthology of testimonies and
    documents about exile, categorized by selected exile aspects.
10 P. Tabori: *The Anatomy of Exile*, p. 35.
11 cf. R. Hexter: *Ovid and the Medieval Exilic Imaginary*; T. Ehlen: *Bilder des Exils*.

Odysseus, but also to Aeneas.[12] Of course, the intertextuality of exile does not confine itself to precise categories, and connects Ovid with say, John of Patmos, not distinguishing the historical context and overlooking the incomparability of Ovid's *relegatio* with political exile in the times of nation states. Even in modern times, Charles Baudelaire presents a complex catalogue of Exiles in his *Swan* poem and connects them with his own person and experience of exile in his own city, Paris.

Documents about different types of expulsion and exclusion date right back to the earliest days and are probably found in most cultures.[13] Paul Tabori cites examples of exile in primitive societies, but also exclusion in the animal world.[14] In ancient documents, the underlying mythical lore is important, and different forms of displacement are at the core of key legends: consider the tale of Odysseus, the numerous tragic heroes Oedipus, Iphigenia, Orestes and others. Sargon (2340–2284 BC), thought to be the founder of the Akkadian dynasty, arrived in a basket down the Euphrates, according to legend.[15] Likewise, the legendary founders of many Greek municipalities were Exiles or migrants; a similar story relates to the founding of Rome; and last but not least the Czech legend of the founding of the state features a migrant-founder (and colonizer). The counterpart of these Greek myths is the Old Testament story of the expulsion of mankind from Paradise, which, along with the legacy of antiquity has fundamentally influenced Western culture since the very beginning of Christianity. Although there was nothing uncommon about exile in antiquity, it was still seen as a mishap, along with other possible misfortunes,[16] while the myth of the fall of man serves-up expulsion as the all-encompassing prerequisite of the human condition.

One of the oldest known written documents about exile goes back to ancient Egypt. The story of Sinuhe dates from around 2000 BC.[17] Contemporary Egyptology regards the story as fiction, albeit earlier authors and more broadly

12   cf. M. McGowan: *Ovid in Exile*, pp. 176–194 for Odysseus; J. Starobinski: *La nuit de Troie*, pp. 307–311 for Aeneas.
13   cf. e.g. P. Tabori: *The Anatomy of Exile*; J. Simpson: *The Oxford Book of Exile*; S. Forsdyke: *Exile, Ostracism, and Democracy*.
14   P. Tabori: *The Anatomy of Exile*, pp. 39–40.
15   see J. F. Gaertner: The Discourse of Displacement, p. 7.
16   E. Bowie: Early Expatriates, p. 50.
17   English translation and comment: M. Bárta: *Sinuhe, the Bible, and the Patriarchs*.

conceived works about exile looked upon it as a genuine autobiographical account.[18] In any case, Sinuhe illustrates the phenomenon of exile, and even in this early text we find the notion of self-identity broken by leaving one's homeland:

> My house is beautiful, and my dwelling is spacious.
> My thoughts, however, are in the palace.
> You god, who have ordained this flight for me,
> have mercy!
> Bring me back home!
> Surely, you will let me see the place
> where my heart dwells!
> For what is more important than to bury my body
> in the land where I was born?[19]

Since the archaic period in ancient Greece we find records of specific persons in exile, among them poets, orators, and politicians: Alcaeus, Xenophanes, Cicero, Ovid, Seneca. As a feature of its time, such exile is not to be regarded as anything exceptional, however, but a common aspect of political practice, a way in which the ruling party removed its political opponents: *"the earliest known Athenian law, the anti-tyranny law dating to the seventh century, enjoined all Athenians to expel the tyrant from the community."*[20] *"Expulsion from their cities,"* writes Benjamin Gray, *"was a perennial risk for citizens of Greek poleis, from the Archaic period to Late Antiquity. This could occur in many different ways, of different frequencies in different periods. Citizens could be sentenced to formal exile by a court; forced to flee their city [...] to avoid condemnation by a court or political persecution; driven out during civil war [...]; or expelled from their city by an exter-*

---

18   cf. M. Bárta: ibid., pp. 9–10. Sinuhe's story is considered authentic by P. Tabori (*The Anatomy of Exile*, p. 43ff.), in whose book one entire chapter is called Sinuhe's legacy, which strengthens the legitimacy of exile in the political subtext of the publication; or the first Czech translator František Lexa, who refers to the text as an autobiography (*Beletristická literatura staroegyptská*, pp. 111–112), translating it as Sinuhe's own biography and argues against the view that it is a 'made-up story', while regarding the tale as 'an account of actual events' (*Výbor ze starší literatury egyptské*, p. 272).

19   M. Bárta: *Sinuhe, the Bible, and the Patriarchs*, p. 20 (B, 155–160).

20   S. Forsdyke: *Exile, Ostracism, and Democracy*, p. 6.

nal invader [...]. *In each case, exile entailed loss of security and status, devastating for those affected."*[21]

Greek poets of archaic and classical times bring to their rendition of exile the significant impulse of their personal history, as opposed to epic legend and myth, though this may be stylized or partly fictional. Some of them (Solon, Theognis) illustrate the adverse or undesirable circumstances they have met with through references to exile. Others speak directly about their experience (Xenophanes, Alcaeus). For poets of the archaic era, exile is not a cardinal theme, given the audience of the symposia where their poems were aired were not interested in the exile topic as such.[22] Nevertheless these poets do cover some notable themes that are seen again in subsequent literary tradition. Solon speaks of forgetting his own language abroad:

> Into our home, Athens, founded by the gods,
> I brought back many sold unlawfully as slaves,
> and throngs of debtors harried into exile,
> drifting about so long in foreign lands
> they could no longer use our Attic tongue;[23]

Theognis also covers themes of homesickness, loneliness, but also changes of identity in exile:

> Never befriend an Exile for the sake of his prospects, Cyrnus:
> > for when he
> goes home he is no longer the same man.[24]

Rome gives the topic of exile the differing topographical framework of a centralized empire, compared to the numerous Greek municipalities interconnected through diverse relationships. Exile from Rome means being forced to stay in some particular part of the empire, sometimes closer to the centre, at other times on the verge of it, yet all the while the exiled person is still tied

---

21   B. Gray: *Stasis and Stability*, p. 3.
22   cf. E. Bowie: *Early Expatriates*, p. 21, 43.
23   *Ancient Greek lyrics*, p. 85.
24   *Greek Elegiac Poetry*, p. 223.

to the centre.[25] When it comes to exile, we need to consider three authors in particular: Cicero, Ovid and Seneca. Cicero takes a view subsequently compared to the term 'internal emigration' (*innere Emigration*), coined during the Nazi Third Reich to characterize the attitudes of some intellectuals.[26] The distinctive figure here is Ovid, whose themes follow up Cicero and earlier Greek authors,[27] though he writes about his exile to an unprecedented extent; above all, his *letters* sent to distant Rome, which also formalize the theme of separation. Ovid's elegies have become a touchstone for later exiled poets, moreover his exile is, in the main, a literary matter – there is no corroborating contemporary evidence that Ovid was sent into exile, except for what we know through his poems.[28]

Plato's *Republic* opens an important chapter on poets and exile. Plato views the topic from the perspective of a community that rids itself of poets, seeing them as undesirables. According to Plato, good poets can dramatize all sorts of love experiences, angers or desires, thereby upsetting the social order that philosophers are there to instil, hence it is reasonable and fully justified for poets to be expelled from the community.[29] According to Eric Havelock, this dispute between poets and philosophers leads to a shift in accepted norms. With the coming of the written word, bards, who represented collective memory in a society reliant on oral tradition, lose their privileged role.[30] There are several important points here for our purposes: the poet has traditionally enjoyed respect, drawing on divine inspiration. Once a society comes to be soberly and methodically administered, the poet represents an irrational element, which the rational state seeks to expel beyond its borders. Plato thus brings to mind the eccentricity of a poet who expounds on matters of import to the community,

---

25   cf. S. Goldhill: Whose Antiquity?, pp. 16–17.
26   see footnote 9 above.
27   cf. J. F. Gaertner: *The Discourse of Displacement*, p. 14.
28   In extremis, this leads to the hypothesis that Ovid was not in exile, that his elegies from exile are pure fantasy. This view is not generally held, but it is demonstrable that few of his exile poems reflect historical reality. For a detailed discussion of the issue, see: G. Williams: *Banished Voices*, pp. 3–8.
29   Plato: *Republic*, 606d–607d, 398a; cf. R. Barfield: *Ancient Quarrel*, p. 13.
30   cf. E. Havelock: *Preface to Plato*, inter alia p. 12ff., 305.

while at the same time flouting its norms.[31] A poet is useful for eulogizing the ruler, but if he crosses the line he can be sent into exile, like Ovid.[32]

The poet thus finds himself banished from his community, in *de facto* exile, excluded from community life, but also in an exceptional position, with the opportunity to speak in a different, *eccentric* way. According to Jonathan Culler, the poet stands apart from the social sphere he inhabits, not bound by its customs, or in opposition to them, undermining official discourse.[33] This stance is well illustrated by Propertius as he celebrates going to war, calls rousingly for combat and yet ostentatively declares that he himself will settle for watching from the sidelines:

> et subter captos arma sedere duces,
> tela fugacis equi et bracati militis arcus,
>   ad vulgi plausus saepe resistere equos
> inque sinu carae nixus spectare puellae
>   incipiam et titulis oppida capta legam!
>   [...]
> praeda sit haec illis, quorum meruere labores:
>   me sat erit Sacra plaudere posse Via.

and captured chieftains sitting beneath their arms, shafts from cavalry in retreat and bows of trousered soldiery, the horses oft halting at people's cheers, and leaning on the bosom of my sweetheart I begin to watch and read on placards the names of captured cities!
[...]

---

31   The history of Czech exile brings an ironic parallel to Plato: in the 1970s and 1980s (at the time of the so-called normalization after the Soviet occupation of Czechoslovakia in 1968), the regime tried in many cases to get rid of uncomfortable writers, forcing them to emigrate by various means. One such case was that of Jiří Gruša, who gave an interview in Switzerland during a legal trip to the West. Prior to his return, he was stripped of his citizenship, i.e. forced to stay in the West. cf. R. Cornejo: *Heimat im Wort*, p. 460 (her interview with Jiří Gruša).

32   Ovid cites two reasons for his exile, *carmen et error* (song and misconduct), the first one being taken to refer to his erotic poems.

33   J. Culler: *Theory of the Lyric*, p. 296.

Theirs be the booty whose toil has earned it: enough for me that I can cheer them on the Sacred Way.[34]

[transl. G. P. Goold]

Thus, at least from Plato onward, the poet theoretically stands some way apart from the State, and such exclusivity can quite easily turn into exclusion.

Simon Goldhill recalls the Greek authors between the first and third centuries A.D. who were active along the boundaries of the Roman Empire and shaped the concept of exile, where greater distance from Rome plays a positive role. They saw freedom as being opposed to the empire's core and as the opportunity to stand up for and express an intellectual position not subservient to political might. *"The philosopher must become an Exile from the norms of his society, an Exile* within."[35] They see exile as an initiation, taking a philosophical stance. The second motive force in their approach was the universality of Greek culture – the philosopher still finds himself within the boundaries of the empire, everywhere meeting with Greek tradition. In that sense, the intellectual is never in exile anywhere. On the other hand, as Goldhill adds, these authors find themselves in the twilight years of classical Greece and base their identity on a relationship with the past.[36] The tendency to a relativization of exile and the relationship to the past foreshadows Christian authors of Late Antiquity and the Middle Ages, while a nostalgia for the cultural past is brought back to life notably in the 19th century by Goethe, the Romantics and later on, Nietzsche.

In the Middle Ages, thanks to Christian universality, the concept of exile is largely recodified. Thomas Ehlen delineates three meanings of exile in the Middle Ages – as a concept based on legal theory, as an exile paradigm based on the Ovidian pattern, and as the concept based on the Christian religious position. Christianity brings to Western thought about exile the theme of expulsion from Paradise as representing the human condition and St. Paul's notions of human life as 'exile embodied': *"Therefore we are always confident and know that as long as we are at home in the body we are away from the Lord."* (2 Corinthinas

---

34 Propertius: *Elegies*, pp. 230–232 (III, 4, l. 15–18, 21–22).

35 S. Goldhill: Whose Antiquity?, p. 18.

36 Ibid., p. 19. Martin C. Putna recalls a nostalgia for the golden age as s widespread phenomenon of late antiquity, cf. M. Putna: *Řecké nebe nad námi*, p. 12ff.

5:6) and as a pilgrimage on this earth and a desire to return home to heaven (Hebrews 11,13–16).[37] For medieval clerics, educated in Latin and often separated from home and family, Ovid represented a paradigmatic separation from Rome and the Latin language. Ralph J. Hexter speaks of nostalgia for Latin culture and Ovid's Rome,[38] which found expression among some medieval poets. This nostalgia for one's native or cultural homeland mitigates the view of the world as a place of exile, as articulated by the oft-cited Hugh of Saint Victor: *perfectus vero, cui mundus totus exilium est* [perfect is one to whom the whole world is exile].[39] In this sense, Ovid's life, as we know it from his exile elegies, has attained apocryphal reinterpretations, where the outcast is transformed into a pilgrim, seeking God.[40]

One key author of the late Middle Ages is Dante, who became one of the exile-poet archetypes for his followers, although exile in the narrower sense is not the main theme of the *Divine Comedy*. The opening verses of the *Divine Comedy* recall the image of human life as a pilgrimage, not being exiled, and for this pilgrimage Dante opts to be guided by Virgil, rather than Ovid, appropriately enough. The latter is of course also significantly present in the *Comedy*, albeit more as an author of the *Metamorphoses*.[41] Dante expresses no nostalgia for his native Florence. In the world of the *Comedy*, the town of his birth has a more complicated role: "*Florence, the far-away town, becomes for Dante a paradigmatic definition of a wicked town, and it may be considered both a historical and semantic counterpart of Ovid's Tomis. The pilgrimage of Dante [...] goes from the deceitful (but concrete) homeland of Florence to the* Ciuitas Dei."[42] Elsewhere, however, Dante also expresses his love for his birthplace: 'Where the lovely Arno flows, there I was born and raised, in the great city.'[43] In the fictional world of the *Comedy*, written while already in exile, the pilgrim Dante sees exile as a future

---

37   T. Ehlen: Bilder des Exils, p. 160.

38   cf. R. Hexter: Ovid and the Medieval Exilic Imaginary, pp. 223–225.

39   cf. ibid., p. 220; R. Tally: Mundus totus exilium est. In his treatise, Tally deals with Auerbach's concept of world literature and recalls his paraphrase of Hugh's words.

40   E. Zambon: Life and Poetry, pp. 24–25.

41   Ibid., p. 40.

42   Ibid., p. 29. cf. Par 31, l. 37–39.

43   Inf 23, l. 93–94, cf. E. Zambon: Life and Poetry, p. 30.

revealed to him by his great-grandfather Cacciaguida in the 17th canto of the *Paradise*. Here Dante writes of Florence as his 'dearest retreat'.[44]

Renaissance exile is reopened by the religious wars that impacted most of Europe and led to great popular upheaval for religious reasons.[45] In the Czech Lands, the commencement of that exile dates from 1547–48, when the protestant Unity of the Brethren was banned and its members were forced to convert, or go into exile.[46] Yet the main waves of Czech Protestant emigration fall into the period after the Battle of White Mountain (8 November 1620) and continue until the 18th century. This period, concluding with the Josephine Reforms and the permission to espouse other faiths (the 'Patent of Toleration' was issued in 1781),[47] coincides with the beginnings of the National Revival, but takes place in a completely different context, having very little to do with the exile literature of the 18th century, for the most part. The concept of exile in the modern sense of the word is closely linked to the growing role of national languages, the rise of nationalism and the emergence of nation states. Johannes Hofer brought in the key concept of *nostalgia* only as late as 1688, prior examples notwithstanding, and thanks to him, homesickness became a term in medical diagnostics for quite some time.[48] Charles Taylor writes about an uprooting, a *"great disembedding"* in connection with changing collective notions *"social imaginary"* in a post-reformist Europe, wherein the individual begins to play a substantial role. At this time, we see the birth of the idea that exile is something the individual can opt for. This makes questions like "Should I emigrate?" conceivable; at the same time, they *"arise as burning practical issues"*.[49]

Miroslav Hroch notes the three necessary conditions for the existence of nationhood: '...firstly, that it is a civil community of equals; secondly, that each or almost every one of these individuals is aware of their affiliation to the nation; thirdly, that the national community has experienced a shared history, has a 'destiny in common', whatever its particular political form may be'. These

---

44   Par 17, 111, "*loco più caro*".

45   cf. P. Tabori: *The Anatomy of Exile*, p. 76ff.; S. Hahn: Ausweisung un Vertreibung in Europa.

46   J. Pánek: Exile from the Bohemian Lands, pp. 35–36.

47   Protestant faith was permitted to only a limited extent and not including the Brethren, which was not re-established in the Czech Lands until the 19th century.

48   cf. J. Starobinski: L'invention d'une maladie, esp. pp. 261–262; H. Levin: Literature and Exile, p. 70.

49   cf. C. Taylor: *Modern Social Imaginaries*, p. 55.

conditions were not met during the period of religious migration, but the key aspect is the collective dimension of exile, notions about a community of Exiles, foreshadowing the later concepts of nationhood.[50]

In 1979, the philosopher Milič Čapek reprinted an extract from the longer Latin composition by Václav Klement Žebrácký in the exile magazine *Proměny* [Metamorphoses] under the name 'The Sigh of the Exiled'. Putting aside its dated poetic vocabulary, this emotive poem resonates remarkably with later poetry, in its sharp contrasting of life back home and an exile-transformed identity:

> Heu! olim fuimus, fuimus! fugimusque fugati
> Jam defloruimus, flos ut fuit ille caducus.
> Sunt pulsi Reges soliis Proceresque coacti
> diversa Exilia, atque alienasque quarere terras,
> incerti quo fata ferant, ubi sistere detur.
> Jam defuncta jacet Patriae spes omnis et Omnis.
> Gloria Czechigenum, libertas corruit alta.
> Religio effertur tumulo tumulanda perenni
> Et Pietas! Et Sancta Fides! Sequiturque pheretrum
> Libertas, duris per colla adstricta catenis!

> Woe, oh, we had lived, truly lived, the banished Exiles we are.
> Our heyday has passed, as what once blossomed doth wither and fall...
> Kings unseated were expelled and leading men
> driven to all parts of the world looking for a new homeland
> not knowing where fate would take them, where to find their home.
> All hope for a homeland extinguished, and the glory of the Czech tribe,
> noble freedom lies trampled.
> Faith destined to be forever buried is being expunged
> with piety and holy fidelity, and behind the bier, heavily shackled
> under the yoke, Liberty makes her way, disgraced![51]

---

50   M. Hroch: *Na prahu národní existence*, p. 8.

51   Klement Žebrácký: Vzdech exulantův. Klement's poem is referenced by Otakar Odložilík in the foreword to the exile poetry anthology *Zahrada v zemi nikoho* [Garden in No Man's Land, 1955]: The Poet's Way, pp. 12–14.

Milič Čapek clearly finds an expression fitting for his time in the poem, and without hesitation connects it with the idea of nationhood: 'The author was so full of sadness and pain over the national tragedy that he put into it [i.e. the poem] a telling passage, which I wrote down, and which has already been translated by Dr Fišer. The historical analogy is too evident for us to regard this fragment as just a documentary piece of history; the sadness of today's exiled poet over our national humiliation is as profound as that of his spiritual brother three centuries ago.'

Klement's Sigh is close to the genre of Czech songs for which Jan Malura coined the term 'exile lament'.[52] Yet there are also evident differences – Klement builds on humanist learning, makes use of secular imagery, writes in cultured Latin and represents the lonely intellectual, while exile lamentations are based on the tradition of Czech religious songs and are based primarily on images from the Old Testament and tied to the exile community. It is characteristic that Klement also expresses his homesickness in the plural, showing the collective dimension of exile and belonging to a community, albeit an entirely imaginary one. As he sees it, the former community has been dispersed all over the world and feels tied to its past homeland, lamenting the past it has lost. While the Czech lamentations likened exile to the Old Testament exodus, by their very function in the religious community they were directed more to the present.

> aj, my vyhnanci rajští
> po zemi putujem,
> pro hřích bídám oddáni,
> pracně se kvaltujem,
> nic v světě nejsouce
> než podruzi tvoji,
> vždy se k smrti nesouce,
> kde cil komu stojí.

> oh, we Exiles from paradise
> the earth we trek,

---

52   cf. J. Malura: *Písně českých exulantů*, pp. 184–204.

for our sin to woes wedded,
strife-hurried there and back,
in the world no worth having
than as thy cotters mere,
ever to death we're heading,
each one's end clear.[53]

The collective dimension and similar references to the Old Testament can also be found in the lengthy epic poem by Martin Kopecký, which depicts the fates of Czech Exiles in Saxony and Brandenburg in the first half of the 18th century.

W roku tisjc sedum set
Třicet a druhého
Dne desátého Řjgna
Tak gmenowaného,
Spolu se shromáždjce
Pjsně gsme zpjwali
W srdečných modlitbách
Na cestu se dali.

Opět nové soužení
Na cirkev připadlo
Že sme všem lidem byli
Za nové divadlo.
Pany za plotem klečic
Žalostně spívaly
(jak slavná krále nevěsta)
Však všecky své těžkosti
Na Boha vkládaly.

Tu nevědouce z místa
Kam zas jíti máme

---

53   J. A. Komenský: *Duchovní písně*, p. 347; the editor Antonín Škarka calls the attribution to Comenius utterly dubious.

Nemajic v světě místa
Jen k Bohu voláme
Aby on nás retoval
Nám hříchy odpustil
A mnohých pánů srdce
K nám zase naklonil.

Za námi byl nepřjtel
Panj Henersdorfska
Užiwagjc fortele
Byla wjc nehezká
Pánům, panjm a stawům
Nás osočovala
Hroznými rebelanty
Lžiwě w psanjch psala.

Ti páni gako hory
Nám po stranách byli
Že sme se uchýliti
Na stranu nemohli
Museli sme skrz moře
K Berlinu se pustit
Ač wody wysušené
Nemohli nám škodit.

In the year one thousand seven hundred
Thirty and two, the same,
On the tenth of October
The month of that name,
Together then assembled
We sang our songs full-hearted
In heartfelt prayers
On our way departed

Once more new tribulations
Our Church did befall

That made all people see us
As minstrels, players all
Maidens knelt behind fences
Sad laments singing
(just as that famed King's bride)
And all their difficulties
To God's will bringing.

We aimless, without notion,
Which way now to go
No worldly destination
Called God, to let us know,
That He may yet redeem us
Forgive us our sins
Melt many noble hearts
Find us a place therein.

Chased by our enemy
Of Henersdorf the Lady
With use of force unyielding
Unpretty though it made her
To Lords and Ladies, Nobles
She denounced us, accusing,
Calling us roguish rebels
In letters false, abusing.

Those Lords like mountain ranges
Flanked our way, whereupon
We could not change direction
We had to go straight on
We had the sea to go through
Toward Berlin to get
Yet dried-up were the waters
And harm us they could not.[54]

---

54   H. Rössel: Der "Schwanengesang" des Martin Kopecký, pp. 310, 316–317 (strophes 77, 137–140).

Goethe's *Italian Journey*, undertaken by the writer between September 1786 and May 1788 was a prelude to the ideology and figurativeness of 19th century exile, though he wrote the book about it based on his diaries only much later, starting in 1813; it was first published in 1816.[55] Goethe perceives Italy as the cradle of European culture and comes to Italy as if it were his homeland, distant in space but also in time. When in the closing part of his travelogue he bids farewell to Rome, Goethe compares himself to Ovid, departing Rome: 'And how I could not recall Ovid's elegy at these moments, for he too was banished and was about to leave Rome on a moonlit night. *'Cum repeto noctem'*– [when I recall that night] his recollection far away at the Black Sea, where he was sad and miserable-kept recurring to me, and I recited the poem, which in part I remember exactly. But actually, it only interfered with and hindered my own production, which although undertaken again later, never came into existence.'[56] Goethe introduces his travelogue with the words *Auch ich in Arcadien!,* evoking Italy as an idyllic or idealized place. The book is thus framed in antithesis to Ovid's poems, in which an idealized and distant Rome compares against the icy wasteland of Tomis.

The theme of a lost or distant homeland that we find in the earlier period takes a new turn with Goethe, and is taken further by the emerging Romantic period – the 'Outcast' still harkens back to an idealized homeland yet also manifests as an individual, "*ego* in Arcadia".[57] The topic of the lost homeland and the poet-as-exile is echoed by numerous leading poets of the 19th century. The figure of Ovid remains central to this imagery, being regarded as the archetype for the modern poet excluded from society. The motif is given graphical form by Delacroix in his famous painting Ovid among the Scythians in 1859, just as Baudelaire references Ovid in his influential poem, *The Swan*.[58] In Czech

---

55 With regard to the genesis of the *Italian Journey* cf. J. W. Goethe: *Italienische Reise* II, p. 1072n. Also cf. M. Putna: *Řecké nebe nad námi*, pp. 25–64; J. Starobinski: La nuit de Troie, pp. 323–326.

56 J. W. Goethe: *Italian Journey*, pp. 447–448. J. W. Goethe, *Italienische Reise* I, p. 596, *Bericht April.*

57 As regards the Arcadia theme and the shift from moralizing to sentimental reading cf. E. Panofsky: Et in Arcadia ego, p. 319; and comments in J. W. Goethe: *Italienische Reise* II, pp. 1168–1170; J. W. Goethe: *Italienische Reise*, p. 539.

58 Baudelaire himself wrote admiringly about the Delacroix painting, Ch. Baudelaire: *Œuvres complètes*, p. 760 in 1859 in letters about the Paris Salon 1859.

poetry, self-comparison to Ovid in exile is made by Jan Kollár[59] and going on to the beginning of the 20th century, we find Jaroslav Vrchlický striking a similar note:

> Jen vyprostit se! To je zákon všeho,
> co k žití schopnost má a k světlu chce.
> Tím kvílil starý Ovid u Skythů
> na pustém břehu moře Černého,
> tím kvílí stejně básník moderní
> v měst pustém ruchu, vřavě, hlomozu.

> Just to make one's escape! That law is universal,
> for all things living, yearning for the light.
> Just like old Ovid at the Scythians
> on the Black Sea, its most forsaken shore,
> just so laments the poet of today
> in urban barren rushing, uproar, din.[60]

On this basis the 19th century notion that a poet is an outcast in his own country, regardless of where he is actually located, took shape. This image of the 'cursed poet', as Verlaine put it, is presented prominently by Baudelaire in his poem *Bénédicton*, opening his *Fleurs du Mal*, 'Flowers of Evil'. Towards the end of the century, Nietzsche, with a nod to Romanticism, typifies the human condition with this nostalgia: 'One is no longer at home anywhere…,' he writes in late fragments published under the title *Will to Power*.[61]

For 20th century intellectuals, this starting point, only underlined by the factual state of exile, takes on a dual form. Many Exiles find their separation from home hard to bear, and their writing is marked by nostalgia in various guises. The major anthology of Czech exile poetry published in the mid-1950s, takes the telling name *Neviditelný domov* [Invisible Home].[62] Conversely, the loss of

59   J. Kollár: *Básně*, p. 191 (*Slávy dcera*, sonnet 332).

60   J. Vrchlický: *Já nechal svět jít kolem*, p. 30.

61   Quoted by S. Goldhill: Whose Antiquity?, p. 1.

62   *Neviditelný domov: Verše exulantů 1948–1953*, Peter Demetz, ed. (1954). The polemic contrast to the book comes in the anthology *Čas stavění* [Time for Building]. *Básně českých exulantů* [Poems

one's home becomes a core characteristic and a motive force. In 1944, Theodor W. Adorno, referring to Nietzsche, states: 'It is even part of my good fortune not to be a house-owner', Nietzsche already wrote in the *Gay Science*. Today we should have to add: it is part of morality not to be at home in one's home.'[63] George Steiner sees the basic stance of Modernism precisely in migration, and sees Nabokov as a paradigmatic author.[64] Both tendencies are present throughout the Cold War, the first of them dominant chiefly in the 1950s, whilst from the late 1960s a second, 'nomadic' tendency comes to the fore, as theorized by some Western intellectuals (Kenneth White, Gilles Deleuze, etc.),[65] but also the (geographically speaking) very trans-national philosopher of Czech origin Vilém Flusser, who belongs to the war and post-war emigration wave, or indeed the writer Věra Linhartová.[66]

II

Even a brief and selective overview shows the historical diversity of exile. Its modern-day meanings started to take shape largely in the 19th century in the context of nation states and nationalisms,[67] and also during this period the word exile covered a whole range of meanings from travels through political exile to metaphorically symbolizing the human condition. It is difficult to think of exile poetry strictly historically, to say nothing of the fundamental difficulties with such delineation, because the different meanings are sometimes only loosely related. However, the link between them remains the use of the word exile, and a conscious referencing and linking to the exile theme. Poems and poets thus create a continuum of different meanings of exile and a joined-up historical network of meanings and depictions. The poetry of exile also forms a certain core, founded on the putative duality of that situation. Ovid sets his

of Czech Exiles], foreword by Antonín Vlach, 1956. For the period context cf. M. Přibáň: *Prvních dvacet let* [The First Twenty Years], pp. 194–198.

63   T. W. Adorno: *Minima moralia*, p. 39.
64   G. Steiner: Extraterritorial.
65   cf. K. White: Esquisse du nomade intellectuel.
66   see Chapter 10.
67   cf. e.g. S. Goldhill: Whose Antiquity?; E. Said: Reflections on Exile.

exile in a mythologized topography, built on the contrast of an idealized centre of the Roman world, and its antithesis, the extremity of Tomis.[68] Similarly, Ovid mythologizes himself as a poet-outcast, and subjects the addressees of his letters to this confabulated situation. Baudelaire's *Swan* refers to a number of mythical characters, and presents Paris in hyperbole as an imaginary place that changes faster than do human memories of it:

> Paris change ! mais rien dans ma mélancolie
> N'a bougé ! palais neufs, échafaudages, blocs,
> Vieux faubourgs, tout pour moi devient allégorie,
> Et mes chers souvenirs sont plus lourds que des rocs

> Paris changes! but naught in my melancholy
> has stirred! new palaces, scaffolding, blocks of stone,
> old quarters, all become for me an allegory,
> And my dear memories are heavier than rocks[69]

[transl. William Aggeler]

Baudelaire more than anyone else perceives the exile as a person living mainly in their imaginings and memories, or rather their illusions and memories prevail over perceived reality. As has been mentioned, Ovid's elegies are very questionable as to their veracity, it is practically impossible to read them as a record of actual events. At the same time, however, there is a consensus that Ovid was indeed in exile. Baudelaire's verses are psychologically unverifiable, yet we read them as the poet's testimony about his situation. Both the *Swan* and Ovid's elegies are worthy of being read as 'true testimonies' rather than as works of fiction.[70] They are not, however, actual description of reality, but a testimony in which *the imaginary* is reality in hyperbole.

In both cases an important premise of poetry is present: in the poem, the poet's voice is that of a public beneficence, the designated progenitor of poetry. It matters not what exactly Charles Baudelaire felt during his walk, but how the

---

68   cf. G. Williams: *Banished Voices*, p. 8ff.

69   Ch. Baudelaire: *Œuvres complètes* I, p. 86.

70   Käte Hamburger uses the term *Wirklichkeitsaussage* in this context. cf. Culler's discussion on the issue, *Theory of the Lyric*, pp. 105–109.

poet Baudelaire expresses some human condition, in a poem. When the first edition of *The Flowers of Evil* came before the courts, Baudelaire was to feel at first hand that, at least in some ways, the poet was still perceived as a public property. The state of exile is symptomatic of this role. The poet is usually connected to a language community and thus in a broader sense also tied to a place, or at least such contact is implicit. Exile, on the other hand, creates often insurmountable distance from both the place and the community and does not allow these relationships to be fulfilled in the usual way. This is what Ovid builds upon in his elegies, wherein places and people represent basic thematic and structural elements. The elegies overcome this two-form distance – they re-establish contact with home and friends, and take Ovid back to Rome, in his mind. Baudelaire's case is different: the poet has not physically left Paris, but experiences a sense of alienation, which he seeks to overcome through construing an imaginary and aesthetised society of Exiles. In Baudelaire's case, the term exile describes how the poet stands apart in modern society. Ovid's elegies seen as nostalgic poems of *de facto* exile on the one hand, and Baudelaire's *Swan* as a metaphorical exile, to represent one's status in the world and in society on the other hand; these are the fundamental bi-poles of exile poetry. There are common points of distance from place and society in both prototypes of exile poetry, in the one case physical, in the other psychological, or existential.

However, the world of the imagination is not exclusively bound up with an exile theme. From a certain point, an *unspecified context* is characteristic of most poetry, as William Waters writes, the poem is not tied to a particular situation, but the context *"as part of its imaginative structure"*[71] is a matter for the reader's imagination to update. Exile poems add to the imaginative context with spatio-temporal distance. For Ovid, Rome is not the setting of the poem for the reader to update, but a place related-to from a distance. Similarly, Viktor Fischl writes of Prague in his *Prague Walks* cycle:

> Na jedné z tisíců procházek
> městem, z něhož jsem odešel,
> na jedné z tisíců procházek
> městem, jež nikdy neodešlo ze mne

---

71   cf. W. Waters: *Poetry's Touch*, p. 9.

On one of thousands of walks
through the city I had left,
on one of thousands of walks
through the city that never left me[72]

In can in many cases be hard to differentiate between the fabulated as *imagined* and as *imaginary*. The collective designation 'we Exiles from paradise' in the song attributed to Comenius may at some point act as a 'fabulated society' in the spirit of Anderson's theory of *imagined communities*,[73] while in the *Swan* the community of Exiles is imaginary in the stronger sense of a personal imagination making up something missing. Similar distinctions, whilst not clear-cut, can be traced to places like *Arcadia* on the one hand, and a *home preserved in memories* on the other, which can easily turn into the *imaginary homeland*, to quote Salman Rushdie.

Baudelaire's *Swan* and Ovid's elegies bring out some telling aspects. The characteristic distance creates the specific standpoint of the excluded poet, an aspect relatively new in Ovid's case, which in addition to the thematic plane also impacts the poem's structure. In addition, this exile theme tends toward a certain isolation, manifested by the repetition of motifs and allusions. The defining thematic and structural elements at the heart of exile poetry are place, community, language and intertextuality. The intertextual dimension of exile is closely associated with the imaginary world: the reference framework for the exile poem is not only the outcast's actual situation, but quite often more to do with the repertoire of motifs drawn upon. If we can say that the exile is characterized by a self unsettled by distance and exclusion, the poem allows the reforging of a new, cultural identity based on the literary exile tradition.

III

A distant home can become the subject of nostalgia and lament. Loss is often compounded with a superstructure: the exiled subject more or less deliberately

---

72   V. Fischl: *Krása šedin*, p. 9.
73   cf. B. Anderson: *Imagined communities* following-on from Taylor's concept of *social imaginary*.

reconstructs a lost or disturbed identity tied to their home and creates a new spatial constellation, changing their relationship to the language and the community, and superimposing this structure onto the real world, creating notions about places, but also places that are completely imaginary. Nostalgia and constructivism also work in the opposite direction, and can shape an imaginary exile situation, a sense of exclusion from society, alienation from the present or nostalgia for an unattainable past. These two perspectives have to some extent a different genesis, but very often meet and complement each other down the ages of cultural history, mutually exchanging motifs.

Exile is connected with two places, *here* and *there*, whereby the speaker is physically located here, but still there in thought. *"An exile is someone who inhabits one place and remembers or projects the reality of another,"* writes Michael Seidel.[74] Martin C. Putna differentiates the topology of exile into a relationship with three lands:

> Russian exile literature works with the theme of a 'land triad': A 'Lost Land' – recalling an unreachable and subjugated homeland, often accompanied by pondering what to do to make the land accessible and free again. A 'Foreign Land' – reflecting the exile situation, sometimes centred on the exile's inability to adapt to the conditions of the host country (most often some 'inhuman' huge city), sometimes generalizing exile into a universal human experience. A 'Novel Land' – a contrasting positive slant on some aspect of the country the exile is living in or travelling through, inspiration drawn from a new reality.[75]

The proffered categories are only elementary possibilities for categorizing the material, the various poets and poems present a number of other standpoints through which exile topology can be nuanced.

The fundamental counterweight that brings a desire for home, a nostalgia, can be found in the oldest written documents (see the quote from the tale of Sinuhe). Ovid brings the contrasts of an uncultured place and extreme climate

---

74   M. Seidel: *Exile and the Narrative Imagination*, p. ix.

75   M. Putna: *Česká katolická literatura v kontextech 1945–1989*, p. 252. Putna introduced this typology in his earlier anthology *U řek babylonských* (M. Putna – M. Zadražilová, ed., 1996).

here in Tomis, as against cultured Rome, as a relationship between the periphery and the centre:

> Frigora iam Zephyri minuunt, annoque peracto
>> Longior antiquis visa Maeotis hiems,
>
> [...]
> Iam violam puerique legunt hilaresque puellae
>> Rustica quae nullo nata serente venit,
>
> Prataque pubescunt variorum flore colorum
>> Indocilique loquax gutture vernat avis;
>
> [...]
> Quoque loco est vitis, de palmite gemma movetur:
>> Nam procul a Getico litore vitis abest;
>
> Quoque loco est arbor, turgescit in arbore ramus:
>> Nam procul a Geticis finibus arbor abest.

> Zephyrus lessens the cold, now the past year's done,
>> a Black Sea winter that seemed longer than those of old
>
> [...]
> Now laughing boys and girls gather the violets
>> that grow, un-sown, born of the countryside:
>
> and the meadows bloom with many flowers,
>> and the song-birds welcome spring, untaught:
>
> [...]
> and the shoots that lay hid, buried in the wheat furrows,
>> show through, unfurl their tender tips from the earth.
>
> Wherever the vine grows, buds break from the stem:
>> but vines grow far away from these Getic shores:[76]

[transl. A.S. Kline]

---

76   *Tristia* III 12 (13), 1, ll. 1–16. [cf. https://www.poetryintranslation.com/PITBR/Latin/OvidTristia
      BkThree.php#anchor_Toc34217030]

Sometimes the two places, two different realities, the home of the past and the present exile overlap in a dual view,[77] but often the duality is based on contrast, antithesis as in Ovid, and in many cases one of the places significantly outweighs the other. In the poems of Milada Součková, American reality is present only marginally, as unimportant, and often only so the poem's speaker can return to her Czech past, which acquires an imaginary nature in her poems. Součková does not deploy the value-contradiction of places, just underscores her anchorage in her old homeland. In Ovid's case, the poem-letter is also a means of returning to Rome, when it cannot be done physically:

> Parve – nec invideo – sine me, liber, ibis in Urbem,
>   Ei mihi! quo domino non licet ire tuo.
> Vade, sed incultus, qualem decet exulis esse.
>   Infelix habitum temporis huius habe!

> Little book, go without me – I don't begrudge it – to the city.
>   Ah, alas, that your master's not allowed to go!
> Go, but without ornament, as is fitting for an Exile's:
>   sad one, wear the clothing of these times![78]
>
> [transl. A. S. Kline]

Like Ovid, Czesław Miłosz perceives the extremes of climate in unspoken contrast to his homeland in the poem *Czarodziejska góra* [A Magic Mountain]:

> Wkrótce po naszym przyjeździe Budberg, melancholijnie łagodny,
> Powiedział, że z początku trudno się przyzwyczaić
> Bo nie ma tutaj ni wiosny i lata, ni jesieni i zimy.
> [...]
> Upalny październik, chłodny lipiec, w lutym kwitną drzewa.
> Godowe loty kolibrów nie zwiastują wiosny.

---

77   cf. D. Bethea: *Joseph Brodsky*, pp. 39–40.

78   *Tristia* I, 1, ll. 1–4. [cf. https://www.poetryintranslation.com/PITBR/Latin/OvidTristiaBkOne .php#anchor_Toc34214733] As to Ovid's letters from exile cf. J.-M. Claasen: *Displaced Persons*, pp. 114–119; P. Hardie: *Ovid's Poetics of Illusion*, pp. 283–285.

Tylko wierny klon zrzucał co roku liście bez potrzeby,
Bo tak nauczyli się jego przodkowie.

Soon after our arrival, Budberg,
gently pensive,
said that in the beginning it is hard to get accustomed
for here there is no spring or summer, no winter or fall.
[...]
Sultry Octobers, cool Julys, trees blossom in February.
Here the nuptial flight of hummingbirds does not forecast spring.
Only the faithful maple sheds its leaves every year.
For no reason, its ancestors simply learned it that way.[79]

[transl. Czesław Miłosz and Lillian Vallee]

However, the topology of two remote locations is just the starting point for diverse and more complex constructs. For many writers, the home country is not the subject of nostalgia, for political or personal reasons, but also of hostility or a source of concern, or of no import at all. In his English seclusion Ivan Blatný built a *shelter* out of words, constructing an imaginary presence intended to cover-up the everyday reality of a mental institution. That's one possible explanation for the vast number of poems he wrote there. Rather than being separate poems, in later years these form a continuum of writing that fills his time and with its imaginative aspect outweighs the reality that surrounds him. This is illustrated, among other things, by numerous examples of Blatný's dread of reality beyond the institution's walls and a degree of sovereignty within his written realm.

Such shelter is close to so-called internal emigration. This concept originated during World War II among German intellectuals to denote voluntarily giving up public appearances and withdrawal into seclusion, or the realm of pop culture. We can find the seeds of this attitude already in Cicero at the end of the Republican regime in Rome.[80] In the Czech setting this could be applied

---

79   Cz. Miłosz: *Wiersze* III, p. 12. [https://www.poetryfoundation.org/poems/49456/a-magic
      -mountain]
80   On the concept of internal emigration, see note 8 above.

to a number of poets who voluntarily, or through compulsion, shunned public life during the Cold War, whether as solitary figures or within various subcultural circles outside the regime – for example, Vladimír Vokolek, Zbyněk Havlíček, Egon Bondy, etc.

Nostalgia can be evoked by a memory of the homeland and a relationship to the past that can no longer be renewed. This theme of a past homeland to which one can no longer return by any geographical move appears already in late antiquity (as aforementioned, see Putna, Goldhill), while its modern-day version comes to life with Goethe in the 19th century, when antiquity itself becomes the idealized past; in Goethe's case, Rome, in Hölderlin's legendary Greece. For a number of German romantics, as well as Mácha, the Middle Ages also take their place. The same authors often also have the opposite perspective of a 'Future Homeland', to use the name of Mácha's poem, in some cases with a revolutionary view or a nationalist revival liberation struggle. A similar theme is featured in Hölderlin's novel *Hyperion*, where the struggle for freedom ends in disappointment and he turns back to the past.

These projections of home border on completely imaginary places, which the poems' speakers no longer cast into history or to the future, but into an imaginary or utopian space – such as Baudelaire's land of plenty in the poem *L'invitation au voyage* [Invitation to a Journey] and in its prose counterpart. In the 20th century, Richard Weiner, a poet who lived much of his life in France in voluntary estrangement from Bohemia, created a poetic Utopia in his collection *Mesopotamia* (1930). Jiří Kovtun's poems of the 1950s and 1960s come close to Weiner in their combination of a utopian setting and incipient speech. Both revive Virgil's prior motif of a Land of Poetry.[81] Kovtun also revives the motifs of an ancient Arcadia as an idyllic space hidden in memory, in other works:

> Umluvme si schůzku v Arkádii,
> když se nemůžeme setkat u kávy,
> kterou za nás jiní lidé pijí
> na počátku jiné výpravy.

---

81   In a key study on the subject, Bruno Snell attributed Arcadia to Virgil, as his discovery. He emphasized the exclusive connection of Arcadia to song: 'You Arcadians, / who are alone experienced in song' (10:32; likewise 7.4); see B. Snell: Arcadia, p. 281. In exile imagining, the theme of death does not play a major role; as written about, among other things by Erwin Panofsky (Et in Arcadia ego).

Když už se nemůžeme setkat na nároží
v ulici s jedinou zahrádkou,
jejíž ploty ověnčilo hloží,
umluvme si schůzku namátkou.

V naší paměti je uschována
nesplněná výzva úsvitů,
šelestící, bílý dopis rána,
škvírou zasouvaný do bytu.

Let's make in Arcadia our meeting,
if we can't do coffee, share a sip,
others in our place drink, take our seating,
at the start of quite a different trip.

If we can't meet on some corner, rather,
in a street with a garden, just the one,
fences decked with hawthorn, let's not bother,
let's agree to meet by chance, anon.

We still have in memory's safe keeping
promising new dawns, as yet unmet,
morning's rustling white slip letter creeping
through a crevice, right into our flat.[82]

The difference between an imaginary place and the imagining of a place (*imaginary* and *imagined*) is not definitive, as already mentioned. The distant homeland can turn into a place of a rather more imaginary nature, and conversely, an imaginary place may be just a pointed metaphor for reality, rather than some fictional place. In Baudelaire's *L'invitation au voyage* the refrain: *Là, tout n'est qu'ordre et beauté, / Luxe, calme et volupté* [There, everything is but order and beauty / Luxury, calm and voluptuousness] sounds more like a spell meant

---

82   J. Kovtun: *Hřbet velryby*, p. 36.

to change reality or summon up a different reality, than as a description of a virtual place.

IV

Apart from the aspect of place, exile poetry reserves an important role for the community, sometimes overlapping (one can be a metonymy of the other), sometimes set apart or functioning in some more complex way, mainly because the community relates to the poem's direct or indirect addressee and this fact sets up the narrative. For example, Dante, in the 17th canto of the *Paradiso*, fondly harkens back to Florence as a place, but is critical of Florentine society. The poet in exile may feel nostalgia for the remote community, but that same community or its representatives may be complicit in his ousting. The poet can relate to a real community, but also to mythical or imaginary characters, such as we find both with Ovid and Baudelaire. Even with seemingly real characters, there is a comparable imaginary duality, as with places – in the conjured-up depictions of real and at the same time distant persons, with whom a direct conversation cannot be established. For Blatný, this imaginary estrangement sometimes conflates with death and grows into a kind of Orphic stage, where the living coexist with the dead. Milada Součková writes in a similar vein to Otakar Odložilík:

> It's strange how by our being cut-off from home even the living are cut-off from us by an impassable border. And so, for us, the line between life and death is blurred to some extent. The living are as if dead to us – and we to them – we don't even know when those who were part of our lives leave us for good. There is a difference there, of course, but not in our mind's eye. In our minds the living are just as unreachable as the dead.[83]

In older writings, for example in Psalm 137 (By the rivers of Babylon) or in songs of post-Battle-of-White-Mountain Exiles, the collective plural stands for

---

83   M. Součková: *Élenty*, p. 336, letter to O. Odložilík dated 12 March 1956.

the community, and the idea of the group as voiced in the poem itself contributes to its formation. This is illustrated by Martin Kopecký's cited epic poem, in which Czech Exiles embark on a journey, to the singing of Liberda's hymnbook *Harfa nová* [The New Harp].[84] The modern poem, by contrast, typically does not relate to the community directly, but as part of 'the public sphere' (as for example defined by Charles Taylor), i.e. anonymously, at least to an extent.[85] The addressed or mentioned characters in a modern poem do not feature as actual and direct addressees or speakers, but as actors on the poetic stage shaped by the reader in the act of reading. Jonathan Culler draws attention to the triangular situation of reaching out in a poem (*triangulated address*): the poem addresses the reader *"by addressing [...] something or someone else"*.[86] Quintilian, whom Culler recalls, defines the apostrophe (literally a 'turning away') as addressing someone who is not the true addressee.[87] Baudelaire, for example, turns to Andromache and other exile characters, but at the same time the whole poem is open to the reader, who reads something more topical into this missive, this imaginary scene in which the poet speaks to people and beings that are not in his presence. Moreover, the *Swan* was dedicated to Victor Hugo, who reflected on the poem in a letter back to its author. Ovid's letters have their own specific addressees (both anonymous and named), but the author's ironic slant envisages a reader capable of keeping up with the apparent dialogue in full, and able to see the irony. The intricate openness of the poem is well evident from the image of writing in solitude as related by Ovid to the letter's addressee. Nevertheless, the poem is accessible to more or less any readers who can understand it, all the while being addressed to a particular person, yet ultimately depicts a poet writing only for himself. The addressee of the letter is not necessarily merely the counterpart *to whom* the poet communicates by letter, but is also the subject *about whom* he communicates something to the reader in this way.

> parvaque, ne dicam scribendi nulla voluptas
> est mihi nec numeris nectere verba iuvat,
> sive quod hinc fructus adeo non cepimus ullos,
> principium nostri res sit ut ista mali,

---

84   cf. J. Malura: *Duchovní píseň v tvorbě pobělohorských exulantů ze Slezska*, p. 43.

85   cf. C. Taylor: *A Secular Age*, pp. 184–196.

86   J. Culler: *Theory of the Lyric*, p. 8.

87   Ibid., p. 186. cf. Quintilian: *The Orator's Education*, pp. 210–213 (IV, 1, 63–70).

sive quod in tenebris numerosos ponere gestus
quodque legas nulli scribere carmen idem est:
excitat auditor studium laudataque virtus
Crescit et inmensum gloria calcar habet.
Hic mea cui recitem nisi flavis scripta Corallis
quasque alias gentes barbarus Hister habet?

I've little or no pleasure, to speak of, in writing,
no joy in weaving words into metre,
whether it's the fact I've reaped no profit from it,
that makes this thing the source of my misfortunes:
or that writing a poem you can't read to anyone
is exactly like making gestures in the dark.
An audience stirs interest: power grows
with praise, and fame is a continual spur.
Who can I recite my work to here, but yellow-haired
Coralli, and the other tribes of the barbarous Danube?[88]

Primarily, the poem as a coherent worded statement aims for some degree of clarity, and so, in general, is open to any reader able to understand its words.[89] In the case of a modern poem, this openness takes place in the public sphere, which does not ensure any immediate contact between the poet and the reader. Osip Mandelstam and, after him, Paul Celan have seen such a situation as analogous to a message in a bottle that can be washed up on some coastline: "*A poem, since it is an instance of language, hence in its essence dialogic, may be a letter in a bottle thrown out to the sea in the – surely not always strongly hopeful – belief that it may sometime wash up somewhere, perhaps on a shoreline of the heart. In this way, too, poems are underway: they are headed toward something.*"[90]

The exile status and theme can indeed be progressed on the basis of images associated with the poem's accessibility and openness: what if the ability to

---

88   *Ex Ponto*, IV, 2, ll. 29–38.

89   cf. W. Waters: *Poetry's Touch*, p. 5.

90   P. Celan: *Gesammelte Werke* III, p. 186. On the image of the poem as a message in a bottle as per Mandelstam and Celan cf. W. Waters: *Poetry's Touch*, pp. 151–152, 158–161. Translation from: W. Waters: ibid., p. 158.

send messages is limited, or almost zero? From this point of view, an exile poem could be seen as that of a prisoner, who has little or almost no scope to communicate. Mácha's protagonist Vilém can speak to the guard, with the clouds, or just with himself, but he lacks that vague horizon of hope represented by the ocean, as in the case of a message in a bottle. It is clear that the basic linguistic coherence of the poem cannot be substantially influenced by such a notion. If so, we would go beyond what is considered a poem, into the realms of personal and private expression, such as when I scream in pain, or mutter to myself, when I recall and hum bits of a melody or note something down as a reminder for later. The more fragmentary the language of poetry becomes, e.g. in the concrete poetry domain, the more it must be accompanied by the framework and signals to mark it out as a manifestation of poetry. For 'exiled' poetry, the basic framework of being a poem is typically not missing, but exile can affect the author's intent, affect the concept of what makes up a poem and its semantic structure.

There are two connected questions here. Ivan Blatný, as an Exile in England, *might be* writing in the belief that no one reads his poems, nor will read them, which *might* show itself in the structure of these poems. In addition, the poetic spokesperson 'Blatný' can lament his loneliness and that his poems are not read, all of which belongs to the thematic plane of the poem, and does not exclude the reader in any way, quite the contrary. How do these two planes relate?

In the traditional critiquing of poetry, there is a significant stream that, unlike Paul Celan, sees some poems as the poet's soliloquy, a monologue manifestation of his solitude. This follows from the romantic aesthetics of poetry as personal expression, as established particularly by Hegel in his *Aesthetics*. J. S. Mill writes that *"Poetry is feeling confessing itself to itself in moments of solitude"*[91] while

---

91   J. S. Mill: Thoughts on Poetry: *"Poetry is feeling confessing itself to itself in moments of solitude, and embodying itself in symbols which are the nearest possible representations of the feeling in the exact shape in which it exists in the poet's mind. Eloquence is feeling pouring itself out to other minds, courting their sympathy, or endeavoring to influence their belief, or move them to passion or to action."* Mill's distinction between poetry and *eloquence* may fall short today, but it does allow us to capture some nuances. A poem is not necessarily a direct report of its content, it is not a rhetorical expression to achieve the given effect, but nor is it closed off from the reader and often conveys an overall meaning rather than just the meanings expressed. The difference lies in the role of time – whether the poem is an expression to be repeated, or a persuasive proclamation, precisely positioned in time. In the case of Ovid's elegies, however, Mill's distinction principle allows us to 'parenthesize' the direct addressee and e.g. to avoid having to view the

T. S. Eliot distinguishes three voices of poetry, the first being *"the voice of the poet talking to himself– or to nobody."*[92] However, contemporary theories of poetry and lyricism emphasize the distinct identities of the poet-as-speaker and the poet as a person. On the other hand, their relationship cannot simply be annulled. The author of the poem is also the author of the 'me' (the lyrical self, the subject), and the older approaches that identify them both only confirm the established convention that it is the poet who speaks through the poem. In other words, the poem's writer takes on a *'poetic pretension'*[93] and becomes a poet *in actu*. This relationship is not a simple one, because only a poet can speak through a poem, but the author is not a poet unless so proved, by the poem.[94]

Staying with exile, we find the extreme position of poems written under the conviction that no one will read them. The poet will be the only reader. In such cases, the expressive speaker in the first person comes close to being the author's *alter ego*. We can clearly see this mirror structure in Milada Součková's work *Sešity Josefíny Rykrové* [The Workbooks of Josefína Rykrová]. The central figure of Josefína Rykrová is a depiction of Součková, reflected in her cultural recollection. Rykrová is *there* while Součková is *here*. The mutual reflection of the two positions is evident in the mirroring of different layers of the work, especially in the comments, written more from the position of Milada Součková the author, as well as in the afterword, called 'The Autobiography of Josefína Rykrová', written in the first person under the name Josefína Rykrová, all the while corresponding to the life of Milada Součková.

Ivan Blatný makes such 'writing to himself' relate to the present, creating an imaginary vista of the present, as synchronous as possible with the reality being experienced and overlapping it with or turning it into a poetic reality that can be put into words. In this take on the fanciful present, the poems become

---

second *Tristias* volume as an obsequious plea to Augustus, but instead as a poem full of ambiguity and irony, intended more for other readers.

92   T. S. Eliot: The Three Voices of Poetry, p. 89. In a similar vein, Gottfried Benn in his *Probleme der Lyrik* [Problems of the Lyric] sees lyrical poetry as akin to a monologue.

93   The term is used by Jonathan Culler in connection with the apostrophe (*Theory of the Lyric*, p. 38), but it also serves well to grasp the first-person role in a range of poems. This pretension is sometimes signalled by the use of one's own name, sometimes with the emphasis on musical and expressive metaphors that characterize poetic expressiveness.

94   For more about this 'expressive figure' cf. J. Hrdlička: *Poezie a kosmos*, pp. 128–148.

a *lyrical gesture*, with the speaker describing their actions.[95] We might call this holding up the present, word by word.

> Michaux only works in the morning, should I go lie down for a while? What would the afternoon be like without writing, I must keep writing, on the way to bed, before napping, for when the towbar reaches the water... [96]
>
> [transl. M. Sweney]

Ivan Blatný stacked his poems with a huge list of names – acquaintances, friends, admired poets. These names are of two kinds: one group includes nurses, patients – people he was in normal contact with; the others were imagined, remembered, reminisced. It is into this second group, the imaginary society of others, that he places 'Blatný the poet'. Blatný made do with distant stimuli from the outside world, hints of interest that keep the imagination going. He seeks to sustain his imaginings of this second group, and the possibility that the two groups will intersect is something the poet sees as a trespass on his here-and-now. He receives letters, which he does not intend to read, and the visit from the poet Jiří Kolář is a cause for concern:

> Jiří Kolář je příliš skutečný
> skutečně snad přijde
> ten balvan neunesu

> Jiří Kolář is too real
> he may indeed arrive
> I can't bear such a boulder[97]

Real visits make Blatný feel unsettled, but his poems are full of imaginary visits by friends, poets. Whereas Součková projects herself into a remembered past, Blatný projects the past into his present.

---

95   The term was introduced by Dominique Rabaté in the book *Gestes lyriques*.
96   I. Blatný: *Pomocná škola Bixley* (2011), p. 229.
97   Ibid., p. 180.

Ivan Diviš in his poem *Konec vidin* [The End of Illusions] from the collection *Odchod z Čech* [Leaving Bohemia] and later in the collection *Moje oči musely vidět* [My Eyes Had to See] turns toward Bohemia and Czech society from exile, and with furious sarcasm criticizes the decline of culture. He takes up the role of a witness with some prophetic powers, indignantly berating his home-land from German exile. Unlike Ovid,[98] Diviš does not berate any particular person, but the collective that has allowed such decadence to set in:

Milovat Čechy znamená přivodit si
a pěstovat svou nemoc,
ničit si poslední zdraví

ⁱ

To love Bohemia means to bring on
and cultivate one's malady,
destroying one's last vestiges of health[99]

V

Exile poetry is characterized by its own specific intertextuality. Thanks to the established notion of the lonely outcast, exile can at first glance seem like a very personal experience and prompt the assumption that poetic expression will also be similarly individual. This does not seem to apply, neither from a histo-rical point of view, and certainly not for a great deal of exile poetry. From the oldest records we see poets trying to express that they are not lonely Exiles, cast out of every society, but that they do belong or intend to return to some com-munity or diaspora. From Ovid onward, at the latest, poets also compare their fate to the fate of other, prior and better known or even legendary Exiles, thus suggesting another kind of kinship. The outcast is akin to earlier Exiles, many of whom were heroes, even the founders of cities. In this way, they integrate them-

---

98   In the poems *Ibis* and *Ex Ponto*, 4,3.

99   I. Diviš: *Odchod z Čech*, p. 70. I am citing *The Lamb on the Snow* and *Leaving Bohemia* from the *Tři knihy. Beránek na sněhu. Odchod z Čech. Thanatea* collection and refer to it by name.

selves into a cultural framework and at the same time gain an identity unavailable through their native community. Indeed, Ovid even compares himself to Odysseus and Aeneas, and is in turn followed by a long line of others who liken themselves to Ovid. In the Middle Ages we find whole lists of Exiles who are in a sense topped-off and transformed by Baudelaire in the *Swan*. Baudelaire does not form this intertextual identity by likening himself to more prominent predecessors, but instead pays attention to neglected and nameless characters. His intertextuality is based on compassionate concern for others, not comparison; The *Swan* opens up the question of countless Exiles of whom no mention has survived, yet can be given some reminiscence.

Baudelaire also more or less ends the typified simplistic comparisons to Ovid, (Vrchlický's poem seems quite conventional in this regard), and the 20th century especially goes on to work with intertextuality in different ways. Karel Zlín hints at Ovid's pages in the quoted poem, but at the same time sets the whole cycle into his own present-day and serves up his own experience of exile in hyperbole. By contrast, Kenneth White, in several Ovidrelated poems, lets the *persona* of Ovid speak out, while in his commentary he sees Ovid's exile as the point of departure for imaginings more along the lines of his own poetics: *"I'm pushing him farther than he ever went. Again, this isn't fiction, it's extension. I'm gathering here all my affinities into one great field."*[100] Meanwhile, the cited poem by Karel Zlín represents more a hyperbolic rendition of his own experience than a contemplation of his own experience through an affiliated character's perspective.

Stanislav Mareš begins his collection *Báje z nového světa* [Fable from the New World] with an ironic paraphrase of Virgil's first Eclogue, moving it toward an allegory of exile, as such. Milada Součková in her cycle of *Ex Ponto* poems very freely takes up some themes from Ovid and speaks with an impersonal or indeterminate voice that cannot be identified as belonging to any particular character or person.

---

100   K. White: *Open World*, p. 622. Poems 'Black Sea Letter', p. 359; 'Found on the Shore' and 'Ovid's Report', pp. 509–514. The commentary refers to the last of the poems from the last section of the book 'Leaves of an Atlantic Atlas'. Likewise in a number of longer poems, White follows up the intentions of his own poetry through a monologue of historical figures.

VI

Going back to the opening questions, we can consider poetry and exile in several ways. It may be (1) poetry written by poets in exile; (2) poems on the theme of exile, whether or not their author is an Exile; (3) and, finally, poems based on the transference or metaphorical treatment of the concept where exile expresses a person's general status in the world, or more specifically, their situation of exclusion from society. In modern times, many prominent thinkers see exile and alienation as the *normal* situation for an intellectual – indeed Baudelaire in that sense predates Nietzsche and Adorno. Such a transposition of the concept can take a variety of degrees from envisaging the present state of the world as exile from the past or from culture, to seeing exile as quintessential, the state of being human in the world.

None of these groups capture the issue in its entirety, and the first two groups also include poems and poets for whom the connection to exile is only superficial or inconclusive. I have tried to contemplate exile and poetry from the standpoint of fabulation. If an Exile is a person living in two places, at home in one of them physically and in the other in spirit, then the difference between the physical, internal and metaphorical exile loses sharp delineation. Nostalgia for *another place* can relate to a bygone and idealized culture or an idealized present. At the same time, notions of what is *not* present or what the exile has limited access to – be it place or community – do come to the fore. Imaginary duality is not peculiar to exile poetry. Ritual or imaginary duality is at work in much of Western lyricism: One has to imagine what the poem is talking about. In addition, the one who gives the poem its voice opens up a fluid field of identities. The *poet* and also speaker of the poem, does, as a social entity, work within the Lacan 'symbolic order'. And it is here that the peculiarity of exile can show itself: it stands apart, because the poet is torn from the symbolic order. Ovid seeks to restore it, while Baudelaire nearly two millennia later makes exclusion his own and shifts symbolism toward his personal envisioning. Some poems can be read as an attempt to alter the situation of exile – to create a new relationship with the homeland (for example, in the form of letters), which break down distance, or to establish a new (imaginary) community or create a new identity for the exile that differs from the identity of the old homeland or the new location's inhabitants.

A key aspect of the whole issue is *language*. Historically, language is an important, albeit not the only factor in national identity as progressively formed

during modern times. Language maintains and shapes a network of relationships with the community, but also shapes the history of the individual and
in this sense shapes their personal identity. Mutlu Konuk Blasing highlights
the profound role of the mother tongue: *"The acquisition of language is a loss of
'innocence', a 'fall' from a deathless infancy that, after the fall, can only be imagined as
a maternal voice."*[101] In her conception, poetry is the expression of this "fall", and
thus, in some respects, poetry itself is the language of exile. The second, factual
exile then means transition into another language and the transformation of the
initial connection with the maternal voice. Writing in one's native language in
a foreign-language environment is another way to define exile poetry. This is
illustrated by the cited verses of Karel Zlín:

> Vždyť mluvím-li rodnou řečí na tomto místě,
> jsem vlastně nepřítomen

> ▪

> Why, if I speak my native tongue in this place,
> I absent myself from it.

In many cases one's sojourn in the other linguistic (and not only linguistic)
environment is of one's choosing, as with Richard Weiner, who lived in Paris
but published in Czechoslovakia and was able to move freely between the two
countries.

Yet language does not come into the thematic plane of poems associated with
exile as often as do place and community. It is more evident when its specifics
are deployed, or disrupted. Especially so, where elements of the other language
associated with the place of exile invade the first, native language. The core
language of Milada Součková's poems in her *The Workbooks of Josefína Rykrová*
is Czech, encroached upon by elements of other languages, not always based
on their relation to the surrounding reality, but often stemming from Milada
Součková's cultural memory. The poems are accompanied by commentary,
mostly in English, as if the Czech poems were a language that needed to be con-
veyed. In the case of Ivan Blatný, Czech, albeit still prevalent, becomes flooded
with English over time, and some poems are written entirely in English. While

---

101   M. K. Blasing: *Lyric Poetry*, p. 138.

the occasional extemporés into German or French are characteristic for Blatný, English does at times take on the role of the core language, at much the same level as his Czech.

In view of this linkage to the language, exile can be a traumatic experience, seeking an outlet in nostalgia, but also by a getting to know of things that cannot be known in the mother tongue setting. *"One can henceforth never know oneself but in a second language, in the words of exile."*[102] The transnational skipping between languages opens up a different field of experience and requires different concepts than exile itself. Since the 1970s and 1980s, the concept promoted in this respect was that of *nomadism*. It was remarkably amply demonstrated by Věra Linhartová in her French-written texts, where prose, essays and poetry meet. Her *Twor* directly addresses the issue of the rebirth of "Me" in another language, the un-natural creation of oneself, which the title itself references.

Another delimiter of exile poetry is to the absence of duality between *here* and *there*. Exile can turn its attention to the discovery and exploration of a new place whose reality fuses with the old homeland, as with Ivan Schneedorfer or Stanislav Mareš, or toward a more exclusive interest in the new reality, without nostalgic ties to 'home'. It's not that the poet would have *forgotten*, but the relationship to their origin or community doesn't bisect their identity. Petr Král points out the finer perception of space by exiled poets: 'I find one feature of exile poetry striking here, its more acute and deepened sense of space — once again certainly both physical and metaphysical; standing out compared to the Czech poetic tradition, let alone the domestic creative works in parallel with the poems of Exiles.'[103] Although the observations of Král and his choice of poets are personal and selective, they do capture that fundamental aspect of exile: greater acuity of perception – not only for places, but also language, home and oneself. In the 1970s and 1980s, Petr Král published a book of studies in which he critiques the imaginary in the sense of the surreal and utopian. He recalls that the various utopias connected with the avant-garde went by the wayside in the post-war period and calls into question the 'romantic desire for some far away "elsewhere"', inasmuch as exile would be better seen as a quest for 'new

---

102 Ibid., p. 85.

103 P. Král: Exil v moderní české poesii, p. 557. *"Zvlášť jeden rys exilové poesie se mi tu zdá nápadný, její zostřený a prohloubený smysl pro prostor – znovu jistě fysický i metafysický; vynikne přitom už ve srovnání s českou básnickou tradicí, natož s domácí tvorbou, k níž jsou básně exulantů paralelní."*

space in the world of the here-and-now.'[104] Král's approach dilutes the distinction between home and exile, taking away its metaphysical value, eliminating nostalgia and the imagined equivocation of exile between *here* and *there*. And anyone who is only present in the *here* ceases to be an Exile in the traditional sense of the word. To look at it another way, we are getting close to Adorno's reflections on the homelessness of the 20th century intellectual – who can have no home to be driven out of.

---

104   P. Král: *Konec imaginárna*, p. 19, 11. The book was published in French in 1993, the bibliography in the book *Úniky a návraty* [Escapes and Returns] dates the essays from 1978–1980.

2. Shaded by Reminiscence

I

In the article La nuit de Troie, Jean Starobinski follows how the image of Aeneas fleeing from burning Troy and the associated motifs keep coming back in Western literature, from Virgil to Yves Bonnefoy.[1] This topic is characteristically linked to exile, and as Starobinski notes, Virgil lays down one of the paradigms of Western literature, 'the simultaneous opening to a remembered past and to the future of forthcoming action.'[2] The first exile as such is only the second author in this series, Ovid, by making this paradigm relate to his own story. In his exile work, however, the past significantly outweighs the openness to the future, and this applies to many later authors, whether applying the exile theme to another's story or perceiving it as their own situation.

Starobinski highlights several other important moments of going into exile, in particular the connection with language and the onerous task of expressing this experience (for the pain of its recollection, its non-transferability and inexpressibility).[3] Taking a comparable view to Starobinski on exile, Edward Saïd says:

---

1   J. Starobinski: La nuit de Troie; the journal publication of this study was entitled *Mémoire de Troie* (2004).

2   Ibid., p. 309. *"l'ouverture simultanée sur un passé remémoré et sur un futur où l'action va se porter"*

3   This is especially at the beginning of a second singing of the Aeneid, when the report of Troy's destruction causes Aeneas unspeakable pain (*Infandum regina jubes renovare dolorem*), cf. ibid., p. 307.

Exile is strangely compelling to think about but terrible to experience. It is the unhealable rift forced between a human being and a native place, between the self and its true home: its essential sadness can never be surmounted. And while it is true that literature and history contain heroic, romantic, glorious, even triumphant episodes in an Exile's life, these are no more than effort meant to overcome the crippling sorrow of estrangement. The achievements of exile are permanently undermined by the loss of something left behind forever.[4]

Unlike Starobinski, however, Saïd underscores the incomparability of the distressing experience with what exile can offer for the future, i.e. not just the conjoining of the past and the future at a crucial juncture, but the driving dominance of the past, ever gnawing at the exile's present. While Starobinski analyses the life-story of one literary paradigm and its context, not transgressing the bounds of literature, Saïd wants to write additionally about the real experience of exile, *"beyond those mapped by the literature of exile itself"*.[5] But facing up to the literary expressions of exile cannot be avoided, not least because exile is *"a potent, even enriching motif of modern culture"*[6] and in some ways being in exile is more favourable to writers, politicians and intellectuals who can go about *"creating a new world to rule"*. *"The exile's new world, logically enough, is unnatural and its unreality resembles fiction"*[7] This connection of exile and culture only underscores the importance of written documents, which are often just literary texts. Without those, we could not even think about exile in times of old.

Starobinski and Saïd, for his part, do also gloss over the fact that many an Exile has had no opportunity to testify, to archive their fate in collective memory, or by writing about their situation to contemplate and process it. Left aside are the fates of those unknown whom we can only guess-at in the hinterland behind the testimonies and literary works passed down to us. Opposite the exile who manages to open themselves a new future or give evidence of their present stands a forgotten figure, always associated solely with the past. Literary texts do still take note of such characters, although their history is frag-

---

4   E. Said: Reflections on Exile, p. 173.
5   Ibid., p. 175.
6   Ibid., p. 173.
7   Ibid., p. 181.

mentary and obscure, since they themselves have kept silent and left us nothing to follow up on their lives.

From the beginning, literary renditions of exile are a blend of different meanings, as exemplified by Ovid and his work. By comparing his departure from Rome to Aeneas' flight from burning Troy and with the Odyssey, Ovid inadvertently places three different routes side by side, but at the same time starts off a long line of continuation, extended by poets up to the 20th century. Ovid, though he seeks and finds predecessors, sets out a new route in one important respect: he compares himself to legendary heroes, literary characters, and thus inscribes his own persona into the cultural memory of the West.[8]

For many later authors from the Middle Ages to the present, Ovid become a paradigmatic exile, even in situations that are 'exile' only in allegory. At the end of his *Italian Journey*, Goethe likens his departure from Rome to exile, although he is returning home, and on that occasion he quotes Ovid's elegy, in which the Latin poet bids farewell to Rome. Baudelaire recalls Ovid in several poems (e.g. *Horreur sympathique*), and the central poem about exile in the *Flowers of Evil* – the *Swan* – revolves around exile, as we are reminded by Jean Starobinski. In the *Swan* Baudelaire remodels the established paradigmatic approach. The poem begins by addressing Andromache, but a whole host of associations are triggered by the recollection of the swan the poet once saw, or more exactly the place where this happened, which no longer exists in its then form. The poet may well take his place alongside Virgil, Ovid and Victor Hugo when it comes to the latticework of ingenious quotes, allusions and references, but his constantly revisited consideration for another prevails over mere recollection, his whole sphere of associations derives from the present emotional moment, making everything palpably present: the suffering swan, Andromache and the others, the unknown. Baudelaire does not compare his fate to the fates of other Exiles, but is mindful of them and joins with them in a conceived community.[9] The pattern or analogy that makes the poet a part of shared memory is not the

---

8 Drawing comparison with some mythical figure is not exceptional in the Greek or later Roman lyrical tradition, but the important thing about Ovid is just how he lays down a functional formula for exile writing. In many other respects, too, Ovid follows-on from earlier authors, especially the Greeks, and in many ways his exile is based on *"reworking of a literary tradition on exile before Ovid"*, J. F. Gaertner: How exilic is Ovid's exile poetry, pp. 156–157.

9 Jean Starobinski writes of the importance of the phrase *je pense à* [I think of], which is repeated several times in The Swan: 'This is no isolated, absolutized 'thinking' in the cartesian sense of

issue here, it is compassion and kinship that preserves the memory of others, as expressed in a letter to Victor Hugo (7 December 1859):

Monsieur,

Voici des vers faits pour vous et en pensant à vous. Il ne faut pas les juger avec vos yeux trop sévères, mais avec vos yeux paternels. Les imperfections seront retouchées plus tard. Ce qui était important pour moi, c'était de dire vite tout ce qu'un accident, une image, peut contenir de suggestions, et comment la vue d'un animal souffrant pousse l'esprit vers tous les êtres que nous aimons, qui sont absents et qui souffrent, vers tous ceux qui sont privés de quelque chose d'irretrouvable.

Veuillez agréer mon petit symbole comme un très faible témoignage de la sympathie et de l'admiration que m'inspire votre génie.

CHARLES BAUDELAIRE

Sir,

Here are verses made for you and thinking of you. You shouldn't judge them with your harsh eyes, but with your fatherly eyes. Imperfections will be touched up later. What was important for me, was to say quickly all that an accident, an image, can contain in suggestions, and how the sight of a suffering animal pushes the mind toward all those beings whom we love, who are absent and who suffer, toward all those who are deprived of something that will never be found again. Please accept my little symbol as a very weak testimony of the sympathy and admiration which your genius inspires in me.

CHARLES BAUDELAIRE[10]

'I think…' Every 'consideration' in the poem is thought *about* unfortunate beings – who are also pensive and grieving for other beings or places', *La mélancolie au miroir*, p. 76.

10   Ch. Baudelaire: *Correspondance* I, pp. 622–623.

II

Baudelaire indirectly posits the inevitable question: How many various Exiles have disappeared in complete oblivion? They cannot serve as traditional role models, but can be thought of with empathy, even if we know nothing about them, and so include even those silent and unbeknown beings in our common memory as its emotional, pathos-filled supplement. We only get a sense of 'the swan' because of Baudelaire, and only thanks to his poem do we remember it. Countless other such fates are completely lost to us. Maybe there's never been the slightest anything to remember them by. But one can give them a thought (as opposed to reminiscence) knowing that such people existed, and disappeared. These figures do not form some continuous sequence, because they are mute, and unconnected with the common pattern. Yet they are united by the shared fate of exclusion and oblivion that can only be overcome by someone else, in giving thought to them. Baudelaire in the *Swan* pointed out a similar *gulf* as in his poem of that name (*Le Gouffre*), but not as an inner divide, but as a deeper abyss of an absent being who can with just a thought be brought closer, spanning and diminishing the subjective divide. The issue of exile in literature borders on this abyss, which is difficult to talk about, but cannot be ignored.

Baudelaire's letter to Victor Hugo confirms a certain ambiguity of the poem. The swan is, on the one hand, *a* suffering being the poet happened to meet (its first appearance in the poem bears the indefinite article), but at the same time is a *symbol*, not only standing in for other sufferers and outcasts in the terms of Baudelaire's poem, but also an emblematic creature with a long tradition, from antiquity, *mythe étrange et fatal* [strange, fateful myth].[11] Appearing in such a poem understandably inclines the reader to see it through these dual lenses, as both a real animal and a symbol.[12] References to Ovid may remind of a lesser-known episode in his *Metamorphoses*, in which Cycnus leaves his country out of grief over the death of Phaethon and turns into a swan.[13] A key angle for

---

11   Michal Švec discusses the symbolism of the swan from antiquity to the present: *Symbolika labutě*.

12   Y. Bonnefoy: *Lieux et destins de l'image* (pp. 220–221) emphasizes that Baudelaire deliberately treats the swan non-allegorically and wants to "show the most ordinary creature, thirsty for water, an anxious, miserable life with a 'bowed neck' and 'frantic movements'."

13   Ovid: *Metamorphoses*, 2, 367ff.; the second Cycnus appears in the 12th book.

reading the poem in its historical-cultural context of exile is the swan's indeterminate gender.[14] The classic exile in Western culture has for a long time been a man, and Baudelaire also dedicated the poem to one such, famous in his time. Simon Goldhill recalls how strongly the discourse about exile, often associated with a heroic story, features maleness: *"the modern superstars of exile form a largely male canon. This is not merely because of the statistical realities of political process, but because, since the Odyssey at least, the values of staying at home and traveling are inherently gendered. It may be that when we move from the commitment to a hero's narrative towards a collective or differently gendered account, it is then that the language of 'refugee' is adopted rather than the language of 'exile'. Pity the refugee, but listen to the exile's story..."*[15]

Baudelaire begins his *Swan* with a female figure in mind, Andromache. In the second part, the list goes on, featuring an unknown black woman, then a reference to Romulus and Remus, and only the final part stays with masculine terms: *Je pense aux matelots oubliés dans une île, / Aux captifs, aux vaincus !* [I think of sailors lost on an island / of prisoners, of the defeated!] – washed up existences, refugees, not heroes prevail. The swan itself, which Baudelaire compares to a human being from Ovid's Metamorphoses, keeps up an ambiguity of gender throughout the poem, but one important feature connects it with both female characters: like them, it is far from its native land, from the idyllic environment in which alone it can live. In so doing he refers to another set of characters than the one which begins with Aeneas and Ovid. These figures have their own myth of someone being abruptly and violently ripped from their environment. Thus is Persephone abducted: the flowering meadow suddenly opens up and Hades takes the girl to the underworld.

> I sing of the revered goddess, rich-haired Demeter,
> and her slim-ankled daughter, whom Hades snatched
> (far-seeing, thundering Zeus gave her away)
> while she and Ocean's deep-breasted daughters played,
> far from golden blade Demeter, who bears shining fruit.
> She picked lush meadow flowers: roses, crocuses,

---

14   In Czech, unlike many other languages, the word for swan, *labuť*, is feminine. The Swan is indeed often regarded as a feminine creature and has kept this ambiguity of gender since ancient times, cf. M. Švec: *Symbolika labutě*, pp. 21, 25.

15   S. Goldhill: Whose Antiquity?, p. 4.

lovely violets, irises, hyacinths— and a narcissus
Gaia grew as a lure for the blossoming girl,
following Zeus' bidding, to please Lord of the Dead.
Everyone marveled at the bewitching sight,
immortal gods and mortal folk alike:
from its root blossomed a hundred sweetly
scented heads, and all wide heaven above,
all earth, and the salty swell of the sea laughed.
Amazed, she stretched out both hands to pick
the charming bloom— and a chasm opened
in the Nysian plain. Out sprang Lord of the Dead,
god of many names, on his immortal horses.
Snatching the unwilling girl, he carried her off
in his golden chariot, as she cried and screamed aloud
calling to her father, son of Kronos, highest and best.[16]

The Hymn represents one myth of the vernal cycle: a young girl embodying the awakening nature of Spring is abducted into the underworld, and the
lifecycle of nature shall be restored only when she is returned to her mother,
the goddess of fertility, at least for a time. The introduction of the Greek hymn
depicts the girl in the idyllic scene of a blooming Spring meadow and in safe
surroundings, among her companions. The abduction into the underworld,
equivalent to death, takes the girl by surprise (although the male powers
behind it all have agreed on everything in advance) thus disrupting the apparently safe idyllic scene. If we continue with the analogy, in Baudelaire's poem,
Paris turns into an underworld, repeatedly – first for the swan in the past,
then for the poet in the present, as he is being made acutely aware of the
disappearance of bygone Paris. The only way to get out of this concatenation
of Exiles, which appears to be a 'fateful and fatal' condition of human life,
seems to be the idea of a community of Exiles, which may be only imaginary
(Baudelaire directly refers to it as exile: *dans la forêt où mon esprit s'exile*, 'in the
forest where my spirit is fleeing') with the added aesthetic of memory's background music. The difference from the male line of Exiles founded by Ovid is
substantial: whilst in that line each is likened to another, here each one *thinks*

---

16   *The Homeric Hymns* [online], p. 17.

of another. The figure of Persephone in Homeric myth is no role model for anyone. Her fate can however be contemplated, with awareness that it touches upon oneself.

III

In 1846, Edgar Allan Poe wrote in his *Philosophy of Composition* the famous words: *"the death then of a beautiful woman is, unquestionably, the most poetical topic in the world."*[17] In so doing he set out the *topos* that has found countless expression in literature and art before Poe, and after him.[18] Many of them have through various themes been revisions of the myth of Persephone. These dying young women are often intimately related to the environment. One example above all is Ophelia, seemingly quite designed for the aquatic element[19] that drowns her. Gaston Bachelard dealt with the 'Ophelia Complex' in his *L'eau et les rêves* [Water and Dreams], highlighting Ophelia's connection to water as the element of death, which appears in many variants of that story.[20] The paradigmatic example of the figure of Ophelia in Czech literature is the similar figure of Viktorka from Božena Němcová's *Babička* [Granny], echoed in several other Czech texts.

In 1909, Teréza Nováková published her leading novel *Děti čistého živého* [Children of the pure life]. She takes an extensive historical look over several decades of the 'East Bohemian Tolerance Sectarians'.[21] The novel describes the gradual decline of this group, their inability to adjust to the ways of the world, the fateful irony with which everything turns against them. The book opens with a scene from a village cemetery in which a gravedigger digs a grave in

---

17   E. A. Poe: The Philosophy of Composition, p. 19.

18   H. Anton deals with the Myth of Persephone and how it has lived on: *Der Raub der Proserpina*; Ch. Brehm: *Der Raub der Proserpina*; G. Kaiser i the book *Vénus et la mort* follows the related theme of the death of a woman, connected with erotica, E. Bronfen: *Over her Dead Body* on the theme of the death of a woman in art viewed from a psychoanalytical perspective.

19   W. Shakespeare: *Hamlet* 4,7, l. 180–181: *creature native and indu'd / Unto that element.*

20   G. Bachelard: *Water and Dreams*, ch. 3.

21   This term is introduced by Zdeněk R. Nešpor in his works, e.g. *Víra bez církve?* [Faith without religion?]

rocky soil for a recently deceased man, Koutný, whose little son Jiřík, the main character of the novel, wraps up the whole book as an older man with his meditations on the ways of the world. In the opening scene, the gravedigger digs up soil full of bones and rotted remains, with hardly any room for other corpses, as if the earth refuses to accept them even after death. The gloomy and despondent scene has its counterpart in the central episode of the whole novel, in which a young girl, Růženka, dies. In describing the death of a young girl, possibly echoing the death of her own beloved son, Nováková shows the world transformed from a seemingly welcoming home into an inhospitable wasteland. The scene is preceded by a timid love story between Jiřík and Růženka, the daughter of a 'Sectarian' family. Jiřík is unsettled by gossip about the sect's orgiastic practices, and after some hesitation talks everything through with Růženka's father. The girl overhears their talk and sobs in distress. Both men hear her sobbing, mingled with other sounds in their surroundings:

> "It did not sound like the wind, but like sighs and crying."
> "The stream is high, blubbing o'er them stones, and the millrace and penstock are overflowin' after them rains – that sounds like crying and the echo from the woods adds to it 'n'all," the miller explained.[22]

The desperate girl is terrified of slander and in her surge of emotion thinks of death:

> [...] oh, who only doesn't know of her shame! How is she now to go on living? [...] If only the stony hillside were to open up and swallow her, right now, how fitting it would be![23]

When she then wants to return home, in the dark the familiar surroundings turn into a strange, hostile environment, and the girl falls into the millrace and eventually drowns.

> Růženka's confused and desperate mind is further upset by fear of the night's silence, the strange surroundings, in which darkness has given

---

22   T. Nováková: *Děti čistého živého*, p. 354.
23   Ibid., p. 362.

every bush, tree and stone a new and menacing, terrifying form. She has to head back to the orchard, once she gets to more level ground, it will all be better, she can already feel the garden's picket fence, now only to pass through the gate and go through the mill room into the house, and to her room. [...]

She made her way down gingerly, but after a few steps cried out in horror: instead of the orchard she found herself in the millrace stream. The running water was almost up to her waist, cold as ice, and flowing as if to take the legs from under her. The girl was shaking, shouting as loud as she could manage and trying to get back up the slope. But what she could easily have managed in broad daylight was now impossible to achieve in total darkness, she could not find any suitable foothold to get up, no branches to grab; she was ever slipping back into the cold, black water again.

[...]

At last she found beneath her a soft patch, which seemed kind to her tired, injured legs, – she was on sand, perhaps, soon to be better off. But the foundation was giving way, she was sinking deeper, the water rising up on her, she could tell it had a foul reek, of mud, water-weed, rot, – she tried to grab onto the bank somewhere, but could not see anything before her, – screaming, groaning — then silenced – – – –[24]

Nováková devoted long and thorough study to her Tolerance Sectarian subject matter,[25] and many pages of the novel are based on this study. Nevertheless, this is not a purely depictive novel, the book has its symbolic plane, which manifests itself especially in this central episode. The theme of the death of a young girl is developed here in a number of motifs traditionally connected with it: the image of the earth opening up, the aquatic element, the voices of nature drowning out the human voice, or the motif of the flowers the dead girl is covered up by and buried under at the funeral.[26]

------

24   Ibid., pp. 363–364.
25   cf. S. Sílová: Dílo Terézy Novákové.
26   T. Nováková: ibid., p. 366. Flowers appear as a central motif in the Homeric Hymn and in Ovid, in his case falling out of the abducted girl's hands, which can be read as symbolizing the loss of virginity; they are likewise important to the image of Ophelia. In the case of Růženka,

Language plays a major role in how the scene unfolds. Jiřík hears slanderous gossip, talks to Růženka's father and acknowledges that he has been deceived. Yet Růženka surreptitiously listens in on only a part of the conversation, which ultimately leads to her death. By the time the two men hear her, her voice is already masked by the surrounding sounds of nature, she already belongs to another world. The slander and (in this case) the man-to-man talk in the scene typify being oblivious to others, self-centred, which is a second factor in Růženka's demise. Jiřík does hear her, but lets himself be persuaded by the miller that it was only the water in the millrace – which not only drowns Růženka's voice but, ultimately, drowns her. From then on, the girl is only present in the memory of those involved, and just as her familiar world had undergone dramatic change, so are their lives radically altered by the accident. Růženka remains inextricably linked with the places she lived in, and after her death these places and the world of her loved ones change, thus her death is symbolic of the entire religious group's downfall. The young girl's death remains an implicit presence throughout the plot and the other events relate to her; ultimately when Jiřík, now as an older man reminisces about her in the epilogue.

Tolerance Sectarianism is closely related to the history of exile. These sects progressively split-off from the furtive groups of Protestants who kept true to their faith after the violent recatholicization of the Czech lands after 1620. They thus 'share the DNA' of the post-White-Mountain Exiles, and we can view them as one form of internal exile or inner emigration. Nováková in her work creates one of the few ties between modern Czech culture based on the revivalist movement, and the religious currents of the 17th and 18th century, not solely factography-based.[27]

---

the flowers from her garden, returned to her after her death, are more a symbol of her being untouched.

27   Going into exile went on constantly until the 18th century, with the undeclared and exiled protestants keeping in touch, cf. E. Melmuková-Šašecí: *Patent zvaný toleranční*, pp. 74–81; particularly the work of E. Štěříková, in summary, inter alia *Stručně o pobělohorských exulantech*.

IV

After the Communist coup of 1948 the short story by Jan Čep entitled *Tajemství Kláry Bendové* [The Klára Bendová Mystery] enters the exile scene. The work of the Catholic Jan Čep resonates in many ways with the motifs of Protestant post-White-Mountain exile. It does so in particular, through its core notion of *'dual-homed cross-pollination',*[28] which is a feature of his prose seen by many as characteristic. In his essay, *Rodný úžas* [Nativity's Amazement] he expresses the life feeling characteristic of his work as follows:

> In this sense, we could say that the world as created, accessible to our natural knowledge, is an illustration and suggestion of reality full and entire, whose form we see in it, as in a mirror. – We are such an image in the mirror unto ourselves. Our inner experience contains in its climatic moments the elements of an existence whose invisible presence surrounds and permeates the realm of our earthly time from all sides.[29]

After Čep's going off into exile we see an understandable change in how his work deals with the topic, whereby the sense of spiritual exile is complemented by material exile.[30] In his short story of 'May Days' *Květnové dni*, Čep describes the liberation of Bohemia by the Soviet army as a less than entirely welcome event, and similarly in the *Klára Bendová Mystery* the joy of liberation alternates with qualms about how Soviet soldiers behave: 'They greeted them with singing, covered them with flowers. But already by evening, the people had become subdued, their faces once again tense with anxiety and fear.'[31] Even the title of the short story strays beyond the outlined theme. Čep makes a very small stage the setting of an unfolding, complex storyline, which turns to the past and at the same time opens up to the future. This may recall the opening--up model referenced by Starobinski. For Čep, however, the effect is rather the opposite – the past (wartime) is dark, and liberation soon proves to be ambiva-

---

28   Čep's 1926 short-story collection bears the title *Dual Home*.
29   J. Čep: Rodný úžas, p. 19.
30   cf. J. Zatloukal: *L'exil de Jan Čep*, p. 38.
31   J. Čep: Tajemství Kláry Bendové, p. 339.

lent, at best. Though the plot opens up in both directions, but the past and the future manifest themselves as hostile and focus the heroine's attention to a more intimate experiencing of the present.

The story begins on a beautiful summer day two months after liberation. While looking at the summer landscape, Klára Bendová recalls recent events – the liberation, immediately followed by the gratuitous arrest of her father, the suspicious looks of the city-dwellers. Her memories take place against the landscape's backdrop, as though human society and nature were inextricably linked:

> She closed the door quietly again and returned to her window. Such a lovely day! The mountains were bluish-tinted on their slopes, their heavy rounded mass suffused with light, lightly projected against the backdrop of a vast, iridescent blue space.
>
> Klára's heart tightened once more. Those mountains and the land were hers, they had always belonged to her, just like her own body. They looked her straight in the eyes, just as she looked into the eyes of people she knew and loved. It wasn't until that terrible event that all those eyes began to look at her like strangers, and the land itself seemed about to sever itself from her heart. For what had happened was wrong, an injustice, intentional, and incomprehensible.[32]

After a series of anxious days, the girl finds solace during Mass, as if she were 'at home, at the very heart of something no one could expel her from [...] She felt that the suffering of the whole world and all people was one, and that her suffering was part of it.'[33] Then Klára goes outside, to the river, in a strangely hallucinatory atmosphere, seeing a Soviet soldier using a rifle to fish in the river, and after that the girl dies. The soldier in the short story resembles a vulgar faun, his actions and appearance are depicted by the narrator as primitive and at the same time strangely vague. All the events of the story are also deliberately without motive – the arrest of Klára's father, her death and the very connection between the events and the historical backdrop. Jan Čep leaves parts of the story unexplained, describing the events from Klára's point of view, but

---

32   Ibid., pp. 338–339.
33   Ibid., p. 340. Jan Zatloukal: ibid., p. 120 highlights this aspect of Christian sacrifice.

she herself cannot see out far enough to grasp their meaning, and in the end, even just to see what is going on directly around her. It remains unclear whether she was struck by a deliberate or accidental shot, or fell onto the rocks. Her death goes beyond simple causality, but makes her being all the more inherently related to events, as their necessary completion, a would-be ritual sacrifice that sanctifies the start of a new era.

In Čep's short story we find a variety of motifs related to the myth of Persephone and its variations. The girl is picking flowers in a meadow, a soldier appears like a spectral being from another world, and his presence disrupts Klára's harmony with her surroundings, the girl loses the firm ground beneath her feet and falls into the water. Flowers have already shown up in the earlier part of the story, when the city's inhabitants were regaling Soviet soldiers with them, and at the story's end they cover the dead girl in her coffin. By his rendition of a beautiful girl's death, Čep achieved a distinctive effect. The mystery of her death pushes back the historical events, casts a different light on them, as though their significance was ultimately not so great, compared with this death that transcends myth and forces us to keep reminding ourselves of the dead girl.

V

The legendary death of a young girl, originally related to observing the cyclical nature of time, does in its modern-day form offer several temporal templates. Above all, its course differs from Aeneas' escape from Troy. Time is also the opening of that narrative, but remains set within it, as a tipping point. The death of the girl is not set in time, because it does not belong to any series of events. It creates a gentle connection with a past dependent on personal, private thoughts, and still at risk of being forgotten. As soon as the death comes back to mind, it transforms the person touched by it, and the atmosphere of the whole story. Edgar Allan Poe in his *Philosophy of Composition* asserts that an abandoned lover should be the one thinking of a dead woman. Such is the case in his Raven, where the poem's speaker remains submerged in the past. In Čep's short story, the death of Klára is an event that stands out against the historical timeline, which puts into perspective the day-to-day happenings and the historical watershed that was to be a new beginning.

In 1922, Robert Musil published the novel *Tonka*. Its eponymous titular character, a Czech girl, exhibits a special malady: she cannot express her thoughts in clear articulated language, she speaks 'a kind of ensemblese', which is more like singing.[34] Yet at the same time she needs someone receptive enough to notice her and able to listen to her speech. What she has to say is more substantial and important than everyone else, even though others look down on her with contempt as if she had no place in their company.

> Seine Verwandten sprachen lebhaft durcheinander und er bemerkte, wie gut sie damit ihren Nutzen wahrten. Sie sprachen nicht schön, aber flink, hatten Mut zu ihrem Schwall, und es bekam schließlich jeder, was er wollte. [...] Wie stumm war Tonka! Sie konnte weder sprechen noch weinen. Ist aber etwas, das weder sprechen kann, noch ausgesprochen wird, das in der Menschheit stumm verschwindet, ein kleiner, eingekratzter Strich in den Tafeln ihrer Geschichte, ist solche Tat, solcher Mensch, solche mitten in einem Sommertag ganz allein niederfallende Schneeflocke Wirklichkeit oder Einbildung, gut, wertlos oder bös? Man fühlt, daß da die Begriffe an eine Grenze kommen, wo sie keinen Halt mehr finden.

> His relatives spoke animatedly with one another, and he noted they were putting their own self-benefit first. They didn't choose their words with care, but they had nimble tongues, bravely lowering the floodgates of their eloquence, and in the end, everyone got what they wanted. [...] How mute Tonka was! She could neither talk, nor cry. But is something that cannot even speak, nor is even uttered, something silently lost in the human multitude, a tiny line scraped onto the tablets of human history, is such an action, such a person, such a snowflake drifting alone to the ground in the midst of a summer's day, is it real, or mere delusion, is it good, worthless or evil? We feel that here concepts have reached their limits, their foothold gone.[35]

---

34   R. Musil: *Drei Frauen*, Rowohlt 1979, p. 53: *"irgend eine Sprache des Ganzen"*.
35   Ibid., p. 57.

When Tonka dies, the narrator realizes that the girl did not impact his life in any tangible way, had no effect on its course, yet he would not be who he is without her. Maybe she was from the very beginning like a memory, which can suddenly enlighten and change a person.

> Wohl war ihm bewußt, daß er geändert worden war und noch ein anderer werden würde, aber das war er doch selbst und es war nicht eigentlich Tonkas Verdienst. Die Spannung der letzten Wochen, die Spannung seiner Erfindung, versteht es sich recht, hatte sich gelöst, er war fertig. Er stand im Licht und sie lag unter der Erde, aber alles in allem fühlte er das Behagen des Lichts. Bloß wie er da um sich sah, blickte er plötzlich einem der vielen Kinder ringsum in das zufällig weinende Gesicht; es war prall von der Sonne beschienen und krümmte sich wie ein gräßlicher Wurm nach allen Seiten: da schrie die Erinnerung in ihm auf: Tonka! Tonka! Er fühlte sie von der Erde bis zum Kopf und ihr ganzes Leben. Alles, was er niemals gewußt hatte, stand in diesem Augenblick vor ihm, die Binde der Blindheit schien von seinen Augen gesunken zu sein; einen Augenblick lang, denn im nächsten schien ihm bloß schnell etwas eingefallen zu sein. Und vieles fiel ihm seither ein, das ihn etwas besser machte als andere, weil auf seinem glänzenden Leben ein kleiner warmer Schatten lag.

He realized that he had changed and was still going to change, but it was his own doing, not really to Tonka's credit. The tension of recent weeks, the tension from his inventions had eased, naturally enough, for he had finished. He stood in the light while she lay underground, but in any case, he felt the light as blissful. As he looked around, he suddenly noticed the head of one of the many children around him; it was brightly lit by the sun, twisting around like an ugly worm: and at that moment a reminiscence called out within him. Tonka! Tonka! He was aware of her from head to toe, he sensed her whole life. At that moment, everything that he had never known welled up before him, as if a blindfold had fallen from his eyes; it was only for a moment, because straight after he saw it was just a thought. And from that moment on, he had many thoughts that made him a little better than others, because his life was warmly and gently shaded.[36]

VI

Poe's account of the grieving lover reminds of the complementary myth of Orpheus and Eurydice, a version of which Ovid included in his *Metamorphoses*. Maurice Blanchot saw it as an archetype of poetic creation, and in his *The Space of Literature* he also presents the motif of singing, akin to Baudelaire's 'Memory blowing the horn'.[37] Baudelaire's Memory is not just a reminder of burning Troy, a ruined past that, at an enormous price, opened up the scope for a new beginning. This memory reminds us that someone is irrevocably lost and that the thought of them, of someone excluded from common memory even, at that moment completely overshadows oneself, the one who remembers and pushes momentous history aside, to consider this case of loss instead. The sadness that Exiles have in common spills out of them, toward others, providing some significant comfort in how it quells the loneliness of the excluded individual, but also opens up and gives a new horizon to exile. The outcast is not just someone cast out of their homeland, or who does not feel at home anywhere, they belong to a community established through compassionate thought.

36   Ibid., pp. 85–86.
37   M. Blanchot: *L'espace littéraire*, p. 227.

3. Exile and Shelter[1]

When we look at the long and complicated history of exile as depicted in literature, from the very beginning we find a whole series of mindsets toward it: from nostalgia after losing one's home (for example in Ovid's poetry) to the discovery of new worlds and the explorer's élan (whose models are the figures of Odysseus and Aeneas). This chapter focuses on one form of the exile space, which the Czech writer Egon Hostovský calls *úkryt* [shelter]. For Czech literature, the basic model in this respect is *Labyrint světa a ráj srdce* [The Labyrinth of the World and the Paradise of the Heart] by Jan Amos Komenský (1623/1631), where the inner space of the heart stands firm against the pandemonium and unfriendliness of the world. Comenius became an emblematic figure of Czech exile in the 20th century, but that is beyond the scope of this treatise. In the 20th century, the idea of innerness as a refuge against the world is revived to a certain extent, and in works by several authors it gains remarkable psychological depth.

I

In the 1940s, Egon Hostovský (1908–1973) published several works of prose set during the period of war-time emigration and in the immediate post-war era: *Listy z vyhnanství* [Letters from Exile; published in Czech in Chicago in 1941], *Úkryt* [Shelter; published in English as *The Hide-Out* in 1945, transl. Fern

---

1   This chapter originally translated by M Sweeney, revised for orthographic and terminological consistency.

Long], *Cizinec hledá byt* [Foreigner Seeks Flat, 1947]. What connects them is
the theme of refuge or shelter, which he refers to in several differing situations,
due also to geopolitical changes. Hostovský is partly building upon his pre-war
psychological novels such as *Dům bez pána* [House without a Master, 1937]
and *Žhář* [The Arsonist, 1935], in which he portrays the break-up of home
and family. As opposed to his earlier novels, historical events play a substantial role in his exile works, intruding into the personal space of the family. His
characters flee Czechoslovakia to avoid the storm clouds of impending World
War II, and the Nazi occupation. The novel *Foreigner Seeks Flat* is set in the
post-war period, and though the historical frame remains mostly in the background (for example the references to the coming Communist government in
Czechoslovakia), it deals with the atmosphere of the new, post-war world, one
which has undergone transformations and in which Hostovský's ongoing exile
is expressed as a normal situation and a diagnosis on human life.

The Hide-Out describes the story of a Czech engineer who has left
Czechoslovakia and after various peregrinations is hiding in the cellar of
a French acquaintance in the occupied part of France. His "hiding place" has
a complex structure determined by relations with the outside world and events.
It is not asylum or refuge, a place that at least partially replaces or represents
a home. Nor is it a hotel, such as that in which Dr Marek in *Foreigner Seeks Flat*
seeks shelter for at least a few days. More than anything else, the shelter resembles a prison: 'I've been living in this prison since mid-June of 1940.'[2] With
one difference, which is primarily psychological – he could leave at any time,
although death awaits him outside. 'You have to exercise your will,' the host tells
him, 'you have to think, 'I know I can go to the light at any time, just take the
handle, but I'm not going to do it on purpose!''[3]

Hostovský in his prose captures something about the complicated topology
of fleeing and hiding, characteristic of the 20th century, which in its complexity
one can find not only in history, but also in literature and language, including
a whole range of terms, often not directly translatable from one language to
another. Shelter is not an arbitrary refuge: it relates to a certain arrangement of
the world, to a certain historico-political situation, and is connected to a certain

---

2   E. Hostovský: *Listy z Vyhnanství. Úkryt*, p. 120; on 121 the word given is 'žalář' (dungeon). The
     quotations herein are not from the 1945 English edition, but have been retranslated from the
     original Czech.
3   Ibid., p. 162; also cf. p. 169.

type of flight or exile. In Hostovský's *Letters from Exile*, the situation is different from *The Hide-Out*. The *Listy* stories take place in yet-unoccupied European countries (France, Portugal); their protagonists flee from one temporary refuge to another. The possibility of arriving at a permanent refuge, casting oneself away from continental Europe, lies on the horizon of these stories as their ideal conclusion; in reality, everything remains temporary and makeshift. In *Foreigner Seeks Flat*, on the other hand, the external danger of occupation and prison disappears: the American world of the novel is not confined by the horizon of the temporary; transience has become the norm, transformed in the ordinary course of time, and in the story of Dr Marek it characterises all of his addresses. The foreigner, Dr Marek, is never looking for a *home*, nor is he looking for any shelter, he is just looking for a place where he could work in peace and quiet for 'a while'[4] – as if the concept of home in this world no longer has a place. It is just about a flat. The temporal horizon is represented by death, which in the novel is allegorical, personified by a mysterious voice on the telephone, offering the foreigner a definitive refuge and at the same time by its expression reminding one of the fleetingness of human existence. The discovery which Dr Marek is working on gradually loses its importance in the story, Marek's journeys from one abode to another come to the fore, as well as how a strange foreigner is not acceptable to everyone he meets. At this point, the novel opens up a double perspective. On one hand, it's about a person seeking a refuge in the world; on the other hand, it is a depiction of a world which, due to its nature, cannot provide such a refuge. The individual characters whom Dr Marek meets in his adventure embody this aspect of the world.

What is it that does not allow a foreigner to remain? At the house of a professor who provides him with shelter, he becomes friendly with the professor's unstable son and his openness brings the hidden conflict between father and son (which the father does not want to admit) to a head; the rich widow, thanks to his initially inconspicuous presence, realises the aimlessness of her life, she falls in love with him and wants to yoke him into a relationship. In one dwelling, he provokes the inhabitant into taking an interest in an elderly Jew; in another, he inadvertently reveals the hypocrisy of the housewife. There is a similar type of conflict in the story *Elisa* from *Letters from Exile*: Rudolf Gruber leaves the flat of a professor who has sheltered him after a conflict with

---

4   E. Hostovský: *Cizinec hledá byt*, p. 35.

his daughter, who was in love with him, but hid her feelings behind an outward enmity. Hostovský's foreigners bring disruption into households. They are considerate to the utmost (behaving as if everything were all right), but actually their perception of what the home dwellers consider normal or suppress, points out what one cannot take for granted about the established way of things and the hidden controlling of one person by another. The refuge is transformed in this moment, due to the tense relationships between people which have come to the surface. 'The household of Prof Backer was transformed for Rudolf Gruber into a prison [...].'[5]

The foreigner here is not the person who has come from elsewhere; rather he is the person who realises that no place is a natural home, and for this reason is always on his or her way *elsewhere*. For those who live or want to live with a feeling of home, the foreigner introduces a disruptive element which reminds them of what they cannot take for granted. The philosopher Vilém Flusser (1920–1991) describes the invasion of the foreigner thus:

> Sociologists would like us to believe that foreigners (such as sociologists or persons without a heimat) can learn the secret codes of heimat, because after all, the natives had to learn them too, which confirms the meaning of initiation rites among the so-called primitive peoples. A person without heimat should therefore be able to wander from one heimat to another and settle in each one, if only he carries with him all the necessary keys needed to unlock them. But the reality is very different. The secret codes are not, in general, conscious rules but rather are spun largely from unconscious habits. What is characteristic of habits is that one is not conscious of them. To be able to settle in a new heimat, an immigrant must first learn the secret code consciously – and then forget it again. If the code becomes conscious, then its rules are exposed as something banal and not sacred. For the native who is settled, the immigrant is even more alien and strange than the migrant outside his door because he exposes as banal what the native considers sacred.[6]

---

5   E. Hostovský: *Listy z Vyhnanství. Úkryt*, p. 27.
6   Vilém Flusser: The Challenge of the Migrant, p. 6.

Flusser, a German Jew from Prague, left Prague in 1938 for Great Britain and later Brazil, where he spent a large part of his life. He later settled in France and wrote his texts in German. In the early 1990s he repeatedly returned to Prague, where he gave several lectures. He died tragically on his way back from Prague in 1991 in a car accident. In his essay *Wohnung beziehen in der Heimatlosigkeit* [Taking up Residence in Homelessness],[7] which he incorporated into his remarkable 'philosophical autobiography' *Bodenlos* [Bottomless, 1992], he poses the pairing of Home (*Heimat*) – Dwelling (*Wohnung*) Contrary to the common idea, their relationship reverses and puts the dwelling first. Home for him represents the place of invisible relationships, "hidden attachments",[8] which root a person, bind him, and at the same time blind him to the rest of the world[9] home represents the place of the relationships he has been thrust into, rather than those he would have chosen freely for himself. For Flusser, home is not essential, because becoming enmeshed in domestic ties is not vital for human life; in this sense, one can be without a home – but not without a dwelling.

> People think of *Heimat* as being a relatively permanent place; a home [*Wohnung*], as temporary and interchangeable. Actually, the opposite is true: One can exchange heimats – or have none at all, but one must always live somewhere, regardless of where. Parisian *clochards* live under bridges, Gypsies live in caravans, Brazilian agricultural workers live in huts, and horrible as it may sound, people had a roof over their heads at Auschwitz. Because a person will simply perish without a home [Wohnung], a place to live.[10]

Hostovský is not far conceptually from Flusser: the hosts of his expats are not able to perceive the foreigner as anything other than a disturber of the peace. In this light, Hostovský's novel *Foreigner Seeks Flat* manifests itself as the pinnacle of his novelistic reflections on home, exile, and shelter, and indicates a similar

---

7   The essay has been translated into English twice: The Challenge of the Migrant, In: Flusser: *The Freedom of the Migrant*, transl. Kenneth Kronenberg. And also Taking Up Residence in Homelessness, In: Flusser: *Writings*, transl. Erik Eisel, pp. 91–103. Kronenberg retained the German terms, Eisel translated *Heimat* as "home" and *Wohnung* as "a home", always in quotes.

8   V. Flusser: The Challenge of the Migrant, p. 4.

9   Ibid.

10   V. Flusser: The Challenge of the Migrant, p. 12.

change in values as in Flusser. What is it that the foreigner is seeking, and what does he not find in the dwellings? Dr Marek does not want to be drawn into the net of domestic ties; and because he perceives them clearly and pretends, and at the same time acts, as if they do not exist for him, he understandably disrupts the stability of the homes of his hosts. He finds friends in a dog, in children, a psychologically frail youth – in creatures whose way of living at home is also like that of a stranger; though unlike him, they are already subjugated by the home dwellers. For these creatures it is characteristic that they do not experience domestic ties as something natural and taken for granted, and therefore they are more aware of them. The foreigner should use the refuge for his work on an important drug; in that sense, it is a place which makes possible relations to the outside world.

From Flusser's point of view, a dwelling is similarly a place where, as an ordinary background, it offers the possibility of perceiving the unusual outside world.[11] 'Without a place to live, without the protection of the usual and habitual, everything that encroaches on one is noise – without information – and without information, in a chaotic world, one can neither feel nor think nor act.'[12] The frame of the dwelling is determined by habit, but on the other hand it is not perceived by oneself: 'Habituation covers all phenomena like a blanket of cotton wool. It smoothes the sharp edges of all phenomena that it covers so that I no longer bump against them, but I am able to make use of them blindly.'[13] And this habit can turn into numbness: through the exchange of a dwelling for a home, and the subsequent inability to perceive the outside world. Dr Marek in Hostovský's novel does not share the secrets and intertwined relationships of a home; for the others he is a person without secrets, living 'in the clarity' (*in der Evidenz*), as Flusser writes: his presence forces the hosts to see the world and home in a different perspective, and it is just that which makes him 'disturbing' to the locals. His mission, which he maintains until the last minute, shows the others that they have shut themselves in at home and have given up on 'living in the world'. Here Flusser indicates very precisely the shift where Hostovský's novel differs from the thematically close *White Disease* by Čapek. The foreigner without a home loses the original secrets of the home and the loss

---

11   Ibid., p. 12–13.
12   Ibid., p. 12.
13   Ibid., p. 13.

'has opened him up to a different sort of mystery: the mystery of living together with others'.[14] This is why the drug on which he is working is not key to the plot of the novel, and does not have the significance of the cure Dr Galén is working on in Čapek's play. Perhaps Dr Marek could cure a few afflicted people, but the principal 'disease' here are the handicapped relationships between people who are shut in their homes and cease to perceive the other.

In the novel *The Hide-Out* (1943), Hostovský points out the conflict between an open place and a closed place in a different situation. The story's protagonist half-leaves, half-flees from the unpleasant atmosphere of personal and family relationships (as do a number of Hostovský's other characters). At the time when, in Paris, he learns of the occupation of Czechoslovakia, his incipient unfaithfulness and all his other personal intrigues suddenly lose their importance to him. The occupation ruined his home; and with it, also nullified the reasons why he left. In the state of occupation, the external world is unfriendly, introducing a threat for home and for dwelling, a time when one can only go into hiding. In the protagonist's memories, the lost home takes on great significance; however, this is because it is threatened or even destroyed. Home in Flusser's conception is broken by the external world, against which it should protect one. Enemy forces are so much stronger than in other times that home becomes a temporary situation – one into which the enemy can suddenly penetrate at any time. One of the few possibilities of staying becomes the hide-out or shelter, and this is in no way a dwelling open to the world, but just the opposite: a defence of life against that which is coming from the world.

This penetrability and inadequacy of all types of dwellings against the world is shown in a key scene in *The Hide-Out*. One day the protagonist sees a person in a German uniform through his window and realises that he knows him from his faraway home town. He does not hesitate to call out to him, and this sets a series of events into motion: the German, Fischer, who outwardly behaves in a friendly fashion, is actually someone he has to kill, in order to save his host. With this of course the temporary shelter ends, and there is nothing left to do but leave the now unsafe shelter and take on a suicidal task, during which the protagonist of the novel will likely perish. The closeness in the relationship of the two characters, or more accurately the protagonist's past relationship with the German Fischer which comes back to life in the shelter, underlines the fact

---

14   Ibid., p. 15.

that Fischer is the only one who calls him by name. The passages in which he decides to emerge from the shelter have, as Vladimír Papoušek has pointed out,[15] ritual and symbolic meaning and expresses initiation, from the shelter into the world, with all the dangers which lurk there. In the retrospective point of view of the narration (*The Hide-Out* is written in the form of letters which the narrator is writing to his wife immediately before he leaves to carry out his dangerous task) all the previous events are shown from the perspective of this final act, and also that of death. And even if the protagonist of *The Hide-Out* could survive and return, home would never be revived: the domestic ties for him vanish similarly as to what Flusser describes in his autobiography.

II

The central scene of *The Hide-Out* has a special dimension. By chance, an old acquaintance shows up in a distant and unexpected place – a seeming miracle, which can evoke the feeling that some hidden causality is at work here. From the standpoint of a realistic story, the coincidence is too great, and Hostovský perhaps should be reproached for fabricating such a storyline. The meeting however has above all a psychological function and proves that verisimilitude is not the most important level of the story. The author's intent is not only confirmed when the protagonist's protector, Dr Aubin, meets him by chance at his moment of need,[16] but also at the ending of the story, when a representative of the underground asks him the question: 'Do you think that everything that has happened to you has been by mere chance? And that it will be enough for your understanding to measure and weigh every event, and then find a perspective on it?'[17]

The protagonist is confined to his memories and thoughts in the cellar shelter for long days; the exterior events of the world practically fall by the wayside to be replaced by his thoughts. In his mind, he returns to his childhood and replays the days of his own past.[18] Even radio broadcasts and the rare conversations

---

15   V. Papoušek: *Egon Hostovský*, p. 137.
16   E. Hostovský: *Listy z Vyhnanství. Úkryt*, p. 154.
17   Ibid., p. 199.
18   Ibid., p. 166ff.

with this host, who shows up occasionally in the cellar, integrate into his mental sphere, and in the shelter act as internal voices. Meeting the Czech German thus works as a catalyst, as an event connecting the internal sphere with the outside world. Fischer, whom the protagonist knows from his past, and the meeting with him, also integrate into the sphere of memories; at the same time embodying the hostile forces of the external world. Through this meeting, the past and the present join and are in conjunction in a way that the protagonist, until now, has never known. In his previous life, he experienced the conflict between the outer world and his interior moods, whereas throughout his stay in the shelter, the two were almost totally separate. Exile in this sense meant banishing a person to their thoughts and memories isolated from the actual world. An event, seemingly inauspicious, actually introduces the protagonist to the fullness of life for the first time, even though death waits on the horizon.

Hostovský in his earlier work was building upon the tradition of the 19th century psychological novel, however he gradually veered away from that toward rather existential points of view. In his war-time and immediately post-war prose, Hostovský also significantly transforms several important motifs found in the works of Franz Kafka. In the story *Der Bau* [The Burrow], Kafka plays with the results of a psychological analysis of a shelter. The narrator, exhibiting several animal traits, describes his long-term attempts at building the perfect refuge, primarily a psychological one. The space of the burrow[19] should offer complete safety, and should conform to an entire series of sensations on the part of its inhabitant. It should not be *smaller*, which would point out its inadequacies, and it mustn't be *larger*, for it needs to conceal its secrets and surprises. It should not be a castle full of hidden rooms, which might perhaps satisfy one's sudden whims; on the contrary it should be a snug dwelling, one which satisfies all the physical necessities and removes all the psychological anxiety which has its source in fear of the outside world. This task however is impossible, and therein lies the feverish, exhausting activity of the narrator. Kafka's creature only dreams about the enemy, he imagines him with every rustle, which could be his own hallucination, for he does not know how to differentiate between interior impressions and outside noises. Hostovský's protagonist, on the other hand, actually meets his enemy, where all his conflicts are personified. Kafka's crea-

---

19 *Der Bau* can be translated from German as "The Burrow", the common title in English, but also as "The Construction", which mirrors the narrator's activities.

ture also in some ways prefigures Flusser's contemplations on home and shelter in the post-war world. His morbid fear is of the outside world and the purpose-built burrow represents the futile attempt to build the perfect shelter, one which is able to completely neutralise the outside world.

The question of home is posed from another side in Kafka's *The Metamorphosis*. Gregor Samsa is fleeing from his home via his transformation into a bug; from the point of view of the other characters in the story, he is rather turning the home upside down, acting hostilely to his 'kin', surfacing like a stranger from the centre of the home itself. Seen from both points of view, Kafka is able to turn his readers' ideas of home, as a firm and natural place for a person in the world, upside down.

III

This method of going into hiding and searching for a refuge in both the world and also in the spiritual space already has a long, changing history in Western tradition, one not without influence on modern philosophy.[20] Jean-Louis Chrétien described the constitution of a model of the inner self, based on the image of the inner sanctum from early Christianity. In this model, which worked in practice for a long time, it was not a refuge in the world, rather it was a functional idea about one's own inner self. This was patterned after an architectural scheme, whereby the person would enter this inner architecture of the mind, wherein to meet with God. The centre of this inner self however was not subjective – it was an empty space which the believer had to free up for God. In this sense, God was more interior and closer to a person than the person was to himself or herself. In Czech literature, this model was made brilliant use of by Jan Amos Komenský (Comenius) in his *Labyrinth of the World and Paradise of the Heart*, 1623/1631. The pilgrim in Chapter 37 of the *Labyrinth* finds his way home by returning to himself, where Christ, expressed as the Saviour within a person's own self, has been waiting for him. It includes a quote ('Return to the place whence you came, to the home of your heart and shut the door behind you')

---

20   For example, Descartes in his *Meditations on First Philosophy* (*Meditationes de Prima Philosophia*, 1641), a key text for all of modern philosophy, situates the beginning of thinking in seclusion.

which is almost verbatim from the Gospel of St Matthew (Matthew 6:6), standing at the very beginning of this tradition: 'But thou, when thou prayest, enter into thy closet, and when thou hast shut thy door, pray to thy Father which is in secret' (KJV).[21] Comenius however inconspicuously connects one more aspect, which will soon prevail. The pilgrim not only returns to himself due to prayer; the return to the self also reveals the entire world and its true form. This motif of the world seen from within brings Comenius close to Leibniz, whose monads represent a certain viewpoint of the world – 'mirrors of the universe' – and at the same time nothing from outside enters them – 'monads have no windows,' as the famous sentence referring to the idea of the inner sanctum of the soul has it – which, in this example and from this perspective, embraces the world.[22]

The end of this model of interior space, according to Chrétien, is indicated by its profaneness.[23] After a certain period, the chamber of the heart ceased to be a place of God and was completely filled by subjectivity. Even in this profane form, the *topos* continued to survive and operate – the model of the house was used for instance by Freud in his *Vorlesungen zur Einführung in die Psychoanalyse* [Introduction to Psychoanalysis, 1917] for a description of the structure of the psyche, and also plays a role in modern literature as an image of the closed psyche. The speaker of Baudelaire's second Spleen compares himself to an old boudoir (*Je suis un vieux boudoir plein de roses fanées*). Huysmans' *Jean des Esseintes* in the novel *À rebours* [Against Nature, 1884] attempts to build a shelter which would become a sort of interior world, into which he can concentrate everything. In the centre of his house is symbolically found a fireplace converted into an altar with three poems by Baudelaire. The collision of the interior space by the exterior world is characteristic of these post-Romantic authors: as if they wanted to help the interior architecture to run the world or to project interior thought outwardly; at the same time however always sensing the real outside, independent of their interior architecture, which it on the other hand often interrupts or disrupts. Kafka's *Burrow* stands at the end of this series of texts, the history of which dates back to the beginnings of Christianity.

Comenius understandably became a handy, emblematic figure in Czech post-war exile writing, especially in its first period, before 1968 (Comenius

---

21   cf. J.-L. Chrétien: *L'Espace intérieur*, p. 30.

22   G. W. Leibniz: *Principes de la philosophie*, pp. 254, 244 (§56, §7).

23   J.-L. Chrétien: *L'Espace intérieur*, p. 84ff.

himself was forced into exile due to the anti-Protestant counter-reformations in the 1620s). It was not only always the figure of the ex-patriot Comenius – some of the topology of his *Labyrinth* was also made use of. The words 'home' and 'alienation' are found in the exile correspondence of the writers Rio Preisner (1925–2007) and Ivan Diviš (1924–1999), who after the Soviet occupation of Czechoslovakia in 1968 left for American and German exile, respectively. Their extensive correspondence from the end of the 1960s until after 1989 was not a systematic development of ideas, rather these were fleeting reflections on events and on personal life; however, they do have a certain integrity. Preisner's contemplations especially could be considered as rather freely-conceived essays which relate to his contemplative work.[24] In a letter dated 4 December 1975, Preisner reacts to Diviš's thoughts on not fitting in, and the phrases which he uses relate to Comenius and indicate that some of his ideas had become communal property for the Czech discourse:

> You say however: I have never been at home. We differ from them [the generation of our parents; *author's note*], in that we don't know where we will live? I know all about that! The Wandering Jew roaming the labyrinth. So few of us understand that home means a condition, and in no way a place. The condition of wandering, of course. The Wandering Jew is always searching just for a place somewhere outside himself: the pilgrim carries his home in his heart; perhaps as those on the road to Emmaus, whose hearts burned within when they heard the Lord on their way.
>
> [transl. M. Sweney]

Less than two years later, in a letter dated 29 September 1977, after his premature return after a visit from Germany back to the USA, Preisner denoted the schism between home and a foreign environment in European countries by the word "chasm". As opposed to this, the USA offered a refuge and shelter, because the feeling of home there has a different meaning:

---

24   Their correspondence is housed in the Archives et Musée de la Littérature in Brussels. Preisner expressed his conservative Christian position in the extensive trilogy *Kritika totalitarismu* [A Critique of Totalitarianism, 1973], *Česká existence* [Czech Existence, 1984], *Až na konec Česka* [To the End of the Czech Lands, 1987]. He devoted to exile his book *Speculum exilii Bohemici* (the book, whose manuscript was completed in 1980, was not published until 2017).

There you ask why the situation in Germany became unbearable for me. That country is perhaps more than disfigured by its anti-historical division: as if in its centre a chasm were opened up. You can find many such chasms in Europe: in the Czech lands – less visible – between the Czechs and the "Czech lands"; in France between the "eldest daughter of the Church" and the "la France douce" of the Jacobins; the English chasm dragging believe it or not Ireland into it; the chasm in Poland, which is like a ripple, recalling one another to the memory of division and the shifting of a proud free country (I am not able to imagine a Polish Švejk). Almost every German seems to be marked by the shadow of this chasm. Germany, in addition to this (and probably because of this), is a country where I would be most "at home" and at the same time (and probably because of this) the most "foreign". This is rooted in – for me – an analogy in my experiences with Czechs; except that in the Czech Lands everything <u>home</u> was without quotation marks and everything <u>foreign</u> was outside of language, nationality, birth certificate – cosmic, vertical. In Germany I felt <u>as if</u> I were in the Czech Lands, i.e. in a <u>perfect</u> ersatz Bohemia, which was simply unbearable. In the USA, home and abroad are reversed and substituted here by a purely <u>rational</u> and <u>voluntary</u> citizenship, the melting pot – the oath of taking citizenship frees one from the schizophrenia of home and abroad. What is missing here is obviously all that which races through the heart. In this perhaps indirectly I am replying to your question: Where do you actually feel at home? That 'actually' feels a bit like a friendly dig. In Germany I felt at home with you in the workshop with the Master of Třeboň – and without any 'actually'. I felt at home there, precisely the way I feel at home in our house in State College [Pennsylvania – *author's note*].[25]

[transl. M. Sweney]

---

25   A reference to *The Good Soldier Švejk* by Jaroslav Hašek (1921–1923; first English edition 1930), the iconic Czech black comedy about World War I, the title character of which is anything but a hard-headed patriot, and whose cleverness in evading power struggles rather than taking a stand has been considered symptomatic of the Czech character. Evidently a reproduction of the altarpiece by the Master of Třeboň (Wittingau) ca 1380; panels from the original are now displayed in the National Gallery in Prague and the Aleš South Bohemian Gallery in Hluboká nad Vltavou, Czech Republic. The underlining is in the original letter.

Labyrinth, heart, wandering: Comenius's words live on, three hundred and fifty years after he wrote *Labyrinth of the World and Paradise of the Heart* within a historical situation, which despite great differences, portrays in the era of the Thirty Years' War a parallel of the ideologically divided world. Preisner found a shelter only in the interior, as if the exterior world were hostile from its foundations. A similar break is delineated in Hostovský. Whereas in *The Hide-Out*, there is an emergence from the shelter to the exterior via resolution and fulfilment of life, in *Foreigner*, the world no longer offers any such hope.

The chasm which Preisner describes in his letter characterises the life-long feelings of a whole series of post-war Exiles. They cannot, or are not able, to live in the country of their origin; however, they do not feel at home where they are living. They seek a shelter or refuge abroad, of a different sort than war-time Exiles – a place where they could be permanently protected from the outside world in the post-war era, when home has become unbearable, or morally unacceptable, as Adorno wrote already in 1944: 'The predicament of private life today is shown by its arena. Dwelling, in the proper sense, is now impossible. The traditional residences we grew up in have grown intolerable; each trait of comfort in them is paid for with a betrayal of knowledge, each vestige of shelter with the musty pact of family interest. [...] 'It is even part of my good fortune not to be a house-owner,' as Nietzsche wrote in *The Gay Science.* Today we should have to add: it is part of morality not to be at home in one's own home.'[26]

To create this kind of shelter, many intellectuals were helped by art and literature, similar as to how the reproduction in Diviš's study brought something of the culture of the lost home into the shelter abroad. These temporary dwellings, whether real or literary (which oft-times cannot be distinguished), are characterised by a certain degree of construction – introducing an image, combined with writing and words, and/or simply finding suitable seclusion, but always also with the complicated relationship to the original "home".

The fates of several similar "emigrants" are described in W. G. Sebald's book of that name. His prose pieces, through the medium of characters one or two generations older than the author's narrator, reflect the situation of the world after WWII and Nazism, times from which he came and at the same time did not experience: "Yet to this day, when I see photographs or documentary films

---

26   T. W. Adorno: *Minima moralia*, pp. 38–39 (ch. 18).

dating from the war I feel as if I were its child, so to speak, as if those horrors I did not experience cast a shadow over me and from which I shall never entirely emerge."[27] The title itself, *Die Ausgewanderten*,[28] which is difficult to translate, for example into English or French (*The Emigrants*; *Les émigrants*), demarks the wide field of exile in the 20th century. Sebald's book should neither be called 'The Exiles' (*Die Exulanten*) nor 'The Emigrants' (*Die Emigranten*). German offers a larger scale of expressions (as does Czech) and differentiates between several close terms such as 'exile', 'emigrant' and 'displaced person', the latter maintaining a closer relationship with his country and his departure, unlike exile, is not enforced by external causes, while an emigrant has a moralizing motive for leaving the homeland.[29] Sebald's emigrants left on their own will; they cannot take Germany for their home, but at the same time they cannot live elsewhere. Dwelling [*Wohnung*] in Flusser's sense is not maintainable for them in the long-run. The main characters of the four stories end in suicide or die in seclusion. Sooner or later they consciously turn their backs on the world,[30] shut themselves up in their atelier, an institution for the mentally ill,

---

27   W. G. Sebald, qtd. in Denham – McCulloh: *W. G. Sebald*, p. 343.

28   W. G. Sebald: *The Emigrants* (New Your: New Directions 1997); *Die Ausgewanderten* (Frankfurt am Main: Fischer 1994).

29   For instance, the words "emigrant" and "emigration" were used in Communist propaganda in Czechoslovakia to indicate Czechs who went into political exile after 1948, and were given a pejorative shade of meaning. Similarly, Martin C. Putna formulates the distinction between exile and emigration in the context of post-February exile, with an emphasis on the relationship to the homeland: 'Exiles flee in order to work for the country and preserve its culture. Emigrants flee to have a better life in a new country, be it political, religious or economic. This distinction is echoed even in the self-reflection of Czech post-February exile. Those who reflect (upon themselves) in this way count themselves as Exiles – who are the morally more demanding (on themselves). Conversely, the term 'emigration' is also used by regime propaganda – in a negative sense', M. Putna: *Česká katolická literatura v kontextech 1945–1989*, p. 237. Alfrun Kliems recalls a similar distribution of words in German and Czech (*Im Stummland*, p. 17) and recalls the meaning of the word Auswanderung / Emigration, largely for economic reasons. Sebald's titular term works with a subtle shift of this meaning.

30   'I severed my last ties with what they call the real world,' W. G. Sebald: *The Emigrants*, p. 21, "*löste ich meine letzte Kontakte mit der sogenannten wirklichen Welt*", Sebald: *Ausgewanderten*, p. 35; 'one day, without preamble, that he would no longer be present at any dinners or gatherings whatsoever, that he would no longer have anything at all to do with the outside world' Sebald, *The Emigrants*, p. 99, "*eines Tages ohne weiteren Vorsatz erklarte, dass er von nun an keinem Diner und keiner wie immer gearteten Gesellschaft mehr beiwohnen würde, dass er überhaupt mit*

or in a greenhouse, living out their lives in deep melancholy and the greatest possible isolation. Filling their days is their one and only impractical activity – raising orchids or painting pictures, as if they were shut-ins from life and were able to maintain themselves only in that melancholy monotony.

IV

The Czech poet Ivan Blatný (1919–1990) went into exile right after the Communist take-over of Czechoslovakia in 1948. For several years he lived precariously, with the help of friends, until he landed in a mental institution, where from 1954 on he spent the vast remainder of his life in a similar condition to Sebald's great-uncle, Ambros Adelwarth. Indeed, Blatný's exile and his way of life are reminiscent of Sebald's emigrants. Blatný shares the same history and the same geopolitical arrangement, only coming from the other side of the Iron Curtain, and bringing with him the experience of the beginnings of Communist totalitarianism. For Czech post-war Exiles, the Second World War and the extermination camps were the recent past, one which substantially influenced the present, and many Czechs in exile had just gone through two totalitarian regimes, the Nazis and the Communists, with some of them, like Egon Hostovský, going into exile for the second and final time.

Blatný was not a politically engaged man, and his departure from Czechoslovakia surprised many of his peers. Certainly, he had many reasons for going into exile, and later he gave different explanations. The primary motivations however remained fear of a Communist dictatorship and artistic freedom. At some point during 1953, reacting to the fake news of his death which was broadcast on Radio Prague, Blatný proclaimed that the Soviet regime meant not only tyranny for the artist, but also the loss of contact with others in the outside world and thus artistic death. Interestingly, otherwise he did not comment on

---

der Aussenwelt nichts mehr zu schaffen haben [...] wolle", Sebald: Ausgewanderten, pp. 144–145; 'I have spent my life out of doors here [...] and I no longer concern myself with what goes on in the so-called real world', Sebald: The Emigrants, p. 110, "lebe ich hier heraussen [...] und kümmere mich grundsätzlich nicht mehr um das, was vor sich geht in der sogenannten wirklichen Welt", Sebald: Ausgewanderten, p. 161.

the political side of things.[31] In a later interview, he revealed that the main reason for his exile was fear of the Communist regime and similar motives are repeated in his poetry.[32] Blatný's mental health was not in question for all of his time in exile, and he could have lived outside the walls of the sanatorium, according to eyewitnesses. But he did not want to live without this shelter which protected him from the outside world, and perhaps he would not have been able to. In a 1982 interview with Lubo Mauer, a Slovak film director living in Norway, Blatný's doctor at St Clement's Hospital, stated, with a certain amazement:

> D: To be honest, you know, I don't know how a sensible person can tolerate that ward. First the fact that you are in the middle of a hospital. It's a long-stay ward, with many cases of chronic schizophrenia and personality disorders and all that. I think they are a sort of closed community for themselves. I thought he was quite rational, and I asked him the question, why don't you live outside? LM: He could do that if he wanted? D: Of course, he's the one who doesn't want to go out. We don't feel that he is too ill to go out and live. I don't see any reason why he can't go to a hostel sort of place, and live with all his own people, you know, in a flat. Even in Ipswich they have a community, a sort of group there. He can always go to a hostel... but he doesn't want to. LM: It is fascinating that the man escapes from a dictatorship to live in a closed society. It is quite interesting and quite unique.[33]

The contradiction, which the doctor did not understand, had an ambiguous logic for Blatný; for while in the 1950s he had already spoken out about freedom and contact with foreigners, at the same time he was worried about

---

31   The text, evidently the basis for the radio broadcast, was found in the papers left by poet Josef Lederer, a friend of Blatný's, with whom Blatný resided for a spell after his departure from Czechoslovakia. Also surviving is the initial part of an interview with Blatný by Josef Lederer intended to be broadcast on the radio, where they both comment on the confabulated reports; whether the two texts were ever broadcast remains unverified.

32   cf. J. Serke: Ivan Blatný, pp. 161–162.

33   Tape transcription. The Czech translation was published as „V současnosti nevykazuje žádné psychiatrické symptomy" ['At present he does not exhibit any psychiatric symptoms'. Interview by Lubo Mauer with Ivan Blatný's doctor at St Clement's Hospital], pp. 93–94.

being abducted and sent back to Czechoslovakia, and went through states of anxiety leading to a breakdown:

> – Fear. For instance, when I was walking home to 50 Avenue Road, somebody was behind me, a solitary walker, and I started to get scared, that he would abduct me and take me back to Czechoslovakia – – And that feeling gradually receded? – It receded later. I felt calm and safe in the hospital. Claybury Hall primarily, then Claybury Hospital main building…
>
> [transl. M. Sweney]

However, he gave an unambiguous response to a question about the contradiction between freedom and life in an institution:

> – Let me tell you also about my perspective: it might seem a bit illogical that a person fleeing from totalitarianism would prefer to live in a protected environment, in a hospital. – Of course. Freedom does not mean being footloose and fancy free. A person can be incarcerated somewhere in a hospital, but living in a free country, where all the news in the papers are real.[34]
>
> [transl. M. Sweney]

The institutions in which he stayed gave him a feeling of safety against the Communist regime, while living at the same time in the free world. This is a similar refuge as to that which Preisner found in his closed shelter, and it is a psychological continuation of Kafka's burrow-construction. Blatný renounces all worries about ensuring his everyday existence and with this a certain portion of a citizen's freedoms; at the same time however, he was gaining a relatively undisturbed refuge – for writing poetry. Blatný's exile poetry from the 1950s to the 1980s has its development; but especially in the period of the late 1970s–early 1980s, it focuses on the situation of shelter. And not only on the level of

---

34   „Dneska bych se omluvil a trochu bych toho už nechal" [Today I would apologise and be a bit more hands-off]. Interview by Lubo Mauer with Ivan Blatný at St Clement's Hospital, pp. 60–61.

autobiography: Blatný at this time was trying to create his *residence* through the help of words; as if writing poetry could form his surroundings.

In fact, the title of Blatný's first collection of poetry in exile was entitled *Stará bydliště* [Old Domiciles,[35] 1979], indicating the past. His second had the title *Pomocná škola Bixley* [Bixley Remedial School, various editions: 1982/1987/1994/2011], referring to the present, and with some irony indicating Blatný's current residence. And also his poetic programme:

> Manya the hen, Vera the cat, are emerging from the shadows in my mind. I'd like to explain the title *Remedial School*. The reader notices sentences which are ordinary facts from geography, history, etc. I get into the mood, the concerto goes on, the police is friendly, it is the police of the democratic free country. Remedial School: Much as he recognizes the necessity of diffuse awareness, Blažej Vilím is on an uphill path to better wisdom. Why? Because knowledge enriches poetry.[36]
>
> [transl. M. Sweney]

A "remedial school" satisfies Flusser's conception of a shelter to a 'T'. An almost perfect defence against the outside world and at the same time it is the one most open to him. In a school all information about the world is accessible; and at the same time, it is not the real world, for these are only pictures of the facts of the world, ones which the poet can freely manipulate. One important information channel which connected Blatný to the world was television. A simplistic map broadcast on television brought him to the cited consideration regarding the remedial school – through his memories he attempts to reconstruct the

---

35 [transl. note: choosing the term 'domiciles' rather than 'residences' (as translated elsewhere), recognizes how the rather bureaucratic term *bydliště* defines 'where one has been living, staying', not necessarily the particular addresses or dwellings]

36 I. Blatný: *Pomocná škola Bixley*, p. 103. This edition contains the samizdat text of *Pomocná škola Bixley* (1982) found in a copy of Blatný's manuscript from 1979, also texts from the exile edition (Toronto: Sixty-Eight Publishers 1987) and a selection from the extensive manuscripts from this period in Ivan Blatný's papers. The original quotation is in Czech, except for the passage "the concerto [...] free country", which is in English. *Pomocná škola Bixley* is a multi-lingual work. Blažej Vilím (1909–1976) was a Czech politician who was in the opposition during the Occupation and subsequently went into exile after the Communist take-over in 1948, to London. Blatný lived with him for a time.

map. This representation of the reality allows Blatný to mingle the past with the present and at the same time also examine his current life (which at the institution was not always idyllic) with a certain internal distance. Blatný's poems are replete with actual names, references to the past, to the contemporary world, and also to his immediate surroundings and everyday routine. Blatný took all these in like "school" facts: everyday details appear as new discoveries as he tries to arrange them into an ideal image, one in which he is the centre. A characteristic example of Blatný's filtering of reality are letters. Blatný expresses the joy from receiving a letter, though he is not up to reading it: "I received a letter, but I am not going to read it."[37] Letters provide an impetus to write, contact with the outside world, but the fact that the letter exists is enough in and of itself for him. Blatný does not intend to let the uncertain content of the letter disturb him and writes, in English:

> Every letter to open
> to see whether perhaps isn't the pound note
> but not to read it
> not to read books not to do nothing
> here I must something write
> because they could force me to make tea-pots or some woodwork[38]

A certain naïveté in his view of the world is reminiscent of Comenius's *Orbis pictus*, a visual textbook based on an idealised and harmonious picture of the world which the teacher would portray to his students in the form of an extensive catalogue of things. To create such a world for oneself is of course an impossible, Sisyphean task, because in time new, intrusive elements will appear. In several poems, characteristic for *Bixley Remedial School*, Blatný attempts to synchronise his writing in real time. It is as if what was happening would be conducted by writing:

> Michaux only works in the morning, should I go lie down for
> a while? What would the afternoon be like without writing, I must

---

37   Ibid., p. 21.
38   Ibid., p. 153.

keep writing, on the way to bed, before napping, for when the towbar
reaches the water...[39]

[transl. M. Sweney]

This creates a space in which the fact is supplemented by its registration.
For Blatný, the notation of all the facts gains importance, and at the same time
writing also becomes an important factor which reality arranges on the fly.
Blatný is not attempting to create an illusory dream space over a blank page
which would replace reality. Rather it is a constant back and forth between
writing and the world. At such times the two levels – written down reverie
and the exterior world – complement each other and it is possible to live on
both levels. One of the shorter poems, named *Změna programu* [Change of
Programme] refers to this constant relay between the real scene of daily work
therapy and the internal scene of reverie and writing.

Holan se právě vrátil ze zdejších polí a luk
já sedím a čekám na occupational therapy

Tesaři stále něco zatloukají sedím jak tolikrát
dnes budeme číst hry

V naší mysli bude malá opona
pro ptačí divadlo v naší mysli.

Holan[40] has just returned from the nearby fields and meadows
I'm sitting and waiting for occupational therapy

The carpenters are still hammering on something I've sat here so
         many times
Today we're going to read plays

---

39   Ibid., p. 229.
40   Vladimír Holan (1905–1980), a major Czech poet.

In our minds there will be a small curtain
For the bird theatre in our minds.[41]

[transl. M. Sweney]

V

Kafka's story *The Burrow* and the post-war reflections of Theodor Adorno refer
to the uncertainty of shelter and homelessness as a state of human existence
in the modern world. In the post-war period, Kafka's psychological parable
has become real in many respects: scores of Exiles searching for a refuge not
because they have been expelled from their home, but because their home has
become an unbearable place to be. The prose of Egon Hostovský does a good
job of showing the dependency and uncertainty of refuge. His characters, in
various situations, vacillate between staying in an isolated shelter and entering the public space, which in the end brings death. The antithesis of home
and residence, according to the philosopher Vilém Flusser, is expressed by
a nomadism without deeper bonds to the original home, which would form
the shelter. At the same time, there is a positive interpretation of exile which
indicates the importance of a residence as a sort of place which establishes
one's approach to the world. Sebald's emigrants (or, *departees*) are on the other
hand maintaining a certain relationship to the home in which they can no
longer live, and search not only for a refuge away from home, but also a shelter
against the outside world in general. Turning their backs to the world leads
them to enclosed and isolated places. In Jana Borová's poem from the early
1950s, an inner space of the heart stands against the cold reality of the refugee
camp, in which the motifs of Comenius remarkably come to life. Ivan Blatný's poetry reflects in the topology of the shelter the complex history of the
post-war world.[42] He is leaving a totalitarian regime and yet hides away from
the free world, too, in his own words finding freedom in the enclosed world
of a sanatorium. In a way, he embodies Flusser's conception of the sheltering dwelling: all the stimuli from the outside world come to him filtered and

41   Ibid., p. 280.
42   Similarly, in the poems of Jiří Kovtun included in the same anthology *Čas stavění*. cf. Chapter 5.

provide him with material for writing his poems. This verbal activity makes the hideaway habitable, giving it an impermanent meaningfulness that can only be maintained by writing.

4. Arcadia, Utopia, Exile

The idea of exile in the 19th century is characterized by a complicated topology, in which reality and imagination are inextricably intertwined. The concept of a homeland based on nationalism clashes with ideas of a spiritual homeland, itself influenced by earlier ideas about an ideal land of art and poetry, as well as the utopian ideas of revolutionary romanticism; realworld political exile crossed with the imaginary, longer journeys take on a touch of exile, and vice versa. Georg Brandes gives exile an important role in his seminal work, the *Main Currents in 19th-century Literature.*[43] which he opens with a piece dedicated to émigré literature, whose history largely began with the French Revolution. Often building on these foundations, exile fiction of the 20th century only moves matters into the imaginary plane.

I

Goethe's *Italian Journey* amounts to a significant overture about exile in the 19th century. Goethe undertook his journey on the eve of the French Revolution: On 3 September 1786 he left Karlovy Vary (Karlsbad), and bade farewell to Rome in April 1788. His pilgrimage belongs to a tradition of cultural journeys to Italy, a phenomenon peculiar to the 18th and 19th century.[44] There is hardly any mention made of the political events of the time in the travelogue, which Goethe prepared and published only much later, after 1815. The whole journey is

43   The work of Brandes is brought up in this context by H. Levin: Literature and Exile, p. 62.
44   cf. M. C. Putna: *Řecké nebe nad námi*, p. 25ff.

undertaken in the spirit of the opening motto *Auch ich in Arcadien!* It begins and ends with a furtive but coveted departure *Früh drei Uhr stahl ich mich aus Carls-bad* [I stole out of Carlsbad at three in the morning][45] and an elegiac farewell to Rome, when Goethe quotes the passage where Ovid recalls his departure from Rome into exile (*Tristia* I, 3).

> Dieses in aufgeregter Seele tief und groß empfunden, erregte eine Stimmung, die ich heroisch elegisch nennen darf, woraus sich in poe-tischer Form eine Elegie zusammenbilden wollte.
>
> Und wie sollte mir gerade in solchen Augenblicken Ovids Elegie nicht ins Gedächtnis zurückkehren, der, auch verbannt, in einer Mondennacht Rom verlassen sollte. Cum repeto noctem! seine Rückerinnerung, weit hinten am Schwarzen Meere, im trauer- und jammervollen Zustande, kam mir nicht aus dem Sinn, ich wiederholte das Gedicht, das mir teilweise genau im Gedächtnis hervorstieg, aber mich wirklich an eigner Produktion irre werden ließ und hinderte; die auch später unternommen, niemals zustande kommen konnte.

> This, being felt deeply and grandly in my agitated soul, evoked a mood that I may call heroic-elegiac, out of which an elegiac poem began to take form.
>
> And how I could not recall Ovid's elegy at these moments, for he too was banished and was about to leave Rome on a moonlit night. 'Cum repeto noctem'– his recollection far away at the Black Sea, where he was sad and miserable–kept recurring to me, and I recited the poem, which in part I remember exactly. But actually, it only interfered with and hindered my own production, which although undertaken again later, never came into existence. [46]

Goethe does, however, ingeniously upturn the topology of Ovid's elegies, when he likens his returning *home* to *exile*. This cross-pollination of imaginary

---

45   J. W. Goethe: *Italienische Reise* I, p. 11, *Den 3. September 1786*, cited from *Italian Journey*, transl. by Robert R. Heitner.

46   Ibid., p. 596, *Bericht, April 1788*.

and real places and their values of home and exile plays out from the very beginning of his travelogue, when he describes Italy as his true home, only now being discovered as such:

> Ich lasse mirs gefallen als wenn ich hier geboren und erzogen wäre, und nun von einer Grönlandsfahrt, von einem Walfischfange zurückkäme. [...] Wenn mein Entzücken hierüber jemand vernähme, der in Süden wohnte, von Süden herkäme, er würde mich für sehr kindisch halten. Ach, was ich hier ausdrücke, habe ich lange gewußt, so lange als ich unter einem bösen Himmel dulde, und jetzt mag ich gern diese Freude als Ausnahme fühlen, die wir als eine ewige Natur-notwendigkeit immer fort genießen sollten.

> I pretend that I was born and raised here, and have now returned from a trip to Greenland, catching whales. [...] If someone living in the south, who was a native of the south, were to hear my raptures over this, he would consider me very childish. Alas, what I am describing here has long been known to me, as long as I have suffered beneath an evil sky, and now I am happy to feel, just as an exception to the rule, a joy which should be ours as a perpetual natural necessity.[47]

The topology is thus a notch more complicated than with Ovid, mixing up the meanings of his real homeland (Germany) and the idealized homeland of the spirit (Italy).[48] The geographical polarity of the North and South as put forward by Goethe corresponds in some respects to the relationship between Rome and Tomis in Ovid's case. The north is full of fog and gloom, compared to the sunny and bright south. Goethe likens Italy to Paradise.[49] Yet in other moments Goethe does recall that his real homeland is in the north, emphasizes

---

47 Ibid., pp. 29–30, *Trient, den 11. September, früh.*
48 A similar shifting of Ovid's topology is seen in Pushkin's poem to Ovid, since he is genuinely in exile in the south and recalls the north as his home.
49 J. W. Goethe: ibid., p. 51, *Verona, den 17. September et ssq.*

his German diligence compared to southern lassitude, and recalls that home is where one was born and experienced one's childhood and youth:

> ... auch mir kommt das Jenseits der Alpen nun düster vor; doch winken freundliche Gestalten immer aus dem Nebel. Nur das Klima würde mich reizen, diese Gegenden jenen vorzuziehen: denn Geburt und Gewohnheit sind mächtige Fesseln. Ich möchte hier nicht leben, wie überall an keinem Orte, wo ich unbeschäftigt wäre.

> ... and to me too the other side of Alps now seems dark; but friendly figures keep beckoning from the mist. Only the climate would tempt me to give preference to these regions over those; for birth and custom are strong ties. I would not care to live here or any other place where I would be idle.[50]

Later on, during his second stay in Rome, he reminds of the close life bond with places of one's childhood and youth and also emphasizes the material side of such places:

> Jetzt fangen erst die Bäume, die Felsen, ja Rom selbst an mir lieb zu werden; bisher hab' ich sie immer nur als fremd gefühlt; dagegen freuten mich geringe Gegenstände, die mit denen ähnlichkeit hatten, die ich in der Jugend sah. Nun muß ich auch erst hier zu Hause werden, und doch kann ich's nie so innig sein als mit jenen ersten Gegenständen des Lebens.

> Only now are the trees, the rocks, indeed Rome itself becoming dear to me; heretofore I have always just felt that they were foreign. On the other hand, I was pleased by unimportant objects that were similar to what I saw in my youth. Now I must begin to feel at home here also, and yet it will never be as close to me as those first things in my life.[51]

---

50   Ibid., p. 104, *Den 12. Oktober.*
51   Ibid., p. 376, *Rom, den 16. Juni.*

The inclination and spiritual need to see Italy is well described by the passage where Goethe justifies his journey. His aim is to see with his own eyes what he had only been able to read about:

> Hätte ich nicht den Entschluß gefaßt, den ich jetzt ausführe, so wär'
> ich rein zu Grunde gegangen: zu einer solchen Reife war die Begierde,
> diese Gegenstände mit Augen zu sehen, in meinem Gemüt gestie-
> gen. Die historische Kenntnis fördert' mich nicht, die Dinge standen
> nur eine Hand breit von mir ab; aber durch eine undurchdringliche
> Mauer geschieden. Es ist mir wirklich auch jetzt nicht etwa zu Mute,
> als wenn ich die Sachen zum erstenmal sähe, sondern als ob ich sie
> wiedersähe.

> If I had not made the resolution I am now carrying, I would simply
> have perished, so ripe had the desire become in my heart to see these
> sights with my own eyes. Historical knowledge was of no benefit to
> me, for while the things stood there only a hand's breadth away, I was
> separated from them by an impenetrable wall. Even now I really do
> not feel that I am seeing the objects for the first time, but as if I were
> seeing them again.[52]

It is only in Italy that Goethe sees things as they are, stripped of the deposits of obfuscation *"diese bin ich nun, Gott sei Dank, auf ewig los!"* [thank God I am rid of these now forever!].[53] On his terms, it is not about discovering something new, it is about finding something already known, as if he were being reunited with it. Goethe's goal is to bring this new way of seeing back north: *"ich [...] habe Hoffnung, auch dereinst in Norden aus meiner Seele Schattenbilder dieser glücklichen Wohnung hervor zu bringen"* [and I hope that I shall be able, even someday in the north, to summon up mental images of this happy domain].[54]

The *Italian Journey* is not a volume about exile, although exile motifs do play an important role in it and Goethe repeatedly returns to them. For him, it was

---

52   Ibid., pp. 105–106, *Den 12. Oktober.*
53   Ibid., p. 94, *Den 8. Oktober.*
54   Ibid., p. 249, *Palermo, den 3. April 1787.*

primarily a formative journey; he speaks several times of a new life and rebirth during his stay in Italy, *"denn ich bin wirklich umgeboren und erneuert und ausgefüllt"* [For I really have been recreated and renewed and completed][55] consistent with the new way of seeing he finds there. So, what then is the significance of the final reference to Ovid and the fact that the whole book ends by quoting his verses about going into exile? While Goethe compares his departure from Rome to Ovid's expulsion, returning home is firmly part of his plans from the very beginning of the journey, as he reminds us every so often. Ovid's verses serve to express the mood of a weighty moment, though not a twist of fate, an uplift, not harking back in nostalgia. In an earlier version of the *Italian Journey*, Goethe writes about a 'pain of a singular kind':

> Bei meinem Abschied aus Rom empfand ich Schmerzen einer eignen Art. Diese Hauptstadt der Welt, deren Bürger man eine Zeitlang gewesen, ohne Hoffnung der Rückkehr zu verlassen, giebt ein Gefühl, das sich durch Worte nicht überliefern läßt. Niemand vermag es zu theilen als wer es empfunden.

> Upon my departure from Rome, I experienced pain of a singular kind. This capital city of the world that one became a citizen of for a while, without giving up all hope of return, evokes a feeling one cannot put into words. No-one has managed to describe the way it felt.[56]

In the later, definitive form of the text, he describes the mood of the moment as sublime and refers to it as heroic-elegiac (*eine Stimmung, die ich heroisch elegisch nennen darf*). This hyphenation only reinforces the inner contradiction of the moment, full of mixed feelings, not just elegiac melancholy. Goethe does not manage to find just the right words, and the unique mood is marked by a compound adjective that combines the sadness of farewell with the hope of return. The exile motifs and topology reminiscent of Ovid serves Goethe to emphasize the ground-breaking and formative importance of his 'Italian Journey' a fundamental change within oneself, which he refers to as a new

---

55   Ibid., p. 413, *Rom, den 23. August 1787*, cf similar motifs pp. 157, 158, 160, 421.

56   J. W. Goethe: *Italienische Reise* II, p. 1156, variant conclusion completed 31. 8. 1817.

life: "*Überhaupt ist mit dem neuen Leben, das einem nachdenkenden Menschen die Betrachtung eines neuen Landes gewährt, nichts zu vergleichen. Ob ich gleich noch immer derselbe bin; so mein' ich, bis aufs innerste Knochenmark verändert zu sein.*" [Nothing can compare with the new life a reflective individual receives from contemplating a new country. Although I am still the same person, I think I am changed to the very marrow of my bones].[57] In a similar vein, he uses hyperbolic phrases elsewhere: "*Hätte ich nicht den Entschluß gefaßt, den ich jetzt ausführe, so wär' ich rein zugrunde gegangen*" [If I had not made the resolution I am now carrying I would simply have perished].[58] That the journey and exile are polar opposites is underscored by the successful return, in that the southern, clear vision is brought back to the fogbound north; theoretically such a journey could also end in a failure tantamount to being exiled in a disappointing world: be it the haziness of the north or the sleepiness of the south. Goethe aims for a fully-formed and rounded persona, and such endeavour needs to reach its end. In that sense, the journey also has its beginning and end. The shaping ends by conjoining two homelands within the same person. "*Meine Kunstkenntnisse, meine kleinen Talente müssen hier ganz durchgearbeitet, ganz reif werden, sonst bring' ich wieder euch einen halben Freund zurück und das Sehnen, Bemühen, Krabbeln und Schleichen geht von neuem an.*" [My knowledge of art, my small talents must be thoroughly perfected here and ripen full, otherwise I shall bring back only half a friend to you, and the longing, striving, creeping, and crawling will start all over again].[59]

In the earlier version of the conclusion as picked out by Jean Starobinski,[60] Goethe does finally manage to express the inexpressible feeling, as brought across to the drama about Torquato Tasso. This happens at the stopover in the Florentine gardens on the way back. Even here, a notable moment in a notable place brings with it a multiplicity of constituent parts: Goethe compares his fate to Ovid and Tasso at the same time.

> Den größten Theil meines Aufenthalts in Florenz verbrachte ich in den dortigen Lust- und Prachtgärten. Dort schrieb ich die Stellen, die mir noch jetzt jene Zeit, jene Gefühle, unmittelbar zurückrufen. Dem

57   J. W. Goethe: *Italienische Reise* I, p. 157, *Rom, den 2. Dezember 1786.*
58   Ibid., p. 195, *Den 12. Oktober.*
59   Ibid., p. 379, *Rom, Ende Juni.*
60   J. Starobinski: *La nuit de Troie*, pp. 324–325.

Zustand dieser Lage ist allerdings jene Ausführlichkeit zuzuschreiben, womit das Stüde theilweis behandelt ist und wodurch seine Erscheinung auf dem Theater beinah unmöglich ward. Wie mit Ovid dem Lokal nach, so konnte ich mich mit Tasso dem Schicksale nach vergleichen. Der schmerzliche Zug einer leidenschaftlichen Seele, die unwiderstehlich zu einer unwiderruflichen Verbannung hingezogen wird, geht durch das ganze Stück.

I have spent the greater part of my stay in Florence in these wonderful park gardens. Here I wrote of places that are still at once evoked by thoughts of that time, of those feelings. The nature of the situation has to be attributed to the small detail the play deals with, in part, and which made it almost impossible to put on the stage. Just as I was able to liken myself to Ovid in terms of location, I could take to Tasso in terms of fate. The whole piece is perfused with the anguish of a passionate soul, inexorably dragged into an irrevocable exile.[61]

In a sense, here Goethe gets close to the ranks of Exiles that started with Ovid. The reason, however, is not only an attempt to join a community of well-known Exiles (Goethe has no need to underpin his importance, nor to shape his identity through exile), but to convey the feeling and mood that gives insight into one's fate and may be held in common. In a way, in so doing he presages Baudelaire's compassionate concerns. Moving from the supposedly autobiographical Ovid to the literary Tasso also inextricably combines the true and the imaginary.

Goethe is no exile, neither in fact nor in any feeling that translates into imaginings, yet the theme of exile plays an important role in his *Italian Journey*. He is neither the first to liken Italy to Arcadia,[62] nor the only one who sees Italy as an idyllic country in which different ideals are to be realized.[63] Unlike most of the Romantics who come after him, Goethe does not treat antiquity and the

61 J. W. Goethe: *Italienische Reise* II, p. 1157, variant conclusion, completed 31. 8. 1817.
62 In German literature, this association following on from early modern ideas about Arcadia appears at the end of the 18th century. cf. comment in J. W. Goethe: *Italienische Reise* II, p. 1168ff.
63 cf. J. Stabler: *The Artistry of Exile*, vii.

idyllic land of art as something bygone, irretrievably lost. He revives and relates the ancient monuments and the Italian landscape to the present, and regards Italy's present landscape as a backdrop that brings Homer's epic back to life.[64] He views traces of the past as stimuli for the present; when he declares himself a citizen of Rome and also connects back to his homeland, neither of these places direct his identity, yet both are integral parts of it. In other words, when he talks about exile, it is not with an overriding sense of *here* and *now,* versus *there* and *then,* but the there-and-then is subordinate to the here-and-now.

Pierre Hadot recalls that for Goethe the present means, above all, a given moment that can encompass the past and the future.[65] In Rome, Goethe tries *"das alte Rom aus dem neuen herauszuklauben, aber man muß es denn doch tun, und zuletzt eine unschätzbare Befriedigung hoffen"* [to sort out the old Rome from the new ...] which can bring 'inestimable satisfaction'.[66] His inspection of the past is all about revival. Art allows him to better perceive nature through the eyes of artists, *"...was jene gefunden und mehr oder weniger nachgeahmt haben, [...] Ich will auch nicht mehr ruhen, bis mir nichts mehr Wort und Tradition, sondern lebendiger Begriff ist."* [...to find and gather what those men found and more or less imitated ... I shall not rest until everything that is still merely words and tradition for me becomes a living concept].[67]

When Goethe bids farewell to Rome, he sums up everything he has experienced into the present moment, Rome becomes the venue that completes the experience of the whole journey. The sense of sadness and nostalgia remains not only in the past, but turns towards the future.[68] The mention of a heroic-elegiac tone at the end of the *Italian Journey* captures this turning toward a new beginning and corresponds to the heroic image of the exile-founder, as represented by Aeneas. In an interview with Friedrich von Müller (4 November 1823), Goethe mentions this productive type of nostalgia:[69]

----

64   J. W. Goethe: *Italienische Reise* I, p. 320, *Aus Erinnerung (den 7. Mai 1787).*

65   P. Hadot: *N'oublie pas de vivre,* p. 63.

66   J. W. Goethe: *Italienische Reise* I, p. 140, *Rom, den 7. November.*

67   Ibid., p. 378, *Rom, den 27. Juni.*

68   He had previously taken a similar retrospective view of his travels through Italy: 'I often kind of stop and look back across the highest peaks of my attainments so far', ibid., p. 143, *Den 9. November.*

69   The passage is cited by P. Hadot: *N'oublie pas de vivre,* p. 73. German text Goethe: *Goethes Gespräche,* [online], 1823, 4. November.

Das uns irgend Großes, Schönes, Bedeutendes begegnet, muß nicht erst von Außen her wieder er-innert, gleichsam er-jagt werden, es muß sich vielmehr gleich vom Anfang her in unser Inneres verweben, mit ihm eins werden, ein neueres besseres Ich in uns erzeugen und so ewig bildend in uns fortleben und schaffen. Es giebt kein Vergangenes, das man zurücksehnen dürfte, es giebt nur ein ewig Neues, das sich aus den erweiterten Elementen des Vergangenen gestaltet und die ächte Sehnsucht muß stets productiv sein, ein neues Besseres erschaffen.

Anything great, beautiful, significant that meets us in life must not be initially re-minded (*er-innert*) from the outside, as if en-snared (*er-jagt*), but must on the contrary be interwoven into our very inside from the onset, to unite with, to create a new and better self in us and so live and create with us forever. There is no past to be longed for, only the eternally new, formed out of extended elements of the past and true nostalgia (*Sehnsucht*) must always be productive, create a new and better now.

Arcadia in the motto of the *Italian Journey* takes on a particular meaning: it is not only a mythical idyllic landscape – lost and long gone – but also an idyllic present during Goethe's sojourn in Italy, and creatively active within himself, as evidenced by the *Italian Journey* published after quite a few years.

II

For many Romantics, Goethe's synthesis ceases to apply. The present moment cannot encompass and integrate a distant past unto itself, and the synthesis shifts towards a level of projection, into the future. A key factor remains that this is no longer just about shaping the self, but also about a collective and often a nationalist dimension, the poet seeing himself as a spokesman for the community. If this role is not fulfilled, a matter which is of course not just in one's own hands, one experiences the present as a time of waiting, of exile. In the symbolism of Hölderlin's poems, this barren time is represented by the night, as in his 'Bread and Wine' elegy:

[...] Indessen dünket mir öfters
Besser zu schlafen, wie so ohne Genossen zu sein,
So zu harren, und was zu tun indes und zu sagen,
Weiß ich nicht, und wozu Dichter in dürftiger Zeit.
Aber sie sind, sagst du, wie des Weingotts heilige Priester,
Welche von Lande zu Land zogen in heiliger Nacht.

[...] Meanwhile I often consider
Is it better to sleep, than to be without comrades,
So to wait; in that time what to do and to say
I know not; who needs poets in more needy times?
But, you say, they are like holy priests of the wine-god,
That went roaming from country to country on Holy Night.[70]

For Hölderlin the motifs of exile relate to a present reflecting on loss (of homeland, community, love) characteristically expressed by a verse in Menon's lament over Diotia – *im furchtsamen Banne zu wohnen* [in dreadful exile to live].[71] Francis Claudon adds that for Hölderlin, exile marks a period of asceticism and preparation for a triumphant return.[72] Indeed, for Hölderlin, the culmination of the process – the return of the gods, the renewal of love – is not of the nature of a current event, it opens up a utopian time and space. In the final strophe of Menon's lament over Diotia, hope, presentiment and desire opens up the utopian world of the blissful *beyond*:

[...] bis wir auf gemeinsamem Boden
Dort, wo die Seligen all niederzukehren bereit,
Dort, wo die Adler sind, die Gestirne, die Boten des Vaters,
Dort, wo die Musen, woher Helden und Liebende sind,
Dort uns, oder auch hier, auf tauender Insel begegnen,
Wo die Unsrigen erst, blühend in Gärten gesellt,

---

70 F. Hölderlin: *Sämtliche Gedichte*, p. 290, ll. 119–124.

71 Ibid., p. 268, l. 19; p. 39. The word *Banne* (damnation) can be paraphrased as exile in the context of the poem, close in meaning.

72 F. Claudon: Exil et création littéraire. Hölderlin et Rousseau.

Wo die Gesänge wahr, und länger die Frühlinge schön sind,
Und von neuem ein Jahr unserer Seele beginnt.

[...] until we are laid in shared common ground,
Where all the blessed wait for their return
Where the eagles, the stars, are heralds of the Father,
Where the muses, where heroes and lovers come from,
Let's meet there, even here, on a softening island,
Where Ours do first bloom, in those gardens yonder
Where the word-songs don't lie and charming Springs linger
And where a new year for our Soul does begin![73]

III

With Czech poet Karel Hynek Mácha, depictions of exile appear in a symbo-lic-allegorical framework akin to Hölderlin.[74] In a series of poems before his famous 'May', he introduces characters mourning their lost homeland, largely seen in terms of a community:

Tak temnou nocí s větrem lká
na pusté skále králověc;
však ne té země králověc,
v níž bydlí, nýbrž vzdálená,
neznáma jemu leží vlasť,
v níž kraluje otec neznámý
synu, jenž *nezná sebe sám.*

By dark night he wails with the wind
on barren rock the young crown prince;

---

73   F. Hölderlin: *Sämtliche Gedichte*, pp. 271–272, ll. 119–124.
74   Michal Charypar suggests such a framework: *Máchovské interpretace*, e.g. pp. 28, 33.

not of that land the young crown prince,
where he lives, of a distant land
his homeland own unknown to him,
ruled by unknown a father king
for his son who knows not himself[75]

Mácha uses such stylization in his own letter to an unknown girl:

Tak se světem v rozepři, se zničeným srdcem, nepoznán od nikoho,
samoten jsem žil v hluku světa, nemilován od žádného a nic nemiluje
jako vyhnanec, jenž na pustou se ukryl skálu, jejížto neprohledná noc
černým závojem ho zahaluje... Tu Vy jste mi vzešla co denice žžoucí.

Thus at odds with the world, with a broken heart, recognized by
nobody, I lived alone in the tumult of the world, not loved by anyone,
and nothing approaches the love of an Exile taking refuge on a barren
rock, shrouded by the black veil of its impenetrable night... Then you
rose up for me, like the day-star, blazing.[76]

We can find a parallel between the two poets in the process of their overcoming the present, which is characterized by loss. For Mácha, as for Hölderlin, this often takes the form of a pilgrimage, being itself a reflection of human
life. In many places, there is the motif of the new dawn, associated with the
hope of return, a new stage of life, but at the same time more clearly than with
Hölderlin, linked to the motif of death and deceptive hope. The hopelessness
of such utopian thinking is expressed by Mácha's poem *Budoucí vlast* [Future
Homeland], inspired by verses from the first part of Byron's *Childe Harold's Pilgrimage*.[77] In this earlier poem, the Page confuses the light of the moon with the
setting sun, representing the homeland. From Mácha's later point of view, his
mistake is twofold: firstly, in confusing the moon for the sun, and also in the fact
that he is giving in to nostalgia and looking back, toward the setting sun, which

75 K. H. Mácha: *Básně a dramatické zlomky*, p. 115 (Královič).
76 K. H. Mácha: *Literární zápisníky, deníky, dopisy*, pp. 342–343.
77 cf. M. Procházka: Childe Haroldovo Dobrou noc a Budoucí vlast; M. Charypar: *Máchovské interpretace*, p. 26, 28ff.

for Mácha corresponds to the past, not the future. In that sense, the poem's title seems ambiguous and ironic.[78]

Mácha shifts the perception of time toward a schematic abstraction, in which the present reduces to a momentary point separating the past and future: *"Minulost a budoucnost, víc a více v hromadu se sráží, – až se zasáhnou, není nic, zhasl čas; životu není přítomnost žádná, lze říci jen bude a bylo, v životě není žádná přestávka".* [The past and the future pile up more and more, – when they collide, there is nothing, the time has been snuffed out; there is no present for living in, we can only speak of was and will be, with no pause for life.][79] For Mácha, the present loses its extent, being akin to a flash of lightning, 'of which it can be said that it has been, and will be, but not that it ever *is* being'[80] thus effectively excluding the possibility of integrating the past and future into the present. *Exile*, exclusion and loneliness are for Mácha determined by this nihilistic concept of time, the result of which is the sheer utopian nature of any homeland, whether it be situated in the past or in the future.

IV

While for the Romantics the community is idealized as a utopian, aspirational project, Baudelaire notes such aspirations tend to fail. In his poem *Le Voyage* [The Journey] Baudelaire belittles the desire for distant and exotic lands, the idea that some kind of Utopia will bring fulfilment. The longest poem in the *Flowers of Evil* allegorically records the collapse of the utopian project:

> Notre âme est un trois-mâts cherchant son Icarie ;
> Une voix retentit sur le pont : « Ouvre l'oeil ! »
> Une voix de la hune, ardente et folle, crie :
> « Amour … gloire … bonheur ! » Enfer ! c'est un écueil !

---

78   Referring to the title issue, M. Charypar: ibid., p. 25.
79   Ibid., p. 307.
80   K. H. Mácha: *Literární zápisníky, deníky, dopisy*, p. 251.

Our soul's a three-master seeking Icaria;
A voice resounds upon the bridge: "Keep a sharp eye!"
From aloft a voice, ardent and wild, cries:
"Love ... glory ... happiness" Damnation! It's a shoal![81]

The image of Icaria, referring to Étienne Cabet's utopian missive of 1840, eventually turns out to be a treacherous jutting reef. The journey ends with an apostrophe of death, which, unlike all parts of the material world, can indeed be *unknown* and revealing of something new (*Plonger au fond du gouffre, Enfer ou Ciel, qu'importe ? / Au fond de l'Inconnu pour trouver du* nouveau ! – 'To the abyss' depths, Heaven or Hell, does it matter? / To the depths of the Unknown *to find something new!*' [transl. William Aggeler])[82]

Nevertheless, the aforementioned *Swan* is central to the exile theme. Baudelaire soon sobered up from the political illusions and projects of 1848,[83] and this multifaceted poem can also be read as 'a hidden expression of the laments of a revolutionary, solidarity of an *internal exile* with the political Exiles after 1851, of which the most famous, let us recall, was Victor Hugo, to whom the poem was dedicated'.[84] In this, Baudelaire establishes a community of Exiles around a compassionate thought originally sparked by a swan seen in Paris. But the poem also fundamentally shifts the temporal and spatial dimensions of exile, by contrast with earlier ideas.

The poem's speaker implicitly likens himself to a number of well-known and unknown Exiles, and in the last strophe directly speaks of being an Exile of the spirit or of the mind: *où mon esprit s'exile* [to where my spirit exiles itself]. Unlike Andromache and other characters, his notion of exile refers to his city, Paris, in his here-and-now as it changes before his eyes: *la forme d'une ville / Change plus vite, hélas ! que le cœur d'un mortel* [the form of a city / Changes more quickly, alas! than the human heart]. The second section begins develops the notion into an introspection in which thoughts are more constant than the surrounding reality:

---

81   Ch. Baudelaire: *Œuvres complètes* I, p. 130

82   Ibid., p. 134.

83   R. Chambers: *Baudelaire's Paris*, p. 108.

84   R. Chambers: *Mélancolie et opposition*, p. 173. Baudelaire not only dedicated the poem, but in December 1859 also sent it to Victor Hugo, at that time in exile on Guernsey.

Paris change ! mais rien dans ma mélancolie
N'a bougé ! palais neufs, échafaudages, blocs,
Vieux faubourgs, tout pour moi devient allégorie,
Et mes chers souvenirs sont plus lourds que des rocs

Paris changes! but naught in my melancholy
has stirred! new palaces, scaffolding, blocks of stone,
old quarters, all become for me an allegory,
And my dear memories are heavier than rocks. [85]

[transl. William Aggeler]

The *Swan* is founded on associations not exactly aligned with the strophes'
sequence; as though the poem were combining several ideas on an enlarged
scale. The poet stands before the Louvre, where he suddenly calls back to mind
the image of the swan he had seen in these places before the reconstruction of
the city. Yet he begins the poems by addressing Andromache and attributes the
reminiscence to the scene of her exile, a landscape imitative of the real Troy:

Ce Simoïs menteur qui par vos pleurs grandit,
A fécondé soudain ma mémoire fertile,
Comme je traversais le nouveau Carrousel.

That false Simois swollen by your tears,
Suddenly made fruitful my teeming memory,
As I walked across the new Carrousel.

So, the association has several components: a place in the present moment, the
same place in the past, when it was quite different in form, the swan that the
poet saw here at that time and its being likened to Exiles:

Je pense à mon grand cygne, avec ses gestes fous,
Comme les exilés, ridicule et sublime

---

85   Ch. Baudelaire: *Œuvres complètes* I, p. 86.

[...] et puis à vous,
Andromaque

*

I think of my great swan with his crazy motions,
Ridiculous, sublime, like a man in exile,
[...] and then of you,
Andromache

It is only the connecting of the swan and Andromache that 'spawns' memory and evokes a sequence of images, and in that regard the association has several origins. It could be said that Baudelaire in this poem transmutes the temporal structure we witnessed with Goethe, and, in a different form, with the Romantic poets, where the present turns back to the past, tries to assimilate it, and turn once again toward the future.

In Baudelaire's poem, however, this is not a case of a noted or known historical past or any concept of the past, merely a past event that suddenly punctures the present when suddenly met with, like a shock experience, as Walter Benjamin put it in his Baudelaire article.[86] In the *Swan*, the event structure is even more complex, because it is an envisaged idea evoked by the present place and its transformation. The abruptly revealed present is not heading toward any particular form of the future, the many characters Baudelaire thinks of, triggered by this meeting, are completely imaginary and taking their place in his mind, thought or reverie. The final strophe also portrays a no less imaginary place of exile of the spirit – a forest resounding with remembrance:

Ainsi dans la forêt où mon esprit s'exile
Un vieux Souvenir sonne à plein souffle du cor !
Je pense aux matelots oubliés dans une île,
Aux captifs, aux vaincus ! ... à bien d'autres encore !

*

Thus in the dim forest to which my soul withdraws,
An ancient memory sounds loud the hunting horn!

---

86   cf. W. Benjamin: Some Motifs in Baudelaire.

I think of the sailors forgotten on some isle,
— Of the captives, of the vanquished! ...of many others too![87]

The image of a memory blowing the hunting horn creates a distinctive transition between the sensory and the cognitive plane. At the beginning of the poem Baudelaire presents the recollection of the swan as being visual (*Je ne vois qu'en esprit*, 'I see only in spirit'), while here at the end memory is characterized with the sound of a horn. In the final strophes of the poem, the depictions of the opening part are joined apace by a medley of other images, arguably not just for their content, but to create the confluence the last strophe calls for. Yet the shift from the visual to the sonorous is more sophisticated. Eugène Minkowski gives a very similar example for his concept of *reverberation/resounding* (*retentissement*):

> c'est comme si le son d'un cor de chasse, renvoyé de toutes parts par l'écho, faisait tressaillir, dans un mouvement commun, la moindre feuille, le moindre brin de mousse, et transformait tout la forêt, en la remplissant jusqu'aux bords, en un monde sonore vibrant [...] le son [...] se reflétant et se répercutant de toutes parts, remplit la forêt, en la faisant tressaillir et vibrer à l'unisson avec lui.

> as if the sound of a hunting horn, resounding by echo from all sides, in its overall agitation made tremble even the smallest leaf, the least frond of moss, while transforming the whole forest, filled to the brim, into a sonorous and vibrating world [...] the sound [...] reflects and rebounds on all sides, filling the forest, making it tremble and vibrate it in a unifying consonance.[88]

Minkowski does not restrict this phenomenon to sounds, but ponders the nature of the sonic metaphor and finds a structural consensus between such an auditory phenomenon and that of 'life synchronism', which he sees as ful-

---

87   Ch. Baudelaire: *Œuvres complètes* I, p. 86.
88   E. Minkowski: *Vers une cosmologie*, Chapter 9, pp. 101, 104.

filment and harmony. Sound in this sense is not a phenomenon in isolation, but a soundscape that one is surrounded and encompassed by. This take on thought/memory fills the present moment and forms its mood. The portrayal in the *Swan* expresses the communal presence of Baudelaire and all the mentioned figures, together in one space.

In Baudelaire's work, imagery has one important correspondent aspect. The word forest appears in a similarly harmonious image of the poem *Correspondances*. In that, the forest serves to epitomize nature, similarly filled with sounds *dans une ténébreuse et profonde unité* [in a sombre and profound togetherness]. The last verse of the *Correspondences* speaks of rapture, the elated carrying away (*transports*) of the spirit and senses; the image in the *Swan* equally combines the senses with thoughts. Unlike the *Correspondences*, however, in the *Swan* we are not concerned directly with nature, but a completely imaginary space, which is only modelled according to the corresponding natural idyll. For Baudelaire, the place of exile is definitely in the mind's eye, likewise employed in the opening poem of *Parisian images* in *Paysage* [The Landscape]. In that, Baudelaire, with gentle irony, subscribes to the pastoral tradition of Eclogue, carried across the city. But as soon as the idyll is to be disturbed by wintry weather, the poet shuts the windows and ensconces himself in his imagination, where he can evoke spring and a favourable atmosphere from his ideas.

V

With Baudelaire, the concept of Arcadia loses its ties with the past and the future, however utopian and idealized they may be, and definitively moves into the realms of the imagination. As imagined in modern terms, it ceases to be the land of poetry, whose inhabitants have a poetic gift, but becomes an imaginary place that poetry creates. For two Czech poets, Richard Weiner and Jiří Kovtun, this idea of a poetic land has a connection to the inception of language and its elementary poetic nature.

Richard Weiner (1884–1937) lived in Paris from 1919, where he made a living as a correspondent for the Czech daily *Lidové Noviny*. It was only shortly before his death in early 1936 that he moved back to Bohemia, where he died in the first days of January the next year. Weiner was not an Exile compelled by external forces, nor a nomad (as the concept was to become understood),[89] his sojourn in Paris was more about keeping his distance from home, albeit maintaining close relations with it from afar. One of the directions of his poetic and prose works could be described as a quest for the idyll of everyday life, on metaphysical foundations. In his poetry after 1927, when he returned to writing poems after a hiatus of several years, we find a number of cosmogonic poems, on the theme of the creation of the world and of primal Paradise. In his last collection *Mesopotamia* (1930) Weiner shifts this focus toward language; in the opening and longest composition of the collection, *Snebevzetí slova Mezopotamie*[90] [The Descent from Heaven of the Word Mesopotamia], the speaker meditates on how the constituent parts of a utopian place, Mesopotamia, derive from language. His reflections start off from some other, real place:

> S místa jež nevím kde už je a klímá
> mžourajíc na sluníčko
> dívám se skrze zakouřené sklíčko
> na náměstí svatého Augustina
> Sedím tu za bíledna na výsluní
> a za rozuteklými dumami si zpívám

> Down from some place I know no longer where and dozing
> squinting at the sun
> I look through a smoked glass
> at St Augustin square
> I sit here in broad daylight in the sun
> after scatty contemplations songs proposing[91]

The poem refers to the biblical motif of the creation of the world from the *Word*, but Weiner does not approach this topic of the power of language as if he were

---

89   see Chapter 10, and the classification of Věra Linhartová, who, like Weiner, lived in Paris and
      devoted her work to him, before her departure.

90   The latest edition of Richard Weiner's work is somewhat unfortunate in its spelling of his lyrical
      work. I refer the reader to this edition, but I take the wording from the first edition. Accord-
      ingly, "Snebevzetí" (Descension, down from), not "Znebevzetí" (Extraction, out of).

91   R. Weiner: *Básně*, p. 355.

some sovereign demiurge, but tries to work in the opposite direction, drilling back down to the roots of speech:

Proto té̌z se říká: Jméno
bylo skutkem učiněno
čili: Rozuměti slovům
může jen kdo znov' a znovu
klne pádu Adamovu

Hence it is also said: the Name
has become deed, one and the same
so: To grasp words can be an order tall,
solely for him who 'gain, again, appalled
castigates Adam's fall[92]

Weiner makes great use of rhetorical figures in this collection. The word Mesopotamia appears in the acrostic of the first and last poems, and, as Josef Vojvodík points out, the Czech word for poetry, POEZIE is also anagrammatically contained within the word ("mEZOPotamIE").[93] In addition to this combinatory spelling exercise, which Josef Vojvodík connects with the mannerist-Baroque tradition,[94] the collection has as its key motif of insight and vision, as associated with the Rimbaud tradition of the visionary poet.[95] Both positions, wordplay and vision, become connected as insight into the utopian dimension of everyday life:

Já snil já snil že kráčím rovnou k ráji
Ó zázraku! Mé sny jež procitají!
Jsem v ráji V ráji Neboť jsem a bdím!

---

92   Ibid., pp. 369–370.

93   J. Vojvodík: *Povrch, skrytost, ambivalence*, p. 138.

94   Ibid.

95   In the second half of the 20th century, Weiner spent time with young French poets from the *Le Grand Jeu* grouping, who were actively signing up to this tradition.

I dreamt I dreamt of walking straight to Eden
Oh miracle! My dreams awakening even!
I am in Paradise Because I am, aware![96]

VI

Weiner's composition is reminiscent of a group of poems by Jiří Kovtun from
the late 1950s and 1960s, which he summarized under the name of one of
them – *Zrození řeči* [The Birth of Language].[97] These were preceded by a series
of poems in prose called 'Sentimental Letters' from the late 1950s, in which
Kovtun takes memories of childhood experiences in the Czech countryside and
adds allusions to the idylls of antiquity. In the opening text *I write letters* he
connects childhood with the rural idyll and the plenitude of the world, while
likening adulthood to exile:

> This was the first stop on the way to the landscape of adulthood and
> exile, to further tables, which didn't belong just to us, and other waters
> that flowed from invisible, bitter springs. But back then, everything
> was still open to being seen, and those who saw were wise. All you
> had to do was watch and be receptive.
> And what had to come, did come: the wheat ripened all too quickly
> in the land of childhood. We live in wonder, and eat the bread of
> memories.[98]

Kovtun, whose early poetic work is distinctly Christian-oriented, does not
explicitly refer to the Paradise legend, but there are evident allusions on this

---

96   Ibid., p. 399.
97   George (Jiří) Kovtun (1927–2014) went into exile in 1948 and initially worked in Germany (in
     Radio Free Europe) and later worked as a librarian at the Library of Congress in Washington.
     Known as an author of books about history, he also wrote two remarkable novels, and trans-
     lated poems by, among others, O. Mandelstam, B. Pasternak, J. Brodsky, P. Celan, E. Dickinson.
98   J. Kovtun: *Hřbet velryby* [Whale Ridge], p. 8.

subject throughout his later work.[99] Contrary to the Christian beginnings of his poetry, his later poems are characterized by the confluence of sources from numerous cultural circles, in which the ancient world plays a great role. The 'Sentimental Letters' title can be read in the sense of a straightforward nostalgic looking back, but also in the spirit of Schiller's concept of a sentimental poet who seeks to restore the natural spontaneity that has been lost in this lineage from Rousseau on, due to culture. In Kovtun's work this finds a corresponding, almost romantic motif, of adulthood as exile.

The first of the letters, which begins with the words *"Milý dome, měl jsi číslo 36, stál jsi v Sousedovicích na kopci nad návsí..."* [Dear house, you had number 36, you stood in Sousedovice on the hill above the village square...], ends surprisingly with the sentence: *"Přišel Korydón, měl nestárnoucí rty."* [Korydon came, his lips ageless.][100] Places and events associated with a rural childhood are characteristically ephemeral, underlined by the fact of their being a memory; the motifs of an ancient idyll bring in a different temporal dimension to this context, transforming the rural images. In another of the letters, Kovtun thus brings together Virgil's Meliboeus with a particular man of the 20th century, and his story. While he does not argue with his being mortal, he gives the man's life a certain idyllic universality, as if he were not just some innocuous 'Václav Zahradník':

> Dear postcard [...] I read in you the ancient tale of Václav Zahradník, who was formerly called Meliboeus and was told one lovely day that he had to leave his house and several fields. In the end, he was lucky, because he came back again, tired of the harvest season heat, and Thestylis once again cooked him a fragrant soup of crushed thyme and garlic. As he was scooped up the mortar with the bricklayer's trowel, he looked behind him and saw the Naiads snatching up the bright

---

99   In 1995, he published his poems in the collection the *Whale Ridge*, in which he no longer included the first collection, *Blahoslavení* [Beatitudes, 1953] or other similarly inclined poems from the late 1940s and first half of the 1950s. A similar shift from the Christian world-view, with an emphasis on humility and suffering, to a more generally oriented and idyllic view, is also evident from the two editions of the poem *The Birth of Language*.

100   Ibid., p. 9.

irises and flowering poppies, tying up the daffodils with fiery mari-
golds and cinnamon flowers. But the idyll soon passed away.[101]

Some of the Letters themes are followed up with three longer poems from the
late 1950s and 1960s written in regularly rhyming strophes of evocative songs
that can be read as a poetic analysis of what the Letters opened up and hinted
at as a whole: the presence of the idyll (Arcadia) as a universal but hidden layer
of human reality. The poem *Kde to bylo* [Someplace] turns to the past as to an
idyllic landscape archived in memory. In the *Birth of Language*, the theme is the
restoration of the first, original language of this idyllic past. In the last of the
letters, one such language is also the language of the landscape:

> Dear landscape, I wanted to write to you in your language. I mean in
> that language into which everything had already been incorporated
> before the first word was uttered, easy to understand from the cry
> of the rooster in the neighbouring yard, from the nocturnal howls of
> dogs, from the murmur of the wind under the old fortress. There is
> no need to worry about the sentence composition in such a language;
> it was taken care of by the one who planted the tree, carved the rock,
> made ripples on the surface of that pond known as Křemelný. Your
> language, my landscape, grows out of the ground like the grass, green
> and clear.[102]

The later poem *The Birth of Language*, features the motif of restoring language
from sources other than just a return to the idyll of nature:

> Teď je to jiné. Zetlely
> na polích dětské luky
> a musíš hledat, dospělý,
> starší svisty a zvuky,
>
> elementární tóninu,
> starší než hybelská včela.

---

101   Ibid., p. 20.
102   Ibid., p. 24.

[...]
Musíš si, němý, osvojit
prvotní hudbu ticha.
Je ve tvé dřeni, jsi jí syt
a nikdy nevysychá.

Co slyšíš kolem to jsou jen
její ozvěny časné.
Strom hoří, zvon bude roztaven,
žárovka vosy zhasne,

ale zbyde tu jako dřív,
míza bez prsu kmene,
horké uštknutí bez kopřiv –
jsi tedy u pramene.

It's different now. They've rotted down
in fields, kids' bows and arrows
and now, as adult, hunt your own,
old whistles, sounds long borrowed,

the elementary tonal key,
older than Sicily's Hybla bee.
[...]
Now you must, mute, to your heart take
first music, of sound abated.
She's in your marrow, brimming, slaked,
and never desiccated.

What you heard round about, you've felt,
her echoes, time-relinquished.
The tree burns, and the bell will melt,
the wasp's bulb glow extinguished,

but all will be restored once more,
sap, without tree bare breasted,

a hot sting, without nettles, sore –
you're at the wellspring, tested.[103]

The shortest and last of the trio of poems, *Schůzka v Arkádii* [Meeting in
Arcadia], hints at the artistic tradition of the Arcadia theme, but also points
to it as the place that forms a hidden foundation stratum for memory, hope or
yearning for an idyll:

> V naší paměti je uschována
> nesplněná výzva úsvitů,
> šelestící, bílý dopis rána,
> škvírou zasouvaný do bytu.
>
> V našich vzpomínkách jsou předsevzetí,
> starší nežli celé naše vědomí,
> [...]
> je to pokyn, který dennodenně
> navrací nám stará zkušenost,
> který píše výstrahu na naší stěně,
> ukazuje směr a splétá most.
> [...]
> Posnídáme jako na pohovce
> v trávě, kolem nás tři pastýři
> budou trylkovat a hlídat ovce,
> ozbrojené rouny jako pancíři.
>
> Celý život bude potom prostý,
> budeme si odměřovat čas
> sluncem, vánicí a letorosty,
> nalezneme život, který v nás
>
> moudré smysly podvědomě žijí,
> najdeme, co ztraceno jest, klid.

---

103   Ibid., p. 48.

Umluvme si schůzku v Arkádii,
nezapomeň se však dostavit.

We still have in memory's safe keeping
promising new dawns, as yet unmet,
morning's rustling white slip letter creeping
through a crevice, right into our flat.

In our memories are resolutions,
older than our entire consciousness,
[...]
an instruction every day, that's all,
brought back by experience, old times,
that writes out a warning on our wall,
shows the way, some suspended bridge entwines
[...]
As if on a couch, we'll breakfast, lounging
in the grass, three shepherds round us, glad,
minding sheep, to their bleats, trills arranging,
in their armour-plate of fleeces clad.

After that life will be truly simple,
we will pass the time, its passing mark
by the sun, a blizzard, tree rings ample,
we will find a life within us, hark,

wisely sensed, subconsciously entreating,
we will find what we have lost, our peace.
Let's make in Arcadia our meeting,
don't forget to turn up, if you please.[104]

Kovtun's body of poetry comes to a close with poems from 1966–1973, collected
under the *Whale Ridge* title. Compared to the early regular rhyming poems, they

---

104   Ibid., pp. 36–37.

are written in free verse, and show a similarly distinct break in content; unlike earlier, they are not a composite whole, but rather a collection of more or less occasional poems from one period. The idyll motif remains, but Kovtun analyses it sceptically and ironically in varying contexts and from differing perspectives. In some poems, he attributes to it the worth of being that which makes other things make sense, even if it does seem random and, in some ways, ephemeral:

> Ale je to tak a nelze to změnit,
> z mimovolné souhry povstal úkol:
> náhodou seděl Dafnis pod šumícím dubem.

> But that is how it is and it can't be changed,
> from involuntary interplay a task has risen:
> as if by chance Daphnis sat under the whispering oak.[105]

In other poems, the idyll is confronted with the violence of the 20th century and by contrast, essentially loses its right to figure in a poem and in human life, seemingly only displacing reality:

> Jako pes po studené lázni
> Evropa se vždycky dovedla otřepat.
> [...]
> Máme však mstivou paměť.
> Otevřete okno v mlze
> a do pokoje se vám vřítí yperit.
> Právě vám dobře chutná
> a vedle vás Ivan Děnisovič
> saje poslední šťávu z páteře slanečka.
> A víte koneckonců po tom všem,
> z čeho je mýdlo?
> Mezi palcem a ukazováčkem si uděláte bublinku
> a v ní se leskne
> oko osvětimského dítěte.

---

105   Ibid., p. 99 b. *Úkol* [The Task].

Co si dnes dáme k večeři?
Kobylky a lesní med.

Like a dog after a cold bath
Europe has always managed to shake off.
[...]
But we have a vindictive memory.
Open the window in a fog
and you'll find mustard gas surging into your room.
You just like the taste of it too much
and next to you Ivan Denisovich
sucks the last juice from the spine of a herring.
And did you know after all that,
What soap is made out of?
Make a bubble between your thumb and forefinger
and shining out of it
is the eye of an Auschwitz child.

What shall we have for dinner tonight?
Grasshoppers and forest honey.[106]

The concept of the idyll, deeply rooted in the Western poetic tradition, remains present even in Kovtun's late poetry, which, above all, reveals how problematic and uncertain it can be. The issue is not about restoring the idyll in primal language; speech is not as eloquent as nature, it is *just* a means of communication among people, cf. the poem *Řekni slovo* [Say the word]. This aspect, hinted at by the 'Meeting in Arcadia', shows the idyll as a value held by people and dependent on their awareness of reality, which is itself a rebuttal of the idyllic. An idyll without such an awareness is a deceptive illusion; yet a consciously grasped idyll is always necessarily rife with nostalgia, which in Kovtun's case is not devoid of some joy. In his later poems we can read this stance, of Man as Exile, uncertain of any solid ground underfoot, but this does not of itself rule out some idyllic element.

---

106 Ibid., p. 84.

Byl to opravdu krásný kout.
Na zvětralých skalách
se dalo dobře žít,
datlovník,
do jehož kořenů se zaplétaly kosti,
živil děti,
byla tam voda a stín,
rána se pravidelně navracela.
Stačila rychlá výzva
a milovali se.

A to všechno
na hřbetu velryby.

I ten, který to věděl,
dělal jakoby nic

＊

It really was a truly lovely spot.
On weathered rocks
life could be lived well,
the date palm,
its roots entangled in bones,
nurtured children,
there was water and shade,
mornings regularly returning.
A quick cue was enough
and they made love.

And all of this
on the ridge back of the whale.

Even he, who knew it,
acted nonchalantly.[107]

---

107   Ibid., p. 96 (poem *Ostrov* / The Island).

VII

Weiner's *Mesopotamia* stems from different literary traditions than Jiří Kovtun's *Arcadia*, but in both cases we are dealing with an imaginary land linked with poetry, and in both cases these imaginary projects retain a feature present in Virgil's *Eclogues* – blending myth and reality.[108] For Virgil, this meant that in Arcadia real people can meet mythical heroes; in modern poetry, Arcadia itself is mythical and gives the scope to fulfil what reality precludes. The beginning of Kovtun's poem can be read as the identification of an imaginary meeting place for people separated by the impenetrable barrier of exile:

Umluvme si schůzku v Arkádii,
když se nemůžeme setkat u kávy,
kterou za nás jiní lidé pijí
na počátku jiné výpravy.

Let's make in Arcadia our meeting,
if we can't do coffee, share a sip,
others in our place drink, take our seating,
at the start of quite a different trip.[109]

Another aspect of Arcadia is the projection of political goings-on and the historical situation into the myth, and vice versa.[110] In Kovtun's *Sentimental Letters*, reality is seen against the fragmentary background of the idyll, gaining an additional time dimension of idealized events in a mythical landscape. This aspect is also evident in the first part of *Báje z Nového světa* [Fable from the New World] by Stanislav Mareš, in which the author updates the first Eclogue with the situ-

---

108   On this, cf. B. Snell: Arcadia; W. Iser: *The Fictive and the Imaginary*, ch. II.
109   J. Kovtun: *Hřbet velryby*, p. 36.
110   On the presence of political events in Virgil's *Eclogues*, B. Snell writes: Arcadia; W. Iser: *The Fictive and the Imaginary*, p. 34–35.

ation in Czechoslovakia after the Soviet invasion. In this case, a modern event benefiting from a previous text shifts to universality and becomes one facet of the great history of Western culture.[111]

---

111   I deal with Mareš's poem in more detail in the Chapter 8.

5. The Invisible Home

I

In 1954, the *Invisible Home* anthology was published in Paris, subtitled *Verses of Exiles 1948–1953*. Peter Demetz is listed as the editor. The book provoked a host of reactions in Czech exile circles, and is probably the most famous book of Czech exile poetry, alongside two collections by Ivan Blatný. From today's point of view, it features poems of unequal merit, in addition to poems by the worthy Ivan Blatný, Milada Součková or Josef Lederer (under the pseudonym Jiří Klan) there are also verses in it, which, seen dispassionately, are no more than a testimony to their time.[1] History has also delivered an unintended tragic blow to the book. The poem by František Kovárna 'The East River' depicts a night hospital in New York in which an unknown man dies. The anonymous observer is watching the patient's wife depart, captures a last few words, and then just records how the personal belongings and the last traces of the unknown's presence progressively disappear, how the hubbub around subsides.

> Už neslyším kroky
> Je půl desáté pryč
> K půlnoci snad usnu
> nad Východní řekou,

---

[1] cf. M. Přibáň: *Prvních dvacet let*, pp. 194–198; D. Šajtar: Neviditelný domov, p. 48; L. Nezdařil: O autorovi, p. 154.

kde před chvilkou skončil
jejich příběh

■

I can't hear any more steps
It's gone half past nine.
I hope to fall asleep by midnight
over the East River,
where just moments ago
their story ended[2]

The poem is dated 7 June 1952 in New York; František Kovárna died twelve
days later.[3] We can only imagine that an insomniac observer is also pondering
his own destiny, and that the East River of the title also represents a foreign,
unknown place where the life of an Exile ends in anonymity:

Kam se až táhne
ta Východní řeka
nad kterou skončil
jejich příběh?

■

How far does it stretch
that East River
over which
their story ended?

II

The exile press reactions to the *Invisible Home* revolved around two key aspects:
that the selected poets were not sufficiently representative of Czech exile poetry,

---

2   *Neviditelný domov*, p. 76.
3   For more about Kovárna see V. A. Debnár: František Kovárna.

and Ivan Blatný's poem *Hřbitov* [Cemetery] seemed to most critics needlessly
provocative. In both respects, the underlying ideas and non-poetic conside-
rations were quite understandable in the politicized setting of exile, but both
were also revealing of a broader context. Ivan Blatný, as one of the few poets of
this anthology (and two other similar ones) displayed a sense of humour in his
poems. In most of the other poems, pathos and nostalgia prevail. The incrimi-
nating second strophe of Blatný's *Cemetery* reads:

> Ležím v posteli s tetičkou Staňkovou
> A smějeme se.
> Paní Nezvalová přináší makové koláče.
> Má se také svléci donaha?
> Za almarou jsou ještě čtyři lahve vína.
> Musím si ukrojit kus masa, říká tetička.

> I'm lying in bed with auntie Staňková
> And we are laughing.
> Mrs. Nezvalová is bringing poppyseed pies.
> Should she strip naked, too?
> There are four more bottles of wine behind the wardrobe.
> I have to cut myself some meat, auntie says.[4]

As to criticism of the poets selected, this had more to do with the persons represented, than their respective poems; it shows that the *Invisible Home* was regarded

---

4   *Neviditelný domov*, p. 23. Mrs. Nezvalová is an allusion to one of the most famous Czech poets,
     Vítězslav Nezval (1900–1958), who was Blatný's mentor and friend; cf. M. Reiner: *Básník*, p. 39ff.
     After Blatný went into exile, Nezval wrote a tendentious ditty *Ach škoda* [Oh, What a Shame] in
     which he distances himself from Blatný in a would-be paternal tone: 'Even in the tiniest village
     of them all / to gather together [with folk] the rye we'll hurry / while you, within the asylum
     walls... / For you I feel, nevertheless, sorry'; Blatný: *Texty a dokumenty*, p. 374. Nezval had no
     qualms about pandering to the regime at the time, writing no shortage of tendentious poems,
     and he probably isn't expressing his true opinion of his friend ('Nezval of course did not stop
     being fond of dear Ivan [...] to the very end,' writes Vlastimil Fiala in his memoir. ibid., p. 413).
     For the exiled community, Nezval was above all a pro-regime poet, which is why his very name
     is a red flag. The name 'Mrs. Nezvalová' also led the editor of the *Tribuna* magazine to believe
     that the author of the poem was Nezval; cf. M. Přibáň: *Prvních dvacet let*, p. 195.

by the exile community primarily as a collective showcase of the nation's Exiles, not as a book that would bring a new or a distinctive poetic testimony. Much of this also applies to the authors and organizers of the *Invisible Home*.

The first signs of the upcoming publication appeared in 1951, in the Geneva published journal *Skutečnost* [Reality], which printed an essay by Jan Tumlíř[5] entitled *Hořká vodo poesie* [Bitter Water of Poetry] (being addressed in the vocative), with examples of poems by several writers, and a challenge to poem-writing emigrants (not poets in exile, etc.) to send their works to a given address. This text by Tumlíř was then re-published without much editorial change as the foreword to the *Invisible Home*. The opening paragraph of the magazine version hints at some of the background to it all:

> As far as we are aware, by means of the meagre sample on the pages of this issue of *Skutečnost*, Czech poetry is making its debut toward its public on this side of the border. Why did it take three years for it to find its voice in freedom, and why is it still speaking in a voice so uncertain and feeble? Any emigrant who would rather lighten his luggage by not packing a pair of warm socks is entitled to ask such a question of a book of verses. Let us try to reply, in the hope that our reflection on the difficulties of a Czech poet of the third emigration wave will capture at least the outline of the more general change that current literature is undergoing. Displacement, the isolation of emigration: herein, poetry finds itself at its limits, opening up so many new vistas to critical exploration. Indeed, is not this displacement, the homelessness of the refugee, one of the most pervasive features of our time?[6]

Tumlíř's essay in this issue of *Skutečnost*, accompanied by a select few poems by various authors[7] were not the first poems published in exile, but it was probably the first joint appearance by multiple poets, and the text also suggests he was trying to take a stand against a certain fragmentation, isolation and 'homelessness'. There were multiple attempts to organize political and cultural

---

5   As to Jan Tumlíř cf V. A. Debnár: Všestranný exulant.

6   J. Tumlíř: Hořká vodo poesie, p. 68.

7   Published under their initials by Jiří Kárnet, Jan Tumlíř, František Listopad and L.S.

life in Czech exile, and a number of institutions established, with greater and lesser success.[8] Tumlíř was more concerned with bringing together exile poets on the basis of their poetry and poetics, regardless of political and personal ties. This might also be borne out by the equivocating title *Invisible Home*, which does not solely indicate the land the poets have left behind, but also extrapolates to a shared, if not obvious interpretation – a certain notion of poetry as a refuge, perhaps. An intention along these lines is confirmed by a revised introductory paragraph, which introduces the Tumlíř text in the book edition:

> The book you are opening is the first anthology of works by a number of Czech poets in exile. We redacted it via letters exchanged between three continents: It is therefore more than likely that many of the poems it might have included have missed our attention. Yet, howsoever incomplete, this anthology does capture several essential features common to the works of all Czech poets on this side of the border.[9]

Tumlíř's foreword represents the first, or one of the first reviews of exile poetry in the Czech diaspora environment, but also reveals some agenda--setting, purposive ambitions. Jan Tumlíř does not provide any synopsis, does not describe the fates of specific poets, but takes a more general contemplative look at exile poetry in its modern context. The text, taking one of Tumlíř's own verses for its magazine version title, addressing the *Bitter Water of Poetry*, and later in the book simply entitled 'Foreword', opens up the question of modern poetry in avant-garde streams that untether language from the confines of logic and break Parnassist rhetoric. Language can enter the poem in the form of words overheard, 'a poem does indeed come about whenever and wherever it chooses: in a railway station waiting room, on the football terraces, at the bar table of a crowded fast-food outlet – anywhere the language lives.'[10] The role of language is all the more important in exile, because now 'the poet is cut off from the most personal medium of his creative work', communica-

---

8   A thorough overview of exile life with a focus on literature is given by Michal Přibáň in his book *Prvních dvacet let* [The First Twenty Years].

9   *Neviditelný domov*, p. 9.

10   Ibid.

ting in a foreign language, availing his mother tongue only intermittently and in its capacity to inform: 'in effect, he is writing in a dead language'.[11] Tumlíř further rejects the notion of a poet working in isolation and for themselves, the anchoring of language in poetry is the contrary quest for 'resonance' with those who share similar words, based on similar experiences and acquired knowledge. Exile poetry is also characterized by Tumlíř as embodying a sense of compelled departure, making it distinct from the works of authors living abroad voluntarily. For this reason, the poetry of refugees is necessarily politicized and filled with an awareness of alienation from the new environment and of being scattered. Here he explicitly compares the situation with the Jewish diaspora.[12] One important point, which Tumlíř finds characteristic of modern poetry in general, is the loss of the idea of a certain harmony between the microcosm and the macrocosm:

> Even before the First World War, people inhabited their private worlds, so cleanly and smoothly integrated into the outside world that they hardly grated. There was no effort needed to make the personal experience of love equate with love, of God with God, of nature with nature; to make one feel one is facing these phenomena in one's own right. The world had its order, within which it moved with such regularity that it stood beyond one's momentary awareness: much as we do not notice the clock ticking on the wall, unless and until we want to know the time. But then it happened: the ticking of the clock turned into gunshots and exploding bombs, order and regularity crashed down upon us, like the house in an air-raid. [...] Personal experience grew to encompass the experiences of crowds,

---

11   Ibid., p. 10. František Kovárna characterizes the situation of poetry in exile in very similar terms, in an undated leaflet as part of the magazine *Stopa* initiative, sometime around 1951: 'There are plenty of opportunities to write or speak Czech or Slovak here, but so far the words have been those of utility, particular and restricted to a given task. It does not matter if we are limiting ourselves or being limited. For the language to live, however, it needs to live in all its registers, and especially in its highest, which culminates in poetry,' cites M. Přibáň: *Prvních dvacet let*, p. 74.

12   *Neviditelný domov*, p. 12.

crises, revolutions and Exiles. Politics cannot avoid breaking into poetry, at the personal level of experience.[13]

If, as Tumlíř summarizes, 'the presence of language and of a conversation partner – are two almost basic prerequisites of poetics', then poems that originated in exile are understandably different from poetry that arises under more normal conditions. Nevertheless, as he adds, these tendencies to varying degrees characterize literature in its entirety, and in the suggested perspective of one's private world having been politicized, and the need to defend the 'inner environs of poetic existence' he finds that 'all today's poets are Exiles'.[14]

Jan Tumlíř aptly characterizes the role of the poet at the beginning of the Cold War, and, as I will try to show, at the same time characterizes his own poetics, having some points in common with the other poets featured in the *Invisible Home*. In so doing he also met with some misunderstanding from other poets and the exile public. There is a core contradiction between Tumlíř's idea that exile is an extreme situation that changes the fundamental conditions for poetry, and the opinion of the more conservative critics, for whom the poet is primarily an Exile and supposed to expound on the subject of exile in an appropriate way.

III

We do not know exactly how the *Invisible Home* came into being, nor what sort of response there was to the call for submissions published in *Skutečnost*. Peter Demetz reports that the impetus for compiling the anthology came from listeners' poems sent in to him while an editor at Radio Free Europe.[15] It seems there were plenty of discussions and controversies around the forthcoming book. Under a review printed in the journal *Sklizeň* was a note that Jiří Kavka and Jiří Kovtun turned down their own participation;[16] in another review

---

13   Ibid., p. 13.
14   Ibid., pp. 13–14.
15   Personal communication.
16   *Sklizeň* 2, no. 6, June 1954, p. 12. Jiří Kavka was one of the pseudonyms of the poet and publisher Robert Vlach, which came to light only after Vlach's death.

Antonín Kratochvil speaks of disagreements about the title: 'The anthology was originally to be named after a poem by František Listopad, *Nazvi to nadějí* [Call it Hope]. That title was undoubtedly much more fitting for the anthology than the clichéd and unclear *Invisible Home*.'[17] The year after the *Invisible Home* came a Czech-Estonian anthology called *A Garden in No man's Land*[18] and the following year another anthology of exile poetry, *Time for Building* (1956). The *Garden in No man's Land* does not explicitly relate to the *Invisible Home*, and with its several forewords in French and English tries to reach an international audience, while involving the authors in the *Invisible Home* and *Time for Building* in equal measure. Conversely, the third Czech-instigated anthology reminds us of a number of authors omitted from the *Invisible Home*, and introduces the works of another fifteen. In the foreword, Antonín Vlach explicitly writes about thirty poets, of whom each 'contributes their free part to the edifice', thus indicating the polemic unity of both books. Unlike Jan Tumlíř, he does not look to find a common theme or to describe the situation of poetry in exile. These are 'thirty poets, thirty individualities, each of whom is earnestly seeking the purest manifestation of their inner self'.[19] Rather than anything in common, Vlach emphasizes he is looking to complete 'the picture of our poetry in freedom', at the same time his words imply trying to give a platform to poets whose opportunity to publish had been limited.[20] Contrary to the *Invisible Home*, this it is not an anthology of exile poetry as such, but rather the showcasing of poets living in exile, so it is not about the state of the world as only a poem can show it, but the voices of poets affected by this state of the world. The title *Time for Building* and the theme of an edifice as mentioned in the foreword are intended as a positive contrast to the seeming nostalgia of the *Invisible Home*, yet the poems of all three books form one body of work, with differences of emphasis, while the theme of construction, as Antonín Vlach understands it, does not in

---

17   A. Kratochvil: Tečka za jednou antologií.

18   The book is titled *Poetae in exilio* and the bilingual name *Rohtaed ei kellegi-maal – Zahrada v zemi nikoho*, edited by Peeter Arumaa and Robert Vlach, who was probably the project's initiator. The book was published as the fifth volume of the 'Knižnice lyriky' compendium, in Stockholm.

19   *Čas stavění*, p. 3.

20   The exception in the *Time for Building* being A. D. Martin, the pen-name of Antonín Bartušek (1921–1974), who was not living in exile. His contribution was probably facilitated by his friend Jana Borová (Aurelie Jeníková).

overall terms mean some net gain added through exile, but rather joint efforts on building national culture.

Anthologies of Czech exile poetry were not exceptional at the time. Draho-mír Šajtar compares the *Invisible Home* to the Polish anthology *Najwybitniejsi poeci emigracji współczesnej* [The most eminent poets of contemporary emigra-tion], published in Paris in 1951.[21] Even the flamboyant graphic design of the book, in a style that harkens back to the beginning of the century,[22] suggests that this was intended to be a showpiece publication, presenting the fruits of exile culture. The very first sentence of the introduction: 'Polish exile poetry has a great tradition,' clearly notes that this is not about any kind of programme or service to poets, but a manifestation of national culture of which exile forms an integral part. The book was also written up in the Polish press back home, something unimaginable in the Czech case.[23] Subsequent anthologies pub-lished in Polish exile likewise testify to this sense of belonging to a joint domes-tic and exile literary scene. The book *Poeta pamięta. Antologia poezji świadectwa i sprzeciwu 1944–1984* [The poet remembers. An anthology of poetry of tes-timony and opposition] produced by Stanisław Barańczak and published in London, brings together Polish poets regardless of whether they lived in exile or in their homeland.

Polish and Czech Exiles differ in this respect, but by making the comparison we can highlight some of the limits and contexts of exile poetry at that time. For poets in the 1950s, the national language is the ultimate limit of their scope,[24] and even international projects like the *Garden in No-man's Land* fail to gain much

---

21   D. Šajtar: *Neviditelný domov*, p. 46.

22   By contrast the *Invisible Home* has a sober modernist design by Miroslav Šašek, who made his name as an author of art books on the world's major cities.

23   cf. D. Šajtar: ibid.

24   The more prominent poets from the East, who would write in another language for their Western readers, come into their own and gained some international acclaim only later, from the 1960s, for example Czesław Miłosz, Joseph Brodsky, in the Czech exile case Petr Král or Jiří Gruša; this also applies to those translated in the West. In this communication towards the West, exile is not always a decisive factor; akin to Miłosz and Brodsky, in the case of Czech literature a similar role fell to Miroslav Holub, who was translated into English from the 1960s and had some influence on Anglophone poetry. cf. J. Quinn: *Between Two Fires. Transnational-ism and Cold War Poetry*. From the 1960s, transnational influxes became more popular, whereby the epithets of exile and exile poetry lost some significance.

traction or follow-up.[25] Restricting exile to the national context also brings its own demands as to what exile poetry should look like, or rather what it shouldn't look like, according to the reviews of the *Invisible Home*. One of the fundamentals is a certain conservatism – a preference for structured and rhyming verse (i.e. criticism of free verse) and a not always voiced, but clearly present regard for continuity with the Czech poetic canon. The first poems published in exile were not poems by Exiles, but the classical Czech poets of yore – Karel Hynek Mácha, Karel Havlíček, Svatopluk Čech, Otokar Březina or Viktor Dyk.[26]

IV

The only positive review of the *Invisible Home* was written by Zdeněk Němeček (1894–1957), who was a noted prose writer of the older generation, and himself contributed two poems to the *Time for Building*. Němeček finds common characteristics in the trauma of exile, sadness and hopelessness and illustrates this by quoting from the poems of ten of the poets involved. As to the five remaining, he adds commentary that clearly puts them in the frame of sadness, trauma and nostalgia, from which there is no escape. It is as though a poet in exile simply couldn't write in any other way:

25　One such attempt to publish exiled poets and writers from the Eastern Bloc is heralded by a notice in Tumlíř's *Bitter Water* collection (1951); but it seems the first volume was as far as it went. Some initiative also came from the international Pen Club. Paul Tabori, the chairman of the PEN Exile Centre arranged for two anthologies of exile authors *The Pen in Exile* (1954, 1956). In the first volume, two Czech authors were represented – Zdeněk Němeček with his short story *Time, The Magician* and Ivan Jelínek with the poem *Battlefield*; in the second volume came an essay by Vladimír Štědrý, *Still Life*. The original idea was to publish a yearbook of exiled authors. Even the fact that only two volumes were issued is indicative of few Western readers taking an interest, and it being relatively restricted to the national 'diaspora'. After that, attempts to reach an international audience remained a matter for the individual authors themselves. Both these anthologies and other Pen Club initiatives gained little traction among Czech Exiles.

26　cf. M. Přibáň: *Prvních dvacet let*, p. 70. The popularity of Viktor Dyk as referenced by M. Přibáň (ibid., p. 67), is paradoxical in a way, because his famous poem *Země mluví* [The Land Speaks] was used by the regime almost as a mantra against Exiles (cf. Přibáň: ibid., p. 319). In an article published later in the exile journal *Západ*, Jan Vladislav shows how this regime-reading is based on a wilful misinterpretation of Dyk's poem (cf. J. Vladislav: Opustíš-li mne...).

Here we find deep clues, if not proof of, trauma. If Tůma adds his poems to them, with profound Hebrew melodies, he cumulates even older, far-from-healed wounds. The same, if we have understood rightly, can be said of Klan's[27] beautiful poem. Junius' simple verses bring only a brief glimmer. Blatný seeks, in vain, a way out through a mixture of images of the homeland and his present domicile abroad, and in all futility wraps the 'wondrous word cemetery' in a cellophane of cynical glistenings. He will not escape. Kovárna, as if he had taken a detour somewhere, writes a gloomy hospital epigram about simple things and people; and one just can't believe how this boisterous, wonderful brain, this diligent hand shortly after falls into an abyss of doom.[28]

Zdeněk Němeček's view is understandable and well-representative of the attitudes evident in other reviews. He is also in agreement with opinions about Blatný's *Cemetery* poem, although he does not write about it belligerently: the review's benevolent tone suggests that Blatný is not only being difficult on purpose, he actually isn't aware of how he is writing – because from Němeček's point of view, under the circumstances of exile, the topic and the tone are inevitably given. Němeček is not mistaken in his overall characterization of the book: one would hardly expect such a publication to include children's nonsense verse or wordplay typical of the Czech 1920s poetistic movement. The book's contextual framework is already prescriptive, albeit less so than its reviewers make out. Němeček's characterization is not entirely misplaced, but in being so unequivocal he does not allow other views of exile and does not take note of the prompts in Tumlíř's foreword.

The expected posture of sadness and nostalgia is represented by poems reminiscing about lost idyllic Czech lands. All three anthologies do contain such, in their more conventional parts. They echo images of an idyllic rural landscape and motifs returning to the symbolic poetry of the turn of the century. Poems of this type include those by Pavel Javor, Václav Michl-Junius or Jaromír Měšťan's poem *Ve vysokém létu* [At the Height of Summer], culminating in the

---

27   Jiří Klan was the pseudonym of Josef Lederer.
28   Z. Němeček: Verše exulantů, p. 23.

exclamatory: 'God, how I pine for the Czech Lands.'[29] The poems of Jan Tumlíř
are marked by another form of sadness. For him, it is more about a sense of
being alone in a foreign country.

Jan Tumlíř published his *Bitter Water* collection in 1951, which includes
poems later selected for the *Invisible Home*. The poems of the collection are
dated 1947–1950 and collate Tumlíř's poetry written after the War while still in
Czechoslovakia, as well as those after 1948 in exile.[30] The title *Bitter Water* references a motif of melancholy, which is echoed in the verses of the poem with
which Tumlíř wraps up the entire anthology:

> Nepoznáš mne nikdy, protože já jsem ten,
> kdo nespí ve svém lůžku,
> plném hořké a slané vůně tvé pokožky,
> kdo sbírá střepy, bázní posunován
> na konec světla, v němž se poznáváme:
> kdo je sám a mluví čirou řečí smutku.

> You'll never know me, because I am the one
> who does not sleep in his own bed,
> full of the bitter and salty scent of your skin,
> who collects shards, nudged along by fear
> to the end of the light, in which we acquaint ourselves:
> who is alone and speaks the pure language of sadness.[31]

In contrast to the conventional idyll of lost Bohemia, the poetry of Tumlíř
takes on board the specific reality of the abandoned home, or the inhospitable
foreign land. Tumlíř does not present us with personal feelings of sadness writ
large, but neither does he pore over the inner workings of the melancholic self,
nor projects his mood onto the surroundings. Even the names of several poems

29   *Neviditelný domov*, p. 93.
30   After this collection, in the 1950s Tumlíř published only a few poems alongside several
      magazine prose pieces (J. Tumlíř: Básničky z Ameriky; Malá noční hudba budoucnosti;
      Namísto nákupu) [Poems from America; A little night music of the future; Instead of buying].
31   *Neviditelný domov*, p. 118.

from his collection evoke rather torpid surroundings: *Vítr utichá, Kamna jsou vychladlá, Okna jsou zavřena –* 'The Wind is Dying Down', 'The Stove is Cold', 'The Windows are Closed.'

> Okna jsou zavřena. Slunce krouží
> nad červenou zemí, plnou prasklin.
> Teprve nyní docházejí dopisy, psané
> přes hranice států a staletí
> a nové se vydávají na cestu.
>
> Zvuk klíče, otáčejícího se ve dveřích,
> paprsek, pronikající pevnou okenicí:
> život se zdá být zpožděn
> o dva, tři lidské věky
> a stále o rok před námi.
> Do tohoto dostihu času
> zaznívá praskot
> hořících lesů.
>
> (Jen balvany zůstávají trčet
> na rozsáhlých spáleniskách,
> očazené a tvrdé odštěpky
> dávných skal či hvězd.)
>
> Studánky načpěly kouřem
> – ty křišťálové, kde nejhlubší byl...–
> a na dně kostřičky ptáků.
>
> (Jen balvany, nejtvrdší víra
> má naději přetrvat.)
>
> Hořká vodo poesie!

The windows are closed. The sun is circling
above the ruddy ground, full of cracks.
Only now are the letters arriving, written

over the borders of countries and centuries
and new ones are heading off on their way.

The sound of a key, turning in the door,
a light beam, piercing the firm shutter:
life seems to be delayed
by two, or three human ages
yet still a year ahead of us.
This steeplechase of time
is filled with the crackling sound
of burning forests.

(Only boulders remain, jutting out
of swathes of cindered ground,
the sooty and hard spalls
of ancient rocks or stars.)

The wellsprings reek of smoke
– those crystal ones, in the once deepest...–
and at their base, the skeletons of little birds.

(Only the boulders, the most hardened faith
can hope to persist.)

Oh, Bitter water of poetry![32]

In the foreword, Tumlíř notes the disintegration of a harmonious cosmos as
familiar from older poetry, his poems manifesting the deconstruction of the conventional idyllicism that sufficed for other exiled poets. The verse 'those crystal
ones in the once deepest...' is an allusion to the opening verses of a famous
poem by Josef Václav Sládek (1845–1912), one of the Czech poetry's emblematic images of idyllic nature: "Znám křišťálovou studánku, / kde nejhlubší je les /
tam roste tmavé kapradí / a vůkol rudý vřes" [I know a glade, spring crystal clear,
/ in deepest woodland, crowned / by shady ferns in silhouettes, / red heather

---

32   J. Tumlíř: Hořká voda, p. 45; Neviditelný domov, p. 113.

all around]. In Tumlíř's poem, the landscape has turned into a wasteland, and the deep woodland is a thing of the past. The disintegration of the world pertains as much to a lost home as it does to contemporary Europe. At the end of Sládek's poem comes a motif of stars reflected in the wellspring, this intimate idyll (itself a reflection of the more complex tragedy of Mácha's *May*) loses its merits in post-war Europe, as far as Tumlíř is concerned, as in the poem *Mapa času* [Chart of Time]:

Ó Evropo, ztrnulá v krátké řeči lásky
[...]
Dáváš si schůzku s hladem, noční Evropo.
Kdy pak chceš spát, jazyky větrů, horké
a drsné, bloudí po tvé nahotě. Hvězdy se přišly na tebe vymočit.

Oh Europe, frozen in terse talks of love
[...]
You're making a rendezvous with hunger, nocturnal Europe.
When you want to sleep, tongues of wind, hot
and coarse, wander over your nakedness. The stars have come to
        pee on you.[33]

In terms of his collection, the 'bitter water of poetry' image acquires dual meaning – poetry can be an 'invisible home', which provides some sort of solace after all, but can also be a sceptical take on the world it is part of.

---

33   J. Tumlíř: *Hořká voda*, p. 19; *Neviditelný domov*, p. 114. The stars, as a traditional motif of European poetry symbolizing the harmony of the world appear already in Mácha's *May* imbued with an ambivalence associated with their falling. In two of the latter, unpublished poems by Otokar Březina, to which many exiled authors make a reference, "*slavnostní jiskření hvězd*" – 'the solemn sparkling of the stars' characterizes the grandeur of the cosmos (in the poem *Návrat*, the Return), but also the loneliness of man, "*když jako zuby v šíleném smíchu jiskří se hvězdy*" – 'when the stars sparkle like the teeth in a deranged grin' (in the poem *Za všechno díky...*, 'Thanks for everything ...'). This image presages the stars of Tumlíř's poem.

Similarly, the poem of Jana Borová[34] entitled *Kasárna* [The Barracks] – a home for refugees, itself the opening poem of the second anthology, *Time for Building*, breaks down the idyll with the reality of exile as having to make-do. Daydreams of home, from within a refugee camp, are suddenly interrupted by German announcements, as an ironic reminder of the realities of the 20th century:

> Co hledají ti lidé chodící sem a tam
> po všech cestách po všech schodištích domů?
> To nejsou domy
> V kterém BLOKU bydlíte? – 8 – 15 – 26?
> Bojím se BLOKŮ
> Chci už bydlet v domě
> domku domečku
> [...]
> *Achtung, Achtung! Alle Emigranten die Kinder unter zehn Jahre haben…*
> Zas už hned ráno teď ráno bičuje tlampač
> Naproti mému oknu rozvěšuje na ostnaté dráty prádlo těhotná žena
>
> Proč jsou ty stromy tak smutné
> i tráva neveselá
> a vůně akátů tak hořká
> a jasmínu vůně bolí
> že zavírám raději okno i srdce?
>

> What are those people after, walking back and forth
> taking every path, every flight of stairs of the houses?
> These are not houses
> What BLOC do you live in? – 8 – 15 – 26?
> I fear these BLOCS

---

34   By her own name Aurelie Jeníková (1905–1994), she also published under the pen-name Reli Bernkopfová; in exile, she published poems and translations of American poets in magazines. She is also the author of the feuilleton *Plechovka* [The Tin], in which, with subtle irony, she describes the reality of refugee camps; printed in M. Přibáň – A. Morávková: *Poštovní schránka domov.* cf. also M. Přibáň: Kdo byla Reli Bernkopfová.

I want to live in a house
a little house, a tiny house
[...]
Achtung! Achtung! Alle Emigranten die Kinder unter zehn Jahre haben...
And again from early morning the morning is whipped by a loud-
speaker.
Across from my window, a pregnant woman is hanging her laundry
on the barbed wires.

Why are these trees so sad
and the grass unhappy
and the scent of acacias so bitter
and the scent of jasmine hurts
so it makes me prefer to close my window and heart?[35]

Jana Borová manages in a single poem to capture the wavering between symbolic generality and specificity, between idyllicised nostalgia and austere reality,
as is typical of both anthologies. 'To close my window and heart' means to keep
safe the idea of home and the identity associated with it, in contrast to the harsh
reality of the camp.[36] A similar contrast appears in, e.g. the poems of Ivan Blatný
and Pavel Javor devoted to cemeteries. Javor portrays cemeteries in Bohemia as
places of rural idyll, associated with safety, tranquility and home (*"zroseny jste*
vonným heřmánkem" – 'dew-dropped you are with balmy chamomile');[37] while
Blatný treats the conventional topos with irony: *"Je to podivuhodné jak slovo*
hřbitov / Ztratilo dlouhým používáním v poesii všecku tísnivost" [It's marvellous
how the word cemetery / Long used in poetry has lost all dolefulness] and with
playful irony follows up with the associated images from his own imagination.[38]

The idyll of the home represents a rather complex plethora of motifs and
stances. Taking the example of a poem by Pavel Javor or by Jaromír Měšťan, we
find, in one aspect, recollection of an absent home being very often idealized as

<hr>

35   *Čas stavění*, p. 6.
36   Borová uses the motif on an inner sanctuary to take up the topic of shelter, cf Chapter 3. Exile
       and Shelter.
37   The poem 'Hřbitovy', *Neviditelný domov*, p. 42.
38   I. Blatný: Hřbitov, *Neviditelný domov*, p. 23.

a fertile rural landscape, in the spirit of 19th-century poetry.[39] The landscape is complemented by a reminiscing figure, fully at home in it. The recollection or reminder setting then creates a polarity between the idyllic completeness back there at home and the emptiness here, which goes for both the landscape-space and the human aspect. Pavel Javor expresses this in one of his poems from the collection put together by Antonín Brousek, which came out not long after the poet's death:

Kdo jsme? Kam jdeme?
Neznámí cizinci,
mluvící, slyšící,
a přece hluchoněmí

Who are we? Where are we going?
Unknown strangers,
speaking, hearing,
and yet deaf-mute[40]

Or elsewhere:

Nic tu nejsem! (Smetí, slepý střep)
Doma aspoň zasadil bych štěp.

I'm nothing here! (Garbage, a shard, blank, ceased)
At home, I'd plant a fruit-tree graft at least.[41]

Javor's verses reveal another, important feature of such poetry. The one who speaks of home identifies with the image of a national poet, that is, one who is or should be able to speak on behalf of the community. One of the reasons why Pavel Javor was described as the 'official poet of Czech exile'[42] might be

---

39   Prague is of course another popular type of home-space (e.g. for V. Fischl, but also Měšťan).

40   P. Javor: *Plamen a píseň*, p. 82.

41   Ibid., p. 112.

42   cf. P. Den: Slovo na cestu; A. Brousek: Doslov, p. 134.

his aspiration to be a spokesman for the group: 'Who are we? Where are we going?'[43] Although such an approach could hardly have any noticeable impact, it expresses the prevailing conservatism of Czech exile poetry at the time. The anthologies are conscious of the fact that exile prescribes a certain scope for the poet, whilst at the same time there was no blanket diaspora whose collective expression such poems could represent.

The agenda of poetry, howsoever engaged it may be, is not the realistic programme of a political community, as modern poetry repeatedly proved to itself when aspiring to be politically activist – whether within the avant-garde, or regime-fostered Communist poetry. The shared cultural memory in Czech exile can be represented by the canonical poets of the past (also published in exile circles) whose connection to the homeland is unproblematic, rather than by contemporaries who bring to the common mind their personal, non-transferable experiences. This disparity is foreshadowed much earlier by the post-White Mountain songs whose voice is always collective and impersonal, like Klement's lament.[44] This corresponds to the Lacanian distinction between the symbolic and the imaginary: in the symbolic order lie the shared values that correspond with the life of the community and are matched by the established and conventional role of the subject, in this case the poet (bard), while in the imaginary order we have portrayals of personal reverie, shaping the particular self.[45] Within the *Invisible Home* context, and not only from this point of view, Pavel Javor and Ivan Blatný are utter opposites.

A certain analogy also applies when comparing to domestic poetry in the late 1940s and 1950s. In the works of Jiří Kolář, Jan Zahradníček or Vratislav Effenberger and other poets a doubt is raised as to whether the poem's speaker may be a poet, i.e. one capable of poetic expression – which is the traditional determination of the poem's speaker. Within the terms of the ethic brought about by WWII and the onset of Stalinism in Czechoslovakia, a testimonial has to come solely from someone who is present first-hand in any given matter, to experience it and suffer it, not one who has merely poetic talents. Similarly, Theodor W. Adorno grants the right to expression to sufferers: 'relentless suffering has the same right to express itself as does a tortured man have the right

---

43   cf. likewise from Junius: "Až se jednou budeme vracet", *Neviditelný domov*, p. 57.

44   cf. Chapter 1, p. 24–25.

45   cf. J. Hrdlička: *Poezie a kosmos*, p. 15ff.

to scream.'[46] This shift only confirms that the modern poem is not an expression of some collective 'us', but a personal one. Some of the poets of the *Invisible Home* and *Time for Building* do try to fulfil the collective representative function, but the reach of their poems is limited, as even the reactions in exile testify. For some of them, there is an obvious shift from the collective to the personal (see below, in the case of Kovtun) and from the general and symbolic to the specific. Over time, many poets who harken back to their homeland create imaginary constructs of the home and exile subject, based on their very specific 'self'. Such is the case with Ivan Blatný's works, starting with the *Old Domiciles*, or Milada Součková, but also with Jaromír Měšťan, for whom the tendency toward symbolism prevails in some poems, while others tend toward the imaginary.[47] In exile, Měšťan wrote and published a free poetic trilogy *Sladká jako med* [Sweet as Honey, 1955], *Útěk do Egypta* [Escape to Egypt, 1957], *Potměchuť svoboda* [Darktaste Freedom, 1962]. Some poems of his Catholic-oriented poetry are surprisingly close to the *poetism* and spatial imaginings of Konstantin Biebl,[48] who, as a member of the inter-war avant-garde, was prone to associate his poems with far-off places. In his poem *Protinožci* [Antipodeans] located in Java, which Biebl visited in the second half of the 1920s, he dreams of a Europe on the opposite side of the globe:

Na druhé straně světa jsou Čechy
krásná a exotická země
plná hlubokých a záhadných řek
jež suchou nohou přejdeš na Jména Ježíš

On the other side of the world is Bohemia
a beautiful and exotic country

---

46   T. W. Adorno: *Negative Dialektik*, p. 355. For more detail, cf. J. Hrdlička: *Poezie a kosmos*, pp. 85–87.

47   Jaromír Měšťan (1916–1965), for more about him cf. V. A. Debnár: *Jihočeský lyrik*.

48   Měšťan wrote a long 'Poem on the Death of Konstantin Biebl' (*Útěk do Egypta*, pp. 28–33), for which R. Vlach reproached him as being an inappropriate celebration of a Communist poet, cf. M. Přibáň: *Prvních dvacet let*, pp. 218–219. Měšťan's poem and reflection on R. Vlach (*Sklizeň* 1957) were printed in the book by Nezval et al.: *Bojím se jít domů*, pp. 123–132.

full of deep and mysterious rivers
that can be crossed dry-footed in the Name of Jesus[49]

In his trilogy, Měšťan, with a similar ease accompanied by the nostalgia of exile, connects together not only places geographically far apart, but also nearby regions separated by another kind of insurmountable distance. From his Bavarian exile he reaches out to the neighbouring landscape of Southern Bohemia, shut off from him by an impenetrable border, and indeed makes his subject the difference between writing poetry while staying abroad, and the exile spoken of by Jan Tumlíř.[50] Whereas Biebl is fascinated by how fantasy can bring two places closer together, howsoever far apart they may be, Jaromír Měšťan uses a similar association to show how two places or landscapes that border each other (Bavaria and Bohemia) are hopelessly separated.[51] In some poems, he sublimates the impenetrable boundary into an invisible and immeasurable distance: where almost everything matches, the landscape is the same, the people are similar, yet it is another place.[52] In the pair of poems *Dopis do Bogoty – Dopis na Haity* [Letter to Bogota – Letter to Haiti][53] he turns to his Czech homeland via far-off exotic regions (with evident allusions to Biebl) and thus makes the impassable border all the wider, by the maximum geographical distance he can, which only intensifies the chagrin of the lonely exile abroad:

Jak duje vítr jenž vane
Sníh do mých oken
Jsem jediný kdo ještě svítí
Protože píši dopis

---

49   K. Biebl: *Dílo* II, p. 84.

50   *Neviditelný domov*, pp. 11–12.

51   Bavaria has an important place in the imaginary topography of Czech exile, as a land that borders home; something that applies for Měšťan, but also for Ivan Diviš (see below). Anastáz Opasek writes in his poem *Vzpomínka z Itálie* [Memento of Italy]: "*Rozhořela se krajina sluncem, / v dáli vyzývá Loretto k pouti // přece však v bavorské zemi / mohu naslouchat borovicím, / dívat se ptákům do očí / a lépe slyšet srdce české země*" – 'The landscape has ignited with the sun, / in the distance Loretto invites a pilgrimage // yet in the Bavarian land / I can listen to the pines, / look the birds in the eyes / and better hear the heart of the Czech Land', *Almanach české zahraniční poezie 1979*, p. 89.

52   E.g. the poem *Babiččin bílý slunečník* [Grandma's White Parasol], *Útěk do Egypta*, p. 12ff.

53   J. Měšťan: *Sladká jako med*, pp. 23–24, 25–27.

Daleko – na Haity
Že budu krčmářem v přístavní čtvrti
Budou tam chlapi tvrdí jak skály
S očima alpských encyán
A budou pít rum
Na vaši krásu mé Čechy
Mé daleké Čechy
S každým si jednu dám
A pak si zazpívám
Tu moji – tu smutnou
Ó hřebíčku zahradnický
Růžičko ty voňavá

How blustery is the wind that blows
Snow into my windows
I am the only one with the light still on
Because I'm writing a letter
Far away – to Haiti
That I'll run the dive bar in the harbour district
There'll be guys there tough as rocks
With alpine gentian eyes
And they'll drink rum
Here's to your beauty my Bohemia
My far-flung Bohemia
I'll have one with each of them
And then I'll sing
My song – the sad one
O my common garden cloves
Oh my Rose, you fragrant one[54]

With an ease typical of Biebl he reminds of Bohemia's proximity in one of the later poems, entitled *Prague*, where the border is not directly mentioned, but

---

54   Ibid., p. 27.

the poetic twist at the end clearly suggests being remote from that dreamt-of place:

V rozhlasové reportáži z Prahy
Vzdálen několik dnů cesty koňmo
Slyšel jsem houkat auta
Na Václavském náměstí

Právě tak houká kapitán lodě
Kapitán tušící neštěstí

In a radio report from Prague
A few days' horse ride distant
I heard cars honking their horns
On Wenceslas Square

Just the way a ship's captain blows the horn
A captain sensing misfortune there[55]

V

The tension between a collective symbol on the one hand and a specificity and detail on the other has its parallel in the movements of domestic Czech and European poetry. Ivan Blatný and Milada Součková were both close to Modernism and 'Group 42', which emphasized the everyday reality of the outside world. For some poets, such as Blatný, Součková or Listopad, the exile environment amplifies their emphasis on specific, non-metaphorical elements, as if that were the only value to be found in this new world, as though the prior stage of poetry, in which things could make sense or have symbolic significance, had come to an end. In her poem *Na troskách básnictví* [On the Ruins of Poetry]

---

55   J. Měšťan: *Potměchuť svoboda*, p. 30.

Součková depicts America as a country where the European tradition of poetry has been made banal, while Europe itself has fallen to ruin:

> [...] Balzacovy sny
> oč vyšší nežli mrakodrapy
> nad krámy Rue de la Paix, Pod Lipami
> lidé nevědí, že v Evropě jsou dávno smeteny
> základy, na nichž je vystavěli
> z babylonských smaltů, ze stél kretských labyrintů
> vysoké jako středomořská pevnost Maurů
> z níž Byron ráno v březnu pátral po lodi
> s nákladem zlata, cinamonu, myrhy
> sirény Hudsonu, East Riveru volají
> Odyssea, který tu někde vlastní restauraci
> unaven velkým dobrodružstvím básnictví
> dožívá v domech, kde jsou smaltované nádržky
> koupelen, odřené, kde se myjí ztroskotanci,
> prodává lehátka, křesla Empiru
> ó, Nausike, na březích Saugatucku
> zda smyješ špínu svého hrdiny?!

> [...] Balzac's dreams
> how much taller than skyscrapers
> above the shops of the Rue de la Paix, of Unter den Linden
> people don't know that in Europe, they've long since swept away
> the foundations on which they were built
> with Babylonian enamels, with the stelæ of Cretian labyrinths
> tall as the Mediterranean fortress of the Moors
> from which Byron spent his March morning searching for the ship
> carrying gold, cinnamon, myrrh
> the sirens of the Hudson, East River call
> Odysseus, who owns a restaurant here somewhere
> tired of the great adventure – poetry
> ending its days in houses with enamelled cisterns
> in bathrooms, scuffed, where the washed-up wash,
> selling sun beds, Empire chairs

oh, Nausike, on the shores of Saugatuck
will you wash off your hero's dirt, I wonder?![56]

František Listopad manifests a great sense for and a fascination with detail.[57] For Listopad, objects lose any semblance of meaning, only their factual purpose remains, which brings a particular lightness to existence in Western exile.

Jen detaily; krásné, hrozné; jen detaily!
Nazývat zátiší pravým jménem: talíř, kost, nepřenosný lístek
Sobota večer děje se kdykoliv: horizont cigaret...
Západní nicota neděle září nám v Paříži.

Zásadní tam-tamy: spravedlnost: Zatmít!
Tragické, že jsme tak snadno zdědili naději.
Déšť zapomněl jméno, poslední abstraktum.
Jen detaily; krásné, hrozné; jen detaily.

Just details; beautiful, terrible; just details!
To call a still life by its proper name: a plate, a bone,
        a non-transferable ticket
Saturday night comes at any time: a horizon line of cigarettes...
Occidental Sunday nothingness glows for us in Paris.

Occasioned tom-toms: equity: Occlude!
The tragic thing is, how lightly we have inherited hope.
The rain forgot its name, the last abstractum.
Just details; beautiful, terrible; just details[58]

---

56 *Neviditelný domov*, p. 100.

57 Born as Jiří Synek (1921–2017) after leaving, he first lived in Paris, then Portugal, where he became a cultural celebrity. He also wrote in Portuguese, but wrote poems only in Czech.

58 Ibid., p. 90. I include the word Sunday in the fourth verse as per the collected works edition Fr. Listopad: *Básně* I, p. 227, published from Listopad's exile collections. The *Invisible Home* contains a large number of printing errors, it could even be an omission here.

One important moment of exile anthologies is the poem's speaker. In the more conservative poetry section, it is all about preserving their identity, founded on their native language and ties to their homeland. On the other hand, as soon as a foreign reality comes into the poem the speaker's identity disintegrates or transforms. In the very first poem of the *Invisible Home* Ivan Blatný analyses the linguistic subject:

> Jako nějaký zlatý roh,
> Lighthorne,
> klímalo mezi svými posadami.
>
> Za shlukem chlévů bylo slyšet z ticha
> *žluté bzučící dřevo,*
> jak rozesychá.
>
> Kraj stál
> jak čerstvě nadojené mléko
> s nehybnou pěnou pahorků.

> Like some golden horn,
> Lighthorne,
> dozed among its hutches.
>
> Behind a cluster of byres from the silence was heard
> yellow buzzing wood,
> drying out.
>
> The land stood
> like freshly drawn milk
> with a motionless light froth of hills.[59]

---

59   *Neviditelný domov*, p. 19.

Lighthorne is an English village where Blatný stayed for a while in 1948, and this short poem depicts the almost idyllic atmosphere of a quiet rural evening.[60] The first verse stands out, linguistically prompted by a shifted translation of that place-name – with equal subtlety, sleight of hand, the subject as speaker is teased apart. The distinction also stands out given the context of the anthology and Blatný's later poems, in which language collages play an important part.

Taking into account the language motifs that appear in relation to exile, these display a dual nature – for Blatný, Jana Borová or Milada Součková foreign words are introduced, distinguished from the language of the speaker-subject. By contrast Ivan Jelínek seeks out the depth in language, thereby also confirming the subject's anchorage and identity in that language, (similar to Jiří Kovtun in *The Birth of Language*):

Tam dolů po koříncích řeči
do hlubokosti
V svit bílých kostí
slov šeptaných do nářečí

Down there along the tendril roots of speech
into the deep zones
The glow of white bones
of words whispered into vernacular reach[61]

Another element taken from the conventional repertoire that confirms the identity of the speaker is the love motif, as a traditional prop of national poetry. František Listopad almost deconstructs the convention of identity and the love motif: his poem's speaker seems to turn away from the world and reality, not insisting on his identity (*"jsem lehká aktovka"* – 'a light briefcase I am now'). In the addressing of a second person, we are tantalized by a residue of love poetry, but the poet is only ironically apologizing, getting carried away:

_____

60   On Blatný's stay here cf. M. Reiner: *Básník*, pp. 289–290; I. Jelínek: Pomocník na farmě, pp. 385–386.
61   *Neviditelný domov*, p. 51.

Tak jako nádraží spolehnu se na tmu
a totéž s budoucnem.
Obrácen zády k filmovému plátnu
jen hlasy slyšel jsem.

Zas jednou časem přijde nový strávník
má čisté knihy bydlet chce nad námi.
Dlouhá je louka. Kriketový trávník
s divnými brankami.

Jsem lehká aktovka. Všechno jsem už prodal.
A je to sen. Odpusť už nežiju.
Plavou podél koše teče do nich voda
spoléhám se zvolna na její přesilu.

Just as the train-station I rely on the dark for my cover
the same for my future world.
With my back to the film screen seeing never
only the voices heard.

In time a new full-boarder will come, beseech
with his clean books wanting to live upstairs
Long is the meadow Long the cricket pitch
with strange gated affairs.

A light briefcase I am now. I've sold off all therein.
It is a dream. Forgive me I no longer live like some.
Baskets float by with water seeping in
By and by I rely on being by its superior power overcome[62]

In another of Listopad's poems, the constant restlessness and sadness disrupts one's essence, only the motion remains:

---

62   Ibid., p. 89. I favour the corrected orthography per Listopad, *Básně* I, p. 193. In the fifth verse the verb *přejde*, (will pass) becomes *přijde*, (will come).

Leč z tesknoty je člověk stále,
z okružních jízd, a prosté jsou.
Podmět už vyprášil se, ale
ne sloveso, ne sloveso.

＊

Albeit of melancholy man is amply ever,
of round sightseeing tours, so simply set.
The subject has been dusted out, but never
no, not the verb, no, not the verb, not yet.[63]

Blatný's *Cemetery* also caused outrage and misunderstanding because the poem deals with a completely different subject than would be expected from the typical image of a poet suffering in exile. He's not alone in this, although other poets do not step forward with such flamboyant provocation. Milada Součková explores non-identity with the speaker in several different ways, in her poems from the 1950s she repeatedly employs a speaking voice in the male gender with some features of the epic bard, and does likewise in some of her prose. In the sample poem *On the Ruins of Poetry*, he is a kind of pilgrim through the ages, witnessing the rise and fall of cultures:

Špinavý chudák plný svrabu vší
znám krásu mrtvých minulostí
viděl jsem parthenonské mramory
trhané lístky jarní anemony
trhané básnictvím a světlem Egey
tisíciletí jsem žebral u školy
když Parmenides, Plato, Svatý Pavel odešli
má milenka se navracela ke mně z podsvětí
zkvétala prvosenkou mezi mramory

＊

A dirty wretch teeming with scabies lice
I know the beauty of dead bygone times

---

63   *Neviditelný domov*, p. 87; *Básně I*, p. 213.

I've seen the marbles of the Parthenon
the torn leaves of the spring anemone
torn off by poetry and the Aegean light
for long millennia I begged outside the school
when Parmenides, Plato and St Paul had left
my lover coming back from the underworld
a primrose twixt the marbles flowering.[64]

Jiří Kovtun gave us a remarkable and at the same time controversial analysis of the exile subject, which well demonstrates the polarity of the *Invisible Home*, in the poem pair *Čas boření – Čas stavění* [Time for Teardown – Time for Building], which gave the name to the third anthology and also appeared in the *Garden in No-man's Land*. In the late 1940s and early 1950s, Kovtun wrote a series of Christian-themed poems. Some of them came out in his collection *Blahoslavení* [Beatitudes, 1953],[65] others in magazines, and yet others remained in manuscript.[66] Martin C. Putna remarked on the initial, debut work *Beatitudes* that 'it was taken to be the calling card of a Catholic poet'.[67] The *Time for Teardown – Time for Building* diptych belongs to this grouping, while at the same time foreshadowing Kovtun's later poems.[68] The pair can be read as a riposte to Tumlíř's claims about the collapse of the world and an attempt to reconstruct a harmonic entity in the symbolic plane. Kovtun takes the view that Man is like a house that can only be rightly built and made complete by God.

Naše tělo – mladé konstrukce a trámy,
naše tělo – nedorostlé lešení.
Nevíme však, zdali strachem, jistotami,
nevíme však, Pane, čím jsme stavěni.

---

64   *Neviditelný domov*, p. 99.

65   [transl. note: *Blahoslavení* could translate as 'Blessings' or 'The Blessed', as well as 'Beatification', or even 'Beatitudinations'. The poems are billed as 'meditations on the eight beatitudes' from the Sermon on the Mount, cf. Matthew 5:3–12].

66   I thank Lukáš Klimeš for the opportunity to peruse Jiří Kovtun's manuscript legacy.

67   M. C. Putna: *Česká katolická literatura v kontextech 1945–1989*, p. 316.

68   *Čas stavění*, p. 15, 15a.

Our body – is but fresh structures, beams,
our body – is just scaffolding incomplete.
But we don't know if out of fear, of certainties,
we know not, Lord, out of what we are built.

The image evokes the old Christian idea of the human heart as a space God resides within.[69] The building only has a purpose when God enters it – such is the conclusion of the first poem, but this arrival and fulfilment is preceded by breakage:

Říkáme Ti: Pane, budu neoslepen,
přijdeš-li. Své plody tedy do mne vlož.

Potom budu cítit bezpečný dům růsti
pod svou kůží. Budu plný koš a číš.
Dosud patříme však k těm, co stojí pusti.
Proto čekáme, kdy nás už rozbouříš.

We say to Thee: Lord, I will be unblinded,
If Thou comest. Place then Thy fruits in me.

Then I will feel a safe house growing
under my skin. I shall be a brimming basket and a cup.
But so far, we stand with others in the desert.
Thus waiting, for Thee to come and tear us down.

The first poem can be read as a spiritual poem not set in any particular time, the *Time for Teardown* is about the cardinal moment in the inner life of a man turning to God. The second poem seems to tell of a different situation, a different state of mind independent of the first poem.[70] In the second poem, the

---

69   On the question of an inner sanctuary cf. Chapter 3, p. 60.
70   In the *Čas stavění* anthology, the pair are listed as one, not two poems, and in *Zahrada v zemi nikoho* the two are given under one joint hyphenated title ČAS BOŘENÍ – ČAS STAVĚNÍ, which is key to further reading.

construct that sought purpose and meaning in the first poem reveals hidden
scope through which the theme of exile and suffering comes in:

> Jak Ti máme říci: Já jsem podkopaný.
> Každý z nás má uvnitř sebe sklepení,
> kam se ukládají bolesti, a rány
> mají tam svou skrýš. A tam jsme ztlumeni
>
> jako výkřik v jeskyni. Tam nikdy, Pane,
> nedoléhá ani Tvoje ozvěna.
> Jak Ti máme říci: Tam je přichystané
> lože utečenců. Němých. Bez jména.
>
> V každém kroku slýcháváme z podpodlaží
> vzdechy toho, kdo se v spánku obrací,
> údery. A to jsou rány, jimiž váží
> tíhu srdce ztrmácení tuláci.
>
> Jsou však jinde lepší, neprodyšné domy,
> měkčí jeskyně a lepší, tišší skrýš,
> lidé, v jejichž krocích nezní podvědomí.
> Proto čekáme, kdy už nás postavíš.

> How are we supposed to tell Thee: I am undermined.
> Each one of us has a cellar deep inside of us,
> where we store pain, where wounds
> have their hideaway. And that is where we are muted
>
> like a scream in a cave. To there, Lord, never
> never even an echo of Thee does reach.
> How are we supposed to tell Thee: There we have at the ready
> a bed for refugees. Mute. Nameless.
>
> With every step we tend to hear from the sub-subfloor
> the sighs of one who is turning in his sleep,

thuds. And by these blows, they weigh-up
the heaviness of the heart, the weary wanderers do.

But there are better, soundproofed houses elsewhere,
softer vaults and a better, quieter hideaway,
of those, whose subconscious does not resound in the steps they take
That's why we're waiting, eager for Thee to build us up.

This place full of suffering, a place without God, is one Kovtun denotes as the subconscious. If the poem is viewed through this psychological lens, then the suffering of other, nameless Exiles enters the mind of each person and constantly calls for their attention. In another time, this domain could be called Hell. While we may regard the speaker of the first poem as showing uncertainty about themselves, in the second the world makes them distraught; the last strophe expresses the desire to have the subject reconstituted, such that suffering is shut out from their soundproof, airtight house. The poem seems at first to be trying to posit an idyllic, unproblematic subject – something similar to Jana Borová's dreaming, shutting herself off from the world while in a refugee camp. We hear once again Kovtun's enduring motif of the idyll, which he takes further, from a reversed perspective. In one of the later poems, the house forms a space that a person can never leave, no matter what, because the structure of the inner space corresponds to their perceptual perspective on the world. The difference reminds of Flusser's distinction between a *home* and an *abode*:

I kdybys dezertoval
na lákavější bojiště vesmíru,
nezbavíš se představy,
že to, co máš a co hledáš,
je dokonale ohraničeno světnicí,
která se za den otočí kolem osy,
za rok proletí jarem, létem, podzimem, zimou.
A bude tě zneklidňovat myšlenka,
že se nikde nesetkáš s větším přáním,
než aby v domě bylo teplo.

Even if you deserted
to the more enticing battlefield of the universe,
you won't shake off the idea,
that what you have and are looking for,
is perfectly circumscribed by a room,
which turns each day around an axis,
in a year flying through spring, summer, autumn, winter.
And you will be disturbed by the thought,
that you will never find any greater desire,
than that the house should be warm.[71]

VI

With more attentive reading, the *Invisible Home* reveals a number of common themes, but also some latent points of controversy in how these are viewed; there are the conservative poetics of exile, wrapped up in straightforward nostalgia, and then the more open approaches that poetically explore the state of things. Some poems also show how difficult it is to keep the two tendencies apart. Notably present is the motif of the contemporary world as a wasteland, the domain of suffering and meaninglessness. This view corresponds to similar apocalyptic tendencies in domestic Czech poetry in the late 1940s and early 1950s. Martin C. Putna regards this apocalyptic stance as a Catholic theme, for example in *Atlantida* [Atlantis] by Vladimír Vokolek or in the compositions of Jan Zahradníček, which is a somewhat reductive view.[72] Among the key compositions that see their time through the apocalyptic perspective are also works by avant-garde poets such as *Prometheova játra* [Prometheus' Liver] by Jiří Kolář or the *Přízrak třetí války* [Spectre of the Third War] by the surrealist poet Vratislav Effenberger. In exile poetry, these motifs appear more loosely scattered, but still clearly shown by Jan Tumlíř, František Listopad, Milada Součková, in allusions by Blatný and the remarkable psychologizing in the aforementioned

---

71   J. Kovtun: *Hřbet velryby*, p. 70.
72   M. C. Putna: *Česká katolická literatura*.

Kovtun poem – as a Hell of the subconscious that everyone hides within themselves. In the *Invisible Home*, the poem by Jiří Klan bears the title *"Apocalypse"*.[73]

Valem se stmívá. Nikdo není doma.
V kuchyni prázdné kape vodovod.
Venku se valí stará nevidomá.
Poslední moře. Průvod důlních vod.

Z ulice Sedmi sester (konec týdne)
radia, lokomotiv dutý dech.
Křik andělů jak hrách. A potom řídne,
haraší chabě na studených zdech.

Odchází alejí a prsty pěti
zažíhá navždy podzim. Motýli
se nedočkají jara. Konec dětí.
Když u nich zvonil, doma nebyli.

A píše na plot kouskem vlhké křídy:
„Blíží se zánik vaší Atlantidy".

Swiftly the darkness falls. There is no-one at home.
In the bare kitchen water drips, no-one's minding.
Outside just an old blind crone shuffles some.
A final sea. A mine-water procession, winding.

---

73   The pseudonym is that of the poet Josef Lederer (1917–1985), who left for English exile as early
as the late 1930s and after the War returned to Czechoslovakia for only a short visit. Lederer
published in magazines even as a young man, and published only one collection in his life,
Sopka islandská a jiné verše [The Icelandic Volcano and Other Verses, 1973], with the unfinished
Elegie [Elegies, 1986] published posthumously. Lederer was, among other things, an excel-
lent translator of English poetry and taught English literature at one of the London colleges.
He published several much-cited studies on John Donne, whose poems he also translated.
cf. Z. Šťastná: *České překlady Johna Donna.* – I thank his daughter Caroline Lederer and
Vladimír Svoboda for access to Lederer's written estate.

From Seven Sisters Street (week-ending, thus)
the radio, the locomotives' hollow huff.
Angelic cries like shrugged-off peas, thrown, sparse
rattling off chilly walls, not loud enough.

Five-fingered, leaving down the avenue
lit for all time by autumn. Butterflies
that will not see the spring. The children's end is due.
When he rang, they weren't home he would surmise.

And with some damp chalk on the fence, he scrawls:
"Your Atlantis is nearing its demise".[74]

The quotation marks in the title of the poem no doubt signal irony; in the second edition the poem was dated 1952, bore the name 'Minor Apocalypse' subtitled 'old and new verses', and was supplemented with a second sonnet dated 1972. There are two handwritten drafts of the first strophe, the first of which links the dripping water with a reference to Mácha's *May*:

Jak shaslý měsíc, provázíš nás, stíne.
Křik andělů a ďáblů houslí svod,
vše jednostejně v uších zní a hyne,
když v prázdném bytě kape vodovod
strom viny útrobné už roste z úst,
a nepřestává, bratří moji, růst.

Shadow, you trail us, like the moon extinguished,
The cries of angels, devils, violins' spree
all alike in our ears to sound and perish,
as in an empty flat the water drips endlessly,
from our mouths the sapling tree of visceral sin
now begins growing, brothers, and will grow ever on.

---

74   *Neviditelný domov*, p. 71.

In *May* falling drops 'sound and perish', indifferently marking time in the prisoner's cell and reminding him of his impending death. In Lederer's *Atlantis*, the original allusion to Mácha is virtually unrecognisable, it is only when we take into account the draft that we can see how the existential motif has become the mechanical dripping of a tap in an empty apartment. There is no clear speaker and probably no human presence in the poem. The 'old blind crone' is more evocative of some element in motion, and the strange figure in the closing part of the poem has something angelic about him, as if another kind of being is somehow nostalgically looking back at an empty world from which mankind has gone, and sees the beginning of the end of this world, in an eternal autumn. The Atlantis motif in the last verse may refer to the Communist state's utopian project and its dead-endedness, but also to the world of Western culture itself.[75] Howsoever multi-faceted Lederer's poetry seems to be, the depopulated world, previously inhabited, gives the impression that the whole human civilization project has failed, with only the empty shells of cities to show for it.

A variation, twenty years on, shifts to a different position. Compared to the first poem, the whole image is filtered by the medium of television, as if nothing were real anymore and everything was happening only on the screen. Things are not coming to an end, but a familiar and senseless circle of repeats. Mankind does not cease to be, but ceases to have any purpose, the great project of Atlantis in the last two verses seemingly just an episode in a series:

Ráj světa odhazuje po ráji
jak sirky, které špatně chytají.

After Paradise, the paradise of the world
like matches that fail to light, away is hurled.[76]

---

75 The poet's daughter said in a personal communication that Lederer referred to Communist Czechoslovakia as Atlantis, although the poem does not make that clear. The motif of Atlantis is quite widespread in poetry of this time, seen with Kavka (Vlach), Měšťan, but also with Vladimír Vokolek, who called his 1947 composition *Atlantis*. Also, Vítězslav Nezval published in 1956 a play *Dnes ještě zapadá slunce nad Atlantidou* [Today the Sun is Still Setting over Atlantis], which is a response to the atomic bomb drop on Hiroshima.

76 J. Lederer: *Básnické dílo*, p. 53; *Sopka islandská*, p. 14.

VII

For Czech exile, the early 1950s were a time for anthologies.[77] It was also a time of attempts at international poetic cooperation, typically never getting beyond the project stage, at least in poetry, seemingly thwarted by the relative isolationism of national Exiles. The contradiction between national interests and attempts at international acclaim is also illustrated by the aforementioned Estonian-Czech anthology, with its four introductions in English and French, only underlining how nationally-anchored Exiles are. On the Estonian side, Ants Oras[78] writes in his *Literature in exile* piece about the greater responsibility of poets in exile, and characterizes their mission with the words:

> It is up to him to demonstrate to his companions in exile the value and vitality of their mother tongue, increasingly obscured to many of them by the unavoidable impact of the alien languages spoken in their surroundings. Only the writer is in a position to create for them a homeland of the mind which they will be free to inhabit, even though their physical existences may be scattered over all the four corners of the world. It is he who is expected to bridge the present sombre vacuum in the intellectual history of his nation.[79]

This mission, essentially to 'hold-the-fort' is clearly linked to the national language. Oras's Czech counterpart, the historian Otakar Odložilík,[80] in his foreword entitled *The Poet's Way* commemorates the Czech humanist poet Klement Žebrácký and his Latin composition addressed in 1627 to The Swedish King

---

77   In addition to the three poetic books mentioned above, there was another anthology of exile prose published as the *Peníz exulantův* [The Exile's Coin, 1956].

78   Ants Oras (1900–1982), originally professor of English philology at Tart, worked at the University of Florida in the 1950s.

79   A. Oras: Literature in Exile, pp. 9–10.

80   Otakar Odložilík (1899–1973) went into exile for the first time in 1938, when he worked at American universities. In 1945 he returned to Czechoslovakia and after 1948 he lived again in the USA, where he taught at the University of Pennsylvania. Even before the Second War, he had dealt with the history of post-White Mountain exile.

Gustav Adolf.[81] Like Oras, he emphasizes the poet's responsibility, but the emphasis is not on preserving culture for a post-exile future, but to encourage, and seek support in the past. According to Odložilík, the conceptual or mental home rests in trying to *"keep alive the memory of happy days and to sing praises of the Paradise lost"*, and although one cannot turn solely to the past, *"the use of the present tense can be limited and reserved for special occasions"*.[82]

A similar sense of mission, motivated by a national duty, influenced the exile anthologies of the 1950s and their critics. A little later, Petr Den still defends this approach in the foreword to the selected works of Pavel Javor *Kouř z Ithaky* [Smoke from Ithaca, 1960], although it is clear from his words that he is reacting to growing opposition:

> Javor's poetic world will not appeal to everyone. It won't appeal to those who only love poetic experiments [...] More likely it will be appreciated by those who love the amorous stream of Czech poetry flowing continuously from the likes of Sládek through Šrámek to Seifert, and who will find in Javor new variations on a well-known and beloved motif. [...] I have said elsewhere that Javor is quite the official poet of our exile, as it were. So as for those who will find in it to their dissatisfaction not only pearls of love for his homeland, but some sentimental smoke, blue-wafting over the roofs of Czech cottages, let them search the conscience of their innermost heart![83]

In the *Invisible Home* and other anthologies and collections of the 1950s, however, this view tends to split into at least to two, often intermingled currents. This is most evident in the depiction of home: some of the poems utilize symbolic images of the homeland and the poet-subject standing in for the collective, while others conversely construct an imaginary home in which the distinctive individual subject takes shape, or the earlier idea of the poet is dismembered. In addition, many poems express a compelling reality of exile – post-war Europe,

---

81   cf. Chapter 1, p. 24–25.
82   O. Odložilík: The Poet's Way, p. 13, 15. Odložilík's assertion can only be sustained as an analogy, the present tense clearly prevails as the main time-setting of lyrical poetry, even in when dealing with remembrance.
83   P. Den: Slovo na cestu, p. 5.

the Cold War, refugee camps. A typical sign of such an insurgence of reality are words cited in a foreign language, as with Jana Borová or even Jaromír Měšťan:

> Srdce mi ztvrdlo v kamení
> *Tschechisch-Bayerische Grenze*
> A jediné slovo *HALT*
> Lesy jsou tady jako u nás
> Ale to není Šumava
> To už je *Böhmerwald.*

> My heart has hardened into stone
> *Tschechisch-Bayerische Grenze*
> And the one single word *HALT*
> The forests here are like ours back home.
> But this is not Šumava
> This here's the *Böhmerwald.*[84]

Most of the time, even in poems by someone like Jan Tumlíř, the ingress of reality conforms to a symbolic or imaginary mode. It is only subsequent poetry, especially with the arrival of the second wave of Exiles after 1968, that puts the surrounding reality and its influences at the forefront, outweighing the imagination. In the early 1990s, this turnaround was taken up by Petr Král, described in his propositional essay *Konec imaginárna* [The End of the Imaginary]. But in his poetry, and in the poems of other authors, it starts showing through much earlier.

In the Czech exile context only one similar anthology was published, by Daniel Strož, namely the *Almanach české zahraniční poezie 1979* [Almanac of Czech Poetry Abroad]. It brings together thirty-three authors, in addition to five poets featured in the *Invisible Home* and *Time for Building*, these being mostly post-1968 Exiles. Even the name of the anthology suggests a certain arm's length attitude to the concept and framework of exile. At this time, exile poetry was being much more influenced by contact with literature back home, as well as by more trans-national impulses. The late 1970s saw the rediscovery

---

84   J. Měšťan: *Sladká jako med*, p. 8.

of Ivan Blatný, whose fate caught some attention in the Western media; there were evidently poets coming out of Czechoslovakia writing and publishing in other languages and not beholden solely to Czech poetry. By this time, the idea that poets had a mission to fulfil had lost its meaning.

6. Ivan Blatný's Orphic Theatre

Myšlenka na smrt potěší
jak sedmihlásek v ořeší

※

The thought of death will cheery prove
like a warbler in a walnut grove[1]

I

Ivan Blatný (1919–1990) is probably the best-known of Czech post-war exile poets. This is partly thanks to his poetry, and to his life story itself. Before leaving Czechoslovakia in 1948 for exile in England, Blatný published four poetry collections: *Paní Jitřenka* [Lady Morning Star, 1940], *Melancholické procházky* [Melancholy Walks, 1941], *Tento večer* [This Evening, 1945] and *Hledání přítomného času* [In Search of Present Time,[2] 1947].[3] In the early years of exile, he published several translations in magazines, and five poems in the *Invisi-*

---

1   Verses from Blatný's manuscript legacy, kept in the Archives of the Museum of Czech Literature, (LA PNP).

2   [transl. note: attempting to capture the inherent ambiguity of the title, literally "Searching for the present tense / the present time / a time of presence" would require a neologism, e.g. 'presentness']

3   Additionally, Blatný published two books of verses for children and a number of poems in magazines. His pre-exile body of poems, including handwritten ones, is summarized in the compendium *Verše 1933–1953*.

ble Home anthology. He then fell silent for a number of years, with only sporadic mentions of him in the exile press. In 1951, Czech Radio reported that Ivan Blatný had committed suicide in England. Blatný reacted to that via a Radio Free Europe broadcast, or intended to, as the surviving script testifies.[4] Martin Reiner notes that 'between 1958 and 1969 we don't have a single tangible report on Ivan Blatný'.[5] In the home press he was sometimes remembered as a poet who betrayed his country; his name all but disappeared in the exile press after reviews of the *Invisible Home*. Blatný at that time was living in various places and mostly in various hospitals and institutions for the mentally ill. 1968 saw a Brno reedition of *Melancholy Walks*, probably Blatný's most famous collection before going into exile. At that time, however, no one seems to know where and how Blatný lives, and there are reports that he is dead. It was only in 1969 that his cousin Jan Šmarda visited Blatný in England, followed by other visitors.[6] As far as we can tell, Blatný returned to writing poems in the interim, but the papers on which he wrote his verse were swiftly shredded by the nursing staff. In the summer of 1977, an English nurse by the name of Frances Meacham became interested in Blatný, started to save his writings and arranged for Blatný to be able to write regularly. That same year, she approached Josef Škvorecký and sent Blatný's poems to him in Canada.[7] As a result, in October 1979, the Škvorecký spouses' exile publishing house Sixty-Eight Publishers in Toronto brought out his *Stará bydliště* [Old Domiciles] collection. It was edited by Antonín Brousek, who selected poems from a more extensive body of poems dating from 1969 to 1977.[8] From that point on, interest in Blatný and his poems kept growing. The German writer Jürgen Serke, who was at that time collecting interviews with exile writers, published his interview with Blatný in December 1981 in Stern magazine. This sparked some interest, led to documentary films about Blatný,

---

4   cf. Chapter 3, p. 86f.

5   M. Reiner: *Básník*, p. 435. Reiner's text, subtitled *Román o Ivanu Blatném* [A Novel about Ivan Blatný] founded on extensive research regarding Blatný, contains a great deal of important information that I rely on in the text, but at the same time it does not give references and the data in it has to be taken with some degree of caution.

6   cf. ibid., p. 450, J. Šmarda: *Ivan Blatný v mých vzpomínkách*.

7   cf. M. Reiner: *Básník*, p. 473ff.

8   Frances Meacham obtained at least some of the poems from Jan Šmarda. cf. J. Šmarda: Doslov, p. 119.

and the poet and his story became relatively well-known in Western Europe.[9]
Emerging almost at the same time as the publication of the *Old Domiciles* came
the *Bixley Remedial School* collection, whose manuscript made its way to Prague
thanks to Jiří Kolář and was published in samizdat in 1982. In 1987, a subset from
this first collection was published, still under the same *Bixley Remedial School*
title, supplemented by further verses as chosen by Antonín Brousek, once again
in the Škvorecký publishing house in Toronto.[10] Later, after 1989, the *Old Domiciles* and *Bixley Remedial School* collections were republished repeatedly, in extended editions together with other choice samples from among Blatný's poems.[11]

A vast set of manuscripts, which Martin Reiner estimates at 280,000 verses
or 5,500 densely written pages, has been preserved in Blatný's manuscript
estate.[12] Despite the collections mentioned, Blatný's exile work remains only
partially processed and mapped, since its editors have either focused on some
portion of the poems (around the *Bixley Remedial School*) or have proceeded
unsystematically; it is also not always clear what the original source materials
looked like.[13] Blatný's poems from his early years of exile also remain an open
question. In 1952, the exile magazine *Hlas domova* [Voice of Home] announced
that Blatný's collection *Jazyky* [Tongues] won first prize in the poetry cate-

---

9   In book form J. Serke: *Die verbannten Dichter*, 1982.

10 cf. A. & A. Petruželkovi: Ediční poznámka, p. 311.

11 The collections *Fragmenty* (ed. Jan Šmarda) and *Domovy* (ed. Petr Král) also contain, apart
    from earlier poems, unpublished poems from exile, the extensive collection *Jde pražské dítě
    domů z bia...* [A Prague child heads home from the movies...] (ed. Martin Reiner) presenting
    Blatný's late exile poetry from the 1980s.

12 M. Reiner: Foreword, p. 9; The Petruželkas estimate the number of handwritten sheets from
    the *Bixley Remedial School* at 2,000. Petruželkovi: Ediční poznámka, p. 311.

13 This is the case of Martin Reiner, who in his book *Básník. Román o Ivanu Blatném*, collated
    a great deal of information, but mixes it with his own fabulation, and unfortunately does not list
    sources. His selection *Jde pražské dítě domů z bia* (2017) is extensive, but textually less reliable
    and does not provide any references to manuscripts. – There are several individual poems from
    the *Old Domiciles* period in Blatný's estate, the poems having been conscientiously saved from
    most likely the *Remedial School* period onward, some on loose sheets, some on hospital forms.
    The poems written in workbooks came later, but the hundreds of workbooks can only be dated
    on a case-by-case basis, sometimes perhaps by the type of workbook, pen, or handwriting,
    but overall the chronology is uncertain. These workbooks seem to cover the 1980s up until
    the poet's death. The poems from these workbooks were first presented in Reiner's edition of
    A Prague child heads home from the movies... – In addition, there are handwritten poems in other
    sets. For example, Petr Král had poems sent to him by Ivan Blatný himself.

gory in a Radio Free Europe literary competition.[14] Martin Reiner reports that, according to Meda Mládková, the publisher of *Invisible Home*, Blatný wrote a compact collection in 1951 entitled *Londýnské jaro* [London Spring].[15] Five poems from that period were published in the *Invisible Home* and six others, including a poem called *Londýnské jaro* [London Spring], in the exile magazine *Proměny* [Metamorphoses] in 1989.[16] The somewhat more extensive typescript ensemble that contains all these poems and several others and is entitled *Jazyky* [Tongues] has also survived,[17] possibly the remnants of two collections or projects, with a degree of overlap. It seems none of Blatný's texts from the first half of the 1950s to the late 1960s have survived, although he probably did write poems at the time. Despite the uncertain date of some of the surviving texts, it can be said that in his first years of exile Blatný conceived one or two collections and also during the *Old Domiciles* period he was collating his poems into

---

14   *Hlas domova*, 2, 1952, no. 11, p. 8; cf. M. Přibáň: *Prvních dvacet let*, p. 93.

15   M. Reiner: *Básník*, pp. 337, 339–341.

16   *Proměny* 1989, no. 4, pp. 142–153, the poems *Podzim v N., Jaro, Londýnské jaro, Jelínek, Jelen I, II*. The note states: 'the poems and translations [...] were sent by Ivan Blatný sometime in the early 1950s for publication in the *Invisible Home* [...] Out of what Blatný sent five poems were selected [...]. The other poems have never been printed, so they are published here for the first time. Their manuscripts were loaned by Dr Meda Mládková from her archive' (p. 143, signed -ds-). Martin Reiner mistakenly assigns the poem *Nikoleta odpovídá ve verších* to this group of poems (*Básník*, p. 340). It belongs among the 'poetic scribbles', which Blatný sent to Petr Král in the 1980s (*Proměny*, ibid., p. 143).

17   A typescript with handwritten notes comprising two differently numbered sets. I thank Petr Král for providing the text. In his words, it comes from the *Proměny* magazine circle. It is probably related to the given poems *Proměny* published. The same edition of *Proměny* (see above) published a study by Petr Král entitled a 'Certificate for Ivan Blatný', in which Král mentions some poems from that typescript. The set contains 25 poems, in three cases being variants of one poem. Judging by the page numbering, these are two different sets, the first of which was called 'Tongues', the second, which is missing its first page, could be called the 'London Spring' (as added by hand to one of the poems). The second set was probably collated later, as suggested by the variant poems, and above all the poem *On the Death of George[s] Hugnet*, who died in 1974. It is true that Blatný wrote the poem *The Death of Klement Bochořák*, which dates from the mid-1930s (Bochořák died much later, in 1981), but that piece takes a rather different, musing stance, than the poem dedicated to Hugnet. Later on, he was prone to react to the death of his friends or well-known poets. If we accept the dating, at least some poems of this typescript belong to the 1970s, this being the *Old Domiciles* period. Conversely, the *Old Domiciles* include the poem *Nokturno*, which was published with slight differences under the title 'Night' in the *Invisible Home*. It cannot therefore be ruled out that the *Old Domiciles* set includes other older poems.

larger ensembles. *Old Domiciles* were apparently assembled and also named by Antonín Brousek, and the name, chosen from one of the poems, seemed to capture a key aspect of Blatný's poetry of that time. According to Jan Šmarda, at that time Blatný himself conceived the collection *Být s matkou* [To be with Mother], much of which went into the *Old Domiciles*.[18] The *Bixley Remedial School* collection came about at the suggestion of Jiří Kolář, in response to the upcoming edition of the *Old Domiciles*. At this time Blatný had the opportunity to write regularly, and his manuscripts were being taken care of. Yet something else was changing. Especially after he started writing in workbooks, Blatný no longer considered making sets of compositions, but focused on the space and time he had to write, both in terms of his daily schedule and at the conceptual level, enticed by the empty space of a freshly opened pristine workbook. This is borne out by, among other things, repeated references that appear at the beginning and end sections of some of the workbooks:

Ó nový sešite jak vždycky miluji tě
Sešit za sešitem se plní mými zvuky
Hle nový sešit mám a nové krásné psaní
Zavírám sešit svůj, do nového chci psáti

v tom jsem si však uvědomil že jsme na konci sešitu.
Hodiny bijí půl.

my Smrtku vyženem, když začíná už tát.
A nové sešity, veliký je náš Sklad.

O my new workbook how I always love you
Workbook after workbook filling with my sounds
Behold the new workbook I have and new beautiful writing
I close my old workbook, want to write in the new one

yet just then I realized we've reached the workbook's end.
The clock is striking the half hour.

---

18   cf. J. Šmarda: Doslov, p. 119; I. Blatný: *Texty a dokumenty*, p. 455.

We will drive out Marzanna,[19] since the thaw has begun.
And as for new workbooks, we have a great Store.[20]

In this respect, sometime during the *Remedial School* period, when Blatný was
still writing on loose pages, his take on poetry changed and shifted from com-
posing collections to a continuous flow of writing. This collection was already
being created against the backdrop of a vast set of poems, of which Blatný's original *Bixley Remedial School* represents only a lesser part. In the following
period, this written textual backdrop becomes the norm, and forms an essential
part of Blatný's daily rhythm or routine.

II

If we accept the names of five exile collections, albeit partly hypothetical, and
not always the author's own (*Jazyky, Londýnské jaro, Být s matkou, Stará bydliště, Pomocná škola Bixley*) and what we know about their content, as well as
the uncertain chronology of the surviving poems, what do these testify about
Blatný's poetry after he left Czechoslovakia in 1948?

Blatný in exile follows on from the poetics of his older collections and with
some irony also from the Surrealism and Poetism he admired.[21] Yet, at the same
time he is changing all this and shifting in a certain direction, and it is these
shifts that find things to say about the influence of exile on Blatný's poetry. Petr
Král writes directly about the 'new way of seeing' which Blatný owes to being in
exile.[22] Some poems from the *Invisible Home* ('Summer Evening', 'Night') have
things in common with Blatný's second collection of *Melancholy Walks*, which

---

19   [transl. note: the original has the colloquialism *Smrtka,* literally meaning Death, feminine,
      but the context makes the chosen translation evident, being the pagan effigy of deadly winter,
      Morena in Czech]

20   Selected verses from Blatný's estate.

21   As noted by Petr Král: Certifikát pro Ivana Blatného, and passim by Martin Reiner and Blatný
      himself, he showed a propensity to both these movements with some humour in several
      poems.

22   P. Král: ibid., p. 565.

was originally and more aptly supposed to be called *Brno Elegies*, with a pedestrian-observer subject linking and combining perceptions and impressions with his physical presence. These poems are tied to a place and a moment, and can be said to keep the unity of place and time, tied to the physical presence of a speaker, who is at times less of a presence but always acts as the originating centre of perception. In his *Melancholy Walks*, Blatný worked with the present and past tense in a certain balance, and both senses of time served mainly to capture the moment. In his exile poetry, the present tense starts to prevail while also changing its function. It is no longer the time of the present moment, but the time of his staged lyrical presence that shapes the poem as an artificial scene. This too has its seeds in older poems, for example, in a poem from *The Lady Morning Star*, which ends with the verses:

> A marnost minulá s vším marným budoucím
> se tiše schází ve mně –
> vše, co jsem uviděl a co kdy spatřit smím
> v divadle této země.

> And past futility with all things future, vain,
> meet within me, discreet –
> all earthly things I've seen, or to see may remain,
> from my theatre seat.[23]

Also, in the poem 'Summer Evening'[24] the speaker does not show his presence and observes the landscape in a panoramic view, as if stood somewhere above it. The simile 'The land stood / like freshly drawn milk / with a motionless light froth of hills' resembles a photographic enlargement, i.e. from a vantage point off-scene, and seeming purposely arranged. Blatný's exile poetry is full of comparison to theatre, the stage, with frequent enclosed scenes such as a park or an interior. All this is closely related to observer poems, where the speaker at some point begins to follow their own ideas, memories and associations and shifts from the real scenery to some other conceptual scene that lacks the unity of

---

23   I. Blatný: *Verše*, p. 31.
24   cf. Chapter 5, p. 152f.

the here-and-now, but is held together only by the associative and constructive motive force of the speaker. Poems of this kind include 'The Cemetery' we have referred to in the Invisible Home chapter, as well as 'The Stage' or 'October'. In 'October', the theatre scene blends directly into the landscape, the mood of the autumn landscape being complemented by quite theatrical props:

> Silnicí ubírá se františkánský mnich.
> Zdá se, že šedá pára stoupá z něho.
> Za plachtou vozu Matěje Kopeckého
> Modré plaménky lihu kloužou po polích.
> Opona loutkového divadla,
> Napjatá mezi skalami, se vznese
> Jak černozlatý prapor v tmavém lese
> nad modré močály a jejich zrcadla.
> Obora jako zlaté hnojiště
> Paří své listí s mokvající hlínou.
> Nijaká, hloupá vrána nad krajinou
> Si sedá rozpačitě na oraniště.

> Along the road a Franciscan monk goes.
> Grey mist seems from his habit to be rising.
> Matěj Kopecký's cart tarp hides disguising
> Blue meth flames as they glide the fields reposed.
> The curtain of a puppet-theatre set
> Lifts up, stretched out between two jutting crags
> Like in a forest dark, a black-gold flag,
> Above blue bogs and their reflections wet.
> A deer-park like a golden midden heap
> Steams leaves with soil that's oozing, weeping slow.
> Nondescript, dumb, over the land a crow
> Sheepishly settles on fresh furrows deep.[25]

---

25   The poem 'Říjen', *Neviditelný domov*, p. 22. Matěj Kopecký (1775–1847) a dramatist and pup-
peteer, an important figure of the Czech national revival. Blatný links him with travelling players
and puppets – cf. the related poem 'November' (*Stará bydliště*, p. 25): "Matěj Kopecký's great
puppets smoulder in parks".

In some of these poems, the speaker makes a direct appearance, commenting on the scene with irony and personal satisfaction, keeping his distance, yet intervening, as if having a conversation with the onlooker and trying out what they will find acceptable and understandable. Most of the time, the subjective comments appear at the end of the poem, such as in his 'Cemetery':

Je to podivuhodné jak slovo hřbitov
Ztratilo dlouhým používáním v poesii všechnu tísnivost
Svatebčané se zvolna svlékají
Hudebníci jeden po druhém
Odcházejí do tmy kralickým návsím

Ležím v posteli s tetičkou Staňkovou
A smějeme se.
Paní Nezvalová přináší makové koláče.
Má se také svléci donaha?
Za almarou jsou ještě čtyři lahve vína.
Musím si ukrojit kus masa, říká tetička.

Jestli se mi to líbí?
To je otázka!
V neděli odpoledne půjdeme do Jinošova.
Otakar Březina je s námi.
Spí.
Důstojný pane, svítá. Podívejte se!

It's marvellous how the word cemetery
Long used in poetry has lost all dolefulness
The wedding guests are slowly disrobing
The musicians one after another
Going off into the dark down Kralice square

I'm lying in bed with Auntie Staňková
And we are laughing.
Mrs. Nezvalová is bringing poppyseed pies.
Should she strip naked, too?

There are four more bottles of wine behind the wardrobe.
I have to cut myself some meat, auntie says.

Do I like it?
That is the question!
We will go to Jinošov on Sunday afternoon.
Otokar Březina is with us.
Asleep.
Reverend sir, it is dawning. Look![26]

The poem spreads out the tendrils of a complex network of references, as is typical of Blatný's later poems. A key motif is that of the already deceased poet Březina, who joins Blatný as if the living and the dead in this poem were living together in a shared space. From this perspective, Blatný sees himself standing apart from the realm of those actively living. The cemetery had been a favourite motif for Blatný since the *Melancholy Walks*, and the first verses of the Cemetery in the *Invisible Home* confirms a conscious connection. A similar view of a cemetery as an idyllic place where the dead are entertained is given by his later poem *Různé názory* [Various Opinions] from the *Remedial School* period:

Motocykl se zeleným přívěsním vozíkem je veselejší
dvacáté století v Lhotákově podání je hřbitov
kde mrtví lenoší v lenoškách pozorujíce balóny
či lépe v skládacích zahradních křeslech.

■

A motorcycle with a green side-car is more cheerful
for Lhoták the Twentieth Century is a cemetery

---

26   *Neviditelný domov*, p. 23. Otokar Březina (1868–1929), a distinguished Czech poet assigned to symbolism, whose name can stand in for the notion of a poet as such. Jinošov, the village in which Březina worked as a teacher, is located near Náměšť nad Oslavou where Blatný spent time as a child, thus in his own way connecting the location with poetry. Jinošov was also for some time the home of Jakub Deml (1878–1961), who was an admirer of Březina in his youth and became a priest at his initiative; he is probably the intended addressee in the last verse.

where the dead lounge in lounge-seats watching balloons
or better still in folding garden deck-chairs[27]

Especially in his manuscript poems Blatný does not fail to mention becoming
aware that someone has died, be it one of his friends or some celebrity, and
does not bother too much about which of the characters in his verses may or
may not be dead. He creates an imaginary space, in which death does not represent an absolute frontier:

Říkali že zemřel Brežněv
Stalin je mrtev
na Hradčanech vládne Masaryk.

They said that Brezhnev has died
Stalin is dead
Prague Castle remains ruled by Masaryk.[28]

In the last verses of his poem *Jeviště* [The Stage], the stage-setter is voiced in the
first person, his relationship to life being more than an observer, more about
participating in it:

V Colombe sur Seine
Zelené rozmazané keře prostupují skleníčky
Stoupající pára
Na okamžik podobná rozvětvené květině
Se ještě dotýká země koncem svého stonku
Ještě žijeme
Ještě slyšíme melodické hádky
Sousedek se slepicemi ráno v Colombe sur Seine a ještě

---

27   I. Blatný: *Pomocná škola Bixley*, p. 216 (the poem is one of a selection of manuscripts found
     only in the last, 2011 edition). Kamil Lhoták (1912–1990), painter, and together with Blatný
     a member of Group 42.
28   I. Blatný: *Pomocná škola Bixley*, p. 77 (the poem 'Rocking-Fair' in the original part of the collec-
     tion).

Kolíky na prádlo nabírané do hrsti a štětce
Vydávají svá jemná zvonění.

Ⅰ

In Colombe sur Seine
Smudged verdant bushes grow through small greenhouses
Rising steam
For a moment resembling a branching flower
Still keeps in touch with the ground by tendril stem
Still we live on
Still we are hearing the melodic quarrels
Of next-door ladies with hens by morning in Colombe sur Seine
            and still
The clothes pegs scooped by the handful and brushes
Tinkle with gentle chimes.[29]

The Cemetery can be read as a metaphor for exile and likening exile to death, which none of the reviewers of the *Invisible Home* have noted. This is in an old--established and repeated motif figuring in exile. Ovid, when addressing the gods, purports to be dead himself:

vos animam saevae fessam subducite morti,
        si modo qui periit, non periisse potest

Ⅰ

Save ye my weary life from cruel death,
        if only 'tis possible for one already dead not to die![30]

---

29   *Neviditelný domov*, p. 20. – The typescript contains an older version of a poem called 'A Small Poem for Heisler and Toyen', which also contains one verse: 'Heisler came out to meet Toyen she put down her brushes in a small studio', before the verse 'Still we live on'. The French town of Colombe sur Seine is probably associated with Blatný's sojourn in France, and in his poem 'May VI' in the *Old Domiciles*, he is featured together with the studio of the surrealist painter Toyen (1902–1980).

30   Ovid: *Tristia. Ex Ponto*, pp. 28–29; Trist I, 4, l. 27–28.

In similar imagery death and life have two often intermingled meanings that establish the pathos of this fabulation. Death means physical death, but also the deprivation of everything that forms the essential content of life, except life itself as a biological fact. By taking a similar figurative approach, in which they do not distinguish between life as such and its content, Ovid, and some poets of the *Invisible Home* thus express sadness and nostalgia.

Ivan Blatný did not accede to the numbing rhetoric of nostalgia, it could even be said that in his *Cemetery* he ironically deconstructed it, but also filled it with fresh content. Being wrenched away from one's past gives life a new content, and if the loss of the homeland and contact with an earlier life is seen as a kind of death, it opens up a new, imaginary space where death no longer implies an insurmountable obstacle. The verses 'Still we live on / Still we are hearing the melodic quarrels' lead us to a finer distinction between life and death. Life is not essentially about any particular content, but the ability to perceive nuances, the intense sensory perception of a poetic observer who hears the 'chiming' of the clothes pegs and the paintbrushes. In a similar vein, in those poems that rely on a stage-setting subject (*October, Summer Evening*) we find atmospheric elements based on fine figurative work, tied to sensory impressions.

Let us take another look at the names of Blatný's collections. *Tongues* evidently points to the theme of foreign lands and foreign tongues. Indeed, in the typescript two poems are written in French and could refer to Blatný's time in France in 1946,[31] while the poems feature foreign particulars and locals. The text, very probably incomplete, does not have much to say about the title, which to some extent corresponds to Blatný's deploying of titles whose connection to the text of the poems is at times unclear or merely marginal.[32] *London Spring* may be associated with his interest in a revitalized perception of the environment or to commemorate his first years of exile as the beginning of a new life. The theme of different languages appears to a greater extent only in Blatný's later poems. In the short poem *Slavnost* [Celebration] from the *Bixley Remedial School* he takes a quasi-macaronic approach, alternating Czech with English and German, and makes direct comments on this multilingualism:

---

31   cf. I. Blatný: *Texty a dokumenty*, p. 452.

32   In the poem 'Tongues' in the *Bixley Remedial School* (p. 34) there is only a mention of Hebrew.

Poetry is a panacea for all illnesses
bratři Marxové vylupují žloutek
Der Dichter spricht in verschiedenen Sprachen
na dně jezera kde vodníci nocují
Volná cesta byla zatarasena
quite blocked by gaiety girls.

Poetry is a panacea for all illnesses
The Marx Brothers spoon out the yolk
Der Dichter spricht in verschiedenen Sprachen
        [The Poet speaks in different languages]
on the lakebed where the Watersprites overnight
the Open road was blocked
quite blocked by gaiety girls.[33]

Characteristically, Blatný is not so interested in the foreign language in the outside world as something for him to hear and record in a poem; this is what some of the *Invisible Home* poets do. On the contrary, his issue is that he himself should speak through his poem in different tongues, as each cited verse demands.

Two other titles – *To be with Mother* and *Old Domiciles* – evoke a tendency to nostalgia, which does not play a major role in Ivan Blatný's older exile poems. Yet the link to *London Spring* is supported by the fact that he feels nostalgia not only for his Czech home, but indeed his 'old domiciles' in England. One of the key words of the *Old Domiciles*, the word 'still', takes on a slightly different meaning in this collection than in *The Stage*, a poem from his early exile years.

III

Old Domiciles came out in 1979, published twenty-five years after the poems in *Invisible Home,* when Blatný seemed to go off the radar, so to speak. The collec-

---

33   I. Blatný: *Pomocná škola Bixley*, p. 16.

tion's editor, Antonín Brousek, aptly called his introduction *Návrat ztraceného básníka* [The Return of the Lost Poet]. By this he meant, above all, the poet returning to his readers, not to writing poems, which Blatný seemed to keep on writing the whole time with just a few breaks. *Old Domiciles* has the feel of a cohesive collection, contrasting with his *Remedial School* by its textual consistency. The reality is more complicated. Leaving aside the uncorrected printing errors,[34] the question still remains how the book came about, e.g. whether the dedication and the prefaced title poem are the work of the editor or the author. Antonín Brousek states that he made his selection from a great many texts:

> Thanks to Ms Meacham, whole reams of Blatný's unexplored texts – being either Czech, or English or 'Macaronic' texts, i.e. Czech-English, or even more linguistically mixed, i.e. Czech-English-French--German – came into the hands of Josef Škvorecký, and from there into my own. Making a selection out of this plethora of texts of very unequal value turned out to be a relatively easy task, and what's more, quite an uplifting one: It was enough to pick out the poems that were in definitive form and finalised shape; and quantity, peeled away, gave forth quality.[35]

Jan Šmarda, on the other hand, writes that Blatný had a ready-made collection *Být s matkou* [To be with Mother] at the time:

> At the beginning of August 1978, we – my wife and I – managed to spend a week with Ivan Blatný in Ipswich. On this occasion, he gave me the manuscript of his recently completed collection *To be with Mother*. Frances Meacham sent a copy of that manuscript of poems dating from 1969-1977 already in early 1978 along with copies of other poems from the same period to Josef Škvorecký's Toronto publishing house Sixty-Eight Publishers. Josef Škvorecký accepted the poems and confirmed receiving them by letter, dated 27 February 1978. He

---

34 Ivan Blatný's estate includes the collection's typescripts with apparently the author's proofreading notes, which have not been implemented to this day, although the collection has already been published in five editions and in some cases the published wording is clearly flawed.

35 A. Brousek: Návrat ztraceného básníka, pp. 469–470.

handed over the manuscripts for editing to Antonín Brousek – which led to the Old Domiciles collection.[36]

Jan Šmarda later published twenty-one poems, which he said belonged to the collection Blatný had in mind but were not included in Brousek's selection, and which, by its poetic imagery do largely correspond to other poems of the *Old Domiciles*.[37] These two testimonies are not necessarily at odds, and with some caution we might surmise from them that Blatný conceived a collection that was not textually far removed from the *Old Domiciles*, but at the same time also wrote numerous texts that defy being singled out and in part seem to have made their way into the body of texts to do with *Bixley Remedial School*.[38] Their connection with older poems from the 1950s remains unclear.[39]

Although today the chronology remains uncertain, the title and title poem form a distinctive thematic core of the collection, which references earlier poems from the *Invisible Home*.

STARÁ BYDLIŠTĚ
6, Brunswick Gardens, Kensington

Maqui, můj kocourku, co děláš, ještě žiješ?
Musíš být velmi stár a znaven, jak je ti?
Je ještě v knihovně ta krásná poezie,
jsou ještě v knihovně Štolbovy paměti?

Brunšvické zahrady. Princ Albert ještě žije,
v Hyde Parku, v Kensingtnu, zde v těchto zahradách.

---

36   J. Šmarda, *Doslov*, p. 119.

37   Other poems ascribed to this period are in the keeping of Blatný's estate. Two of them, *To město To* [This City This], *Šlechta* [Nobility] have been published by Šmarda, two remain unpublished, *Koňak* [Cognac], *Neděle v říjnu* [Sunday in October].

38   In his foreword to the *Old Domiciles*, Brousek mentions a poem dedicated to Martina Navrátilová (*Návrat ztraceného básníka*, p. 479), which it seems he later included in his edition of the *Remedial School* (p. 146, 2011 edition).

39   These clearly include the aforementioned poem *Nokturno* (as *Noc* [Night] in the *Invisible Home*); the poem *Nápoje* [Drinks] literally quotes several poems included in the typescript of *Jazyky / Londýnské Jaro* [Tongues / London Spring].

A žije starý dvůr, a žije Viktorie,
umíme setřít prach, umíme setřít prach.

Žije jak Chitussi, jak Štolba na jevišti,
žije jak minulé, žije jak všichni příští,
žije, jak v Anglii ožívá národ náš.

Pouť budoucí je tvá, zbavena zemské tíhy,
pouť budoucí je tvá, obrazy, básně, knihy,
pouť budoucí je tvá, a ty ji uhlídáš.

OLD DOMICILES
6, Brunswick Gardens, Kensington

Maqui, my little tomcat, how's things, still alive?
You must be very old and weary; how d'you feel?
Did that fine poetry in the library survive;
are Štolba's Memoirs in the library still?

Brunswick Gardens. Prince Albert is still living,
in Hyde Park, Kensington, in these gardens, I trust.
The old court, Victoria still living breathing,
we can wipe off the dust, we can wipe off the dust.

He lives like Chitussi, like Štolba on the stage,
lives like bygones, lives like all future ages,
lives, like in England our nation reviving, see.

Your future pilgrimage, cut free of Earth's pull hooks,
the pilgrimage to come, your pictures, poems, books,
the pilgrimage to come is yours, you'll oversee.[40]

---

40   I. Blatný: *Stará bydliště*, p. 9.

Old Domiciles may surprisingly mean places from the first years of Blatný's exile, not his Czech home. After all, domicile evokes a certain transient quality, and rather than a home, reminds of Flusser's concept of some *abode*. The poem is steeped in light nostalgia, to the times when Blatný's first poems in exile were emerging. It also features two key Czech words which strangely resonate together with the poems of this group – *"ještě"* [persistently, still] and *"jeviště"* [drama stage]. Blatný lived at the poem-subtitle address from February 1951, after staying for a time at Claybury Hospital.[41] If we consider in turn the names Blatný mentions in the poem, they are all deceased. The name Prince Albert, seemingly the poem's centrepiece, may in fact refer to King George VI. He had one of his residences in nearby Kensington Palace and died in February 1952. This date marks the time the poem relates to and from there reveals a more distant, deeper past – 'we can wipe off the dust'. All the others mentioned are long dead by that year.[42] The opening recollection of Maqui, the little tomcat, turns to irony in retrospect, because the words 'still alive' in this poem refer only and exclusively to the dead, rounded off by the completely unreal verse of the penultimate strophe: 'like in England our nation reviving, see'. The progression toward the past and the dead, the 'dust-wiping', creates the kind of perspective in which you can communicate with the dead or bring them to light in a poem that sets its own stage or scene. The revival of the nation alludes this memorial revival of the dead, measured against a relatively immortal, or long-lived royal dynasty. Other poems reveal that Blatný idealized England into a kind of fairytale and idyllic land of regal monarchy, order and security: 'This greenhouse-seeming England.'[43] This idyllic nature underlined by the 'English' adjective brings with it the quiet depiction in the poem *Ohrady* [Fenced Enclosures]:

> Vyšla jste vraty ohrad
> do březnového světla anglické neděle

---

41   cf. M. Reiner: *Básník*, pp. 325, 328ff. and further to the poem on pp. 333–334.

42   Prince Albert (1819–1861) may also be the husband of Queen Victoria (1819–1901), the painter is Antonín Chittussi (1847–1891), the writer Josef Štolba (1846–1930).

43   I. Blatný: *Stará bydliště*, p. 24; similarly 'In this land we still have fairy tales', p. 14 and other poems especially in the first section of the collection.

You came through the gates of the fenced enclosures
into the March light of an English Sunday[44]

Blatný's stays in seclusion correspond with this desire for an idyllic scene, which is very often enclosed, like the sanatoriums where he lived.

Ivan Blatný returns countless times to the idea of invoking the dead, a regular prop feature of his poems; such as when, in another poem from this time, he writes 'Nezval is alive'.[45] The word 'still', repeated in other guises, carries within it the contradictory cognisance that those referred to are no longer among the living, while at the same time entailing imagination's denial of reality or taking issue with it. Only rarely and in significant cases are the dead not admitted onto the poem's set or stage, and turned away. Such is the case of the poet Jiří Orten, Blatný close friend, whose tragic death during the occupation seemed to sweep him away beyond the reach of poetic imagination, although Blatný recalls him under no fewer than three poetic names:

Ohnice kvete, smutný světe.
Orten a Jakub pijí z Lethe,
nikdy se neshledáme, žel.
A Jílek na nás zapomněl.

The Pyre is blooming, sad world, aching,
Orten and Jakub from Lethe drinking,
We'll never meet again, alas.
And Jílek forgot about us.[46]

In one of the poems of the *Bixley Remedial School* collection, the connection between death and the theatre is quite explicit:

---

44   Ibid., p. 13.
45   I. Blatný: *Fragmenty*, p. 97.
46   I. Blatný: *Stará bydliště*, p. 59. Jiří Orten, properly Ohrenstein 1919–1941 was a poet of Jewish descent and also published under the names Karel Jílek and Jiří Jakub, so that all three names in the poem indicate the same person. *Ohnice* [Pyre] is the name of Orten's collection from 1941, which was published under the name Jiří Jakub.

LÁSKA

Uvaděčka smrt usazuje návštěvníky Velkého divadla
říkali jsme někdy ve Velkym
zde v Brně bývaly Hradby
stál jsem před nimi s Vítězslavem Vejražkou
navěky Sukův Radúz
navěky Mahulena.

▪

LOVE

The Usher death seats the visitors of the Great Theatre
we used to say sometimes in the Big one
here in Brno there used to be the Ramparts
I stood in front of them with Vítězslav Vejražka
forever Suk's Radúz
forever Mahulena.[47]

What does this Orphism presented by Blatný mean? Blatný continues to craft the concept of the poem as a stage set or theatre scene onto which people and things are summoned to appear, whether recalled from memory, or evoked from the imagination, or whether Blatný simply knows them off the TV. The poetic setting resembles the TV screen, a framework within which an event or character shows itself while also being highlighted, brought to the fore. It's not just about remembering, but rather about cross-fertilizing all possible sources, including memories, historical knowledge, television updates and the real world around. Present on the set are the dead and the living whom Blatný knew personally, as well as those he only heard of, temporarily. Temporarily, that is, for the duration of the poem, while it is being read or written. In the first case, for the benefit of the reader, in the second for Blatný himself as the author, which also explains his intensive writing and frequent revisits: the set needs to be kept freshly dusted.

---

47   I. Blatný: *Pomocná škola Bixley*, p. 25.

An important counterpart to this stage is the speaker. In some poems, the speaker is impersonal, elsewhere drawing attention to themselves with some irony. From this point of view, Blatný's long-term seclusion can be seen as a realm between life and death. In this vague and ambiguous position, the poet remains on the border, as if belonging to both the living and the dead, and in the spirit of Rilke's sonnet, capable of finer and more reconciled perception:

Nur wer mit Toten vom Mohn
aß, von dem ihren,
wird nicht den leisesten Ton
wieder verlieren.

Who with dead men would down
from their realm, poppy bane,
even the faintest of tones
will ne'er forget again[48]

In the *Old Domiciles*, the speaker holds one more important role – a curling up and regressing into a prenatal state, which corresponds to the alternative name of the collection *To be with Mother*.[49] The poem 'Football', filled with evocations of Moravian football matches, oscillates between a past full of memories, the present of the observer and the future of his fantasizing about football. With this movement, space is divided into the past around Brno and the present, in England, from where the regressive reverie unfolds, attempting to reconcile and bring the two places together:

Budeme celý zápas sledovat
z daleké Anglie za zavřenými víčky
Na této televizi uvidíme snad
penalty, ofsajdy a nemotorné kličky.

---

48   R. M. Rilke: *Die Gedichte*, p. 726 (Die Sonette an Orpheus I, 9).

49   The motifs of regression, huddling, closeness to the mother appear in various guises in the poems *Na verandě, Fotbal, Vánoce, Vilému Bräunerovi* (*Stará bydliště*, pp. 15, 49–50, 51, 88) and *Opona ještě nepadla...* (*Fragmenty*, p. 100).

Tam vidět fanoušky a jejich pěstní hádky,
tam zůstat, zůstat tam – zápas je příliš krátký –
pod celou kupou klubů vyšších tříd.

Tam zůstat, zůstat tam, poblíže řeky Svratky,
poblíže fotbalu, fotbalu naší matky,
a nemuset se narodit.

We'll watch the game in its entirety
from distant England from behind eyes closed
on that TV screen, hopefully we'll see
penalties, offsides, clumsy heel-to-toes.

There we'll see fans their fisticuffs besport,
stay there, stay there – the match is far too short –
below, away from higher league clubs' scorn.

Stay there, stay there, by Svratka riverbanks,
near football, by our mother's football ranks,
and save having to be born.[50]

The memory collage turns into a visual broadcast watched in spirit, but trans-mitting one 'there' (repeated several times like a spell); and the running time in which the match cannot be stopped ('the match is far too short') concluded by the motif of returning to motherfootball and the wish to 'save having to be born'. For Blatný the imaginary prenatal place is outside the reach of temporal events, and also beyond life and death. It is, or is supposed to be the ideal observation room, protected from time, but allowing events in time to be monitored. Blatný leaves the time contradiction unresolved, because he longs to some extent for both: to stop time and to observe events in time. The poem Na verandě [On the Porch] does at least in the wishful thinking sense reach for a certain balance, as if to stay in the mother's womb could in its way freeze time and give events an infinite duration, an eternally captured snapshot:

---

50   I. Blatný: Stará bydliště, p. 50.

Na verandě v šelestu starých fazolových lusků a semenářských ceníků
mladý Everár čte staré detektivky
Edgar Wallace Agatha Christie Simenon
Dvacet tisíc mil pod mořem
Veranda odplouvá jak léto poslední léto
kapitán Nemo je mrtev v písku pod mořem

Kéž by to nebylo ještě poslední léto
kéž bychom zůstali navždy
šťastni v matčině lůně
v šelestu semenářských ceníků.

On the porch to the rustle of old bean pods and seed pricelists
young Everard reads old whodunnits
Edgar Wallace Agatha Christie Simenon
Twenty Thousand Leagues Under the Sea
The verandah floats off like the summer the last summer
Captain Nemo is dead in the sand under the sea

If only it wasn't the last summer yet
if only we could stay forever
happy in mother's womb
to the rustle of seed pricelists.[51]

But it is not just about observation. From the more distant vantage point outside time and events one can very easily and readily identify with every incoming stimulus, and vice versa, allow oneself to be carried away by events, engrossed, but no longer having a time of heaviness and nostalgia, but a time of distraction. It opens up opportunities for a never-ending identity game. As a poet, Blatný, for example, declares himself a surrealist: 'I am a surrealist and will never be any different',[52] and a Poetist: 'I am a poetist / I play with hues

---

51   Ibid., p. 15.
52   I. Blatný: *Fragmenty*, p. 97.

and sounds',[53] but also quite lightheartedly, a ruralist: 'I am also a ruralist / I am a miller, the Agrarians are my party; / from England Ivan sends his greeting'. Some of these claims have local support in the poem, but elsewhere, Blatný is just ironically playing out the association.[54] In some poems he observes himself, as if he were a third person:

> Hubené ubohé tělo Ivana Blatného
> neustále zraňované těmi kteří vidí
> tělo plné studu pohlaví
> začíná svoje šedesáté narozeniny

> ▪

> Ivan Blatný's wretched and skinny body
> ever being hurt by those who see
> a body full of abashed sexuality
> embarking on its birthday, the sixtieth[55]

Elsewhere again, he takes on the curious identity of one Josef Kunstadt:

> Hra na básníka pokračuje
> jsem Josef Kunstadt publikující v magazínu Roztrhané panenky

> ▪

> The game of being a poet carries on
> I'm Josef Kunstadt publishing in Torn Doll magazine[56]

He toys with him: 'we must create the image of Josef Kunstadt',[57] in places he turns to Blatný as Kunstadt, elsewhere he mentions both in the third person:

---

53   I. Blatný: *Stará bydliště*, p. 53 (the poem *Manifest poetismu*).
54   I. Blatný: *Fragmenty*, p. 99.
55   I. Blatný: *Pomocná škola Bixley*, p. 110.
56   Ibid., p. 207.
57   Ibid.

Svět se boří a staví
mladý Ivan očekává Josefa Kunstadta
který podepsal v létech třicátých manifest české surrealistické skupiny

The world is breaking down and being built
young Ivan is awaiting Josef Kunstadt
which in the thirties signed the Czech surrealist group manifest[58]

However, behind the variability the stage-setter stays firmly present, the one who brings all these 'fantasies' onto the scene, and is the commentator, dispassionately observing. Quite often he speaks in an impersonal plural, which may well have multiple meanings, but in many cases, he personifies the speaker as if he was not physically present on the spot, even though closely following everything:

Několik narcisů na pokraji lesa který jsme
málem pokládali za divokou přírodu
svědčí o vynalézavé jemné práci zahradníků.

Several daffodils on the edge of the wood that we
almost considered to be nature, wild
testify to the gardeners' inventive art.[59]

I have mentioned the reservations expressed by reviewers about Blatný's poems in the *Invisible Home* anthology. Conversely, *Old Domiciles* were enthusiastically received. This contrast of critical response is mainly down to changing times and how poetry was viewed, Blatný's poems themselves are not so very different. In the larger ensemble it also becomes apparent how Blatný took exile nostalgia to its imaginary consequences. It remains somewhat of a paradox that of all the poets of the *Invisible Home*, he is perhaps the most consistent in that respect. In his conception of the scenic poem, the primary

---

58   Ibid., p. 280.
59   I. Blatný: *Stará bydliště*, p. 17.

distance between home and the place of exile is transformed. The scenic stage
of the poem is the showground for it all, and at the same time a 'glasshouse', an
isolating environment that acts as the enabling medium. It is not only home
(and all it entails) that is remote, but everything, including one's own person, is
observable with all detachment. No thing or person or place is any more distant
than any other. The imaginary scenic stage of the poem can also accommodate
what is irretrievably lost in the nostalgic world, allowing new lives to be lived,
trying out all sorts of roles and constructing an otherwise impossible idyll.

IV

The scenic nature of his works is characterized to a great extent by Blatný's poems from the *Old Domiciles* period and with some degree of shift also the
Bixley Remedial School period. At the same time, however, it divides into several
types that correspond with the different roles of the speaker. Especially so in
the early poems, a key aspect is the *place* the poem reminds about or constructs,
somewhere relatively cohesive and typically physically enclosed.[60] In the poem
Ohrady [Fenced Enclosures] several independent movements and intentions
intersect. By intersecting more or less randomly, they delimit the scene and
form the location's associative structure:

> Stála jste ve dveřích chodby vedoucí k nějakým dílnám
>
> Kdosi si prohlížel předměty odložené na smetiště
> železné tyče papírové růže kusy skříní
>
> Někdo jiný přešel po dvoře
>
> Vyšla jste vraty ohrad
> do březnového světla anglické neděle.

---

60   For example, in the above cited poem *Mýtus* [Myth], ibid.

You were standing in the door of the hallway to some workshops.

Someone was browsing through things that were dumped
iron rods paper roses pieces of cabinets

Someone else walked across the yard

You came through the gates of the fenced enclosures
into the March light of an English Sunday[61]

In these poems, the stage-setter brings the scene to life rather passively, without necessarily bringing anything else onto the scene. In other poems, consciousness projects onto the scene, memory, figurativeness and the scene connects with multiple places distant in space and time – as in the poem 'Football', where the speaker projects the scene from England. Another such is the poem *From a Terrace in Prague*, in which several places cross in a complex way, the reference point being the initial reminder of the past.

Můj dědeček byl optik
kdykoli jsem šel v Československu v nějakém jiném městě
kolem optického obchodu
myslel jsem na rodinu jeho majitele

Za Karlovým mostem za Mosteckou věží na Malé Straně
je také optický krám
Snad se jeho majitel vracíval domů přes Kampu
po Mostě legií kolem Národního divadla
snad měl byt v Novodvorské ulici pod Petřínem

Dnes kdy píši tuto báseň Seminářská zahrada kvete a to
co Součková vídávala z terasy
se vlní koléba zní drobnými zvuky od starých zámeckých schodů na
      Malé Straně

---

61   Ibid., p. 13.

My grandfather was an optician
whenever in some other Czechoslovak city I went
past an opticians' shop
I thought about the family of its owner

Behind Charles Bridge behind the Bridge Tower on the Lesser Town
    side
is also an opticians'
Maybe its owner used to go back home through Kampa
over the Legions Bridge and past the National Theatre
maybe his apartment was in Novodvorská street under Petřín hill

Today as I write this poem the Seminary Garden is blooming and
what Součková used to see from the terrace
swing sways small sounds from the Lesser Town Old Castle Steps[62]

The name of the poem highlights the motifs of the last strophe, in which the said "Součková" used to watch from the terrace; but the time tense of the poem at that moment switches to the present and the atmosphere of 'back in the day' is transferred to the present by the act of writing. Yet the whole scene is defined by a few places and characters at certain different times. The past in Czechoslovakia is crossed with the present in exile, the past space includes Brno, where the Blatný's grandfather had his shop, and Prague, which the shop evokes. Despite the association of places, the poem gets as far as Milada Součková, who, like Blatný, went into exile, and lived in the USA.[63] In the figure of Součková, distant in time but at the same time also close-by in the exile domain (on the same side of the border as Blatný), the past meets the present. In the associative arc of the last verses, Blatný connects different spaces and times through England and America and brings onto the poem's scenic stage the atmosphere of the Seminary Garden, paraphrased in a remarkable syne-sthetic image: 'what Součková used to see' – 'swing sways small sounds'. The poem's keystone are words 'today as I write this poem' – which not only tie it to

---

62   Ibid., p. 86.
63   They both knew about each other for a while at least. A letter from Blatný to Součková from his early years of exile has survived (I. Blatný: *Texty a dokumenty*, pp. 240–248), Součková in her turn reacted to the publication of *Stará bydliště*. Blatný mentions her in several other poems.

a particular moment, but also show the possibilities of poetic scenography: to conjure up in one place and time something from a distant time and place. The one who 'writes this poem' composes this complex space while also present on the poem's stage. The scene is neither the Prague of back then, nor the England of 'today', but a locus where spaces and times come together.

Some of the places in Blatný's poems and sometimes whole poems do necessitate some explanation. It isn't just about content, but more about the way Blatný connects together the individual motifs, and often people with places, to create scenic constellations. Without knowing the context, we may miss the poem's constructive meaning – for example, in the poem *Old Domiciles* you need to know who is who, to realize that only the dead are spoken of. Jiří Trávníček drew attention to this 'encyclopaedic' work, and saw it as a remembrance.[64] It would be more accurate to say, however, that memory here only serves as a reservoir of themes (and not the only one); and, above all, with the aim to shape the present scene. The poem *From a Terrace in Prague* shows that the 'stage' need not be some specific place, it can also be an imaginary place combining different space-time aspects, and ultimately can become the only link between the various images of Blatný's associative thinking. Even in this role the poem retains some scenic features, but the aspect of scene-setting prevails over the space itself.

V

Blatný repeatedly claimed an affinity to Surrealism in his poems. Sometimes there is an irony present in such a declaration, and certainly we are not dealing with Surrealism in its classic pre-war form, but Blatný's quirky interpretation of it. In addition to this irony and humour, literally embodied by the bizarre figure of Josef Kunstadt, we are of course faced with his attempt to give a name to his own poetry. Antonín Brousek recalls the poem *Starosurrealismus* [Old Surrealism] from the *Old Domiciles* as well as a whole range of typically surrealist

---

64   J. Trávníček: Pod sankcí paměti, p. 170ff.

verses, but also speaks of Blatný's 'inner distancing from this [...] movement'.[65]
Petr Král mentions the importance of 'spontaneity and free-flight of thought
associations' in Blatný's poetry, but notes the rare presence of 'purposely *auto-matic* texts' that 'jut out inappropriately from the whole body of work; they are
suddenly unexpectedly abstract, the will that controls them does not seem to be
free, but on the contrary wilful, a voluntarist imposition'.[66] What Blatný employs
in his poems can be described as reverie, in the sense used by Gaston Bache-lard. Contrary to a dream, reverie involves a certain degree of conscious aware-ness, albeit relaxed and guided by various stimuli. Blatný himself makes several
mentions of what he calls *"nejasné vědomí"*, a vague or diffuse awareness, or of
"nízké vědomí", a low or germinal level of consciousness, as a necessary condi-tion for him to write poetry: 'God leaves me with a diffuse awareness, because
it is impossible to live without that, it is impossible to write surrealist poetry.'[67]
In the poem *Nesmělé námluvy* [Timid Courtship] with the Breton International
Surrealist Group, as quoted by Petr Král, Blatný comments on his 'method' by
asking: 'Will he mind that I make rhymes?', which aptly captures his associative
thinking. The cues for linking words and images may be random initially, but
then they turn into a deliberate playing with words and using a broad regis-ter of figures – rhymes, puns in one language and between different languages,
and very often, *double entendres* whimsically reflecting on the poem's message,
deliberately letting himself be taken off by them in a different direction. The poem
André Breton, one of the first in the *Bixley Remedial School* as Blatný conceived it,
shows this 'method' or Blatný's interpretation of surrealism quite illustratively:

ANDRÉ BRETON

> Z úrodné prsti nejasného vědomí
> rodí se silokřivky
> silokřivky železných pilin magnetických polí Duchamps

---

65   A. Brousek: Návrat ztraceného básníka, pp. 474–475. How Blatný relates to surrealism is dis-cussed by M. Reiner, who emphasizes how it influenced or rather dazzled the young Blatný
       (*Básník*, p. 33ff.), and by Petr Král, who also recalls the differences and Blatný consciously dis-tancing himself (P. Král: Certifikát, p. 563).

66   P. Král: Certifikát, p. 564.

67   I. Blatný: *Pomocná škola Bixley*, p. 103. Further as, 'diffuse awareness', pp. 10, 103–104; 'we must
       regain our diffuse awareness', p. 143; 'I am calling from an inkling', p. 24.

Byl šachovým hráčem a dovolil mi vyhrát šustermatem
vydáme se na cestu
půjdeme ukázat tyto básně mladému Blatnému

Jsem pilina jste magnet.

▪

ANDRÉ BRETON

From the fertile loam of diffuse awareness
force-field lines are born
force-field lines of iron filings in magnetic fields Duchamps

was a chess player and let me win with a fool's mate.
we will set off on a journey
we'll go to show these poems to young Blatný

I the filing you the magnet.[68]

The beginning of the poem evokes an emergence and focusing of images, as is characteristic of Blatný. The combination of *Magnetic Fields*, Marcel Duchamp (*champ* = field in French) draws a whole network of significant connections into play, with several layers, letting the game of different themes unfold. The final verse summarizes the workings of 'diffuse awareness' attracted by various stimuli.

Especially during the *Remedial School* period, surrealism had a broader meaning for Blatný, as if it were the very essence of poetry as such or underlying the poet's view of the things that give rise to poetry. In one poem of this collection we have the surrealist poetry of a radio broadcast: 'We have no silence here / Wogan is spewing surrealist poetry out of the radio.'[69] It is during the *Remedial School* period that the scenic approach changes, whereby the location, as an evoked

---

68   Ibid., p. 10. The last verse 'I [am] the filing you [are] the magnet' also appears in Blatný's poem
      Chleba [Bread] (*Fragmenty*, p. 98), once again in connection with Breton.
69   Ibid., p. 234. Terry Wogan (1938–2016), a well-known Irish and British radio and television
      announcer and commentator.

imaginary stage, becomes much less a foundation for the poems, although not disappearing completely. One reason is that the ubiquitous setting of his poems is now the institution where Blatný lives, and writing poems is his daily routine in this very place. In some poems, the stream of associations relates to the immediate surroundings, the daily regime; in others he lets himself drift off without any relation to the place. This approach is well characterized by the name of one of the poems – *Myšlenky na procházce* [Thoughts on a Walk].[70] At this time, Blatný is attending to his 'project' of the School, of which it might be said that it is a space where the world is construed and renewed by words. In many poems, starting with the *Old Domiciles*, we find verses that mimic the speech of children's textbooks or illustrated children's encyclopaedias, in which individual things are put side by side with a certain naïve matter-of-factness that has no need to explain anything. In one of the poems of the *Old Domiciles* dedicated to the Škvorecký couple, the impetus for the schooling tone is a contact with Czech, the alliteration in the fifth verse reminding of the 'living alphabet' used to teach children to read:

> Trošku psát česky znova,
> chybí mi česká slova,
> peří a lupení
> těch krátkých letních dní.
>
> Kůň kluše, kovář ková,
> v měknoucím soumraku lípa je fialová.

> To write a little Czech again,
> I am missing Czech words, plain,
> feathers and the leafy haze
> of those short-lived summer days.
>
> Bronco bucking, Blacksmith bashing,
> in the softening dusk, the linden tree mauve blushing.[71]

---

70   Ibid., p. 87.

71   I. Blatný: *Stará bydliště*, p. 42. The alliterative 'bronco bucking' part of the verse, though literally 'the horse canters' is a quote from an earlier Blatný poem, cf. *Verše*, p. 219.

The notion of a school and a place of shelter built with words conjoins the duality of Blatný's exile. On the one hand, this scenic poetry creating imaginary places, on the other a geographical move projected into poems and leading to these imaginary places. Blatný's exile can be read as a search for a quiet and undisturbed location – Blatný is fleeing to England from the Communist regime, and sees England as a 'greenhouse' with an artificial atmosphere of timeless history.[72] Staying in institutions only rounds off Ivan Blatný's poetic life and his idiosyncratic concept of freedom.[73]

Intersecting here are two topologies, and two stances of the speaker – as an observer and as the architect and scene-setter, choosing who moves and dreams upon it. In some poems, Blatný manages to flourish a gesture that connects the two positions. In moments like that, what is happening in the poem is what its words are saying. At such times it is not about capturing the atmosphere or mood of the moment, he wants to write what is going on just then, even at the risk of sometimes slipping towards everyday banality – be it about food, money, cigarettes, erotic dreams or physical needs: 'I wrote a book in Czechoslovakia, *Tento večer, teď právě teď* [This Evening, Now Right Now], and so I will at some time insert notes about what I am doing right now: I need to pee, I'll go and have a pee …'[74]

Antonín Brousek recalls in the foreword to his editions of Blatný, that he had to make choices, and not everything Blatný wrote could be considered fully-fledged poems. In the second Blatný book, there is already a noticeable shift in Brousek's approach, toward more free-form poems and prosaic texts. Zbyněk Hejda notes that the quantity of written records has merit in its own right – something a selection focused on individual poems cannot fully capture.[75] Of all the editions of the *Bixley Remedial School* the latest one best testifies to the sheer volume of it all, with its scope and selection and arrangement of the texts showing the overflowing streams of motifs and how much the writing is bound up with its real-time. In this late poetry, Blatný tries to translate reality into words or have words stand in for it. When we read these entries, they seem an unending stream of speech, a monologue the author is writing down, but at

---

72   Elsewhere, he likens England to Paradise: *"The country is England / the green Paradise of twice harvesting fields"* [sic], *Pomocná škola Bixley*, p. 219.

73   cf. Chapter 3.

74   I. Blatný: *Pomocná škola Bixley*, p. 265.

75   Z. Hejda: Čteme jakýsi deník, p. 90.

the same time listening to, speaking to himself, while embodied in this speech. Underlying the words we can often feel anxiety about reality as such, as well as institutional reality, complete with an occasional beating: 'a pity that we are all alive, it is such an anxious nuisance'.[76] But it is precisely at times like this that language makes things a little more bearable. Blatný often repeats himself, often banal and simple, but he always manages to shape and furnish his abode.

> Moje filosofie zůstává neustále otevřena
> nemohu udělat tečku
> všecko je jenom evidence, nic se nemůže dokázat
> ani positivisté nevěděli nic positivně
> *there should be every day a christmas party like yesterday*
> můj problém je zda mám dokouřit cigaretu bez psaní
> nebo přerušovat psaním
> rozhodl jsem se nepřerušovat.

> My philosophy remains open all the time
> I cannot make a full stop
> Everything is just evidence, nothing can be proven
> even the positivists knew nothing positively
> *there should be every day a christmas party like yesterday*
> my problem is whether to finish the cigarette without writing
> or to keep interrupting it by writing
> I have decided against interrupting[77]

Along with this being drawn into the present moment we can also find places where Blatný seemingly comments on his poetics: not as a proclamation about the whole, but as a statement of the momentary state. Thus, he is here and there a Surrealist, a Poetist, or a Ruralist in the particular poem developing that motif. We find not only *"der Dichter spricht in verschiedenen Sprachen"*, but 'I am only a poet of one language / but I love foreign language inserts',[78] as befits the

---

76   I. Blatný: *Pomocná škola Bixley*, p. 286.
77   Ibid., p. 166.
78   Ibid., pp. 16, 62.

context of one or other poem.[79] Sequestration gives Blatný great freedom to be at any moment at one with his current state, albeit only at the time of writing the poem, and not to worry about holding together as an integral person exposed to the direct influences of the outside world. His shelter allowed him to filter out these influences to a large extent and make them subordinate to his poetic work.

Such freedom has its pitfalls, in Blatný's case the mechanical obsession with which in later years he filled one workbook after another with hundreds of verses. Oftentimes this was only automatic rhyming without much invention, out of which would emerge an exceptional portrayal or grouping of verses, forming a distinct poem. The exile works of Blatný's in his last years are more akin to a continuous stream of writing, in which even the separating out of individual poems is of diminished worth, enfeebled. Going back to his older exile poems, there is an evident gradual transition from formalised and thought-encapsulated poems to a stream of writing. In the *Old Domiciles* we repeatedly find the sonnet form, going back further, in the *Invisible Home* there is a type of poem inclining toward a six verse, largely unrhymed form, and one that Blatný continues with in variant ways in the *Remedial School*. In addition, that collection also features longer poems, often with rhyming couplets, whose thematic context and composition tends toward free associative sequences, as well as occasional longer prosaic texts.

VI

Despite his singular fate, Ivan Blatný is a central figure of Czech exile poetry after 1948. In his early exile years, he was not given much credence by critics, but it was just about that time that he took the situation of exile to its logical conclusions and created the contemplatively scenic type of poem. Since the late 1970s, Blatný was once again in the forefront, known and written about, his poetry was being published and read; Blatný was being visited by friends. And by contrast with the first exile years, we can also find parallels to the activities

---

79 The changes of attitude in Blatný's poems are highlighted by Zbyněk Hejda: Čteme jakýsi deník, p. 92.

and writings of Ivan Blatný with other poets. Milada Součková had already put in writing her certain affinity to him, given the important role the setting of an imaginary scene or space takes in her work, though differing from Blatný's, differently organized. Ivan Diviš also uses scenic staging in his exile poems, in yet another form. The poetic gesture of Ivan Blatný's later years has its equivalent in the prose of Věra Linhartová.

7. The Case of Milada Součková's Poetry

I

Milada Součková (1899–1983) was born into the family of a Prague real-estate magnate and builder, studying at the first Czech Grammar School for Girls and later at the Science Faculty. She made her debut in 1934 with the distinctive experimental prose *První písmena*, meaning first letters (of the alphabet), enthusiastically welcomed by Roman Jakobson. Before the war and during the occupation she published several other books of prose, the last of them, *Hlava umělce* [The Head of the Artist], in 1946. From September 1946 she worked as a cultural attaché in New York, resigned from her post in April 1948 and stayed in American exile until her death. She was active in several US universities, and since the 1970s worked in the Slavic studies department of Harvard College Library. Before the war, she also participated in meetings of the Prague linguistic circle, whose activities she supported financially.[1] Her husband was the painter Zdeněk Rykr (1900–1940), who inclined toward the avant-garde. In Milada Součková's literary works, poetry was initially only a fringe component, but in exile it outweighed her prose. Součková also published literary historical works of some merit, in English. Her family background and history, as well as all these influences and interests, are all notably reflected in her literary work.[2]

---

1   Součková writes about the Prague Linguistic Circle in an eponymous article.
2   Among other things, her book about Vrchlický (*The Parnassian Jaroslav Vrchlický*, 1964) and the Baroque (*Baroque in Bohemia*, 1980), whose themes are also prominent in her poetry.

Součková made her debut as a poet with the bibliophile publications *Kaladý* (1938)[3] and *Mluvící pásmo* [Talking Zone, 1939], and later published the collection *Žlutý soumrak* [Yellow Twilight, 1942]; in exile, four collections of her poems came out: *Gradus ad Parnassum* (1957), *Pastorální suita* [Pastoral Suite, 1962], *Případ poezie* [The Case of Poetry, 1971] and *Sešity Josefíny Rykrové* [The Workbooks of Josefína Rykrová, 1981] with an afterword by Roman Jakobson.[4] All four collections can be read through the prism of exile and exile poetry, but the stylized nature of the poems and their mutual interconnectedness and certain introspection, set within their own world, do not always allow us to clearly distinguish what of their content may or may not in fact be influenced by exile, and where Součková is following on from her pre-exile poetics. In his afterword, Jakobson also recalls the homogeneity of Milada Součková's work and this book's resonance with her earlier texts.[5] From a certain point on, Milada Součková's work consistently refers to her personal, familial and cultural history, and only some aspects hint at her then exile, as a point of reference. Yet there are points where exile is evidently a topic and a reference space. One section of the *Gradus ad Parnassum* collection carries the Ovidian title *Ex Ponto*, and the last collection draws attention to the status of language in exile: most of the poems were supplemented by Součková with a largely English commentary, which seems to suggest the language of the poems themselves needs to be explained, transposed to a known reference language. It is of course very much a game, but this is precisely how Součková characterizes her imaginary space of exile, by using almost a private language, which in the USA the Czech language very much is.

---

3   *Kaladý* is an old name for the village of Koloděje nad Lužnicí in Southern Bohemia, which she often visited.

4   Součková also met with Jakobson in exile and was grateful to him for his support in her early exile years. – The collection was first published under the title *Sešity Josephiny Rykrové* (Toronto 1981), and the later two Prague editions (1993, 2009) contain handwritten poems that Součková conceived as part of the collection, as well as the prose piece 'The Autobiography of Josefína Rykrová'.

5   R. Jakobson: Afterword, p. 215.

II

Like Ivan Blatný, Součková published her first exile poems in the *Invisible Home* anthology and was the only one who defended Blatný in the controversy this anthology evoked: 'There is certainly a lot of bad poetry in exile, and more importantly it is awash with weeping sentimentality and an unprecedented lack of artistic discipline; yet there is one genuine poet living in exile, and that is Ivan Blatný.'[6] The two poets had previously had friendship ties, signalled rather at a distance in exile, as well as their affinity to Group 42.[7] Součková did not include any poems from this anthology in her collections, but some of their motifs are close to the *Ex Ponto* section of her first exile book of poems. First and foremost, the home and exile spaces are juxtaposed. This motif later turns into a stable feature, in which a short reference to her American present serves as an impetus for evoking images from Bohemia. In the poem *Zrání* [Ripening/ Maturing], this is more a case of confrontation between two spaces that intersect, whereby the American framework retains the upper hand:

> Na padesáté sedmé ulici je v srpnu k večeru
> jak na mezích, jež svážejí se k Smutné, k Lužnici
> tu chvíli v žlábku u chodníku by mohly vonět laty tolijí
> však válí se tam zbytky cigaret a papíry
> balady říkají: v pasekách v hloubi lesa tančí víly
> již jako dítě pátral jsem jak dělají se pohádky
> až uviděl jsem v padesáté sedmé ulici
> jak símě vrbin letí srpnovými světly
> pozvolna jako pohyb času pavouka
> zrcadla křesla mahagony
> pokryté „vybledlými vzpomínkami" —

---

6   M. Součková: *Nezval nebo Blatný?*, p. 12. cf. M. Přibáň: *Prvních dvacet let*, p. 195.

7   cf. the letter by I. Blatný to Součková. Součková dedicated to Blatný her article *"Říkám, že každý verš je hoden básně!"* [I say that every verse is worthy of a poem!], whose title is a modification of a Blatný verse.

On fifty seventh street it is an August evening
as on the verges sloping down to Smutná, to Lužnice
the sidewalk gutter now could smell of Parnassia penicles
but is instead filled with cigarette ends and papers
telling ballads: in woodland glades where elven girls are dancing
back as a child I wondered just how fairytales are made
until I saw in fifty seventh street
how willow pollen flies through August lights
slow as the crawl of the time spider
mirrors armchairs mahogany
covered with "faded memories" —[8]

As the poem unfolds, the speaker marvels at the non-existence of poetry about the American city:

ptám se: Kde je epos velkoměstských subwayí
proč nenapsal je žádný Amerikán
proč nenapsal ho ani Walter Whitman
i ten psal epos světlem srpna sežehnutých trav
proč nikdo nepsal epos velké hemisféry
kde pod prérií srpnů duní metra subwayí
proč není báseň o mazu, jež potí kámen, dřevo, kovy
57, pět a sedm, *fifty seven*, sloky opakují
Times, čas, Čas, až zmizí v podzemí
pro lidi, bez lidí, jež žmoulají
oříšky, gumu, cukrovinky, ženy

I ask: Where is the epic on big city subways
why is it still unwritten by any American
why left unwritten even by Walter Whitman
yet he wrote an epic on August light blanched grasses
why have none written the epic of the great hemisphere
where under a prairie of Augusts the subway tunnels boom

---

8   *Neviditelný domov*, p. 97.

why still no poem about ooze from stone, wood, metals
57, five and seven, *fifty-seven*, the verses repeating
Times, time, Time, till it vanishes underground
for people, without people, who are chewing
whatever, nuts, gum, sweets and candies, women

As evidenced by the author's correspondence, the poem was written before 1948, when Součková resigned her diplomatic post, and probably refers to New York, where she was cultural attaché.[9] Within her body of work, this represents an attempt to write poems in an American setting, as borne out by the somewhat later published poems entitled 'To Whitman'.[10] But there were to be none beyond this trio of poems. In her doubts about American poetry, however, Součková is wrong – we need only remind ourselves of Hart Crane's *The Bridge*, indeed dedicated to New York, where for instance the subway plays an important role. But the poem *Zrání* suggests a strange conclusion: as if the absence of poetry made the space inhospitable, compared to the idyll of the Czech countryside, American reality does not appear gloomy on its own, but because it has no poetry to go with it.[11]

There is another important element here. Součková in her poems makes considered use of an impersonal, distanced speaker. In this we can see some influence of her prose and the similarly distanced narrator, who is however altered by the shift to poetry, gaining new possibilities. In some cases, the poetic speaker is more confident and begins to resemble a distinct figure. Součková treads carefully as to just how much definition she gives that figure. It could be said that these figures emerge from language, thanks to occasional hints given by the properties of the language: sometimes the speaker shifts into the first person and so clarifies that what seemed to be impersonal speech does have a specific voice, sometimes the speaker uses the

---

9   In her letter to Jindřich Chalupecký of 29 October 1946 she speaks of writing about America, mentioning the poem *Na troskách básnictví*, i.e. the poem *On the ruins of poetry*, the second poem in the *Invisible Home*. At the beginning of 1947 (on twelfth night) she writes: 'America gets more and more interesting. [...] I've written three or four 'American' poems. When they ripen, I'll send them to you,' M. Součková: *Élenty*, pp. 30, 33, 38.

10   M. Součková: Whitmanovi.

11   While Součková occasionally mentions some American authors, there is no indication that she has consistently followed American poetry.

past tense and identifies with a gender – typically masculine, which gives a would-be impersonal statement a certain tint. In her prose, this stance is best illustrated by the *Neznámý člověk* [Unknown Man] in whose guise the narrator reveals very little about himself, and acts primarily as a witness and a reporter of events. In doing so, these 'figures', albeit mostly male, have some autobiographical features and express something of the writer's attitude. This striving to keep a distance from oneself, and yet to bear witness, is characterized by the beginning of the poem 'My biography' from the 'From My Life' section:

> „Já" zůstaň nenáviděné!
> a žádný jiný výklad nechci
> než verše nejasné a nezřetelné
> jak pro mne byla kdysi slova Aeneidy
> jíž překlad čte věštkyně z předměstí

> "I" remain ever hated!
> and I want no other interpretation
> than verses vague and indistinct
> as were the words of the Aeneid once to me
> translation read by a sibyl from the suburbs[12]

The poem and the whole 'From My Life' section are written in the masculine. These transformations of gender and shifts of identity are subtly topped-off by the last collection of *The Workbooks of Josefína Rykrová*, in which Součková uses a heteronym, composed of the names of her relatives, presenting Josefína in the third person in the poems and comments and in the prose text entitled 'The Autobiography of Josefína Rykrová' she presents her own memories in the first person.[13] In her two 'American' poems from the *Invisible Home* the speaker is

---

12   M. Součková: *Případ poezie*, p. 124.

13   As to the collection in more detail cf. J. Hrdlička: *Poezie a kosmos*. In this fractured autobiographical perspective, she may have drawn inspiration from Gertrude Stein's book *The Autobiography of Alice B. Toklas*, in which Stein writes from her girlfriend's point of view. The book was translated into Czech (1968) by Jiřina Hauková and an afterword written by Jindřich Chalupecký. Součková's was friends with both and they kept up correspondence.

also masculine. In the first one, he only announces himself in a single verse, in the second he represents the much more apparent figure of a pilgrim down the ages who has witnessed ancient poetry and now traces its decline in pragmatic America. The male voice is characteristic of Součková from this *Unknown Man* period onward and in addition to the autobiographical motifs (in the 'My life' section) he also features in her purposive poems. In terms of its themes and speakers, the 'Ruins of Poetry' work is closely matched by the poem *Velký Podzim* [Great Autumn][14], which features an abstracted spirit of poetry, permeating and reviving everything:

> Jsem v zavanutí větru, měním zvíře v bajku
> zažíhám hvězdy v prachu Východu
> přes pěnu vln, hor, hřbety pasátů
> rybářské sítě stínů mraků v oceánu
> rád měním barvy listí, srsti, kontinentů
> v cypřiši Arna, atlantickém cedru
> jsem hudba divu světa na pobřeží Rhodu
> kudy se sunou stíny impérií, křížů
> jsem v soli slz, slin, moří kontinentů
> v rybářských sítích, očích dobrodruhů
> jsem v kroku, který praská větví v stopu
> duch, který změnil zvíře v bajku
> rád měním barvy srsti, kontinentů
> spočinu v hlince, prachu azuru
> v cypřiši desky kdysi v quinquecentu
>
> ▪
>
> I'm in a gust of wind, I turn animal to fable.
> I light up stars in far-flung Eastern dust
> over the sea foam, mountains, Passat ridges
> fishing nets of cloud shadows in the ocean
> glad to change hues of leaves, fur, continents
> in Arno cypress, the Atlantic cedar

---

14 [transl. note: given Součková's American context, there may be back-translation wordplay on 'Great Fall']

I'm music of world-wonder on the shore of Rhodes
where shadows of empires, crosses, pass
I'm salt in tears, spittle, seas continental
in fishing nets, in adventurers' eyes
I'm in the footstep cracking sticks, trail-making
a spirit turning animal to fable
glad to change hues of leaves, fur, continents
I dwell in art, in pastel, azure dust
in cypress boards erstwhile in quinquecento[15]

The *Great Autumn* opens the section called 'Ex Ponto' in the *Gradus ad Parnassum* collection and, unlike her 'American' poems, expresses a positive view of poetry and art and grants them a reviving power. This may be why Součková did not include both poems from the *Invisible Home* in her collections. The given *Ex Ponto* section of the *Gradus ad Parnassum* collection is immediately preceded by a poem called 'Linguistic Ode', which wraps up the previous section 'From My Life'. In this, Součková also expresses scepticism or disbelief in poetry, but substantially differently in not aiming at the state of things in the American domain, but rues the insufficiency of languages, and also notes how ideal poetic diction ought to work:

Básnit mou řečí, je mi věru málo
vždyť ani nechci, aby měla slova
ať je jen slaná jako pokožka
průzračná jako živý rosol v moři
[...]
nač ještě básně moje souložnice
ty prodavačko veršů, kterým všude rozumí
nač ještě hlásky, slova, verše, rýmy
literatury?! Smlčím je, smlčím.

◾

Poetizing my language falls short for me

---

15   Ibid., p. 131. As to the poem cf. K. Suda: Krátká „povídka", pp. 48–49.

indeed, I have no wish to give it words
whether they be like skin, as salty-tasting,
transparent like live jelly in the sea
[...]
whyever more poems, my concubine
peddler of verses, understood everywhere
whyever sounds of speech, words, verses, rhymes
of literature?! I'll keep them silent, hush them up.[16]

Kristián Suda reads the opening verses of the poem as 'expression of a desire to break free of the present netting snares of language' and makes a comparison with the distrust of language expression in the work of Jiří Kolář and, overall, with trends in post-war Czech art. This somewhat relativizes the character of the speaker-poet, formed by the relationship to a 'concubine' lover, who in this case does not seem to be the author's pure alter ego. As part of *Gradus ad Parnassum* (the title, referencing traditional textbooks for beginners suggests a progression towards some pinnacle), the poem also opens up the issue and indicates a new option (or 'gradus'). If we take the initial verses literally, then the language of the poem should not only name things, but directly bear and embody sensory qualities, be 'like the skin, salty-tasting'. Yet, taken literally, such a requirement cannot be met, albeit this criss-crossing of the linguistic with the sensory lies at the core of Součková's poetry. In addition, the saltiness motif links the piece with the immediately following *Great Autumn*.

III

The *Ex Ponto* section is made up of four poems. The *Great Autumn* is a kind of more general prologue, followed by three poems dedicated to three persons, each introduced by a motto from Ovid's *Epistulae ex Ponto*, just as is the entire section. The formal framework suggests that these poems are meant to repre-

---

16   Ibid., p. 126. In this poem, the male gender of the speaker is revealed by the appelation 'my concubine', but both the characters are very vague, and the 'concubine' in some respects evokes a personification of poetry. – As to the poem cf. K. Suda: Exil a svět v poválečné tvorbě Milady Součkové, pp. 69–70.

sent letters addressed from exile. Indeed, the 'addressees' are salient: The first is Jindřich Chalupecký, who sent Součková a carefully worded letter in 1948 whereby he broke off contact with her – but the poem testifies to a deeper relationship between them. Later, in 1967, Součková renewed correspondence with Chalupecký, sending him her texts.[17] The second poem is dedicated to Ivan Blatný, at that time lost somewhere in distant England, whom Součková valued as a poet and befriended (there is a surviving long letter from Blatný to Součková sent from Claybury Hall in November 1948).[18] The third of the poems bears a dedication to Z. Rykr, the husband of Milada Součková who died in January 1940. In all cases, the addressees are distant and beyond reach, in the last case, absolutely so.[19] No less significant are the quotes themselves. In the poem dedicated to Chalupecký (*Fort George*), Součková seems as if renewing their interrupted conversation, from afar: *"Accipe conloquium gelido Nasonis ab Histro, / Attice, iudicio non dubitante meo".*[20] In the poem to Ivan Blatný *Na pražském předměstí* [In a Prague Suburb], it seems to evoke the shared fate of a poet in exile: *"ad laetum carmen vix mea versa lyra est".*[21] The third poem recalls the constant presence of her late husband in her mind: *"ante oculos nostros posita est tua semper imago".*[22] The trio of poems-letters can stand comparison with Blatný's poems, in which he elicits distant and dead friends and celebrities. Like him, Součková perceives the place of exile as remote from everything

---

17   cf. S. Hadžagić: *Paměť v exilu*, p. 37.

18   cf. I. Blatný: *Texty a dokumenty*, pp. 240–248. Chalupecký's letter is kept as part of the literary estate of Milada Součková in the LA PNP, Blatný's letter also as part of his estate ibid.; After Součková's death, it came out in the exile magazine *Proměny* in 1989.

19   The choice of addressees also suggests drawing a parallel between exile and death, something already done by Ovid, a constant presence in Ivan Blatný's work. Součková lists them in a letter dated 1956 (cited *in extenso* in Chapter 1): 'The living are like the dead to us,' *Élenty*, p. 366.

20   Ovid: *Ex Ponto*, II, 4, 1–2: 'Let Naso converse with you from the freezing Hister, Atticus, friend whom judgment should not doubt'. Ovid: *Tristia. Ex Ponto*, p. 339.

21   Ibid., III, 4, 46, p. 401: 'my lyre [...] could scarcely turn to a song of rejoicing'.

22   Ibid., II, 4, 7, p. 339: 'before my eyes your image ever stands'. The entire *Ex Ponto* section opens with this quote: *"Naso Tomitanae iam non novus incola terrae / hoc tibi de Getico litore mittis opus"* – 'Naso, no recent dweller now in the land of Tomis, sends to you this work from the Getic shore' (*Ex Ponto*, I, 1, 1–2, p. 265), Součková contemplated Ovid while in exile, as confirmed by her letters with Latin quotes, *Élenty*, pp. 199, 356–8. Both the letters, the first to Olga and Ladislav Radimský, the second to Otakar Odložilík, date from January 1956, which may broadly correspond to the poems' inception timeframe.

and everyone. Yet she approaches separation and remoteness from almost the opposite angle – to her, exile is not a place or a condition that allows everything a paradoxical immediacy, the distance of exile can be overcome through the medium of poetry, but never annulled, and, in keeping with all of Součková's poetry, a poem is a means and a way of overcoming this distance. Corresponding to this is the format suggestive of a letter, and if we consider the motif from the dedication to Chalupecký, the chilly Danube of Ovid's topography evokes the realm of the dead, from which there is no return.

Yet the letter represents only an external format by which to span distance, and it is only within this framework that Součková develops her technique, heralded by the opening poem of the *Ex Ponto* section. This is remarkably embodied in the final poem dedicated to Zdeněk Rykr:[23]

> Letní vítr čechrá platanové listí
> na náměstíčku vytvořeném Brodwayí
> letní vítr v červnu, v neděli
> obrací na rub listy lipoví
> pohybem, světly letních nedělí
> jímž čechrá, hladí trávy v poříčí
> Hudsonu, Labe, Seiny, Vltavy
> tím štětcem v plátno letních nedělí
> pohybem, kterým vlaje prapory.

> A summer breeze ruffles the sycamore leaves
> on the small square bounded by the Broadway
> a summer wind, in June, and on a Sunday
> flips overleaf the leaves of linden trees
> with its strokes, with light Summer Sunday glints
> while ruffling, caresses the grassy riverbanks
> of the Hudson, Elbe, Seine, the Vltava
> with that brush on the canvas of Summer Sundays
> with its strokes, serving to make the pennants wave[24]

---

23   The painterly motifs in the poem refer to the fact that Zdeněk Rykr was an artist.

24   M. Součková: *Případ poezie*, p. 134.

There are some subtle shifts between the two poems. In the *Great Autumn*, the spirit of poetry or art permeates everything, it is in a gust of wind, in footsteps and finally in the materials of a Renaissance painting. In the poem dedicated to Zdeněk Rykr, the action is transferred to the breeze blowing and becoming visible to the observer: 'when summer wind in June and on a Sunday / turns with its brush the grass over the graves', yet both poems retain an important relationship to painting. The spirit in the first poem manifests itself in various things in various places, converging on the Mediterranean and Italy, and the ultimate connecting link comes to be art, as that which embodies or captures such a spirit 'in cypress boards erstwhile in quinquecento'. In the second poem, the wind first shows itself in a particular place and time, but then evokes associations of various places that the same wind blows through, and manifests itself with an artistic, aesthetic effect: 'while ruffling, caresses the grassy riverbanks / of the Hudson, Elbe, Seine, the Vltava / with that brush on the canvas of Summer Sundays'. Contrary to some hints of scepticism in the *Linguistic Ode*, there is an obvious shift here: only art, in the paradigm of painting, can preserve and pass-on sensory values, conveying in time and space a remote impression or experience. The material of art itself and the overtness of that medium notwithstanding; the material is also not just the bearer, but a participant in the effect. As the sensory values are made aesthetic, the art medium transitions into the matter-of-fact plane of perception, and the one stands next to the other. Summer Sunday turns into a canvas, and the spirit of art permeates reality. Součková develops this 'aestheticization' technique in a number of aspects in her other books. In the *Pastoral Suite*, the all-pervasive element is music: it is present in the evoked scenes, it penetrates through ordinary sounds and visual perceptions and makes them aesthetic:

Na tržišti
mezi stánky
tenory, basy
jarní zeleniny
z balkonu opery
mandolíny!

In the market
between stalls
tenors, basses

of fresh spring greens
from the opera box
mandolins![25]

The backdrop of this collection, as the name suggests, is an idyll largely set in Czech countryside in an indeterminate idealized past. The sounds heard, turning into music and lingering in the scene as if made tangible, evoke the timelessness of the pastoral scene:

v tichu zahrady
v jilmu zašumí
v jedli hvizd ptačí
v trávě svist kosy
v trámech stodoly
sluneční svity
pálí letopočty

in the calm garden
in the elm a rustling
in the fir tree a bird squawk
in the grass a scythe swish
in the barn on the timbers
sunlight with its light beams
branding-in calendar dates[26]

The following collection, *Alla Romana* (1966) is dedicated to Italy. During her exile, Součková made two trips to Italy, and they left a permanent mark on her poetry – there are sections related to Italy also in *The Case of Poetry* and *The Workbooks of Josefína Rykrová*. Součková first visited Italy in 1960, when she received a Guggenheim Scholarship, and while in Italy took an active interest in the time spent there by Jaroslav Vrchlický, about whom she was writing a book.[27]

---

25   Ibid., p. 199.
26   Ibid., p. 188.
27   cf. M. Součková: *The Parnassian Jaroslav Vrchlický*, p. 5.

She made her second trip in March 1976.[28] There are even earlier Italian motifs in her poems in connection with Goethe, with whose journey she compares her own: 'I also wrote, every day: verses [...] and, of course, my own Italienische Reise – with drawings, too!!'[29] The poem *Gradus ad Parnassum II* from the first exile collection describes a visit to Goethe's house in Weimar.[30] Like many other poems, it features an understated observer who shows his persona only in subtle hints about his designs: 'perhaps the doorman will yet open up'. In other respects, the poem is descriptive: approaching Goethe's house through the Harz landscape, walking around and going in. The first part is evocative of a summer landscape, nature and the park around the house. Some of the motifs ('the greenhouses have dried up') gently give the impression of dilapidation, which the interior makes plain in full: 'inside is emptiness, the salons / are without sofas, tables, chairs'. The art objects kept in the house seem to be stuck in some living past:

> jen na zlomených sloupech mramory
> klasické rysy apollinské hlavy
> napojeny září letních odpolední
> v tom míru, jenž se snáší z pohoří,
> mramorovým uchem lastury
> naslouchá Lisztově rapsodii
> tou lyrou kterou drží v ruce
> uťaté od ramene hlavy

> only on broken columns marbles
> the classic features of the head of Apollo
> filled with the glow of summer afternoons

---

28   'I was in Italy in March. One week in Rome, two in Sicily, in Taormina. It is still pastoral there, I liked the lemon groves the most,' *Élenty*, p. 486, to Oldřich Leška, 6 July 1976. Poems inspired by this journey appear in the third section of *The Workbooks of Josefína Rykrová*.

29   M. Součková: *Élenty*, p. 399, letter to Otakar Odložilík, 27 June 1960. Some of the drawings related to Italy were included by the editors in the post-exile editions of *The Workbooks of Josefína Rykrová*.

30   Another reminiscence of the trip to Weimar is the poem 'Harz Zween Satyri' in *The Workbooks of Josefína Rykrová*, where Součková writes [in English]: "It was beautiful June day. We went to Goethe's House; it was already late in afternoon and we were the only visitors. The year was 1934," *Sešity Josefíny Rykrové*, pp. 84–85.

in that peace that drifts down from the mountains,
the sea shell's marble earlobe
listening to Liszt's Rhapsody
through the lyre he's holding in the hand
of the head severed from the shoulder

The poem's ending relates the motifs of abandonment and absence to Goethe. The house feels empty and deserted due to his absence, he is the would-be giver of life to the exhibits and art objects.

Zpeřené listy přerostly
z morfologie nazpět do zahrady,
za skly etruské zlato, horniny
z italské cesty, římských elegií.
Zřítelnice mramorových očí
po slepu židli hledají
kde stávala, vykládaná perletí,
zde byla pohovka, zde stály svícny
prsty v prázdnu hmatají – odejeli
do Teplic, do Mariánských Lázní?
EGO ETIAM IN ARCADIA...

The feathered leaves have overgrown
out of morphology and back into the garden,
behind glass Etruscan gold, rock minerals
from the Italian Journey, Roman elegies.
The pupils of marble eyes
blindly look for a chair
where it used to stand, inlaid with pearl,
here was the sofa, here the candelabras
fingers grope emptiness – have they moved on
to Teplitz-Schönau, to Marienbad?
EGO ETIAM IN ARCADIA...[31]

---

31   M. Součková: *Případ poezie*, p. 142.

The last line is a variation on the traditional Latin inscription *Et in Arcadia ego*, but also Goethe's German motto from the Italian Journey *Auch ich in Arcadien!* The *etiam* that Součková provides in the sense of 'still' connects Goethe, as the absentee actor of the poem, with Italy. For the first time in the whole poem, first-person speech is heard, and this *ego* thus revealed draws in the poem's speaker, making Arcadia-Italy the reference space of the whole poem. Italy is featured here as a land of art, like in the *Great Autumn* poem, and quite contrary to contemporary America.

The poems of *Alla Romana* evoke various images of the past bound up with Italy. The basic element on which the evocation stands is the sensory experience, linking the imaginary rather than the historical past with the present. *"Memory relies on the sensual element,"* writes Součková [in English] in her book on Vrchlický. As regards Vrchlický's poetic memoirs of Italy, she goes on to point out: *"It is not the power of memory over the poet as Proust wanted it, but the power of poetry over the memory to which Vrchlický's* Vzpomínka z jihu *testifies."*[32] Something akin to this applies to her own poems, with the corollary that for Součková, evoking the past is almost a given. In some poems, she follows in the footsteps of her predecessors (Goethe, Zeyer[33]) and connects places with their former presence or present absence: 'He lived here, upstairs, apparently'.[34] Sometimes the absence of the poet in here-and-now reality is precisely the point from which her poem unfolds:

> V šumu vodotrysku *aquatici*
> *mostricciuoli* dovádějí
> na Janiculu maňásci
> své nesmrtelné drama hrají
> bez Goetha, bez Génia křesťanství.
> Torquato Tasso, Múz tiburských med
> a mantovanských vlil mu do šalmaje
> maňásci si šalmaj vypůjčili
> pro *primavèra*, pro děti
> ve vzduchu šumí, v Poussinově modři.

---

32   M. Součková: *The Parnassian Jaroslav Vrchlický*, pp. 26–27.

33   Julius Zeyer (1841–1901) was a Czech prose writer, poet, and playwright.

34   M. Součková: *Případ poezie*, p. 210.

In the fount's spuming whoosh the *aquatici*
mostriciattoli are frolicking
on Janiculum hilltop glove puppets
play out their immortal drama
without Goethe, without the Genius of Christianity.
Torquato Tasso poured honey of Tiburtine
and Mantovani Muses into his shawm reed-pipe
the glove puppets have since borrowed his shawm
for the *primavèra*, for the children
the air is spuming, full of Poussin blue. [35]

At other times, Součková turns to the Christian past (the closing poems) or to works of art (some poems of the section *Per imagines et per verba*). Art, tied to sensory experience, is always the backdrop on which her evocations unfold. Art is the element that can renew the past in the experiential plane.

IV

The exile poems of Milada Součková feature very few asides or innuendo as to the then political and social situation. That is not the case in her earlier works. *Neznámý člověk* [Unknown Man] testifies, as a witness, about key events in Czech history, and three texts from 1938–1939 – *Kaladý, Svědectví, Mluvící pásmo* [Kaladý, Testimony, Talking Zone] – commenting on a critical period of Czech history. In her chronicle *Testimony*, Součková records the events of 1939 and speaks quite openly about them.[36] She repeats several times that she is going to stop writing her journal notes, although she still returns to them, the main reason being a mistrust of the written word:

In these last days I've been reading a modern German novel (von Mechow). It is a nicely, it could almost be said, modernly written

---

35   Ibid., p. 211.
36   In a preface written after the war, she speaks of her then fears that the manuscript might be discovered by the Germans.

book. But how dead every word of it is, how stillborn. Because it is written in the language of a nation that has dedicated words to lies and locked them up behind bars. [...] I want to keep quiet about it and think about living words. About words through which to express an idea of use to everyone.[37]

More final-sounding are her sentences dealing not so much about the deceit of 'the word' become untruth, but the need for something else right now, for words to be reborn as deeds:

I feel that this chronicle, in which feelings, thoughts and words are raging, is now closed. The time is night when words shall become deeds. I summon that time; I want to invoke it with my words.[38]

Milada Součková, although very little has been said about it, was active in the anti-Nazi resistance movement, and so we can take her written remark quite literally.[39] Her *Testimony* represents an exceptionally open and unstylized text within her body of work, which the author did not even consider a 'work of art', but attributed to it the worth of a 'true and first-hand account'.[40] All three texts, including the slightly later *Unknown Person*, indicate how intensely she was experiencing events, as an engrossed participant. After the war and going into exile, Součková's attitude or mood fundamentally changes, and an interest in things to do with memory comes to the fore (although that is by no means a novel side to her). Milada Součková's last political act is her documented resignation from her diplomatic post in New York.[41]

All of Součková's exile collections connect the foundations of poetry with the past, the *Pastoral Suite* and *Alla Romana* find it in music and art; in Milada Součková's fourth exile collection, *The Case of Poetry*, attention turns to the

---

37   M. Součková: *Kaladý, Svědectví, Mluvící pásmo*, p. 158.

38   Ibid., p. 159.

39   She hints at her participation in the resistance in a memoir about Vladislav Vančura, M. Součková: In memoriam Vladislava Vančury.

40   M. Součková: *Kaladý, Svědectví, Mluvící pásmo*, p. 19. This presages to some extent the post-war diary texts of Jiří Kolář.

41   cf. Czech Diplomats Resign, *New York Times*, May 7, 2015 /PR/ (1948) p. 13; reproduced by S. Hadžagić: *Paměť v exilu*, p. 189.

nature of the poetic language and what it is founded on, is given more complex guise in the *Linguistic Ode*, since the present also enters the scene as the starting or entry point of the poem. Here too, there is a change of perspective compared to the active interest in things before her exile. Now, Součková faces her present-day world as a stranger, without a place in it.

In the poem *Apollo* she evokes futuristic poetry invoking modern technology, from there it moves to the destruction of the present world through modern technologies and weapons, and holds up in contrast a certain idyll associated with poetry before the World Wars:

> že v umění plyn nerozslzí?
> hmat prsty nespálí, bez chuti?
> neusmrtí choré smysly?
> volný verš, Whitmanem okouzlený
> měl ještě na zahrádce bezy
> nesežrané chemickými louhy
> atom ještě nebyl rozbitý
> slyšel déšť jak myje listí
> přilévá dlaní vodu do nádržky
> v dešti, zašeptaly konifery
> Whitman, Marinetti naslouchali.

> will gas not bring on tears, in art?
> will touch not scald, and taste go bland?
> be the death, end of ailing senses?
> free-form verse, as by Whitman enchanted
> who in his garden still had elder bushes
> unseared by chemicals and lye
> the atom being then as yet unsmashed
> he listened to the rain washing the leaves
> with palm-held water topping up the cistern
> in the rain, as the conifers were whispering
> Whitman, Marinetti listening.[42]

---

42   M. Součková: *Případ poezie*, p. 289.

The past tense at the end of the poem is less typical of Součková than the present, characterizing the distance between the past, in which verses and the world were in harmony, and the present, in which order in the world is shaken to the core ('the atom being then as yet unsmashed'). The last four verses evoke the harmony between the listening poet and the world at the sensory level. In addition to the older poems around the *Ex Ponto* section, in which American exile was portrayed as an alien place, now all of the here-and-now appears to be a foreign land, not geographically, but due to the historical events of the 20th century. These set an epoch in which the nature of the world no longer corresponds to what the senses may perceive.

Součková also returns to her present-day goings-on in the poem *V srpnu* [in August] with the subtitle "(1968)", which evidently corresponds to the August occupation of Czechoslovakia by Warsaw Pact armies. The poem is set in the typical rural environment of other Milada Součková poems and does not contain any direct references to events, yet indirectly refers to them very clearly: via several connected motifs of a conflagration, St. Florian (the patron saint of firefighters) and geese on the Capitol:

> den celý v ohni
> Florián potlučený
> nejasně vzkazy tlumočí
> jez, splav ho překřičí
> z mlýna husy zaječí
> prý kapitol je v nebezpečí.

> the whole day on fire
> Florian brow-beaten,
> passing on muffled messages, obtuse
> is the weir, outshouted by the sluice
> from the mill the sound of honking geese
> claiming the Capitol endangered is[43]

---

43   Ibid., p. 304.

In a depopulated scene, the backdrop loses its idyllic nature, people are passing each other by, and the alarmed honking of the geese is stifled by the roaring weir; the last verse lacks urgency, as if it were just hearsay. As in the poem *Apollo*, the event shifts to a plane beyond human comprehension, into the conflagration of the day.

The third of the poems, *Žluť, modrá, zelenavá, sieny* [Yellow, Blue, Greenish Hue, Siennas], which has the contemporary world in its sights, takes art as its theme. In the first part, Součková develops the image of a mosaic in which the stones shine with all the colours of the world, as retained from their original, natural place, and through sensory sensations still preserving this original or earlier state of the world. The live sensations are kept in play by the transition between the natural state and a work of art, both states co-existing in the minds of the onlookers, and from the perspective of the present day indeed enlightening the eyes of the audience:

> Kostky mozaiky než se složily
> v pobřežním písku svítily
> žluť, modrá, zelenavá, sieny
> i nejsytější barva v závoji
> mořské pěny, v zobrazení
> zázraku San Marco na náměstí
> dnes světla oči promítají
> obrazy na sítnici, kostky
> v obraz tehdy nesložený
> zelené, modré, žluté, sieny
> spojeny v obraz uctívaný

> ∎

> Mosaic cubes before they were arrayed
> shone out of coastal sand there laid
> yellow, blue, greenish hue, siennas
> even the strongest colour in the veil
> of sea foam, in the portrayal, rendition
> of the miracle in the piazza San Marco
> today lights up the eyes as they're projecting
> images on the retina, those cubes
> into a picture back then unassembled

of green, of blue, of yellow and sienna
combining into a revered depiction

In this game, nature, that is, the original state, mixes with art, that is, culture, and the one predicates the other – nature adds sensory vibrancy, culture provides a framework and the subject of perception. In images such as 'the eye-siennas' Součková blends both into an inseparable amalgam, draws one state into another, the ideal past of nature into the era of culture:

sieny očí s příbojem si hrály
s kaménky, v závoji mořské pěny
než je ruce k sobě přitáhly
přivinuly, v stěnu promítly
u toho pobřeží jsme oba stáli
v pláštích na benátském náměstí

the eye-siennas with the surf did play
with those small stones, in a sea foam veil
before hands drew them up, gathered, collected
closely embraced, and on the wall projected
that shore by which the two of us did stand
wearing raincoats on the Venetian square

Into the temporal layers of the poem now encroach sensitive people, whose experiencing references the past: not to the pre-cultural state of nature, but a past of personal history, a subjective epoch of unsullied perception. The game of nature and culture within this framework in its own way becomes akin to a bygone state or event, added to which is one more layer of the here-and-now:

tehdy jsme, ach, spolu nešli
hustým mlázím, u stolu nejedli
z dubové, vyhlazené desky,
Ruskin, Butor? Lloyd Trieste
na laguně slupka od ovoce
žluť, modrá, zelenavá, sieny
kostky slov pevné, bez hnutí.

> back then, oh, we did not go together,
> through dense young brushwood, nor ate at a table
> made of a polished board of solid oak
> Ruskin, Butor? Lloyd Trieste
> on the lagoon the floating peel of fruit
> yellow, blue, tint of green, sienna
> dice of words firmly fixed, quite motionless.[44]

At the end of the poem, the present seems immobile ('dice of words firmly fixed') and a washed-out condition (peel on the lagoon). The turning point comes pre-announced by the crucial verse, made up of the three names. Both Ruskin and Butor are authors of books on Venice and its works of art, and belong to those upholding the vibrant tradition of art dating back to the primal, natural state of colours.[45] Contrary to the questioning mention of both names, we see the name of the shipping company Lloyd Trieste, which Součková may have seen in the Venetian lagoon. That name represents the present and complements the dirty lagoon awash with rotten fruit. In contrast with the beginning of the poem, where the unarrayed 'mosaic cubes' shine in vivid colours, at the end the colours are 'dice of words' and instead of being taken up with intermediaries in the course of time, it is commercial shipping of the present day that grabs attention. As in the Apollo poem, the present is detached from the even quite recent past in which art was still alive. Ultimately, the here-and-now is posited as colourless, rigid and isolated.

With the exception of the group of poems from the section *Ex Ponto*, Součková does not draw attention to her exile nor explicitly opens up the exile topic.[46] Yet, in her collection *The Case of Poetry* she depicts the present time as

---

44   Ibid., pp. 357–358.

45   John Ruskin: *The Stones of Venice* I–III (1851–1853), Michel Butor: *Description de San Marco* (1963).

46   In Součková's written estate are typescripts of two unpublished poems, which are more open in that direction. Both express a certain mistrust in the scope of art in the present, which could date them to around the time of the Linguistic Ode in *Gradus ad Parnassum*, but another poem from the same file and on the same paper bears the more likely date of 1981. The first of the poems begins with these verses: 'You'll never manage to do it / perhaps just in the mind / to cross that border, boundary / that people vanish behind / you had been living with them, / what will you say then, what?', the second: 'No, it is pointless / to speak, to write verses / except maybe Homer, on Troy / not behind Stromovka park. / Odysseus did make it home / and so

some place where one is in exile from art and the living culture which propagates said art and maintains its connection with primal impulses. Compared to the poems from the 1950s that referred to the Ovidian space of *de facto* exile, in *The Case of Poetry* the place of exile is not just America, nor is it about exile from a place, but rather, time. In this, Součková approaches the Baudelaire type of exile and presages her particular idea of an aestheticized utopia.

The motif of guides and mediators, represented in the cited poem by Ruskin and Butor is further developed in the Dante-attuned poem *E quindi uscimmo a riveder le stelle*. In it the central motif of the stars is represented by the convergence point of poetry, currently lost or obscured:

> O hvězdy ochudili poezii
> jen v písničce se zatřpytí,
> tu vyšli jsme a spatřili zas hvězdy
> hledejte svící ve dne v noci
> skřípe to, chrastí bez myšlenky
> zrůdy se rodí z utrpení
> leč vyšli, spatřili zas hvězdy
> verš, slovo, nápěv, obrazy?
> v sedmdesátých letech poezie?

> Star-impoverished they have made poetry
> only in a song do they sparkle now
> we went out and beheld once more the stars
> seek out the candles lit by day by night
> life screeches, rattles given lack of thought
> out of the suffering are monsters born
> but emerged, once again they saw the stars
> a verse, a word, a melody, images?
> in the seventies, poetry, seriously?[47]

---

enabled the Odyssey, / Hugo wrote after returning from exile / (he didn't say emigration) / one thing for him to write "allons", "la patrie" / it is pointless today.'

47   M. Součková: *Případ poezie*, p. 383.

The motif of stars does, however, connect together more meanings – the stars are a constant light, linked with a vibrancy akin to the colours of the previous poem, and associate with Dante and through him to the poetic tradition that conveys such values. Součková also borrows from Dante her key motif of being guided, much as many poet-Exiles before her have invoked their poetic predecessors. But for Součková the guide is not only the one leading the way in exile, but also one who can lead out of it. In this poem, Dante, one of the emblematic poet-Exiles, fills this role, becoming a guide for Jaroslav Vrchlický, his translator into Czech, as well as a poet, in turn followed by Součková.[48] Yet Dante is not a guide just in the sense of a figure mentioned in a poem, but above all through his poetic works. It is his verses that allow the stars to be seen:

> kde Vrchlickému průvodcem je Dante
> žasne, až pozdě ví, kde chybily
> Múzy honosné jeho století
> zláká, kam se všichni hrnuli
> však přece jednou uzřel hvězdy
> vzhlížeje k básnickému mistrovství
> v té noci, básník veden básníky
> kdy verše v úctě vidí hvězdy.

> whereas for Vrchlický the guide is Dante
> he marvels, knows too late, just where they erred
> the ostentatious Muses of his century
> he tempts, to where all others just rushed in
> but yet there was that time he saw the stars
> looking up to poetic mastery
> that night, a poet guided by the poets
> when in their awe the verses see the stars[49]

---

48 Vrchlický also wrote a poem in which he likens the position of the poet to Ovid's exile (see Chapter 1, p. 30).

49 M. Součková: *Případ poezie*, p. 384.

The guide theme is also brought up in the first of a pair of poems, called *Kanzona*. The title and Dante motto (*O voi che per la via d'Amor passate*) clearly points to the tradition of Italian love poetry. Within Milada Součková's body of work, this takes up the rarer stance of a speaker of feminine gender, which hints at some unknown love story in the background.[50] The 'Poetess' is addressing an absent and distant man, and uses verses to evoke his thought image:

> Podej mi ruku Karle
> pojď se mnou verši v řeči
> [...]
> podej mi ruku k poezii
> radosti mých očí, dost už hry
> kde smysly barvy rozvíří
> pojď se mnou v poezii myšlenky
> v úzkosti, zmatku mysli
> tvar nevidíš, slovo beze zvuku
> verš úsměv bez doteku
> jen obraz tvůj v mé mysli
> srdcem hne aniž tě vidí

> Lend me your hand, Karel
> come with me through verse to language
> [...]
> lend me your hand toward poetry
> the joys of my eyes, end the game
> where the senses just stir up the colours
> join me in thought-minded poetry
> in anxiety, turmoil of mind
> see no shape, nor word without sound
> a verse as a smile without touch
> only your image in my mind's eye
> moves the heart without your being seen

---

50   In its tone, the poem resembles a similar backstory as the *Žlutý soumrak* [Yellow Twilight] collection, as Kristián Suda writes.

For Součková, an exceptionally overt love poem combines feeling with the power of poetry. In this case, speech works in the opposite direction than the fixed 'dice of words', becoming the means to bring a person to vivid memories:

> Den, jen žádné vzpomínky
> říkáš: nepamatuji, jinde žijí
> napsané v kterékoli řeči
> to nezapomeň, Karle, v onom kraji
> pro něž mají slova: v ráji,
> jen v pekle jazyky jsou zmateny

> A day, just no reminiscences
> you say: I don't recall, they're living elsewhere
> written in whatever language
> don't ever forget Karel, in that some-land
> for which they have words: in Paradise,
> only in Hell are the tongues all confused[51]

Poetry is, according to this poem, the language of Paradise, verse being the form that gives sight, as in the close of the cited poem: 'when in their awe the verses see the stars'.

The Case of Poetry concludes with the poem *Brána k Východu* [The Gate to the East], which also completes the arc outlined in the last section of the collection. This arc stretches from living nature, through art and its tradition to the present world, deprived of poetry, and from it through the motifs of poetry and guides on to the poetic Utopia of the language of Paradise and to the East. It is in the figures of guides that a substantial poetic operation takes place. The poet-as-guide is metonymically bound to their verses and shows the way by means of them.

---

51   M. Součková: ibid., pp. 377–378.

V

Milada Součková in her exile body of work developed her own special versification technique.[52] The outcome is particularly seen in *The Workbooks of Josefína Rykrová* a typical dactylo-trochaic verse, which, unlike the common norm of Czech verse, is not syllabotonic, but instead more tonal, based on the number of stresses. Součková compares the forming of verses with weaving and her loose syllabic framework can give the impression of a canvas unrestricted by a solid outer frame:

> Obraz tkaniny
> trocheji tkaný daktyly
> v karmínu zlatém protkaný
> hedvábím bourců

> An image of fabric
> of trochees woven with dactyls
> in crimson with gold interwoven
> with the silk of the mulberry moths[53]

In *The Case of Poetry*, this type of verse is often supplemented by working with a bidirectional enjambment, in which the indented word grammatically fits two verses, yet which are not related to the plane of one testimony, but rather act in parallel. This creates a condensed expression that makes it difficult to read some passages at times, but it also allows words and images from different planes to merge. This type of verse does on the one hand maintain a certain form, but in addition evokes the constant overreaching of frames, also manifested by a reversibility between sensory perception, and art, as if only art was able to keep past perceptions alive and preserve nature within culture.

---

52   Several sketches with notes on the form of verses, the number of syllables in Součková's written estate also testify to a cohesive concept.

53   M. Součková: *Sešity Josefíny Rykrové*, p. 12.

The poetic works of Milada Součková conclude with the extensive collection *The Workbooks of Josefína Rykrová*, written during the last years of her life. One of the keys to it lies in the finale of *The Case of Poetry*. The poem *The Gate to the East* presents the motif of entering poetry, which for Součková is linked with the rapture of Paradise that poetry is able to draw from memory and cognisance:

Zlatou bránu střeží
Golden Gate
na svitku paměti
Connaîsance de l'Est
poznání básnictví.
Z horniny, hloubi
vzduté ostrovy
pteroplazů kůstky
z doby, kdy byli anděly,
stromy rajští ptáci
palmy, eukalypty zelení
drahokamů dosud hrají

The gold-gate sentry
Golden Gate
on a scroll of memory
Connaîsance de l'Est
unearthing poetry.
From the bedrock, deep
emergent islands
bonelets of pterosaurs
from the time they were angels,
trees birds of paradise
palms, eucalyptus greens
of gemstones as ever still playing

The central motif of the poem is an entranceway into poetry, which is symbolized precisely by the Golden Gate. Entering through it are Teilhard de Chardin or (consular officer) Paul Claudel as guides, and at the end of the poem, the speaker is also preparing to do so:

kněz (Teilhard de Chardin?)
snad úředník konzulární
Zlatou branou prochází
střízlivě v poezii.
[...]
válečná loď v přístavu kotví
předkům mého rodu světla rozžíhají
v loďce tančí v stínu Zlaté brány
v hodině zlaté,
dej mi projít.

a priest (Teilhard de Chardin?)
or perhaps a consular officer
pass through the Golden Gate
sober in poetry.
[...]
in the port lies a warship at anchor
to my ancestors raising a light
who dance in a boat in the Golden Gate's shade
in that golden hour,
let me pass through.[54]

In her letter to Jindřich Chalupecký of 13 September 1972 Součková mentions
some motifs not unrelated to this poem:

> [...] it was beautiful there, an earthly paradise [...] But what caught
> my eye the most was that daily view of San Francisco bay, the Golden
> Gate. I kept thinking about Claudel, Teilhard de Chardin and my
> mother (she came by here on her journey around the world) [...]
> Especially in the summer, I often think about back home. [...] and
> I see that undulation of the land around Bechyně circulus Bechy-

---

54   M. Součková: *Případ poezie*, pp. 386–389.

nenais – above the Lužnice river valley, to Kristle [...]. Where am
I more at home? There or by the Golden Gate? In poetry?[55]

Her most important guide is Paul Claudel, who also appears in the *Workbooks*. In a fictional scene in the poem *Sometime at the end of January*, Claudel
meets some godparents on the steps of a church who are carrying a child in
for baptism, and he inadvertently picks up the role of another godfather, introducing Josefína Rykrová to art.[56] The poem rests on the complex interplay
of multiple times and places: Claudel was actually active in Prague (but only
a few years after the birth of Milada Součková) and he knew and admired the
Church of Our Lady of Victory, where Součková was baptized; and likewise,
both poets lived awhile in Boston: 'We missed each other in Boston, too.'[57] The
poem cites Latin passages from the Easter liturgy and thus likens the baptism of
the child to the baptismal vow made by adults; one's birth, to one's commitment
to poetry. The poem *The Gate to the East* also adds to the theme with a reference
to Claudel's famous book, *Connaîsance de l'Est*.

The *Workbooks* give one possible answer to the question 'Where am I more
at home?': Josefína Rykrová[58] is a kind of heteronym of Součková, her alter
ego living only in the sphere of poetry. We can well imagine that it was indeed
exile that brought the crystallization of this question and as such an answer to
it, i.e. an attempt to properly separate civil life, which includes the publication
of poems, and an imaginary poetic existence in which boundaries in space and
time can be crossed that would remain impenetrable in the normal world.

---

55   M. Součková: *Élenty*, pp. 110–111.
56   M. Součková: *Sešity Josefíny Rykrové*, pp. 29–30. I dealt with this poem in detail in *Poezie
      a kosmos*, pp. 120–123; also cf. M. Němcová Banerjee: *Sešity Josefiny Rykrové*.
57   M. Součková: ibid., p. 300.
58   The Rykrová surname resembles that of Milada Součková's husband, being also her unused
      civil name, cf. *Élenty*, pp. 333. Josefína is the first name of Milada Součková's grandmother, Jose-
      fína Horová, cf. M. Němcová Banerjee: ibid., p. 36.

8. Ivan Diviš and Leaving Bohemia

I

Going into exile is one of the defining elements in an outcast's story. It is not always crucial to exile poetry, but once the idea of leaving turns into the notion of exile, it gives the topology of exile tangible concrete form, with the chief role played by a directionality, toward or away from the homeland. Leaving is not only a prelude to separation and life elsewhere, but also creates a specific connection to home, sometimes even demonstratively so, when the exile turns their departure into a judgemental gesture about their homeland. In Czech poetry, the theme came to life after the occupation of Czechoslovakia in August 1968. The coming of foreign troops and the tightening-up of the relatively liberal situation of the late 1960s to a softer version of totalitarianism, as well as the bringing back of censorship[1] prompted a number of literati to emigrate. In this situation, the theme of leaving stands in pronounced opposition and as a counterweight to the arrival of foreigners who are taking hold of the country, as well as a response to the deference of those compliant with the new circumstances.

---

1   After censorship let-up somewhat in the 1960s and was in effect abolished at the end of the decade, the works of some exiled authors were published in the then Czechoslovakia (Ivan Blatný, Egon Hostovský, Jan Čep, Ivan Jelínek, Zdeněk Němeček; cf. M. Wögerbauer et al.: *V obecném zájmu* II, p. 1159). After the Soviet occupation, censorship was progressively reintroduced, a number of magazines ceased to publish and book publishing was greatly curtailed, the publication of many upcoming books stopped altogether. As to post-1968 censorship cf. ibid., p. 1161ff.

Now it is not just about escaping the country from the Communist regime, as in 1948, when it was indeed a matter of life or death for many Exiles, but above all, this is a statement of taking a stand, of dissent, and a breaking-away from those who have occupied the country and seized power. In the exile poetry tradition, this is another case where linking with predecessors fills a great need: Ovid compares himself to Aeneus fleeing Troy, thus assigning his departure the weight of a significant event and imbuing his own person with significance.

In Roman poetry, the theme appears more often, and some of these texts represent an important inspirational source and moment of comparison for later poetry. In addition to Ovid's Tristia I.3, quoted by Goethe at the end of his *Italian Journey*, Virgil's first Eclogue is important, and also worth a mention is Horace's *Epode 16*. In each of these poems, departure has a different meaning. Virgil's Eclogue, as Curtius points out, is one of the basic texts of Western education, indeed 'one key to the literary tradition of Europe'.[2] The poem consists of a dialogue between two shepherds, Meliboeus and Tityrus. The first of these is leaves his homeland after the triumvirate splits the land of former owners among their veteran soldiers, Tityrus, who did not forfeit his property, devotedly expresses gratitude to Octavian (who is not directly named). The Eclogue reflects to some extent Virgil's own fates (the poet also lost his farm, which was returned to him after an intercession), but in the *Eclogues* everything is situated in Arcadia, and historical events and the political situation are reflected in this scene only obliquely. Arcadia in the *Eclogues*, unlike the landscapes of the idylls of Theocritus, as Charles Paul Segal writes in the wake of Bruno Snell's landmark study, represents a completely artificial world. While the contemporary political reality has remained completely out of the frame for Theocritus, the Arcadia of Virgil is, on the other hand, touched by a whole series of motifs that recall the fragility of this poetic world.[3] While Virgil does not show unequivocal political preferences, in the dialogue his sympathies are more on the side of the departing Meliboeus,[4] and in view of the political situation this rather underscores the helplessness of poetry and the songs falling silent during the civil war.[5] Meliboeus' lament at

---

2   E. R. Curtius: *European Literature and the Latin Middle Ages*, p. 190.
3   Ch. P. Segal: "Tamen Cantabitis, Arcades", p. 254; B. Snell: Arcadia.
4   Ibid., p. 264, note 9.
5   Ibid., p. 258. In the ninth Eclogue, a counterpart to the first, one of the shepherds notes the helplessness of poetry: 'But, Lycidas, against the will of Mars / Our songs are powerless, / as Chaonian does "Gainst swooping eagles."' [transl. John William Mackail]

the end of the first Eclogue *carmina nulla canam*[6] can be read as poetry falling silent when leaving the homeland, which in this case is even the idealized land of poetry.[7] Departure from Arcadia means breaking up with the very homeland of poetry, which finds its equivalents among modern Czech poets.

In his poem, Horace follows the political poetry of ancient Greece and creates the figure and stance of the poet-oracle (*Vates*, l. 66). He takes on the role of a paradoxical political authority that is able to judge the community as 'ungodly children of evil blood' and calls on his fellow citizens to travel on the utopian 'Isles of the Blessed'.[8] Horace in his poem responds to Virgil's renowned fourth Eclogue, wherein predicted is the arrival of a golden age, but unlike him, he sets this new golden age on a Utopian island outside the real world. [9]

Ovid, on the other hand, portrays departure from the personal perspective of his actual exile, as also reflected in the topology: his idealized place is not Arcadia or the blissful islands, but Rome; a city which is for Virgil beyond his Arcadia setting, and for Horace, just the place that people depart from. Yet, Virgil's Meliboeus does hint at a topology similar to Ovid's subsequent one, in which extreme polar opposites stand in contrast with a mild and harmonious centre. In other words, Ovid's fabled Rome has something of Arcadia about it:

> At nos hinc alii sitientis ibimus Afros,
> pars Scythiam et rapidum cretae veniemus Oaxen
> et penitus toto divisos orbe Britannos.

> But we must go hence – some to the thirsty Africans,
> some to reach Scythia and the chalk-rolling Oaxes,
> and the Britons, wholly sundered from the world.[10]

---

6   L. 77: 'no more songs shall I sing' transl. H. R. Fairclough [https://www.theoi.com/Text /VirgilEclogues.html#1]

7   In the 10th Eclogue Virgil names the Arcadians as the native speakers of singing, i.e. poetry: 'Yet you, Arcadians, will sing this tale to your mountains; Arcadians only know how to sing ...' transl. H. R. Fairclough [https://www.theoi.com/Text/VirgilEclogues.html#10] cf. B. Snell: Arcadia, p. 281.

8   see H.-Ch. Günther: The Book of Iambi, pp. 191–192, 208–210.

9   Ibid., p. 209.

10 L. 64–66 transl. H. R. Fairclough [https://www.theoi.com/Text/VirgilEclogues.html#1]

In the case of Czech poetry, two poems from the 19th century on the theme of departure have been of lasting significance. One of them is repeatedly referred to by later authors, whilst the other ironically itself harkens back to antiquity. The first is the *Cesta z Čech* [Going from Bohemia] by K. H. Mácha, evidently written in response to Polish emigration in 1831.[11] As Michal Charypar recalls, the poem was often read metaphorically, whereby the motif of saying farewell to one's homeland stood for leaving this life. Such a reading of the poem was also helped by its being supposedly Mácha's last poem, the draft of which he carried with him in the last days of his life.[12] Nevertheless, the final verses of the poem are imbued with a more polemic or ideological undertone about reviving the past, i.e. following up the homeland's heritage (unlike Mácha's *Budoucí vlast* [Future Homeland] poem):

> Taký hrad – to vlast je tvá!
> Hrdé stavby sešlé rumy,
> Pohleď na ni zdaleka,
> Snad tvé žalující dumy
> Z tuhého ji zbudí sna!

> That castle – that's your homeland, yours!
> Proud buildings tall in fading ruin
> Look from afar back now and pause
> In hope your plaint, your brooding ruing
> Its waking, from deep-dreamed sleep, will cause!

As for the second poem, these are the *Tyrolean Elegies* by Karel Havlíček Borovský (1821–1856). A very active politician and journalist of his time, in 1851 Havlíček was transported under police escort to Brixen, Tyrol, where he lived in forced stay until 1855. Aside from his public life, Havlíček wrote three renowned satirical poems, one of them being the *Tyrolské elegie* (dated 20 June 1852).[13] By using that title, Havlíček is referencing Ovid's Exilics, clearly

---

11   cf. M. Charypar: *Máchovské interpretace*, p. 21.

12   Ibid., pp. 21–23.

13   Havlíček certainly found his being cut-off from political life, friends and partly even from his family not at all easy to bear. He was later mythified as a martyr, whom the Austrian authorities

giving the piece a parody dimension. His 'elegies' are not written in the elegiac couplet, but with the flourish of a folk song, from which he also cites the first verse 'Shine, my own dear moon, and lightly'.[14] Further references to Ovid, with a comic tone, can be seen in the nocturnal departure from the house, saying goodbye to his wife and home region. The ride through the night, during which the horses take fright and the gendarmes jump off, while the deported Havlíček coolheadedly guides the carriage to a post office can be read as a ridiculously heroic equivalent of Ovid's turbulent sea voyage.

II

The *Fable from the New World* composition by Stanislav Mareš (1934–2005) came about in Australia from 1970 to 1972, and the author elucidates some of his motifs in his afterword to the first, exile edition, published in 1983. Mareš in his composition relies directly on quotes, allusions and their variations. The work is not only full of references to other poets, some parts of it are direct ironic paraphrases of older poems. He opens with a persiflage of Virgils *Eclogues* in accentual hexameter, all-too-evocative of Otmar Vaňorný's Czech translations of Virgil:

> Tityre, rozvalený tam, kde stín, tam, kde vánek a tráva,
> píšťalou rákosovou pěstíš si náklonnost Múz.
> Nám bylo opustit vlast; ty, Tityre, v chládku se váliš
> jak krotký a bachratý Pan, jak vepřík v osení.
> Cizí a podivný kraj nás čeká; ty tiše si pískáš,
> opatrnosti prý jednomu nezbývá.

drove to his death. The reality is somewhat different, as evidenced by the revealing research works of Jiří Morava (collectively, in *C. k. dissident Karel Havlíček*); but the tragic side was more his returning to Bohemia, learning of his wife's recent death; and living in isolation and without the opportunity to continue his work. He died soon after, in 1856.

14   In the eighth part, Havlíček changes the tone of the poem 'Now, my little moon, let's leave the elegy / and move on, to a more heroic tone', which is another obvious reference to Ovid's contrasting elegiac distachyon with epic hexameter (e.g. in *Amores* I, 1). As to Havlíček's studies of folk songs and his use of it in the *Tyrolean Elegies*, see A. Stich: *Básník Havlíček*, pp. 279–282.

Tityrus, lounging, in shade, there, in the breeze and grass,
there with your reed flute cajoling, coaxing the Muses' favours.
We had to leave our home; while you, Tityrus, lounge in the shade
like some tame and pot-bellied Pan, like a hog in a cornfield.
A foreign and a curious land awaits us; you are softly piping,
one cannot ever be careful too much, or enough, as they say.[15]

Josef Jedlička notes in the review of the first edition of Mareš's book that this part of the poem is more Ovidian than Virgilian, but the shift is more complex and is aimed chiefly toward a more contemporary rendition.[16] Virgil's original dialogue turns into Meliboeus' monologue, and the roles of both characters reflect political circumstances in Czechoslovakia after 1968. While Virgil's Tityrus is not portrayed unequivocally in an adverse light, Mareš turns him into a cynical freeloader, exploiting the situation. When it comes to Meliboeus, on the other hand, Mareš depicts a person who sees no other choice and ultimately decides to leave. The final conciliatory invitation to spend the night at Tytirus' place is completely absent, the poem ends in a breakup. Anachronically, Ovid is also brought up, in passing:

Že v chládku se pískalo líp? Že aspoň to stádo?
Že Augustus Oktavián vždy k pasáčkům uznalý byl?
Tityre, na hlavě nech, vždyť on ti tu lehárnu nedal
pro nic a za nic, jen tak, tvůj mecenáš, vladař a pán.
(Nebo jsi zapomněl už, jak tehdy nám vykázal z Města
přítele Publia? A Publius, chudák, pak z Mostu
bláboly v dopisech psal. [...]

So, in the shade the piping went better? So, the herd found at least?
So, Augustus Octavian was always kind to the shepherds?
Tityrus, on your head be it, for he didn't give you the lie-in
without good cause, for no reason, your patron, your ruler and lord.
(Or have you forgotten that time, how he drove out of the City

---

15   S. Mareš: *Báje z Nového světa*, p. 13.
16   J. Jedlička: Stanislav Mareš, Báje z Nového světa, pp. 359–360.

> genial Publius? And Publius, wretch, from the Bridge
> wrote letters with gibberish laden. [...][17]

In this part, Mareš refers to Mácha's poem 'Going from Bohemia'. In it, Mácha uses the word *"mez"* a baulk between fields, or a boundary, in the now unused meaning of a state border: 'The baulk is now crossed-over, / our land behind us now.'[18] In modern Czech, however, the word *mez* also has the meaning of the limit of what can be tolerated, as in the proverb *"překročit všechny meze"* literally to exceed all limits, or 'to go too far' in the English idiom. This updating is now clearly echoed in Mácha's poem and combines the departure (crossing the border) with the impossibility of staying within the given state of affairs (exceeding all bearable limits). Mareš writes in his poem, 'I have said nothing for ages, but there's a limit, a line not to cross, / Tityrus, I just don't like it when the altar smells putridly sweet.'[19] The word *mez* (likewise used by Ivan Diviš) also refers to an inner, spiritual breakup that is not necessarily accompanied by or preceded by actual exile. Unlike Virgil's (and here our modern concepts of poetry come to the fore) Mareš's Meliboeus reminds us of the inner, ethical or existential value of poetry: He sounds a 'thin and cautionary tone'[20] that affirms the poet's identity, precisely by the act of leaving.

In a comment added later, Stanislav Mareš pointed out some of the quotes in his poem and briefly also how he had paraphrased the original poems of Virgil, Erben or Halas. In the second part of the composition, which touches on his temporary stay in Paris before going on to Australia, he cites the political poems of Halas, and takes them further, into the realms of intense personal experience: 'And even though in France we were so manifestly unwanted [...] one felt such a strong impression after a mere six weeks in Paris [...]'.[21] The first verse of the fourth section: 'In my mother's land, the hilltop Džbán' in turn parodies and creates a rhythmic analogy with the all-too-widely known verses of

---

17   S. Mareš: *Báje z Nového světa*, p. 14.
18   K. H. Mácha: *Básně a dramatické zlomky*, p. 194.
19   S. Mareš: ibid., p. 14.
20   Ibid., p. 15.
21   Ibid., p. 37.

Erben's ballad *Zlatý kolovrat* [The Golden Spinning Wheel]: *"Okolo lesa pole lán / hoj jede, jede z lesa pán"*.[22] The third strophe brings another, updated variation:

> Okolo lesa pole lán
> a jedou jedou z lesa tanky
> To sedlák sedlák velký pán
>
> ▪
>
> Around the woods broad acres lie
> And tanks come out of the woods nigh
> The farmer, the farmer is quite some guy. [23]

The evident word play involving proverbs, and a mention of Jan Palach, who martyred himself by self-immolation in protest at the Soviet invasion, fundamentally transforms Erben's verses of rustic lore. Mareš points to his departure into exile in a whole series of quotes that, change their meaning in this new context and the significant shifts in meaning highlight the growing distance from the native land and culture of the old continent to which their original meaning was closely tied. The third and fifth cantos, which are not based on a paraphrase of another poem, describe the foreign territory as the 'New World'. A solitary quote from Mácha's *May* distances us from his lake, placing it into an alien space:

> Zvučelo temně tajný bol
> jezero solné v křovích nehostinných
>
> ▪
>
> Tenebrously voicing secret pain
> a salty lake among the scrub unshady[24]

---

22   [transl. note: translated by Susan Reynolds as 'Around the woods broad acres lie; / A lord comes riding, riding by' in *Kytice*, Jantar Publishing 2013, p. 85]

23   Ibid., p. 26.

24   Ibid., p. 23; Mácha: *"Jezero hladké v křovích stinných / zvučelo temně tajný bol"* – 'The smooth lake among the shrubs so shady / tenebrously voicing secret pain'. [transl. note: the translation attempts to keep some of the wordplay on stinný = shady vs nehostinný = inhospitable]

From the beginning, in Mareš's poem departure means a journey abroad into a foreign land that never ceases to be foreign, but at the same time distances one from home and attracts by its immediacy and presence; a journey marked by the transformation of poems, which in a foreign environment become more and more one's own private matter: *"cizí a podivný kraj, kde nestojí o naše písně"* – 'a foreign and a curious land awaits us, where they don't want our songs'. The concluding part only confirms one's alienation in a new world.[25] Life brings the same goings-on here as anywhere else, only the 'here' is forever strange, right until death:

> Host nebo rukojmí posléze sůl
> také budeš tomu písku Tady
> jsi zplodil syna tady přejel psa a tady málem
> pochoval dceru
>   trpělivost ti záhy opatří
> domovské právo na hrobeček šest krát tři

> A guest or hostage and after that salt
> you too will be to this sand right Here
> you fathered a son here ran over a dog and here nearly
> buried a daughter.
>   patience will soon enough provide you with
> resident rights to a small grave six by three[26]

III

Ivan Diviš (1924–1999) went into exile in Germany in August 1969, at a time when he had more than ten collections behind him and was one of the best--known Czech poets. He carried on writing in exile, with unabated verve, although he spoke of the initial period until his *Beránek na sněhu* [Lamb on the

---

25   Ibid., p. 13.
26   Ibid., p. 30.

Snow] collection, dated October 1979 and published in 1981, as a time when 'poetry was denied to him'.[27] In Diviš's literary estate are manuscripts of several large sets that originated during Diviš's exile, only a small part of these poems having been published in various exile magazines.[28] An author's opinion of his own creative activities carries substantial weight, but the surviving texts testify to continuous and intensive writing, itself an important feature of Diviš's output. Part of his work comprises a kind of poetic diary, which is not just a simple record of events, but above all an excited poetic commentary and figurative development of ideas. This side to Diviš's writing resonates with his extensive prose notes called *Teorie spolehlivosti* [Theory of Reliability].[29]

One of the manuscript files, which Diviš himself carefully organized, carries the name *Posthuma* (posthumous writings) and contains poems from the late 1960s before exile and from his early years in Germany. The extensive convolute is marked with several attempts at its arrangement, two components bear the names 'Farewell, Exile'; another sheet has a draft index of contents: *PRVNÍ POSTHUMA: 1) Tušení, 2) Loučení, 3) Odchod; DRUHÁ POSTHUMA: 1) Vyhnanství, 2) Nález* – [FIRST POSTHUMA: 1) Notion, 2) Farewell, 3) Leaving; SECOND POSTHUMA: 1) Exile, 2) Discovery]. Diviš retroactively attached the word farewell to some of the poems dated back to Prague, before going into exile. All this illustrates how Ivan Diviš honed his image of himself as a poet, and at the same time just how important his departure was to him, and in his poetry domain. In 1969, while still in Czechoslovakia, a second edited edition of *Uzlové písmo* [Knot Script or 'Quipu'] came out (a collection first published in 1960). The motif of leaving versus staying appears in the final verses of both editions, in the first of which the decision to remain rests on hope:

---

27   cf. J. Zizler: *Ivan Diviš*, pp. 92–93.

28   The bibliography in Zizler's monograph on Diviš does not register them, for the most part. Ivan Diviš's written estate contains unidentified clippings of poems from exile magazines. Much of this estate, mostly from the exile period, is stored in the *Archives et Musées de la littérature* in Brussels. cf. the catalogue compiled by Jan Rubeš: *Ivan Diviš. Catalogue.*

29   A sample selection from his *Theory of Reliability* first came out in 1972 in Munich. The most comprehensive edition of his notes, from 1960 on, came out in 2002, and this too is an incomplete extract. cf. J. Zizler: *Ivan Diviš*, pp. 121–125. Zizler emphasizes that the *Theory of Reliability* is not a diary, as commonly understood, but a very involved composition, an 'autonomous work of the chronicle type', p. 122.

Hle, a to je vše.
Bylo by možno odejít,
ale proč –

Právě teď je nutno zůstat,
když už není cel zoufání,
když jsou odemčeny
a zality světlem…

Look, here's the gist.
One could just leave,
but why –

Right now, to stay's the thing,
when gone are the jailcells of despair,
when they're unlocked
and flooded with light…[30]

In the second edition, from the year the poet left into exile, Diviš has deleted the optimistic verses and staying is a matter of willpower only:

Hle, a to je vše,
bylo by možno odejít –
Ale právě teď
je nutno zůstat.

Look, here's the gist,
one could just leave –
Except that right now
to stay's the thing.[31]

---

30   I. Diviš: *Uzlové písmo* (1960), p. 105.
31   I. Diviš: *Uzlové písmo* (1969), p. 126.

The fact that Diviš's did leave Czechoslovakia after all is not of fundamental importance *vis-a-vis* these verses. The key thing is that he made a topic of
leaving and separation and placed these in the imaginative field of his poems.
The tension between the facts and the imagination is always there. In fact, Ivan
Diviš did go into exile, but in his thoughts, he stayed in Czechoslovakia, or
more exactly in the image of Czechoslovakia shaped by his exile imagination.

One of the poems of the *Posthuma* manuscript, in the section called *Exile*,
makes departure into exile its main theme. Its first part depicts a night awakening and being dragged out of the apartment:

> Mezi půlčtvrtou a půlpátou ranní
> byl jsem vyvlečen ze svého bytu a
> postaven do pozoru pod sochu Karla IV
> naproti Křižovníkům; naproti od trafiky
> vynořily se dvě postavy
> přistoupily ke mně a provedly věc
> úměrnou mému i jejich postavení
> i konstelaci hvězd:
> jeden mně žabkou odřízl ušní boltce
> druhý vytáhl a vyříz' jazyk
> za dvě vteřiny nato jsem stál v kaluži vlastní krve
> obdarován: boltce i jazyk
> vloženy mezi dva oschlé chleby
> a vráceny mně k přemítání.
> [co předmět doličný mezi poezií a exilem]

> Between half past three and half-past four in the morning
> I was dragged out of my apartment and
> made to stand to attention under the statue of Charles IV
> opposite the Knights of the Cross with the Red Star; opposite
>   the newsagent
> two figures appeared
> approached me and did the thing
> commensurate with theirs and my position
> and the constellation of the stars:
> one of them cut off my earlobes with his pocket knife

the other pulled out and cut out my tongue
two seconds later I stood in a pool of my own blood
given gifts: of my earlobes and tongue
laid between two stale bread slices
given back, for to ponder upon.
[as criminal proof in the case between poetry and exile][32]

Leaving by night, dragged out of the apartment, and the scene in its emblematic national history setting, are all evocative of some motifs from the nocturnal departures at Ovid or Karel Havlíček Borovský. But both the mood and style differ considerably: the two anonymous men evoke rather the *Trial* by Franz Kafka, who was a guiding-light author for 1960s Czech literature, and do of course remind us of ever-present State Security. But the physical torture goes beyond these references, into the hyperbolae of the imagination. The mention of the stars shifts the whole act into the plane of Fate, the severance of his ears and tongue, being organs of hearing and speech, symbolically depriving the poet of his faculties, and their being handed back between slices of bread completes the whole scene with a grotesque debasement, into utter humiliation and banal insignificance. According to the last, crossed-out verse of this part of the poem, for Diviš exile amounts to forgoing poetry or at least being far removed from it. The motif of poetry lost is a distant analogy of Virgil's motif of song falling silent with departure, but with Diviš, unlike Virgil's artistic Arcadia, the homeland has a profoundly ambivalent role: it is the land with which poetry is associated, but also the country of a secret police, which, taken to an extreme, cuts off poets' tongues and ears.

The face-off between the poet's privileged status and importance versus the all-levelling banality of an uncultured society is referenced in the poem's conclusion:

Pár dní po tom, co jsem opustil zemi,
v jiné požádal o azyl a moji drazí dorazili za mnou,
v poslední vteřině hořícího domu Evropy,

---

32   The poem is dated 1969 and is the first poem of the exile-titled collection titled *Vyhnanství* /1969–1975/. The typescript bears handwritten corrections, which the transcript has kept-to; the last verse of this passage, set out in square brackets, is crossed out in the typescript.

nastěhovali jsme se do penzionu Alba
dali na hromadu těch pár věcí
a ukládali se ke spánku se srdcem vzedmutým,
spjati láskou právě tak nerozbornou jako rozraženou –
Žena se synem usnuli já ale ne –
Když tu náhle uslyšel jsem pod okny
zavolat svoje jméno hlasem tak hrůzně zrůzněným
že už se nikdy nedovím zda to byl opilec
vražda
anebo Erýnie.

A few days after I left the country,
applied for asylum in another, and my loved ones arrived after me,
in the last second of Europe's burning house,
we moved into the Pension Alba
put our few things in a heap
and settled to sleep with a heart wide awake,
locked in love as much intact as shattered –
My wife and son fell asleep but I didn't –
When at once I heard under the windows
my name called in a voice so horribly made strange
that I'll never know if it signified a drunkard
a murder
or the Furies.

Even here, the poet is an outsider, listening while others sleep, hearing more, but at the same time unable to distinguish between the call of fate and drunken yelling. Once again, we have here the motif of having lost hearing, unable to determine the sound, and ultimately having lost one's voice, unable to answer the call.

IV

Like Ivan Blatný, Ivan Diviš wrote very intently during his exile. Naturally enough, it was not all-day writing, but judging by the dates of some poems,

he wrote daily.[33] Unlike Ivan Blatný's continuous writing, in which it is sometimes difficult to separate individual poems, for Diviš a poem was an occasional sudden surge of inspiration, even though the poems were coming at a brisk
pace:

v roce exilových veder, v šestasedmdesátém,
zažil jsem pět šest i sedm básní za den,
rozplozovaly se mně jedna po druhé před očima
a pod rukama
v knize JDA KRAJ DECHU,
kterou mně nebožtík Jedlička překřtil na PRŮVAN,
já ho poslechl a to jsem neměl

in six-and-seventy, the year of exile heat,
I lived through five six seven poems a day,
they spawned one-by-one before my very eyes
and underneath my hands
in the book JDA KRAJ DECHU,[34]
which dear late Jedlička rechristened PRŮVAN, draft,
I listened to him and I shouldn't have[35]

---

33 For example, the collection *Přece jen…* 'Nevertheless' arose out of poems that Diviš sent to his
     future wife every day in 1972 (cf. I. Diviš: *Obelst, Přece jen…, Průvan*, ed. note, pp. 119–120).
     The sixteen poems selected for the collection arose between the 8th and 12th of March 1972,
     they are dated inclusive of the hour. – Similarly chronicled are Diviš's late poems, written in the
     1990s. cf. J. Zizler: *Ivan Diviš*, p. 193.

34 [transl. note: 'Jda kraj dechu' is a dated-sounding construction, meaning 'While walking the
     Land of Breath']

35 I. Diviš: *Poslední básně*, p. 12. The quote is from one of Ivan Diviš's last poems, from a longer
     composition, the Consilium abeundi, dated 19/20 March 1999. The collection *Průvan* was
     published as an extract from a significantly larger ensemble, which in its two typescript files
     comprises 135 and 107 sheets. The second set contains a note: 'The original text of *Průvan*
     [Draft], which was to be called *Jda kraj dechu* and which was stripped down on the orders of
     Mr Pokorný from roughly this extent to a slim volume. But it can be ditched! That Slendraft
     was typeset in India, and dismembered by a typhoon and thirteen proofreadings.' J. Rubeš: *Ivan
     Diviš. Catalogue*, p. 15.

Unlike Blatný, Diviš also wrote for the reader's sake, not just his own, going back to his poems, crossing out, remedying, composed various groupings of them, which overlapped in time.[36] Diviš put dates to the greater part of the poems and one could speak of a kind of poetry diary supplementing the likewise ongoing *Theory of Reliability* notes in prose, maintained from 1960 on. This chronicle does not record events, but above all expresses ideas and an unending and re-refined train of thought about poetry, through the prism of poetry. We might say, albeit loosely, that two tendencies are apparent: on the one hand, ad-hoc poems that comment on private and social events, and on the other, efforts to write longer compositions that in larger imaginative blocs give a personally slanted portrayal of the times. In both cases, the speaker is often in the first person, sometimes experiencing, but above all commenting on events in an expressive and participative manner, brimming with ideas. Especially the longer poems of his exile books resonate twofold with Czech poetry.[37] The *Lamb on the Snow* invites comparisons with the visionary compositions of Jan Zahradníček, *Rouška Veroničina* [Veronica's Veil] and *Znamení moci* [Sign of Power]. In the second, the speaker as a witness wanders the totalitarian world of Czechoslovakia in the late 1940s and early 1950s, and self-assuredly casts judgement from the irreconcilable perspective compelled by his Christian world-view.[38] Unlike Zahradníček, Diviš is more personally drawn into the action, and although the speaker's attitude in his poems is clearly critical, he does not judge from an extra-worldly perspective, but instead berates, mocks sarcastically and gets carried away by expressive figurative associations.

The second important parallel is with the poetry of Zbyněk Havlíček, a surrealist poet of the war- and post-war generation. Havlíček, with reference to the earlier surrealist concepts, developed an associative method, which he called *Monte Carlo*, inspired by the mathematical simulation of random processes.[39] The approach is the figurative development of fragments of reality the poet encounters, which become pieces of the poem; in the second stage,

---

36   cf. I. Diviš: *Teorie spolehlivosti*, p. 340.

37   Diviš thought highly of both the poets mentioned, Jan Zahradníček (1905–1965) and Zbyněk Havlíček (1922–1969), as well as their works, mentioning them in the *Theory of Reliability* and in his poems. He met Zbyněk Havlíček probably around 1965 (*Slovem do prostoru*, p. 211).

38   [transl. note: another ambiguous title, *Znamení* can also mean 'Stigmata']

39   Monte Carlo appears in one of Diviš's manuscript poems.

he then transforms them and integrates them into more complex compositions. This work is a conscious process, but takes place at the edge of consciousness: 'The state in which this integration takes place, I called it delirious. Consciousness is present, but it is constantly flooded with irrational sentence segments.' This relates, as Havlíček notes, to a diversification of personality: 'it is a method for the artificial alteration of consciousness; a method of desystematization of personality into a confusion and at the same time a method of systematization of that confusion'.[40] This aware susceptibility towards external stimuli is captured by verses from Havlíček's *Kabinet dra Caligariho* [Dr Caligari's Cabinet, 1951]:

> Stal jsem se průchodem živlů
> Bitevním polem
> Kde ostré obrysy padlých vnucují svou vůli příštímu nočnímu nebi

> I have become a thoroughfare of the elements
> A battlefield
> Where the sharp outlines of the fallen impose their will on the next
>   night sky[41]

Diviš follows up Havlíček with his specific breakdown of the person-subject of the poems. Although he displays very expressive opinions and attitudes, unlike Zahradníček in the *Sign of Power*, his speaker also reveals internal uncertainty, alternating between different attitudes. The desystematization of personality, which is to say the poetic self, appears frequently in Diviš's poems, and above all in the plane of physical suffering, as though every encounter with reality were a physical, bodily-felt impact that tears the speaker asunder. In one of the poems of the collection *Obelst* [Guile] written partly in Bohemia, partly in exile, he writes:

---

40   Z. Havlíček: Metoda Monte Carlo, pp. 32–33.
41   Z. Havlíček: *Veškerá poezie*, p. 288.

Jsem toho svědkem, a kdybych to neřekl,
syn by mně naplil do očí a zkažen by byl
ten vyměřený zbytek času.
[...]
Jenže jsem toho svědkem, takže původně jednolitý člověk
událostmi byl rozštěpen na pijáka v hadrech
a směrovače ke světlu,
toho, který jednou rukou přijímaje dar,
druhou je hotov mrštit kámen.

I am a witness to it, and if I didn't tell,
my son would spit me in the eyes and ruined would be
that measured-out rest of my time.
[...]
Except I am a witness to it, so the original integral man
has been split by events into a drinker in rags
and a guider toward the light,
of the one, who while with one hand accepting a gift,
is about with the other to smite, hurl a stone[42]

Diviš's later collection, written mostly in exile, bears the distinctive name *Moje oči musely vidět* [My Eyes Had to See], and as with earlier poems, its testimony reflects mainly physical suffering, an inevitable part of life. It testifies about poets of the late 1940s and 1950s, for whom testimony is itself fundamental – Zahradníček, Kolář, and also Havlíček. Havlíček's recurring 'I saw' in *Dr Caligari's Cabinet* comes to mind when reading similar openers in Diviš's late 1980s collection. Whereas the 'eyewitness' of Kolář is to an extent ethically motivated[43] to testify, Diviš's tendency to mythologize sees life itself, what it brings and what the poet verbalizes as brimming with evil and suffering.

Diviš also resembles Havlíček with his figuratively expressive associations that turn away from the main topic, or rather allow these strands to mark out

---

42   I. Diviš: *Obelst. Přece jen... Průvan*, p. 39.
43   Jiří Kolář wrote the collection *Očitý svědek (Deník z roku 1949)* [Eyewitness] in 1949, and saw it published in 1983 by the exile publishing house Arkýř in Munich.

its limits. His composition *Lamb on the Snow* (dated October 1979) reminds in some of its verses of the gloomy atmosphere of the *Sign of Power*, which opens with the verse 'It was to choke-up on'. But while Zahradníček's speaker has the course of the poem under control, taking a coherent attitude, with Diviš it is as though he were falling apart under the weight of events. The composition begins with an inkling of events, the opening 'I noticed' that unfolds the poem's events can relate to virtually anything, as if the speaker could specify the suspected events only via unrelated, secondary circumstances:

> Po čase, taženém v takou šňůru, že dávno z ní spadalo prádlo,
> v měsících, kdy dělal jsem cokoli mimo bytování v žití,
> chodě nikudama, sádrou cáklá mátoha, povšim' jsem si
> že menstruuje podzim; v platnéřství zazvonily puklice –
> i v leku optal jsem se kdo jsem, a zjistil
> že nevím! že to nevím že jsem jen starší,
> starší a setrvale otrlejší,
> a protože mne to podráždilo, píkatě jsem si povšim'
> jak v čistírně nějaká mrcha arogantně vypnula srnčí strůnu,
> a protože z toho na mne padl smutek i děs,
> prudce dojalo mne na refýži, kde jsem se octl,
> dospívající nehezké děvče,
> rozpaky doničující tak už sešmaťhané střevíce...

> After a while, pulled like a washing line that had long since dropped
>   its laundry,
> in the months I was doing whatever far from settled living,
> walking through nowhereways, plaster-bespattered wraith, then
>   I noticed
> that autumn was menstruating; the armour-plating shop ringing
>   with wheel-hubs–
> In a fright I asked who I was, and so discovered
> that I did not know! that I don't know I'm just older,
> older and unremittingly getting more calloused,
> and since it peeved me, I pointedly noticed
> how in the dry-cleaners' some cocky bastard had stretched a deer-
>   wire,

a because of all this, a sadness and terror fell on me,
I felt suddenly moved, on the stop platform where I found myself,
by an adolescent and unpretty girl,
coy, shuffling feet in already quite scrunched-up shoes ...[44]

Unlike Havlíček, with whom figurative associations often build up, Diviš is characterized by often bringing an anti-climax, ending up wedged into something banal, which corresponds to his scepticism:

[...] – zjevení odešlo: zbylo
jen odprejskané zrcadlo hříchů, pokrápané mušinci,
žárovka na nástupišti nádražíčka v Pečkách ve tři ráno,
anebo mastný papír poletující po peróně,
        kde špalky podepřeno vaklá deset šlísfachů, opatřených nápisem:
                v prípade výpadku prúdu
skrienky batožinu nevracajú...

[...] – the vision had gone: left behind
just a flaky old mirror of sins, dotted with fly-shit,
a light-bulb on Pečky branch station at three in the morning,
or greasy paper fluttering over the platform,
        where on blocks wobble ten locker-boxes, bearing a sign:
                in the event of a failure of power
the lockers won't give luggage back...[45]

For Diviš's poetic style, hyperbole is characteristic, at two levels, as seen in the opening verses of his *Lamb on the Snow*. Firstly, in the typical exaggeration of the motif, where the hyperbolic tendencies are illustrated in other tropes (e.g. 'menstruating autumn'), or in a form that signals excessive quantity ('a washing line that had long since dropped its laundry'). At the second level, Diviš highlights and generally draws attention to events that would otherwise remain unnoticed or not even pass the threshold of consciousness ('I noticed'). In this form, the

----

44   I. Diviš: *Beránek na sněhu*, p. 7.
45   Ibid., pp. 17–18. The last two verses are in Slovak, easily understood by a Czech reader.

banal and negligible becomes characteristic and significant. This trait, which Jonathan Culler considers to be one of the constitutive elements of the lyric,[46] shapes the essential plane of Diviš's poetry. It is not just about 'observation', but a statement of facts the poem's speaker sees and perceives unlike others around him whom he reminds them of their loss of memory. The poem's speaker is often hyperbolic, too: setting himself up as important, so that everything he can draw attention to is thus vested with greater importance and momentousness. The hyperbolised speaker becomes a Judge of Bohemia, of Czech, but also of broader, more general history.

V

In Diviš's poetry, we have to distinguish between the motifs of exile and leaving. He makes the distinction himself. 'But if only I had had an inkling what awaited me, / *among the Czechs, there is my home* – / I would have again bought a return ticket'.[47] For Diviš, exile is not only a strange land or some unknown and inhospitable space, but above all a world deprived of any sense, in which little details gain significance:

Život nošení břemen
zvlášť rozviklané schody emigrace
vedoucí na půdu [...]

Venku lije na objednávku
do baráku zahnané masařky
jebají a oždibují:

---

46   J. Culler: *Theory of the Lyric*, p. 259: "... *form of an underlying convention: that apparently trivial observations are of considerable significance*". Culler presents his thesis only in brief, and some of the questions he implies are left untouched. Lyrical poetry has a number of traditional themes, where it would be difficult to talk about hyperbole in the same breath. How hyperbolae and vision relate is also worth considering, which seems to go beyond the scope of Culler's take on poetics.

47   I. Diviš: *Odchod z Čech*, p. 45.

objednal jsem velbloudí trus
tatarský biftek ruská vejce

A life of carrying loads
particularly the wobbly stairs of emigration
leading to the attic [...]

Outside it's pouring as if made to order
Indoors-banished flesh-flies
fucking and nibbling:
I have ordered camel droppings
steak tartare and eggs a-la-Russe[48]

In his poems, the image of the emptiness of the consumer world (places of exile) repeats: *"Lidé dál čtou Abendzeitung, spřádají sny o hovně / a večer s flaškou mezi nohama čumí na debiloskop"* [People keep reading their Abendzeitung, weaving dreams about bullshit / and in the evening with a bottle between their legs gawp at the dunceoscope].[49] Elsewhere, we find the image of a meaningless journey whereby one will eventually 'disappear' (*"Ujedem do Austrálie // Třicet hodin se budem dusit v letadle"*– 'We'll get away to Australia // for 30 stifling hours on a plane').[50] Similar motifs also appear in works by other poets after 1968 and represent a certain contrast with the poetics of the 1950s, when exile was perceived in the context of a more acute political and, above all, historical perspective. It features in one poem from 1972 by Josef Lederer, the counterpart to an older poem originally named the *"Apocalypse"*. In Antonín Brousek's poem *Sem a tam v lehátkovém voze* [Here and There in a Sleeping Car] exile is typified by a senseless train ride through Europe of the 1980s:

---

48   I. Diviš: *Žalmy*, p. 22 (no. 12). cf. *"takzvaný exil, / šoulání nicoty mezi mlknem a plknem"* – 'so-called exile, / the shuffling of nothingness between stifling and waffling', *Obrať koně!*, p. 56; *"moje oči viděly exil navěky, / navěky, takže nedává smysl"* – 'my eyes have seen exile for ever, / for ever, so it makes no sense', *Moje oči musely vidět*, p. 26.

49   I. Diviš: *Obrať koně!*, p. 39.

50   I. Diviš: *Žalmy*, pp. 53, 35 (no. 40, 25).

Hluchý k záhrobním hlasům,
přec jasně vidím duši, kterak se stěhuje.
Dostala vyhazov. A zítra do nečasu,
a slyší šicí stroj, jak chvatně stehuje

šev kolejí, v němž vedví roztrhla se
státníky zflikovaná Evropa.
[…]
Spálenou zemí budoucího míru
táhnou pacifičtí havrani.

Smrdutou vodou opláchlá, otřená do papíru,
řadí se dušička, nejistá v denním jasu,
k ospalcům, kteří na běžícím pásu
jak do krematoria se sunou na ranní.

Deaf to the voices from beyond the grave,
I still see the soul clearly, moving house and home.
She got kicked out. So off into bad weather, the next day,
hears the sewing-machine's swift-stitching tone,

the seam of tracks, where rent-asunder caved
Europe, by statesmen tacky-tacked.
[…]
Through future-promised peace scorched land now fly
flocks of black pacifistic rooks adrift.

With rancid water splash-washed, paper-dried,
the soul, unsure in daylight's dazzle bright,
joins sleepy heads, who on conveyors quite
crematorium-bound shuffle to morning shift.[51]

---

51   A. Brousek: *Vteřinové smrti*, p. 19, the poem is dated 'Kolín – Berlín, spring 1982'.

The contrast of leaving and exile is formed against a more complex background of historical-geographic fabulation. Leaving is chiefly associated with the Czechs in the period immediately after the Soviet occupation, and Diviš's poems are still thematically going back over this event, while exile represents space-time in the longer period of the 1970s and 1980s; reflecting, naturally enough, consumer society's lack of interest in any Exiles.

Leaving, not just the motif but also the essential theme of Diviš's poems, differs from exile in that it articulates a lively and complex relationship, one that creates and shapes purpose and meaning or seeks to do so. The explicit motifs of leaving appear in Diviš's poems from the 1960s onward. They do not concern themselves so much with recording any biographical fact, but about shaping and formulating a poetic stance taken towards the 'homeland'. In this case, the inverted commas are quite appropriate. Diviš uses various words – country, nation, homeland, tongue – and often gives them a distinctive meaning. Unlike Blatný or Součková, who construct imaginary communities, and contrary to the nostalgic tendencies that revert to an idyllic rural image of Bohemia, Diviš makes refence more to the nation, which emerged from the National Revival programme in the 19th century. A community closely tied to its language that has its cultural and historical work cut out, but also has its religious tradition. A community that had at one point failed, and forgot its mission. The portrayal is not unambiguous, variously accented, but the main difference lies in the type of stance taken: Diviš does not put forward an ideal community as the imaginative compensation or counterweight to exile. He approaches the community and its image as someone who evaluates, judges it, and experiences these values physically, bodily, first hand. Leaving or breaking-up creates a special relationship topology in this constellation. The poet is, geographically-speaking, out of it, his homeland, attached to it from abroad, but at the same time sharing and representing his country's and nation's values; those that are, or are meant to be their founding values, although forgotten by a large part of the community at home and perhaps in exile, too.

The decisive event for Diviš was the insurgence of Soviet troops, the occupation of Czechoslovakia in 1968, and, above all, the all-too-rapid acquiescence to new circumstances and the onset of 'normalization'. Occupation is a fate-altering historical event, but Diviš sees what followed as a failure and a betrayal, and carries this trauma with him throughout his exile, setting the tone of his poems. In one of his 'Psalms', the occupation is tellingly-enough not only an event, but rather a metaphor for an ever-returning threat:

Odkvetly lípy ve šrotu rezavějí
je třeba připravit se na vstup vojsk –

Past blossom linden trees are turning rusty
it's time to get prepared for troops to come –[52]

Diviš's ambivalent relationship with Bohemia is well expressed in his 'Psalm 99':

Přece jsem neopouštěl Československo
ten bílek se žloutkem šlehanými notoricky
na první bublaninu Německa
na druhý svítek Ruska

Přece jsem neopouštěl Čechy
zpřerážené ve Vltavině páteři vodními díly
Přece mně srdce nekrvácelo
za žárovkou pokrápanou mušinci
na perónu nádraží Velim-Pečky
přece jsem neopouštěl odborníky
na kurvení Babiččina údolí

Opouštěl jsem přece Prahu
opouštěl jsem rudolfinský pentagram
opouštěl jsem srdce Svaté Říše Římské
a snad bělohorskou pláň
leč tím si nejsem jist

Surely I did not leave Czechoslovakia
that egg-white with the yolk whipped inveterately
to go first in Germany's cherry souffle
to go in Russia's follow-up omelette

---

52   I. Diviš: *Žalmy*, p. 48 (no. 36). Diviš reminds of the occupation in numerous other places, e.g.
      "Když nás přepadli, / ..." 'When we were ambushed, / ...', *Odchod z Čech*, p. 48, and pp. 45, 71.

Surely I did not leave Bohemia
broken-backed Vltava severed by water-works
Surely my heart would never have been bleeding
over that fly-shit peppered lightbulb there
over the platform of Velim-Pečky station
surely I did not leave to leave the experts
screw-up Babička's vale of rustic lore

What I was leaving after all was Prague
I was leaving the Rudolfine pentagram
leaving the Holy Roman Empire's heart
and maybe the White Mountain battlefield
although I can't be sure[53]

Diviš inadvertently posits a paradox: ostensibly he was leaving Czechoslovakia, which was first occupied by the Germans and then the Soviets, yet, on the contrary, in his thoughts he remained present in that Bohemia defined by history, language and culture. In *Leaving Bohemia*, where he refers to Mácha's poem 'Going from Bohemia', he expresses his mind's persistent presence in that country:

Jen pryč z Čech! Mez překročiv, je ztrativ,
teprv jich nabudeš *in pectore*

Out, flee Bohemia! Boundary crossed, gone too far, it lost,
only then get it back *in pectore*[54]

VI

Leaving Bohemia, first published in 1981, has a motto, taken from Mácha's poem 'Going from Bohemia' which apparently inspired the title of the book, and it

53   I. Diviš: *Žalmy*, p. 130 (no. 99).
54   I. Diviš: *Odchod z Čech*, p. 62.

opens with a shorter poem by Diviš foreshadowing its theme: an ironic and angry view of Bohemia. It is not about leaving in a literal sense, but passionate vituperation by one who feels betrayed and offended by his land:

Se sleděm líplým mezi lopatky
    do žeber bruslí strčen,
zíral jsem na ten stůl:
on mně připomínal karamílek strunkaře,
on mně připomínal hořčák ze stlačeného skla,
připomínal mně vše, což ovšem není plnost,
naopak osiřelost ve vánici při vědomí Sibiře.
Neměl jsem sil to zapálit, nebylo čím –
    a náhle místo vidění tu stálo vědění:
ten stůl, ten zabryndaný vál bez obsluhy,
ten přiboudlý zink bez opilosti krásné,
to jsou dějiny mého hynoucího národa,
nejapná jeho mluva, sirky bez škrtátka,
vešken jeho osud bez mužů, žen,
    vojáků a krve –

With a herring stuck between my shoulder blades
    shoved in the ribs by an ice skate
I stared at that table:
reminding me of a luthier's caramel,
reminding me of a pressed-glass false boletus
reminding me of it all, albeit that's not wholeness,
but being orphaned in a snowstorm thinking of Siberia.
I had no strength to light up, nothing to hand–
    and suddenly seeing became knowing:
that table, that spill-stained table, unwaited on,
that mottled-zinc[55] yet without drunken bliss,

---

55 [transl. note: "*přiboudlý zink*" can mean literally a 'congenered secret sign' where *zink* is slang from the latin *signum*, cf. J. Hugo: *Slovník nespisovné češtiny* (entry 'cink') or may be meant literally as a stained galvanised metal sheet. Or both.]

> such is the history of my perishing nation,
> speaking inanities, matches without a strikeboard
> its fate sealed, without men, women,
>   soldiers and blood – [56]

A physically humiliated speaker, out in the cold, – whose situation is reminiscent of the poet's torture in an earlier poem – is facing a bespattered table, the embodiment of his country and its history. The nation (perishing) and its speech (inane) remind of the failure of the National Revival project commenced in the 19th century; the poet putting himself in a position of observing and passing judgement from a distance. This constellation – humiliation, exclusion and distance, which exposes the original relationship and allows a range of ironic and objecting expressions to develop – characterizes the entire volume.

The visceral attitude to Bohemia is well expressed by the second poem called *Samomluva když vane fén...* [Soliloquy while the Foehn Blows...]. Words spoken in 'Bavaria' into the wind are set in a complex geographical fantasy, whose distant centre is Bohemia, laced with due sarcasm:

> Tady vládne každý den jinačí počasí,
> bavorští patrioti to označují co dramatickou proměnlivost –
> dávám přednost Mongolsku s jeho mrazy a žáry –
> [...]
> Jsem rozštěpen? Kdo mne má zcelit? [...]
>
> Prosím!? S tebou nemluvím, kde bych na to bral sílu –
> vane fén – Čechy, střed světa:
> z ŤanŠanu Sněžky zřít:
> tu dalajlámu, an se drožkou vrací do Tibetu,
> tu Castro Fidéla s nezbytným zánětem sviní,
>   Čechy, pupek světa, v němž celá Brodway poletuje,
> mastnej papír od japonskýho buřta,
>   po hot dogs sebevrahů: rozhledna!

---

56   I. Diviš: *Odchod z Čech*, p. 32.

Here different weather dominates each day,
in Bavarian patriots' words dramatic diversity –
I'd rather have Mongolia with its frosts and broils –
[…]
Am I split apart? Who's meant to bring me together? […]

Pretty please!? I am not talking to you – where would I find the
    strength –
the Foehn is blowing – Bohemia, world's centre:
oh to see from the Tian Shan of mount Sněžka:
at once the Dalai Lama, Tibet-bound in a cab
at once Castro Fidel with due swine foot and mouth
    Bohemia, world's navel, where all of Broadway flutters,
greasy paper from a Japanese fatty sausage,
    to suicides' own hot dogs: a lookout tower![57]

The speaker's characteristically evocation of being physically 'split apart' corresponds to the diversity of the pronouncements: Diviš alternates the first and second person, asking himself questions in the style of a banal journalistic conversation ('And why did you leave?'),[58] in places as if shouting down the inane interviewer.

In the ensemble, Bohemia features in several guises. In the poem *Renety u babičky v Přelouči* [Rennets at Grandma's in Přelouč], as idyllic memories of childhood, in which, as a chorus, warning tones return in forewarning of a near-future 'national history' event:

Všichni židovští kluci ještě brebentili
Hitler kousal třepení koberců
Sovsvaz tomu přihlížel hadíma zorničkama.

---

57   Ibid., pp. 38–39.
58   Ibid., p. 44.

All the Jewish boys were still chattering
Hitler as yet biting at carpet tassles
SovUni lookin on, with snake-like pupils.[59]

The poem *Požár Národního divadla* [National Theatre Fire] figuratively shifts the bombing of Prague to a national catastrophe level, while in the 'Bartered Bride' Diviš conversely creates a kind of Czech pantheon, gathered in the National Theatre, a symbol of the National Revival, all during a concert where Christ holds the baton. The Project of Bohemia, the restoration of the country in the sense of national culture: 'Establish a New Bohemia!', is repeated several times in the volume, in the collection's finale with an ironic question mark and a fairytale reference:[60] *"Čechy ale? sbohem – / české moře."* [Bohemia, yet? Farewell – / Bohemian sea].[61]

A substantial part of *Leaving Bohemia*, if not the whole collection, is characterized by dreaming, in a conscious but partly spontaneous work of the imagination. The 'Soliloquy while the Foehn blows…' and the 'National Theatre Fire' both begin with a very similar image:

rád bych, po směru lupenů hvozdíku,
proti sobě viděl plout Ludmilu Maceškovou,
[…]

Jektaje Ječnou, chtěl bych
proti sobě vidět vzduchem plout
básnířku, vyvedenou z jiřinkového bálu
[…]

I would like, aligned with Dianthus petals,
to see floating toward me, Ludmila Macešková,
[…]

---

59   Ibid., p. 52.
60   Ibid., p. 75.
61   Ibid.

> Blundering down Barley street, I would like
> to see floating toward me through the air
> a poetess, escorted from a Dahlia ball
> [...][62]

Dreaming can be seen in Diviš's poems as the relaxed confluence of images drawn from memory, history, the imagination, which share a certain intent, that certain 'I would like'. This clashes with a disruptive element – the reality of the situation, a contrasting tragic recollection or notion. The clash is given by recognizing the complexity of things, especially that dreaming – that desire, the recollection of a harmonious childhood, comes up against harsh reality. In both poems, after the opening reverie come the elliptical words: 'which happens not'.[63]

> což nestává: zato určitě míjím vilu Heinze Grázla

> Což nestává: zato z Melounové, zprava,
> vidím Liputina, Ljamšina a Tolkačenka,
> tlačenku krvavou cpát do střev.

> which happens not: but sure I pass by the villa of Heinz Grázl

> Which happens not: but from Melon street, from the right
> I do see Liputin, Ljamshin and Tolkachenko,
> stuffing stuffed bloody brawn into their guts.[64]

---

62 Ibid., pp. 37, 58. Ludmila Macešková (1898–1974), [transl. note: whose flowery surname speaks literally 'of pansies'] was a Czech poetess and mystic who wrote under the pseudonym Jan Kameník [i.e. John Stonemason]. Ivan Diviš writes about her with admiration in the magazine *Souvislosti* no. 3, 1991; and in the book *Slovem do prostoru*, pp. 178–181. He also aptly prefers her floral name over an austere pseudonym.

63 The ellipse combines two slightly different meanings, the first of which refers more to the real plot, the second to the work of the imagination: *"což se nestává"* – *"což nenastává"*, 'which seldom happens' – 'which does not happen'.

64 I. Diviš: *Odchod z Čech*, pp. 37, 58.

The first mentioned and derogatory-sounding surname, denoting a villain in Czech, points to his Bavarian exile reality,[65] the second-mentioned names are characters from Dostoyevsky's *Demons* and point to the occupation of Czechoslovakia – both contrasting with the admired poet and mystic Ludmila Macešková, whose floral name evokes idyll and Paradise. The complementary notions of ideality and reality are prominent throughout the collection at various levels: the quoted refrain from 'Rennets at Grandma's in Přelouč' disturbs the idyllic picture of childhood; the 'National Theatre Fire', itself a symbol of the Czech National Revival, forms the antithesis to his utopian 'Bartered Bride' and hopes for an eternal Kingdom of Bohemia ('after all, Bohemia as a kingdom is not ended').[66] These are accompanied by invectives about Bohemia as a land of oblivion, destroying its leaders; reveries of a revived Bohemia are framed by the motif of awakening from a dream and by ever-present irony. The fanciful reverie of an ideal homeland quite simply collides with the recognition of a reality incompatible with such a dream.

The earlier *Lamb on the Snow* collection is also distinguished by a similar complementary aspect, in which the revelation of the Lamb, being of course an arcanely contrived symbol from Christianity, is accompanied by an unconscious, instinctive act of violence. Overall, the envisioned *Lamb* and *Leaving* both contain a positive idealized aspect, complementing reality, namely being in a state of exile, while Diviš's musings during this period correspond to portrayals of an absolute exile, whose ideal counterpart carries some of the motifs of Paradise. In the later composition *My Eyes Had to See* a pessimistic tone is already gaining the upper hand. Here, too, are motifs of leaving Bohemia, and the invectives directed toward it are sharper than in the previous books. This growing abusiveness tells of a figurative world that is losing its positive pole, where exile is no longer counterbalanced by an idealized counterpart. In the fifth section, this change manifests itself in the motif of leaving, which is evoked by the end exclamation in his *Uzlové písmo* [Knot Script], except that the values and decisions are now reversed:

---

65   The word Grázl – in Czech a thug or villain – derived from the surname of erstwhile robber Johann Georg Grasel (1790–1818) does not have this meaning in German.

66   I. Diviš: *Odchod z Čech*, p. 46.

Řekl jsem si zůstaň! zůstaň! jsou věci,
které může poskytnout jen vlast
[...]
a řekl jsem si zděšen:
z této země odejdu –
Odejdu z ní nerad, ale navždy,
a to abych si zachránil život,
který nepatří nikomu leč Bohu a mně
a který je jen jeden, a krátký
jak prásknutí bičem

I said to myself stay! Stay! there are things
that only your homeland can provide
[...]
and I said to myself, aghast:
I will leave this land –
I will leave with regret, and yet forever,
the simple reason being to save my life,
which is rightly but God's and mine alone
and which is just the one, and is short-lived
like the crack of a whip[67]

My Eyes Had to See represent an imaginative history of grief in Diviš's body of work. The speaker, as we've been saying, is witness to all sorts of human suffering and wickedness at different times, taking on a whole range of different identities, and whilst these are mostly impersonations of Diviš himself, he sometimes speaks through the mouths of his characters: The whole cycle begins with 'I am a Princess and the Queen of Subat'.[68] The unifying element is not some identity or other, but the intensely physically experienced testimony about suffering. Whereas the in the prologue to *Leaving Bohemia* a physically degraded speaker observes an equally debased image of his country, he goes

---

67   I. Diviš: *Moje oči musely vidět*, pp. 15–16.
68   Ibid., p. 7.

on to witnesses suffering all over the world, and his physical experience of it reaches a point of utter dismemberment:

> Odpadávají šupiny, oškvarky,
> loupe se ze mne kůra jak z kmene platanu,
> až zbývá jen holý peň,
> maso na kostech,
> maso už nechráněné kůží.
> Pak odpadává i to maso, maso v kusech,
> vyletují ze mne vnitřnosti,
> zbývá jen kostra,
> která časem vybělí
> jak písek na břehu mořském.

> They're dropping off like scales, like cindered greaves,
> bark peeling off me like a plane-tree trunk,
> Until there's nothing left but bole, smooth, bare,
> flesh on the bones,
> flesh that's no longer protected by skin.
> Then the flesh starts to come off, chunk by chunk,
> my innards eviscerating out of me,
> till just the skeleton remains,
> which will turn white with time
> just like the sand upon the ocean shore.[69]

Whereas in *Leaving Bohemia* the notion being exercised was that of a project, in *My Eyes Had to See* the same flowing reverie turns into a nightmare, for which there is no longer any positive counterbalance, however ideal-imaginary it would be:

> Plul jsem špínou sna, najednou vidím
> valit se sklepní chodbou oživlý brambor,
> obrovský šišatý s očima komára, muříma nohama,

69　　Ibid., p. 13.

brambor světélkoval a namířil si to k nám
a ke mně jako k prvnímu.

▪

I sailed through murky dreams, saw suddenly
a living spud roll down the basement aisle,
huge, wonky with mosquito eyes, fowl feet,
a spud effulgent making its way toward us
and going for me first.[70]

VII

Ivan Diviš went into exile in August 1969 and spent the period between 1969 and 1997 living in Munich. Following the upheaval and fall of the Iron Curtain in November 1989, Diviš was no longer under any imposition to stay in exile and after 1990 often visited Prague, published books in the Czech Republic, and was the subject of several TV documentaries. In 1997 he made a final return to Prague, where he died in 1999.[71] Ivan Diviš is not the only poet-exile for whom 1989 opened up the possibility of return, and in any case the nature of his staying abroad changed.

How does such a change manifest itself in the envisioning of exile poetry? Exile is a factor that influences poetic imagination, as is evident from numerous examples in this book. At the same time, it is also clear that biographical particulars need not play any kind of major role. In Ovid's case, exile substantially sets out the thematic and certain structural elements of his poems, but the individual facts are often and deliberately contrived, and indeed one cannot read the testimony of the poems as some sort of historical record of exile life. Much the same applies to returning. If we can say that exile and leaving do contribute substantially to the shaping of the speaker and to the thematic aspect of Diviš's poems, something along those lines also applies to the period after 1989.

---

70   Ibid., p. 17.
71   cf. J. Zizler: *Ivan Diviš*, p. 214 (calendarium).

In his poems of that time Diviš does not talk about returning,[72] and especially not about returning in the sense of a reconciliation, still keeping his distance from Bohemia to a degree. What does come to an end is the complementary figurativeness of longer poems as developed in the *Lamb* and *Leaving*, by way of a project where the poetry is seeking to fulfil a mission, while reflecting the real state of things. Even back in his *My Eyes Had to See*, which in this regard marks the transition from exile to post-exile poems, Diviš cites the motif of eternal exile, which corresponds more to the state of things in the world rather than to being outcast as such:

> Moje oči musely vidět někdejší básníky trouchnivět ve slovaře,
>   moje oči viděly exil navěky,
>   navěky, takže nedává smysl

> My eyes had to see erstwhile poets moulder into wordsters,
>   my eyes have seen exile for ever,
>   for ever, so it makes no sense[73]

For Diviš's poems written in the 1990s, the characteristic perspective is that of hindsight and recapitulation of the past. In a number of his poems, Diviš revisits the subject of his departure, repeats motifs from older poems, but no longer takes the position he took with *Leaving Bohemia*, but instead that of an 'elder', who looks back on his near-completed life, rather than asking questions of the present. The speaker's perspective is well summarized by the title of one of his last collections, *Verše starého muže* [Old Man's Verse]. In one of his poems, there is a short depiction summing up the basic contradictions of his *Lamb on the Snow*. That piece was most marked by a pressing expectant tension born of immediacy, the envisaged present, whereas now the motif of Paradise and its destruction was described as a fact, a done deal, augmented only by a great scepticism towards man:

---

72   *Returning to Bohemia* was the name given to a selection of his letters from the 1990s published
      in 2011.

73   I. Diviš: *Moje oči musely vidět*, p. 26.

Veškerá nádhera světa a jeho rozlehlost
člověku nestačí.
[...]
Nejzapadlejší kout a ráj,
kde se ještě pasou jeleni,
pročesá a tu zvěř složí.
Teprve pak je ukojena
prokletá složka jeho povahy,
kterou nelze změnit
ani kdybyste jí nabídli Ráj.–

All the beauty of the world and its vastness
is too little for man.
[...]
The most remote corner and paradise,
where the deer are still grazing,
prompts him to flush out and kill this wild game.
Only then has he sated
that accursed part of his nature,
which cannot be changed
even if it were offered Paradise.–[74]

Now Diviš keeps his distance, given the political circumstances his stance has a different structure; he is not an Exile living outside the homeland and speaking into the wind, into the blowing Foehn, from a heterotopic external place. His 'place' is now more abstract, not bound geopolitically, but shaped by personal history. The subject of leaving is dealt with in another of the *Old Man* poems, whose title is the matter-of-fact name: 'The Poet JOSEF SUCHÝ plus my exit from the country'. It repeats the previously cited inscription, which was to Diviš (and characteristically in Slovak), a symbol of Czech reality:

Muselo to být v červenci roku šedesátdevět
a tedy pár týdnů před mým osudným rozhodnutím opustit vlast,

---

74   I. Diviš: *Verše starého muže*, p. 33.

kdy pobýval jsem v Horním Smokovci v literárním domě
[...]
a pak jsme šli na nádraží Poprad Tatry
čekat na rychlík od Košic–
Na asi deset skříňkách na zavazadla
visel nakřivo mongoloidním písmem načmáraný nápis:
V PRÍPADĚ VÝLUKY PRÚDU
SKRIENKY BATOŽINU NEVRACAJÚ.
Ten nápis způsobil můj raptus
a destiloval poslední kapku rozhodnutí
opustit tuto nesnesitelnou zemi
a zachránit si život.

It must have been in July of sixty-nine
so a few weeks before my fateful decision to leave my homeland,
when I was staying in Horní Smokovec in a literary house
[...]
and then we went to Poprad Tatry station
to catch a fast train from Košice–
On about ten luggage lockers
hung a wonky inscription, scribbled by a mongoloid hand:
IN THE EVENT OF A FAILURE OF POWER
THE LOCKERS WON'T GIVE LUGGAGE BACK...
That sign was my last straw
and distilled the last drop of my decision
to leave this execrable country
and save my life.[75]

Ivan Diviš represents the case of a Czech poet, whose work remains governed by exile even after returning from exile. Leaving Bohemia fundamentally shifted Diviš's poetry toward a personally distinctive, almost prophetic vituperative stance. Unlike Jan Zahradníček, whose critique of the world and its sorry state is impersonal, as if representing some higher instance, Ivan Diviš experiences

---

75   Ibid., pp. 112–113.

everything first-hand with all the uncertainties and fluctuations such a personal approach entails. Not only his leaving, but also his break-up with Czech reality and convention in its debased form stayed with him until the end. His actual exile came to be the existential exile of a man in this world (*My Eyes Had to See*), but also to the internal exile of a man in his hang-dog days (late poems).

9. In the Space of a Day

In the already cited poem Ivan Diviš reacts to Bavarian consumer society with disdain:

Lidé dál čtou Abendzeitung, spřádají sny o hovně
a večer s flaškou mezi nohama čumí na debiloskop

People keep reading their Abendzeitung, weaving dreams about bullshit
and in the evening with a bottle between their legs gawp at the
dunceoscope[1]

There is a certain paradox in it. Contemporary Czechoslovakia could certainly offer very similar images. This is not to say that reasons for emigration were lacking – there was no censorship in West Germany, there were no occupying troops present and there was no State Security. The shift also derives from the way that Diviš, like many other Exiles, brought with him to Germany, the 'baggage' of an idealized image of his homeland, against which he compared everyday reality abroad; albeit in other poems such comparisons serve to justify his leaving Bohemia. Many other poets perceived exile and their homeland more soberly, so that in their poems no significant role was played by

---

1 I. Diviš: *Obrať koně!*, p. 39.

some idealized image of home nor some sharp contrast between *there* and *here*. If we look at similar points in Diviš's work with different eyes, his disgust also reveals exile as a foreign space that does not provide refuge from the otherness of everyday life, does not protect from foreign customs, which at the time still feel less than obvious, while in the home environment this side of things remains tacit. There is a reminder here of the distinction between a *home* and an *abode*, as noted by Vilém Flusser. An abode or stay in a foreign environment brings the opportunity to better perceive some otherwise not obvious habits, and life's backdrop, as well as the details of the foreign environment. But the exile's abode also confronts them with a situation completely laid bare that must be endured and lived within. In connection with Flusser's distinction between a home and an abode, it turns out that an abode does not serve as a refuge, but lets the unpleasant or simply alien and odd sides of the foreign setting impinge on one's heightened awareness. In this sense, exile is similar to travelling[2] and both aspects affect each other. For some poets, unlike Ivan Diviš, this opens up an opportunity, but also the urgent task to map out a new space and find a contextual framework for it.

In September 1765, Jean-Jacques Rousseau, who had at that time been under attack right across Europe for his writings, found a refuge at Île St Pierre on Lac Bienne in Switzerland, having made a short trip there in July of that year. He writes about his stay, which lasted less than two months, in the twelfth volume of his *Confessions* (completed in 1770) and later in *The Reveries of a Solitary Walker* (which he completed in 1778). The fifth walk of his *Reveries* returns back to the days on St Peter's Island and portrays them in a distinctive way. Among his activities were botanical walks, in which he divided up one part of the island 'into small squares, intending to go through them one by one in each season.'[3] Rousseau tells of daily events in the past imperfective tense that emphasizes the repetitive nature underlying events. Nothing in his narrative reveals whether he carried out the activity repeatedly or only once, as if everything he was doing on the island was inclined toward a daily repeating routine. He dealt with time on the island in just the same way as his exploration of it, as if space and time had fused into one single big Day on the island, within which everything takes place

---

2   cf. J. F. Evelein: *Traveling Exiles, Exilic Travel.*

3   J.-J. Rousseau: *Les Rêveries du promeneur solitaire*, p. 98. The chronology of Rousseau's life and works is presented by Jacques Voisine in J.-J. Rousseau: *Les Rêveries du promeneur solitaire*, pp. 7–13.

in a trusty permanence. This day-frame allows Rousseau temporarily to build up an idyll of undisturbed life, uninterrupted. For later exile poets, a similar diurnal framework is utilized, into which the events of a foreign, unknown exile domain can be set.

In 1941, the French poet Saint-John Perse[4] wrote a composition called *Exil*. In it he captures human existence as exile, making use of mythologised images: '*Exile* is not an image of Resistance. It is a poem of the eternity of exile within the human condition. A poem born of nothing and made of nothing.'[5] The poem begins by opening to a new space:

> Portes ouvertes sur les sables, portes ouvertes sur l'exil,

> ▪

> Doors open to the sand, doors open to exile.[6]

This is not about leaving home or some imaginary Arcadia, land of songs and art; this topology upturns our values in favour of exile, even though exile is no new home. Going off into, or just becoming aware of the human situation as exile is what underlies the birth of a different poetry. Jean Starobinski adds: 'In *Exil*, it is not so much about a threshold that has been crossed, as about stepping into a new space, a wasteland conducive to song being born.'[7] Exile is depicted as a desert or a wasteland, unstratified by old customs; poetry that is born here is new, unmarked by what has gone before, starting anew, out of nothingness. Contrary to the concept of Arcadia, which underscores tradition, in the poem of Saint-John Perse exile means a fundamental restoration of poetry in a foreign environment, not shaped by tradition:

> Ma gloire est sur les sables ! ma gloire est sur les sables ! ... Et
> ce n'est point errer, ô Pérégrin,

---

4   [The pen name of Marie-René-Auguste-Aléxis Saint-Léger Léger]

5   "Exil n'est pas une image de la Résistance. C'est un poème de l'éternité de l'exil dans la condition humaine. Un poème né de rien et fait de rien," quotes Jean Starobinski: Le jour dans *Exil*, p. 650.

6   Saint-John Perse: *Eloges*, p. 150.

7   J. Starobinski: ibid., p. 651.

Que de convoiter l'aire la plus nue pour assembler aux syrtes de
l'exil un grand poème né de rien, un grand poème fait de rien...

My glory is on the sands! My glory is on the sands ...! And that
is no wandering lost, Oh Pilgrim,
When you're looking for a more naked space where to put
together in the moving sands of exile, a great poem made of nothing ...[8]

In this space, existence is uncertain, the pilgrim settles on nothingness and
builds on unstable terrain:

J'élis un lieu flagrant et nul comme l'ossuaire des saisons,
[...]
J'ai fondé sur l'abîme et l'embrun et la fumée des sables. Je me
coucherai dans les citernes et dans les vaisseaux creux,
En tous lieux vains et fades où gît le goût de la grandeur.

I have chosen a flagrant nothingness as the ossuary of the
seasons,
[...]
I have built on the abyss and the spindrift and the sand-smoke.
I shall lie down in cisterns and hollow vessels.
In all places vain and bland, where the taste of greatness lies.[9]

The identity of the exile, whom Perse's poem addresses by numerous names:
the Pilgrim, the Rider, the Stranger, the Prodigal One, remaining ever vague,
and this motif of uncertain identity also concludes the whole poem, which ends
with an ellipsis, as if the poet had yet to find his name:[10]

---

8   Saint-John Perse: ibid., p. 151.
9   Saint-John Perse: ibid., pp. 150–151. The theme is noted by P. Baker: Exile in Language,
     pp. 208–209, and J. Starobinski: ibid., p. 651.
10   P. Baker: ibid., p. 208, 207.

Et c'est l'heure, ô Poete, de décliner ton nom, ta naissance, et ta race...

And this is the hour, Oh Poet, to declare thy name, thy birth, and thy race ...[11]

Jean Starobinski deals with the day theme, crucial to the fifth canto of Perse's *Exil*. In it the Day represents a form of experience: 'the description of the day is inseparable from the ontological experience in which one's personal lasting and cosmic time are closely linked'.[12] The desert is not by any means some randomly chosen space in Perse's poem; it represents a type of *Cosmic Landscape* in which *"the complexities of our concrete life-world are reduced to a few, simple phenomena"*[13] or a smooth, nomadic space, as Deleuze and Guattari write.[14] This unstructured 'featurelessness' calls out for the frameworks the exile uses to delimit the space, 'pitting consciousness against the day.'[15]

II

The poems of Petr Král are very far removed from the mythical pathos of Perse's *Exil*. Where Perse speaks of 'princes of exile', thus underlining exile's importance, Petr Král contrastingly notes that 'heroes have gone' and 'kings have turned away'.[16] Yet his poems seem to have certain points in common with Perse's composition: they feature the theme of emptiness, which Král denotes with a rather urban environment, or more precisely a scene created out of urban inspiration. While Perse develops his myth in a featureless wasteland space, Král stays in a highly organized urban space in which the void equates

11   Saint-John Perse: ibid., p. 171.
12   J. Starobinski: ibid., p. 652.
13   cf. Ch. Norberg-Schulz: *Genius loci*, p. 45.
14   G. Deleuze – F. Guattari: *A Thousand Plateaus*, ch. XIV. 1440: The Smooth and the Striated, p. 474–500.
15   J. Starobinski: ibid., p. 654: *"la conscience face au jour"*.
16   P. Král: *Prázdno světa*, p. 47; *Sebrané básně* II, p. 254.

with a loss of meaning. The 'featureless smoothness' of this space signals, among other things, motility: 'a man knows he is a mere nothing, a nothing naked to the marrow of his bones and the walls dutifully sliding alongside'.[17] Day also plays an important role in his poetry, and Petr Král talks about a quintessential, not just a factual exile.

Král does not make a theme of exile as a situation he would have to endure against his will and something he would somehow have to suffer; he does not experience it as a loss.[18] He sees it from a poet's point of view, as an opportunity to rethink his situation. In his 1988 study, he writes:

> [...] I am doubtless beginning to suspect that my true fortune is not of the nature of some thing: that what I possess is not some tangible fetish, but only my restlessness and movement, from buoy to buoy, or to put it better perhaps, from nowhere to nowhere. The emigration experience here reaches a recognition of 'existential' exile, which befalls any human being.[19]

In a text devoted to Czech exile poetry, Král emphasizes precisely the role of awareness, revived:

> What is surely important here is how the exile experience enriches – and shapes – poets at the level of their self-perception and particular viewing of things. One feature of exile in particular seems striking to me here, its sharpened and deepened sense of space – again certainly both the physical and the metaphysical.[20]

Petr Král's poetry is not based on large-scale portrayals and projects, as is the case with Ivan Diviš, or on the construction of visionary space as with

---

17   P. Král: *Prázdno světa*, back cover; *Sebrané básně* II, p. 181.

18   cf. e.g. P. Král: *Úniky a návraty*, p. 92.

19   P. Král: *Sebrané básně* I, pp. 524–525. The quote is from the foreword to the book *Chimeras and Exile* dated 'Paris, March 1988'.

20   P. Král: Exil v moderní české poesii, p. 557. Originally a lecture, in the first version dated 1985. In it, Petr Král focuses on exile and exile motifs in Czech poetry since the 19th century. He reminds of the motifs of fearing exile among poets of the first half of the 20th century and takes the experience of exile to be primarily existential, not only in the sense of factual exile itself.

Součková, or as with Blatný, in a different aspect. Petr Král explicitly rejects the imagination of grand projects[21] and instead emphasizes an envisioning that inclines toward banality, to expanding the perceptual reach of everyday reality, rather than constructing a domain fundamentally different from it. Král perceives this situation against the background of a loss of meaning, which in his case brings some liberation from constraining values, with the emphasis on more acute perception and on discovering the new. Some words from the essay *Vidět* [To See] capture Král's own poetry more than any: 'In a time without transcendence, all we have left is joy. Joy or grace.'[22] This opening up to the surrounding space is apparent in the second poem of the *Prázdno světa* [Emptiness of the World] collection:

PSST, S.O.S.

Světlo se vzdává,
taky máslo balí svou svatozář,
za třaslavou kulisou chrabře haraší
už jen pár párátek v rukou posledních pobledlých;
i bez mrtvé váhy dědků nejsme o nic blíž východu,
definitivnímu pádu na užaslou hubu
z bedny prohnilého rychlíku.
Zatímco telefon parku ponuře mlčí
(mezi scvrklými špačky je zas vidět až do předpeklí),
rukou od herynků neoblomně tápem
po zmrzlém štukování,
pilně se ujišťujeme o vlastní existenci.

Navždy rozběsněné maso, i kdyby už jenom
v posledním zpitomělém úsměvu.
Než se nám zas na jaře zazelenají uši
(na novou ostudu, nový kabát),

---

21 cf. *Úniky a návraty*, p. 121, 127; and *Konec imaginárna*.
22 P. Král: *Konec imaginárna*, p. 164. But the word 'grace', with its history of transcendence, keeps a certain degree of ambiguity here.

naše vlažná míza diskrétně šumí
v lese zežloutlých Koh-i-noorek.

Pozorně jako nikdy kladu svá anonymní vejce
do zahradního Kiosku Zeměpisných délek.

PSST, S.O.S.

The light is surrendering,
and butter too is wrapping up its halo,
behind the shaky stage screen there's a brave rustling
only a few toothpicks in the hands of the last pale-faced;
despite the dead weight of old men, we're no closer to the east,
in an ultimate fall onto a gob-smacked gob
from the crate of a rotten express train.
While the park telephone remains grimly silent
(between shrunk starlings, Hell's limbo visible once more),
with pickled-herringed hand we relentlessly fumble
over the frozen stucco
busily making sure of our own existence.

Forever enraged flesh, even if it were only
in the last doltishly stupefying smile.
Before our ears turn green again in the Spring
(decked in new turncoats, ready for new disgrace),
our indifferent tepid sap discreetly fizzing
in backwoods of yellowed pencils, Koh-i-noor branded.

With care as ne'er before I lay my anonymous eggs
into the garden Kiosk of Terrestrial longitudes.[23]

The poem repeatedly goes from a collective and historical experience to the
personal level: as the light and a halo are withdrawn, left still standing on the

---

23   P. Král: *Prázdno světa*, p. 11. The collection, dated 1981, was first published in Munich in 1986.

scene are the last pale-faced ones and ancestral heritage, the 'dead weight of old men', does not prevent falling flat 'on the gob', which fact hits each individual hard and with all immediacy. History comes down to the harsh collision of the human body with the material world. If Diviš treats physical suffering as a way of perceiving historical events, i.e. a metaphor, for Král similar shocks only signal that all grand history has its place somewhere beyond the limited horizon of the human body. At the end of the first strophe the speaker tells of reassuring ourselves of our own existence, in the plural, but the fumbling along the wall only emphasizes this is not some collective identity, but is indeed a physical existence, the right here and now. This gets underscored in the last strophe by switching to the singular, replacing the general and collective plural. The strangely cryptic name of the poem "PSST, S.O.S." evokes a situation in which a call for help is vying for our attention, as if the need for it was not at all self-evident. The distress signal acquires a comical dimension, and is lost in the meaningless fizz of background noise. As much as the first part of the poem is characterized by retreat, absence, collision or uncertainty, the conclusion becomes a gesture of confident flair, albeit limited to its own autonomous sphere, where a kiosk encompasses the whole world. A similar but sharper-edged sense of taking issue with grand and overarching events comes in the poem *Poklona* [Tribute], in its contrasts between You and I:

> Tak jo, vykřesali jste oheň, vyčmuchali brambory a uhlí,
> vynalezli jste pádlo i kolo kulatý, stloukly sáně malovaný,
> [...]
> Ušili jste tepláky, palčáky, letní i zimní dresy,
> nabrousili jste vidličky i břitvy, vybílili Pankrác, zapálili Operu a zas
>   ji uhasili,
> nadělali jste voňavku z nafty a mejdlo ze Židů,
> vyšly vám umělý plíce i sádrový hovna
> [...]
> Skřípli jste blesk do kleští, praskáte pilně v nábytku a mručíte
>   v potrubí,
> děláte už na jaře děti na zimu,
> bravo dámy, díky pánové.
>
> Já tu zase nechávám klouzat pár průsvitných pěšců
> po prázdné stránce dálek,

vykukuju nyvě do modra z bílých míst na mapě
a roztržitě přikusuju rozměklý Klíč z chleba.

Alright then, you've sparked a fire, sniffed out potatoes and some coal,
invented both the paddle and the round wheel, knocked together
        a painted sledge,
[...]
You have sewed sweatpants, mittens, summer and winter jerseys,
sharpened up forks and razors, whitewashed Pankrác jail, set fire to
        the Opera and put it out again,
made perfume out of diesel and soap out of the Jews,
had luck with artificial lungs and plaster turds
[...]
You've nipped lightning with pliers, and diligently now crack-on in
        the furniture and gurgle in the pipes,
you get on with it in the spring making children for the winter,
bravo ladies, thank you gentlemen.

Whereas I am letting a couple of translucent pawns slide here
over the empty page of far distances
I'm peeking out into the blue from the white spots on the map
and distractedly nibble on a softened Key made of bread.[24]

The 'ladies and gentlemen' are responsible for great discoveries and collective crimes, for the course of civilization; they could be described as the stuff of history-making, while their counterpart is a poet whose gesture is ostentatiously to ignore the bipole of benefit vs crime. Král is clearly not making excuses to distance himself from mankind, as if he was not personally responsible for anything. Instead, he notes that at this point, some daydreaming human gesture no longer has a role in events purposeful for human civilization, whether they bring benefit, or are crimes; poetry finds itself beyond the zone of historical purpose. The perspective of pushing back grand time, focusing on the present moment, is summed up by the verse: 'life behind your back and the forenoon

---

24   Ibid., pp. 18–19.

ahead of you'.[25] As Král sees it, the morning or forenoon, and indeed the space of one day intertwines with an empty page and form an opposite partner to consciousness, that 'day-facing awareness' that Starobinski finds in Perse.

Most often or most significantly, the exile motif appears precisely in Král's *Emptiness of the World* collection.[26] We are not dealing with poetry marked by or defined by exile in the sense of losing one's homeland, Král's body of work gives us nothing of the kind. His poetics only takes in the impulses of exile and is inspired by them. It never ceases to have a hint of irony, downplaying any take on exile that makes it seem tragic:

> Někde si občas buchar bouchne do peřin,
> támhle české ptactvo straší pilně v korunách
> a tady já se tomu tiše chlámu.

> Sometimes a drop-hammer bashes the snow-down out of duvets,[27]
> there, Czech birds busily scaremongering in tree-crowns
> while I here gently snigger about it all.[28]

Petr Král himself states that emptiness, the titular and key motif of the collection, was one of his exile revelations, even foreshadowing it: 'The discovery of the void underlying an image and of the silence behind a word is not only the fruit of meditation, but also of the kind of brutally immediate shock my exile stems from and, in a sense, only continues to deepen.'[29]

The notion of emptiness and silence in Král's poems leads to an awareness of the world as a realm of things and an object-seeking vision, characterized by great specificity and sharpness of detail. This awareness is not a purely mental act, but it is something intrinsically corporeal, and by the agency of the body open to physically making contact with the world. As a result, one important aspect of Král's work is movement; characterized by walking and distinctive

----

25 Ibid., p. 45.
26 This is also the only collection that Král published in Exile in Czech; before 1989, he published three more collections in French.
27 [transl. note: *"bouchne do peřin"* can also be meant idiomatically as a sudden snowstorm]
28 Ibid., p. 26.
29 P. Král: *Sebrané básně* I, p. 518.

physical gesture in later collections. The author himself summarizes it with the term 'pedestrian metaphysics'. In some aspects, the object-seeking vision also impacts the speaker, as if movement was to mean merely some physical clash:

> Mám hlavu, svou skleněnou kouli
> – v poledne, hlavně symetricky –
> rozkřáplou zvučným pádem lžíce na ledovou dlažbu
> kuchyně, dalekého mauzolea.

> I have a head, my own vitreous ball
> – at high noon, most symmetrically –
> cracked by the sonorous fall of a spoon on the ice-tiled floor
> of a kitchen, in a far-off mausoleum.[30]

These sought-for objects are often fleeting, much like the 'translucent pawns' in the *Tribute* poem, being products of the imagination interspersed among the objects observed. Stood back behind them all, part-revealed, part-hiding is the author's consciousness, always slightly different from the physical speaker, who is himself contrived. In this expanse between physical experience and the shaping of imaginary scenes, an aesthetic sense typical of Petr Král is manifest. Integral to it is the existential aspect of shaping one's life as that of a poet, not to live up to moral imperatives, but poetic ones, which also holds for the poems themselves.[31] In this, Král is not unlike Ivan Blatný. In the following expression the emptiness of the real world and the void within the medium of art characteristically converge:

> The dizzying sensation we get from creative work, with every thought and action that takes us off the beaten path, is the vertigo of the void. That blissful and exciting awareness of being alive that makes our cheeks flush is only the rush of the wind we feel caused by the tem-

---

30   P. Král: *Prázdno světa*, p. 24. In a similar vein, the spokesperson of the poem *Autoportrét v nedělním* [Self-Portrait in Sunday best] comprises a number of objects (p. 12).

31   cf. the author's foreword to the collection *P. S. čili Cesty do ráje* (written between 1969 and 1979), *Sebrané básně* II, pp. 11–12. The acronym P.S. here also refers, ironically, to the motif of an 'empty world', (*Prázdno Světa* in Czech).

porary acceleration of our fall to nowhere. There are no poems, paintings and films, only an immeasurable and blinding white plain – a canvas just like paper – from time to time sprinkled with a translucent rain that leaves no trace behind. There are no events, there is only one continuous happening, a stream without beginning and without end, relentlessly washing away the forms of beings, objects and phenomena, out of whose volatile constellations it is recreating itself.[32]

In these quotations, spatial formulations prevail, which is not to be taken as covering up the void's presence as a space-time backdrop, because, after all, motion amounts to time and space being inseparably in concert. Day in Král's poetics gives emptiness a crucial boundary, including the way time and space are bound up within it. One of the poems in the collection carries Day in the title:

ROZLOHA DNE
(*Jeanovi s Raquel*)

Už od svítání neúprosná modernost stromů.
Černých drápů zaťatých v nepřítomném masu
nebe, dokud se nezablýskne třpytkou existence.

Hluboko ve zdi, v dřevě pod kůrou,
rozžíhá se slunce v bohorovném
neklidu, zvedá se z trosek, pokročilé, leč neposkvrněné
bitvy. Na naše omyly se zapomíná, bez pokřiku.
V pravé poledne sestoupit dolů do sklepa,
seriózně jako se člověk noří
do plesnivých kapes trenčkotu mrtvého.

Z rukávu vyhoštěná ruka
pluje nenápadně ve stojatých vodách aleje, podél stínů,

---

32   P. Král: *Sebrané básně* I, p. 519. The author cites this passage as an excerpt of his contemplations from shortly after his emigration.

hbitá a samotná. „Jsme si podobní",
osleplí. V nejtemnější chvíli nahé
kůže.

V návalu ticha společné zranění obzoru.
Bez odpovědi, až na hlaveň prázdné konve
trčící z kopřiv.

■

DAY SPAN
(to Jean and Raquel)

From earliest dawn the unwavering modernity of trees.
Black claws stuck fast into the missing flesh
of heaven, until it flashes forth its glimmer of existence.

Deep in the wall, in wood under the bark,
the sun grows more alight in pontificating
restlessness, from wreckage, of an advanced but spotless
battle. Our mistakes get forgotten, without shouting.
At high noon, to descend into the basement,
as gravely solemnly as one would delve
into the mouldy trenchcoat pockets of a dead man.

An out-of-sleeve expelled and outcast hand
floats low-key in an avenue's still waters, along shadows,
nimble and alone. 'We are alike,'
gone blind. In the profoundly darkest moment of naked
skin

In rushing silence, the shared wound of the horizon.
No reply, just the barrel of an empty watering-can
sticking out of the nettles.[33]

---

33   Ibid., p. 31.

The poem, abundant with evocative imagery (morning, noon, the injuring of the horizon with a blood-red sunset) evokes a time frame, a day's expanse, which also has its spatial layout on the book's page. The first strophe captures with some exactitude the way time is held immobile in the world's objects; the trees, introduced as being there 'from earliest dawn' are described like a lasting painting, under a prolonged observation when nothing happens but things are there. This temporal silence is disturbed by the flash of the sun, a characteristic reminder of existence that pops up in other poems. The claws and flesh of heaven give the impression of a grave burden, perhaps even the cruelty of the world, chasing the man there present, and impatiently dispersing the sun. In the second strophe, man does, however, appear to be just one of the mirages in the day's projection. The lack of involvement, the almost total absence of a moral or humanizing view is underlined by a floating hand— as if the human body was not held together in a man's image, but along with other things and parts floated around in the light of day. The poem's ending articulates a leap from 'we' to a more impersonal observer, a more abstract consciousness for which this whole compact but sensory scene is expressed by the pointedly protruding muzzle of a watering can.

III

If Petr Král's approach is in many ways typified by the verse quoted: 'life behind your back and the morning in front of you', which already implies movement and walking, Ivan Schneedorfer's *Básně z poloostrova* [Poems from the Peninsula] are characterized by another image: 'I stand here, a man under a tree...',[34] which speaks of standing still and a light melancholy, whereby Schneedorfer observes himself and the outside world, as if standing on the very edge of what is happening in it: 'As always, I am sitting / as close as I can to the door ...'[35] In his poems, a stranger observes, sees and hears, but is himself seldom seen or heard:

---

34   I. Schneedorfer: *Básně z poloostrova*, p. 40.
35   Ibid., p. 51.

Křičíme na plavce:
Teď pozor na běsy!
Ale vítr nám trhá
naši řeč na kusy.
Mořeplavce varujeme,
ale s naším přízvukem
jako bychom mlčeli...

We're yelling at the swimmer:
Beware the surges, now!
But the strong wind is tearing
our speech to shreds, and how.
We're warning the seafarers,
but, with our accent strange,
it's as if we were dumb...[36]

Ivan Schneedorfer left Czechoslovakia after the August 1968 occupation and ever since 1979 has been living on the Tsawwassen peninsula on the Pacific coast of British Columbia. This is where his collection of *Poems from the Peninsula* originated, published in Munich in 1987. *Tsawwassen* is the native name for a land facing the sea, and this border gives Ivan Schneedorfer's collection an important reference frame. The second setting frame is the day – his poems and sections roughly follow the course of a day, starting with morning themes in the opening poems and progressing through the 'Canadian afternoon' section toward the 'Evening Sun'. While Petr Král's space-time day-frame is abstract, the time and place of Schneedorfer's peninsula is by contrast very specific. It is the grounding foundation and basis the speaker of the poems has beneath his feet as he moves. Grounded on the peninsula the here-and-now combines with memories, and images of the past associated with home emerge from the mist of the present, in nostalgic spasms. It is in this spirit that the collection opens, with its first poem:

---

36   Ibid., p. 119.

Zde u moře čekáme
na ranní slunce
mnohdy až do půl jedenácté.
Z mlhy zatím vystupují
rozostřené obrazy
stromů, krav a koní...
Jako když je prodloužena noc,
hromadí se sny a otázky:
Kdepak je teď přítel Dvořák?
Je-li dosud živa
jeho hezká maminka?
A jak to, že jsme tenkrát
cestou do Plzence
minuli pivovar
jakoby nic...

Here by the sea we wait
for the morning sun
often until half past ten.
So far, coming out of the fog
are blurry images
of trees, cows and horses...
Just as the night is extended,
dreams and questions multiply:
Where is my friend Dvořák now?
And is she alive still,
his lovely mother?
And how could we, long ago
on our way to Plzenec
have gone past the brewery
without a second thought...[37]

---

37   Ibid., p. 7.

Ivan Schneedorfer leads a rural existence on the peninsula, as he put it in the 1990s, writing to his friend in Bohemia Emil Juliš:

> It's a January morning. Outside it is still dark. There a pinkish tint to the darkness from the lights of the city to the north. The city of Vancouver is quickly, frantically growing. Fortunately, there is still a good distance between our peninsula and Vancouver, numerous fields, gardens, bridges over the individual strands of the Fraser river delta, and even one underwater tunnel. It still feels like being in the countryside, surrounded by people who don't interfere in each other's lives. No one seems to care I have an old car or that I go for a walk in a ridiculous coat and hat.[38]

The poet on the peninsula, hidden in such a disguise somehow does not belong to his past, or his present world. His cagey distancing allows him to watch everything around more intently:

> Vidím ty muže
> a není mi do smíchu.
> Noviny čtou a všemu věří...
> Jsem ještě cizinec?
> Jako vždy sedím
> co nejblíž u dveří...
>
>
> I see those men
> and I don't feel light-hearted.
> They read the news and believe all the more...
> Am I still a stranger?
> As always, I am sitting
> as close as I can to the door...[39]

---

38   I. Schneedorfer: *Básně*, p. 470.
39   I. Schneedorfer: *Básně z poloostrova*, p. 51.

One important thing remains unspoken in Ivan Schneedorfer's poems, but keeps cropping up between the lines. He has managed to bring to his point of view that special peninsular mood that is inherent in the old expressive name Tsawwassen. It is as if he were constantly standing with his face turned toward the sea, and everything he experiences, what he sees and what he remembers takes place against the backdrop of a ubiquitous ocean:

> Okno máme na západ.
> Když otevřu oči,
> vidím tím směrem
> jen konec pevniny.
>
> ⁕
>
> Our window faces west.
> When I open my eyes,
> in that direction I see
> just the firm mainland's end.[40]

The ocean doesn't even have to be explicitly mentioned, it is enough to let the poem remind of a small detail, a seabird or a fisherman, and we know right away that we find ourselves in another place. The boundaried land opens up our mind's eye to the past, but its ever-evident limits also presage an enclosed framework. In terms of a day, its span becomes an analogy of human life – as if Ivan Schneedorfer was being ironic and bringing into play the old Baroque and Romantic motif of comparing the course of life with times-of-day, as has been developed in Czech poetry by Mácha:

> Zdá se, že homo sapiens
> svět pozoruje kukátkem.
> I když slunce už zapadlo,
> nic není docela ztraceno...
> Konec konců, bude-li tma,
> může otočit knoflíkem
> a usednout k obrazovce...

---

40   Ibid., p. 89.

Může a nemusí. Zatím
tu a tam ještě odkládá
dobrovolnou smrt...

It would seem that Homo sapiens
watches the world through a peephole.
Though the sun's already set,
nothing's yet hopelessly lost...
Why, if there is to be darkness,
one can just turn a knob
and sit down by a screen...
Can, with no obligation. So far
here and there, still postponing
voluntary death... [41]

Schneedorfer does not, however, paint an allegorical image of life, the repeated
alternation of days, hours, minutes creates his living space:

Co chvíli se opakuje týden,
dvacet čtyři hodiny
a šedesát minut.
Už si nevšímáme vteřin...
Každý večer dobrovolně
pokoušíme smrt,
ale předtím, opatrně,
natahujeme hodinky...

Again and again the week repeats,
twenty-four hours
and sixty minutes.
We don't notice the seconds anymore...
Every evening voluntarily

---

41   Ibid., p. 88.

we tempt death,
but before that, with all care,
we wind up our watches...[42]

Schneedorfer does not push the day toward an abstraction counterbalancing awareness, but instead moves through the days, from a hint of dawn, over the morning's fixed point: *"Miluji ráno, ten pevný bod / v neklidném prostoru a čase..."*[43] [I love the morning, that fixed point / in restless space and time...] and right up to the night, which, in an almost Baroque spirit, is akin to death, though lightened-up with contemporary detail.

Not only the *Poems from the Peninsula*, but also Ivan Schneedorfer's other poems, are a kind of notepad diary, recording observations from idle moments. The speaker of these poems being more a narrator of 'micro-stories', who is a lover of 'the melodies of stories'[44] pauses, strolls on slowly, watches his surroundings from some corner seat, from a moving train or bus. He seeks out moments of inactivity, and then, going unnoticed himself, looks around. If one can talk about the meaning of exile as expressed in Ivan Schneedorfer's poems, it lies in this slightly melancholic exclusion: He observes others, listens to their conversations, mostly at a slight distance, as one who likewise observes himself. He's always a bit of an outsider. At the same time, however, what we have here is not an Exile isolated in an alien environment, because his images of the peninsula meld with memories of home, his exile being above all the distance of one looking on and experiencing. In one of the poems, being 'cast out' is on a par with the natural elements, an act of nature, on the frontier between birth and death.

Den se někam poděl.
Ležím. Noc mne zastihla.
Vidím z okna pod měsícem
vysoký trs pampí trávy.
Jak původní pán peninsuly
nehnutě tam stojí...

---

42   Ibid., p. 76.
43   Ibid., p. 8.
44   Ibid., p. 11.

O půlnoci slyším hlasy,
ty z prvních kapitol.
Slyším dobře, sám nic neříkám.
Jako bych už nepatřil.
Jako by mne příliv vyvrhl,
tu ležím...

The day has gone who knows where.
I am lying down. The night has caught up with me.
I see from the window below the moon
a tall clump of pampas grass.
Like the peninsula's primal lord
standing there, motionless...
At midnight I hear voices,
the ones from the first chapters.
I hear well, saying nothing myself.
As though I no longer belonged.
As if the tide had cast me out,
I am lying here...[45]

In 1990 Ivan Schneedorfer wrote the collection *Návrat* [Return], in which he depicts his trip to Europe and finally to Bohemia. The encounter with the European space, with the places kept in his imagery, reveals only new discrepancies but, above all, uncertainty about 'What am I, indeed?'[46] The focal point of the *Return* is his visit home: everything is familiar, and at the same time changed:

Řeknu kdo jsem
    a paní Králová
    pozve mne na kávu
Místnosti poznávám
    nábytek nikoli
    a sebe také ne

45   I. Schneedorfer: *Básně z poloostrova*, p. 33.
46   I. Schneedorfer: *Básně*, p. 207.

V kulatém zrcadle
    je cizí tvář
    a už ani slovo...

     ⸗

I'll say who I am
    and Mrs Králová
    will invite me for coffee
I recognize the rooms
    not the furniture
    and neither myself
In the round mirror
    is some stranger's face
    And not another word now...[47]

IV

Václav Hokův (1932–1986) went into exile in Switzerland in 1969, and afterward spent some time in the United States, from where he returned seriously ill. While in Switzerland, he studied for a time at the C. G. Jung Institute; this interest is manifested in his work by numerous references to Jungian terminology, but also to Eastern thinking and the Western mystical tradition. In a commemorative piece, Jaroslav Vejvoda portrays him as an outsider and at first glance a typical washed-up exile, unsympathetic to his compatriots,[48] Hokův, with some irony, portrays himself in the same vein, in poems from the 1980s:

nebyl jsem oblečen zvlášť salónně
v darované bundě
vyšlé již z módy
dobrých patnáct let
v kalhotách ještě z doby

---

47   Ibid., p. 211.
48   J. Vejvoda: O sladkém neštěstí Václava Hokůva [On the Sweet Misfortune of Václav Hokův].

druhé pražské spartakiády
opíraje se o deštník
unavený čtyřicátník

I was not too well dressed for high society
in a donated jacket
that had gone out of fashion
a good fifteen years ago
in trousers dating back
to the second Prague Spartakiad
leaning on an umbrella
a tired fortysomething[49]

In his collection *Curych: trojrozměrná mandala* [Zurich: a Three-dimensional Mandala] written between 1973 and 1976, Hokův took a quirky approach to raising-up and recodifying the city of Zurich as a readable chart. In contrast to his later poems, the collection exudes a certain vigour, stimulated by discovering a new space.[50] In his poems Hokův intently assert his interest in Jungian psychology, esoteric and Eastern thought, and views various places in Zurich as signals and symbols from this perspective. Whilst the place of exile is a foreign land, in this collection it is also a text-space, in all its details imbued with meaning. Zurich is mysterious but at the same time readable. As he walks around, visiting places, the poet reads their meanings, and through these places he also reads himself.

ULRICHSTRASSE 18

Slepá ulice, která nikam nevede. Černá
panterovská kočka mně přeběhla přes cestu,

---

49   V. Hokův: *Lebka k líbání*, p. 16, the poem *Dopis místnímu básníkovi I*, also cited by Vejvoda.

50   To the extent that we can judge from the published fragements of his work and data available from sources including one publication dedicated to Hokův, Z. Jonák: *Václav Hokův, imaginární portrét básníka a esejisty* [Václav Hokův, an Imaginary Portrait of a Poet and Essayist], it is in the later poems that an ironic and skeptical tone is promoted, a selection of them published as *Lebka k líbání* [A Skull for Kissing].

když jsem sem prvně vstupoval; vysoké
studené zdi činžáku mého dětství,
s exteriérem Maxe Ernsta na dvorku.
Včelí královna tu má svůj úl,
Velká Matka se svým klínem naděje
uprostřed rajského paláce
Šípkové Růženky.

Vracím se tu denně ke svým předkům,
temným a hbitým obyvatelům rodičovského domu,
když se šátrám po chladných schodech
do mé světničky ve třetím poschodí.

ULRICHSTRASSE 18

A dead-end street, not leading anywhere. A black
panther-like cat had run across my path,
when I was first getting off here; high
cold walls of the tenement house of my childhood,
with a Max Ernst exterior in the back yard.
Here is the place the queen bee has her hive,
The Great Mother with her vee of hope
in the midst of the paradisal palace
of Sleeping Beauty.

I'm coming back each day here to my ancestors,
the dark and nimble dwellers of the parental house,
as I am fumbling up the chilly stairs
to my small single room on the third floor.[51]

In his evidently later poem *Popeleční středa* [Ash Wednesday], Hokův, in a dream, requests a consultation with 'renowned Professor Jung', whose secretary fobs him off, and the dreaming poet leaves:

---

51   V. Hokův: *Curych*, p. 12.

Tak namísto
k psychiatrovi
šel jsem
na konzultaci
do pivnice Am Egge
s hlavou zmotanou
provazy
které ze mě
Amnesty International
mezitím sňala
ve spánku
straší mě dál
dračí smyčka

◾

So rather than
to a psychiatrist
I went
for a consultation
to the Am Egge beer cellar
with my head tangled
in ropes
that were taken off me
by Amnesty International
in the interim
as I slept
it continues to haunt me
the bowline, dragon loop[52]

In this poem, the foreign land appears as a space that refuses to accept one, and offers no other reading, the dreamer does not get even as far as the foyer of C. G. Jung, that authoritative reader and decipherer of esoteric signs. In these poems, the foreign land's places are at times discoverable and decipherable as

---

52   V. Hokův: *Masopustní nokturno*, p. 21

in the *Zurich: a three-dimensional mandala* collection and at times merely the ironic self-reflection of a man in an alien and impenetrable environment.

V

For the poets of this chapter, exile is characterized by their relationship to the foreign country, whereby the foreign country need not be either friendly or hostile, but remains, above all *foreign*. Foreignness leads to ordinary things and ways of behaving, manners, being perceived as strange, suggesting otherwise invisible or unnoticed frames of reference. It is not unusual to find in modern poetry a similar attitude to perceiving everyday reality, as something unknown: in this particular point, exile and modern poetry make contact. The poet-exile makes apparent and highlights a reference frame we tend to overlook, but also, looking in the opposite direction offered by this situation, we see that awareness of the setting – its space and time, once highlighted, can lead to a sense of exclusion and exile. When Baudelaire in his *Swan* experiences his Paris as estranged, it fires his imagination toward the motifs of exile.

10. Exile, Nomadic Life and Language

When Ivan Blatný sought shelter in various institutions over many years, he was not just looking to counter home and exile. So much is apparent from his comments about reports of his alleged suicide five years after he left Czechoslovakia:

> Quite apart from the political reasons and political sense of my decision to stay in England five years ago, I consider living abroad to be something that might certainly benefit a person in some other time and some other situation, in the sense that whenever people have had the good fortune or made the decision to do so, they gained through that experience of something very valuable, and there was always a big difference between them and the *less mobile inhabitants of homes*, in terms of their awareness of the world, that kind of education that can't be acquired either from books or cinemas. All the more, people whose life interests include literature or art in any sense, tend to have such *nomadic tendencies*, even if they were not driven out like Comenius or Heine or all of us who are here today, for political reasons. Antonín Dvořák in America, Bedřich Smetana in Sweden, Vítězslava Kaprálová in France, dozens of foreign artists in Paris, – they did not perish for having left HER, while SHE, the motherland not only did not perish, of course, but rather gained, if indeed it can ever be said that the mighty mother country can be

dependent on the lives of her individual insignificant cosmopolitan sons.[1]

In this passage we find probably one of the first mentions of a nomadic life anywhere in Czech post-war exile writing. Blatný here sets out the quite unpolitical antithesis of the nomad and the 'less mobile inhabitants of homes'[2] much like Vilém Flusser. In addition to the spatial *home – exile* polarity that drove the exile poetry of the 1950s, we have here more of an existential duality *home – nomadic life*. Of course, home does not have the same meaning in both cases: for an Exile, home is the centre of their world and the point of reference that defines the nature of their exile. For a nomad, it is merely a stop along the way. In the given geopolitical constellation, home is occupied by a totalitarian state, which one is not allowed to leave, or is forced to, but has no right to depart and return to at will. Whereas an Exile is eager to return, the nomad, on the other hand, hankers after the freedom to move and the chance to take a break in some temporary abode. In the end, Blatný retreats into seclusion even from the state apparatus in England, or rather from the aspect of it that does not benefit his approach to life. To paraphrase Deleuze and Guattari, he would be a nomad who doesn't move around and lives *in intensity*.[3] If we take the antithesis of home and exile to a logical conclusion, exile is almost the mirrored opposite of the homeland, only devoid of territory: the exile community seeks to establish its own institutions, preserve its home culture, with the political aim to return to the homeland. By contrast, the nomad transcends this polarity and seeks a space beyond the structure of a state. In this sense, the term 'nomadism' became established mainly in French philosophical thinking from the late 1960s on, and a little later among some Czech exile authors, too.

The figure of a poet moving between different places and not hamstrung in their actions by ties to some fixed home is after all a very old concept. It is spoken of by Plato when he speaks of itinerant poets, travelling from village to village. In the Homeric Hymn to Apollo, the rhapsode refers to the tradition of singers wandering among the villages:

---

1   Typescript from the estate of Josef Lederer, my italics.
2   [transl. note: the option to translate "*méně pohyblivými obyvateli domovů*" as 'less mobile inhabitants of homes' is a half-way house between the more outlying possibilities, ranging from 'less mobile stay-at-homes', to 'incarcerated inmates of residential institutions']
3   G. Deleuze – F. Guattari: *A Thousand Plateaus*, (Treatise on Nomadology), p. 381.

"Girls, which man's song is sweetest to you
of those landing here, and who delights you most?"
Then you all answer so well about us:
"The blind man, who lives in rugged Chios,
whose songs all remain the best forever."
We will carry your fame so far over the earth
as we travel about the crowded cities of people.
They will be persuaded, since it is the truth.[4]

Just as Odysseus, Aeneas and Ovid differ in regard to the nature of their travels, so does nomadism cover multiple types of movement: the rhapsode of antiquity moved among a relatively finite few municipalities and stayed in his own linguistic environment, it seems; the medieval Latin-speaking poets were able to travel all over the continent, and for them the word exile had a wider, and indeed a different meaning than in modern times. For the poets of the Eastern Bloc during the Cold War, such a journey could even be imaginary, and be more about alternating between two or more languages rather than changing places.

II

The word *nomad* refers in its original meaning to a travelling herder,[5] and only with time has its meaning broadened and shifted to encompass the ways of

---

4   *The Homeric Hymns* [online], pp. 40–41. Likewise, in the Old English poem *Wídsíð* [Widsith], the wandering singer speaks: 'Widsith came to talk, unlocking his wordy hoard, / he who had travelled furthest across the earth / among men and tribes and peoples—' and the poem concludes: 'So the minstrels of men turned to leave wandering / among the created world, throughout many lands, / talking at need, speaking grateful words, / always to the south or north, / measuring out / a certain wise song, unstingy of their gifts—' transl. Dr Aaron K. Hostetter, [https://anglosaxonpoetry.camden.rutgers.edu/widsith/]

5   Rejzek's etymological dictionary gives the following entry for nomad: 'from lat. *Nomades*, greek *nomádes* (pl.) itinerant 'travellers' from the lat. *nomas*, gr. *nomás* 'grazing, travelling around' from the gr. *nomé* or *nomós* 'fodder, pasture', from *némó* 'I allocate, inhabit, manage', *némomai* 'I use, graze', p. 413. He expounds on the Czech term *kočovat* thus: 'Adopted during the national revival from the Polish word *koczować* or the Russian *кочует*, there from the Tatar. *köc* 'wandering, resettlement', p. 283.

life and intellectual attitudes of modern man – to such an extent that nowadays it seems a cliché.[6] In the post-war period, the words nomadism and nomad occur more frequently outside their original historical context, and in many cases serve as the counterpoint or anthesis to a settled way of life or type of existence, one not based on the opposition of home versus exile, but instead founded on a constant migration, without anchorage to a fixed home. The Scottish poet Kenneth White, based in France, writes about 'intellectual nomadism' and begins the genealogy of nomadism with Ralph Waldo Emerson, who used this phrase in his essay *History*,[7] and extends the lineage to include Nietzsche, Spengler, Lyotard, Foucault or Deleuze and Guattari. White dates the growing interest in the term in France to the late 1960s.[8] For White, who himself did a lot of travelling, it is not just the purely intellectual attitude that Deleuze and Guattari expose, for whom 'the nomad is more like one *who lives without relative movement*',[9] but the concept of nomadism remains associated with geography. He treats it primarily as a poetic concept and only briefly mentions the Second World War as an event that 'ended all cosmopoetic speculation and this whole nomadizing movement'.[10] He does, however, leave important historical and political contexts aside. Jacques Attali recalls the hostility of the Soviet and Nazi regimes toward nomads and describes these regimes as 'forms of totalitarian sedentariness',[11] which escalate a tendency already evident

---

6   One of the writers addressing the present burgeoning of the term is P. Kannisto: *Global nomads*.

7   K. White: *Esquisse du nomade intellectuel*, p. 50. White cites an earlier version of the essay, in the later edited version Emerson makes more explicit the antithesis of the nomadic and settled ways of life, without expressing any obvious preference: "*A man of rude health and flowing spirits has the faculty of rapid domestication, lives in his wagon, and roams through all latitudes as easily as a Calmuc. At sea, or in the forest, or in the snow, he sleeps as warm, dines with as good appetite, and associates as happily, as beside his own chimneys. Or perhaps his facility is deeper seated, in the increased range of his faculties of observation, which yield him points of interest wherever fresh objects meet his eyes. The pastoral nations were needy and hungry to desperation; and this intellectual nomadism, in its excess, bankrupts die mind, through die dissipation of power on a miscellany of objects. The home-keeping wit, on the other hand, is that continence or content which finds all the elements of life in its own soil; and which has its own perils of monotony and deterioration, if not stimulated by foreign infusions*" (R. W. Emerson: History, p. 247).

8   K. White: ibid., p. 59.

9   G. Deleuze – F. Guattari: *A Thousand Plateaus*, (Treatise on Nomadology), p. 381.

10   K. White: ibid., p. 59.

11   J. Attali: *L'homme nomade*, pp. 288–290.

in democracies before the Second War. The totalitarian state becomes a prison for its citizens, who cannot abandon it of their own volition.

Maurice Blanchot, in a 1962 essay entitled *Être juif* [Being Jewish], explores the issue of Judaism and substantially links exile with the relationship to truth: the idea of exodus and exile represents a 'righteous movement', in which the 'experience of foreignness' is affirmed as fundamental and the meaning of this experience is for us to learn to speak, with its 'authority'.[12] Nomadism, which Blanchot treats as synonymous with exile, is a relationship to the truth that cannot be had by an existence linked to a firmly established place and to ownership. Exile means distancing oneself from one's origin, but this separation makes apparent a 'truth of origin' beyond anything an ownership relationship can encompass. Exodus is not personified by a man who has lost his home, but one who has felt its true remoteness and is aware of an insurmountable separation. In this situation, the role of language comes to the fore:

> We would expect at this point to bring in the great gift of Israel, the teaching about one God. To put it very bluntly, I would say we owe thanks to Jewish monotheism not so much for the revelation of a single God, but for revealing the word (*parole*) as the point where people hold dearly onto something that excludes a relationship: to the infinitely Distant, to the absolutely Alien [...] Speaking to someone then means I accept I shall not draw them into a system of knowable things or knowable beings, that I accept them as a stranger, without forcing them to eliminate their otherness. In this sense, the word (*parole*) is a promised land in which exile culminates in residence, for it is not about being with oneself, but always Outside, in motion, when the Otherness generously gives, without denying itself.[13]

Blanchot's essay reflects the Holocaust and at the same time the status of post-war intellectuals, including Adorno, who declares in his *Minima moralia* written at the end of the war that: 'it is part of morality not to be at home in one's home.'[14] Also playing a role in transferring the concept of nomadism to

---

12   M. Blanchot: L'indestructible, p. 183 (the essay *Être juif* forms the first part of this text).
13   Ibid., p. 187.
14   T. W. Adorno: *Minima moralia*, p. 39.

philosophical and political discourse is the need to express the status of an intellectual as one who may be living within a state, but in his world-view is beyond its apparatus. This is also the central aspect of the aforementioned study by Gilles Deleuze and Félix Guattari. A similar positional staking-out is seen in Petr Král's cited poem, the *Tribute*, when he is listing all sorts of inventions by human society, which he addresses by the pronoun 'you', creating the space to keep his own inner distance.[15]

Of course, we can also find authors in Czech culture from the 19th century who might take their place in the genealogy of intellectual nomadism, but a notable reflection on the phenomenon does not appear until the 1980s and 1990s, and does so in the Czech cultural exile setting; which means, by contrast with French and Western discourse, with some delay. These aspects stem from the ongoing history of Czechoslovak exile since 1938, especially after the Communist coup in 1948, and to some extent also are a reflection on this history and what an Exile from Communist Czechoslovakia can achieve, and last but not least also reflect something about the personal history of the authors. There is a palpable French influence here, not least by offering a suitable concept. This is borne out by an increasingly frequent use of the word, since the term *"nomad"* had no firm rooting in the Czech vocabulary, and had earlier kept itself aligned with the original Czech word *"kočovník"*.

III

The issue of nomadism appears prominently in the works of philosophers Vilém Flusser and Václav Bělohradský (1944) and in the writings and essays of Věra Linhartová (1938) and Lubomír Martínek (1954). Toward the end of the Cold War, Václav Bělohradský published his study *Příchod doby cikánské aneb Evropou se jen potulovat...* [The Coming of the Gypsy Era, or, Just Wandering around Europe...] a text that influenced then Czech reception of postmodernism.[16] In it, he characterizes the Philosopher as 'Mankind's Gypsy' who 'just

---

15   Jacques Attali ascribes most of the key inventions to nomads, while their destructive power, characterized by the invention of gunpowder, becomes the property of the state that adopts them. The gesture of Král's poem also goes against ownership, toward inner freedom.

16   V. Bělohradský: Příchod doby cikánské.

wants to roam' and not be some 'official' beholden to society. In his essay the term 'gypsy' is linked to a statement from Husserl's 1936 lectures, that wandering gypsies 'do not belong to Europe, in its spiritual sense',[17] but also to the proven persecution of the Roma during World War II, in which Europe suppressed its own spiritual sensibility, as well as to their discrimination under socialist Czechoslovakia.

While Bělohradský's piece was an ad-hoc study clearly following on from Western philosophy that charted the prevailing trends, for Flusser, who lost his whole family after his escape from Prague, exile and migration were personal, existential issues, and nomadism became one of the key themes of his philosophy. One of the chapters of his philosophical autobiography ends with the words:

> What follows is the result of this back-and-forth, the theme being to cut free of the burdensome outdated premise that the 'Prague Jew' has to be a Jew from Prague, and to swing over the abyss of Auschwitz and everything that followed, to reach other places; always in danger of falling uncontrollably into the abyss. One must undertake this risk, so as not to be precluded from ever really being able to gain a foothold in these other places (despite having already found oneself in them)[18]

Flusser addresses issues of exile and migration since at least the 1970s, when the text *Für eine Philosophie der Emigration* [Towards a Philosophy of Emigration] was written, though published only posthumously.[19] The term nomadism itself appears only in a few late texts, but in a number of other texts he takes his own original approach to developing the concept of 'intellectual nomadism' albeit without using that term. Flusser's concept of *Wohnung beziehen in der Heimatlosigkeit* [Taking up Residence in Homelessness], which he formulated in the mid 1980s and which later came to form part of Flusser's exceptional philosophical autobiography *Bodenlos* [Bottomless], is where he delivers an important distinction between 'home' in terms of belonging, and 'a home' in terms

---

17   Ibid., p. 217.
18   V. Flusser: *Bodenlos*, p. 272.
19   see V. Flusser: *Von der Freiheit des Migranten*.

of just a dwelling or abode.[20] Characteristically enough, Flusser separates this distinction from the moralizing stance taken by nostalgia, which does, after all, belong to the domain of *home*, which he takes to be about perception and recognition. In terms of the emphasis given to perception, vision, his approach corresponds with that of Petr Král.

> Although the migrant, this human representative of a beckoning future without heimat, carries in his unconscious bits and pieces of the mysteries of all the heimats through which he has wandered, he is not anchored in any of them. In this sense he is a being lacking in mysteries. He becomes transparent to others. He lives in clarity of the fact of being, not in mysteries.[21]

IV

Lubomír Martínek emigrated to France in 1979, made his living in a number of ways, including as a sailor, and travelled through a range of countries. His prose draws greatly from the French essay tradition in particular. At the turn of the 1980s and 1990s he devoted some of his thinking to 'the nomad' and nomadism. In his *Palimpsest* (1996), Martínek takes us through a progression of life attitudes experienced by a travelling person: as an alien, a nomad, a straying fool; not as a typology, but rather as a gradual deepening of experience over time or the gradual detection of layers of existence that present themselves only during a period of intense experience. Martínek, like Flusser, bases his contemplation on his own life experience, which is, of course, very different from and lacks the tragic element of Flusser's. The *Palimpsest* could be read as a self-assured atheistic variation on the quest in search of one's true self, as was established in the Czech tradition by the *Labyrinth of the World and the Paradise of the Heart* of Jan Amos Komenský (Comenius). The pilgrim, which is how Martínek aggre-

---

20   For more, see Chapter 3.
21   V. Flusser: The Challenge of the Migrant, p. 14.

gates all three positions,[22] ultimately arrives at being himself alone, escaping all categorizations and conceptual distinctions:

> A nomad does not regret the step by which he finally detached himself even from the community of strangers, but progressively comes up with newer and newer reasons for yet another departure. This does not have to equate with any physical relocation. Quite often, his resentment materializes into a virtual departure, fleeing into another language, art or even madness. The parting ways run in an infinite number of directions. An already incomprehensible stranger, transformed by a geographical move into a nomad, fades in the distance of ever more unintelligible forms.[23]

Věra Linhartová published several volumes in the former Czechoslovakia of what were at the time quite singular examples of experimental prose and sets of poems, examining the boundaries of narrative and language. In 1968 she left for France, where she studied Japanese and as a theorist devoted herself to Japanese art and thought, as well as translating texts from Japanese. After she left Czechoslovakia, she carried on writing mostly in French. Linhartová devoted one shorter essay to her reflections on exile *Pour une ontologie de l'exile*, in which she contemplates her exile experience twenty-five years on. She starts off by expressing some reservation about the word exile, taking it to be a concept complementary to a settled life, while she, on the contrary, subscribes to nomadism concept. Referring to older history that knew only of forced exile, she also makes the distinction about the modern form of voluntary exile, when the exiled person is not a banished outcast but one leaving of their own volition, and goes on to subdivide this latter form into exile as an escape from adverse circumstances, and exile 'to a place essentially unknown, open to all possibilities'.[24] It is this second, 'transforming' exile that she refers to as nomadism. The first type, a 'suffered exile', is 'experienced as a period in which time has stopped, or time is on hold in the interim, awaiting a putative return to the place and time before the upheaval (i.e. the 'going into exile')'. Nomadism,

---

22   L. Martínek: *Palimpsest*, p. 15.

23   Ibid., p. 130.

24   V. Linhartová: Pour une ontologie de l'exil, p. 67/72.

on the other hand, is something she characterizes as 'time fulfilled, a beginning without a certain goal but especially without the deceptive hope of return.'[25]

The literary concepts of nomadism lead us to an important distinction, quite well represented by Martínek and Linhartová. We can see nomadism as a lifestyle and way of existence associated with travel, as found in Lubomír Martínek's work. Its antithesis is nomadism in language. While Martínek writes his prose in Czech, with few exceptions, Linhartová does not shy away from journeying, but is more intent on nomadic writing, opening up shifts between languages. In this, her experience corresponds to the concept of Maurice Blanchot's 'literary space' and its notable interpretation by Michel Foucault in his essay *Maurice Blanchot: La pensée du dehors* [The Thought from Outside]. Linhartová's ranging around the language field, whether in her deconstruction of Czech or the opening up of the French space, means opening up to the external and unknown, as enabled by language.

V

We can find a number of authors among pre-1989 Czech Exiles who left the Czech language behind and adopted another as their literary tongue. Before 1968, this includes e.g. the novelist Jan M. Kolár (1923–1979), who published several novels in French.[26] After 1968, alongside Milan Kundera we have e.g. Libuše Moníková (1945–1998), who began writing and publishing only in German, after her departure in 1971.[27] When it comes to poets, among whom switching languages is not so common, we have Jiří Gruša (1938–2011) who wrote in Czech and German, and Petr Král, in Czech and French while abroad.

The exiled poets' approach to a foreign language or foreign languages reflects to some extent Flusser's abode/home distinction, as well as other stances mentioned elsewhere in this book; often, and understandably, nostalgia. For some poets in the *Invisible Home* and *Time for Building* anthologies and thereabouts, some foreign language words appear, signalling an alien, even hostile

---

25   Ibid., pp. 67/72–73.
26   cf. V. Košnarová: *Ztracen v dějinách.*
27   see L. Martínek: *Nomad's Land*, pp. 119–126.

environment and at the same time being far away from home. The exception among them is Ivan Blatný, for whom other languages were a challenge, a call to expand the poetic field. One verse from *Bixley Remedial School* which reads *"Der Dichter spricht in verschiedenen Sprachen"* [The poet speaks in various languages] describes his approach to foreign languages, adopting them for his own.[28] Petr Král perceives French without nostalgia as just a part of the environment in which he lives, and thus writes poems: 'Although I knew few words, French was now my language, and one *in which poems came to me.*'[29]

Jiří Gruša,[30] as he tells us in his writings, found freedom in the change of language: 'the language of my exile, the language that saved me from falling into nothingness, the language that gave me the inner freedom I still live in today.'[31] Gruša's change of language is deeply rooted in Czech history, closely related to German history. Gruša recalls the difference between territorial and linguistic patriotism: 'linguistic and cultural spaces need not blend.'[32] This distinction has since the 19th century fundamentally influenced prevailing circumstances in the Czech Lands, until language-based identity finally prevailed after the Second World War. Jiří Gruša met the territorial concept of patriotism after 1989 as a diplomat and an important mediator between Bohemia, Germany and Austria, as well as a literary man.

Gruša's poems in German benefit from this doubled, Central European anchorage. Even in his German, many Czech specificities abound, memories of Czech friends etc. The German reader is thus often put in the peculiar role of an observer who understands the language, but not always what it is saying. Also paradoxical is the message itself, directed to a Czech addressee, in German. Gruša thinks his poems through, in both languages, even while writing in only

28   I. Blatný: *Pomocná škola Bixley*, p. 16.
29   Quoted by A. Stašková: Die Geschichte begehen, p. 165, based on her correspondence with Petr Král (re-transl. from her German translation).
30   Jiří Gruša (1938–2011) lived in Germany after a scholarship stay in the United States in 1980. He published his German-written poems in two collections, *Der Babylonwald. Gedichte 1988* (1991) and *Wandersteine. Gedichte* (1994); at least some part of the first of his books originated before 1989. At that time, Gruša also wrote poems in Czech, to a lesser extent (in several cases there are versions in both languages), and these were included in the collection *Grušas Wacht am Rhein aneb Putovní ghetto* [Gruša's Watch on the Rhine, or, the Travelling Ghetto]. *České texty 1973–1989* (2001).
31   J. Gruša: *Eseje a studie o literatuře a kultuře* II, p. 193.
32   Ibid., p. 206.

the one, and one needs to know the other language to gain a full understanding of some of his poems, the German of his poems 'ought to be Czech', but precisely because it is not, his poems testify to something familiar, yet alienated:

KAPITÄN NEMO

Ein fremdstern
als axthieb in dem tisch der kneipe
mit blühenden fischen hinter dem nachtfenster
und du
du tödlich erstaunt
über das deutschwort
zeitmesser

CAPTAIN NEMO

An alien star
like the notch of an axe in a tavern table
with flowering fish outside the night window
and you
you astonished to death
by the German word
zeitmesser[33]

Oft cited is Gruša's poem *Wortschaft*, in which the paradoxical nature of shifting between languages is perfectly summed up:

WORTSCHAFT

Erst im stummland
bin ich stumm geworden

---

33   J. Gruša: *Básně*, p. 334, poem is from the collection of *Der Babylonwald*. – Gruša's poetry bears clear marks of Paul Celan's influence, short verses, fragmentation and typical compositions. One of his poems begins with Celan's verse *Ich hörte sagen* (*Básně*, p. 448). – As to Gruša's poetry in German cf. texts by Renata Cornejo and Alfrun Kliems.

erst im stummland
verstand ich
das tier
das schweigsam
bedeutet
und wacht

unsagbar
im raum
des redens

WORDXILE

Only in Stummland[34]
did I fall mute
only in Stummland
did I appreciate
the animal
that staying silent
has meaning
and watches

speechless
in the space
of speech[35]

The word *Stummland* is a literal back-translation of the Czech word *Německo* which literally means the country of non-speakers, mutes. It can thus translate meaningfully into Czech, except that today's Czech speakers practically do not perceive the etymological meaning, which comes to life only in translation but belies the original not being Deutschland, and therefore it is also not possible to

---

34 [transl. note: keeping the original word is at least suggestive of Germany, albeit in English the idiom 'keeping stumm', variously also spelled schtum, shtum, shtoom etc., means keeping silence so as not to give any secret away]

35 Ibid., p. 403 (coll. *Wandersteine*, 1994).

adequately transfer it back to Czech. The poem is thus hopelessly in-between the two languages, and understandable only if seen from both sides. But the paradox does not end there: the speaker of the poem notes that he did not fall mute 'until in Mute-land (Germany)' yet is self-contradictory by speaking in this foreign country and language, as though he had learned to speak once again. The change of language thus connotes a loss of (prior) identity. The second part of the poem sharply, but at the same time on the verge of articulation, points to the unspeakableness within the language that this transformation allows us to see. Only the second, adopted language, only one's exile reveals the speaking 'self', to uncover the non-equivalence of the primal, animal power of speech with any language in particular.

VI

Věra Linhartová represents a characteristic case of linguistic nomadism. After her departure to France, she wrote several French texts on the cusp between poetry and prose. If we read them through our exile-focused lens, her topic here being partly and quite idiosyncratically that of exile, though keeping in mind an inherent ambiguity, we could say that Linhartová has transposed to the linguistic plane the external topology of exile, i.e. her relationship to the homeland, the host country and everything foreign.[36] The first of these texts, *Twor* (written in 1971) can be read as entering the unfamiliar zone that French as a foreign language opens up; a little later *Lieux errables* [Errant Places, 1976] or *Intervalles* [Intervals, 1977], as her perception and awareness of this space and the late *Portraites carnivores* [Carnivorous Portraits, 1982], as delving into the depths of nomadic existence. There is also a progression, going from *Twor*, the text of which strongly draws attention to its linguistic nature, to the prose of *Carnivorous Portraits*, at first glance quite lucidly written.

   Twor is a fragmentary text made up of shorter passages that sometimes seem like a record of observations, a condensed reflection on events, or some una-

---

36   On the subject of exile in Linhartová's case cf. the study by Z. Stolz-Hladká: Human Existence as Strangeness, to which I owe much inspiration; V. Košnarová (Jinde) discusses Linhartová's French written texts as a whole.

ttributed quote, thoughts jotted down, a fragment of a poem or a word association. Nevertheless, the text exhibits a degree of coherence or connectedness
not entirely due to the reader's involvement, as if it were capturing the different
formative stages of an entity that emerges or is born out of fragments of language. Here, language is the medium within which the identity of the speak-
er-self takes shape, and the gradual sounding-out of French and venturing into
a new space also means transforming the identity of that self. The text itself is
at times fragmentary even at the sentence level: words are separated by larger
gaps, and punctuation is reduced to colons and question marks, which disturbs
the impression of a finalized pronouncement and emphasizes the motility of the
language itself. In one place, this deconstruction of the language is marked with
the figural expression *"labyrinthe ombilinguiste"* – 'umbilicolingual labyrinth'
evoking the process of birth in the language zone.[37] The beginning of the text
presents a key motif, the cross-pollinating duality of the world,[38] subsequently
and repeatedly returning in variations on how paths and language divide and
double up. The speaker is trying to deal with these bifurcations, not to have to
choose one of the paths but to always keep all the possibilities open, as if aiming
for a place before any directional run-up, some kind of place of origin.

The title of the text is significant in itself: *Twor* resembles the Czech word
tvor, creature, while the letter *w*, seldom used in current Czech, evokes older
orthography and makes the word seem archaic. *Twor* also encompasses the
English word *two*, which hints at duality. The word thus carries both the theme
of duplication and descent into the depths, to a pre-duality state. At the end of
the text, the word *Twor* appears in this passage:

> Dégoût infini de parler   de laisser des mots s'écouler encore   de perdre
> les mots   Fini les tentatives épuisantes de passer inaperçu   Fini les
> travestissement   J'irai au fond du mot aussi sûr que je vais au bout du
> monde
> *Persona*   l'hai saputo   ne veut dire pas plus que *larva*
> *Personne   je le suis   Stvůra   Twor   Sattvara*

37   V. Linhartová: *Twor*, p. 38.
38   Ibid., p. 8.

Endless disgust to speak   to let the words flow out again   to lose
the words   No more gruelling attempts to pass unnoticed   No more
disguising   I will go to the bottom of the word as sure as I go to the
end of the world
Persona   l'hai saputo   means no more than *larva*
Person   that I am   Monster   Twor   Sattvara[39]

In the vicinity of the title word we find the words *persona* and *larva*, evoking the
motif of a mask, the Czech word *stvůra*, monster, etymologically related to *tvor*,
which means creature, and *tvořit*, to create, and to *nestvůra* as a misfit creature,
a failed creation. The word *sattvara* may be a compound Sanskrit word, but at
the same time it sounds like the Czech word *stvůra*, and in this constellation it
also indicates a descent to delve in the archaic layers of language.[40] *Twor* here
means some indeterminate person and at the same time something created,
something that is born or changed. The way language is being worked with
here, sets the text in dual motion. On the fragmented syntagmatic axis, we have
a story about undergoing change, but at the same time, on the paradigmatic
axis, updated by the play on words, their analysis, we see the deeper experience
of a multi-lingual language space. Seen at this level, we are dealing with the
birth of an entity out of language; a creation that goes against the natural order,
because it is wilfully made, and because no language in Linhartová's work is her
mother tongue.[41] Zuzana Stolz-Hladká also recalls that for Linhartová the issues
are not so much about different languages facing off one against the other, but
about a kind of unified pre-language, *Ursprache*.[42] This makes for a continuous,
albeit intricately articulated array of different languages, in which the subject
is formed or transformed. In terms of the relationship of language, home and
exile, this space has no fixed core, but offers local refuges with varying degrees
of detached autonomy.

If *Twor* describes the translocation stemming from language itself, in which
the nomadic subject takes shape, the fragmentary notes and utterances through
which the subject arrives at themselves, then the somewhat later texts examine
the similar progression of the already formed self that still keeps a certain degree

---

39   Ibid., pp. 76.
40   Z. Stolz-Hladká: Human Existence As Strangeness, pp. 174–176.
41   Ibid., p. 173.
42   Ibid., p. 162.

of life motility in its unification of language with awareness, that is, of body with language. The subject makes their own inception and at the same time is carried forward by the motion s/he evokes:

> Vivre à l'abri de toute stabilité, se soustraire à chaque tentative de définition, traverser sans demeurer. Je suis à l'origine de mon temps et de mon espace confondu qui progressent par vagues, me basculant dans le creux comme dans le trop-plein, m'emportant tantôt avec une violence inouïe, tantôt plus que doucement. Je m'abandonne au mouvement que j'ai déchaîné, je consens à assumer mon impossible rêve en passe de se réaliser ; à m'introduire pour reculer, à plonger pour ressurgir selon le rythme qui d'avance abolit toute fin. Rien ne me porte – sur quoi appuyer mes pieds ? – même le vent se dérobe. Le solide peu à peu se crée, la démarche paraît d'autant plus assurée qu'elle se hasarde vers l'inconnu.

> To live out of the reach of all permanence, avoid all attempts at definition, to traverse, but not stay. I am at the origin of my flowing time and space that proceed forward on the waves, throwing me into upwelling and overreach, snatching me off at once with unheard of violence, at other times more than tenderly. I abandon myself to the motion I have let loose, content to accept my impossible dream as I make the realization; being brought in only to back away, submerging diving in to re-emerge in a rhythm that nullifies any aim in advance. Nothing is bearing me – what am I to press against with my feet? – even the wind shies away. A solid foundation is gradually forming, progress seeming the more certain, the more it dares into the unknown.[43]

The subject's peregrination is still clearly tied up with the language, and what is being said (*to live out of the reach of all permanence*) is only the status right now, a point through which the journey passes, to move on, toward a firmer basis. In her prose pieces Linhartová sometimes attains a similar sweep of gesture as Ivan Blatný, when what is being said coincides with the motion of the speaker,

---

43   V. Linhartová: *Mes oubliettes*, p. 15 (text *Lieux errables*).

who is taking shape and arising from the text. But what Linhartová is doing differs in scope. Blatný strives to cover his presence in a particular place, while for Linhartová the aim is to move across an indeterminate, an imaginary, or in Blanchot's terms a literary expanse. The speaker of her prose takes shape out of the consciousness of the moment, often only in fragmentary form, as in *Twor*, which does, nevertheless, easily convert into physical movement, because this consciousness is always evidently physical. It is open to a reality, which always remains unresolved, a question, always to some extent external; the place toward which the movement is directed. Here, reality is not the outside world, but what is real for the conscious mind, what is making an impression at this very moment, in this heated awareness of immediacy:

> Comment pourrais-je douter que le réel non seulement se passe en--dehors des apparences, mais encore qu'il les contourne avec mille précautions. Je vis dans l'invisible. N'existe que ce qui est scellé, enfoui dans l'immédiat.

> How could I doubt that the real not only takes place beyond mere appearances, but indeed that it anxiously avoids them? I live in the invisible. All that exists is that which is sealed, secreted in immediacy.[44]

VII

Considering nomadism in Czech exile expands the concept of exile and identity, as established in the prevailing nostalgic type of poetry of the 1950s. When it comes to nostalgic exile, Věra Linhartová writes of a make-do or makeshift 'interim time'. In his poetry Ivan Blatný took the interim fully on board and turned it into his fundamental life regime. Yet for him it does not mean waiting for the return of the past or a yearning for home, but life in an everyday routine present, sometimes especially intense, sometimes banal, wherein the past is

---

44   Ibid., p. 17.

integrated as its indivisible layer. In the definitive temporariness of his shelters, Ivan Blatný protects his identity from anything that might perturb it. Vilém Flusser developed an anti-nostalgic philosophy, of a migrant who does not cling to any place and changes abodes as needed. His character is enriched by it, but cannot be fully defined by any of his partial identities. For Lubomír Martínek, estrangement and nomadism are a way of progressively making one's way toward one's own true self, seeking to see what cannot be seen except at a distance.

> I see leaving as one of the best means of telling apart the essential from the inessential, distinguishing what one can do without, and what one finds inextricably inherent. It is only by getting rid of the commonplace, hidden in everyday routine, that one gets the opportunity to realize what it is that permanently connects one to one's point of origin.[45]

Here, Martínek edges toward Flusser's nomad, who is living 'in the evident', in clarity (*"in der Evidenz"*). But for him, identity does not mean so much the accumulation of experience from different abodes, but rather the detection of hidden layers on his quest in search for himself, and this journey, as Noted by J. Czaplińska, is never at an end.[46]

Věra Linhartová has made a very earnest and thorough attempt at a nomadic exploration of language. The identity of "Twor", the speaker in her eponymous prose work, derives from intently stepping out of the given language and literary space. This particular nomad is leaving the past behind moment by moment and opening up to the outside:

> Je retrouve cependant l'appesanteur d'un voyageur qui, les mains vides, arrive dans un endroit inconnu, sans obligation aucune, sans lettres d'introduction, étranger à tout, sauf à l'imprévu qui ne saurait tarder à se produire.

---

45   L. Martínek: *Nomad's Land*, p. 69.
46   J. Czaplińska: Experimenty Lubomíra Martínka, pp. 114–115.

Once again, I find myself in the weightless state of a traveller who comes empty-handed to unknown places, without any obligations, without letters of recommendation, a stranger to everything but the unforeseen, due to happen at any moment without fail.[47]

Mutlu Konuk Blasing writes about the importance of the mother tongue for poetic language. She recalls that *"language is emotionally charged because it has to be acquired"* and this *"socialization into language"* happens under some duress. For this reason, as she writes, *"poetry lives only in its native tongue; it does not translate without a loss of its emotional charge".*[48] What gets lost in translation amounts to the 'emotional history of individualization'. However, a change of language in the case of exiled poets may represent a slightly different case than translation. The poems of Jiří Gruša and the poetic prose of Věra Linhartová serve as good illustrations. In both cases, we see them adopting a new language, as if one is learning to speak all over again. This is why, paradoxically, when it comes to the new language, Gruša brings in the idea of becoming mute and Linhartová descends to the 'prenatal' layer of an 'umbilicolingual labyrinth'. This amounts to a rebirth, in a language charged with new and different emotions.

---

47   V. Linhartová: *Intervalles/Mezidobí*, p. 8.
48   M. K. Blasing: *Lyric Poetry*, pp. 13, 16, 11.

11. Conclusion. Exile and the Imagination

I

The preceding chapters have been devoted mainly to Czech exile poetry during the Cold War. My original intention was to evaluate Czech poetic exile in a broader comparative take on the Exiles of other countries in the Eastern Bloc. It slowly became apparent, however, how little of Czech literature has been dealt with to-date, which eventually led me to focus mainly on Czech authors. Nevertheless, the comparative inclination remained at the heart of the matter: this was primarily about the poetics of exile poetry, and as such, looking into the history of exile cannot be avoided. Taking this approach shows quite clearly how substantially Czech exile poetry is inherently part of the poetic tradition of the West. This no doubt applies in varying degrees to the exile poetry of other countries in the former Eastern Bloc.[1] Thanks to this belonging, predicated and reliant on older models and approaches, Cold War exile poetry is not just a closed chapter in recent history in terms of its poetics, even though it originated in a particular geopolitical situation.

It seems paradoxical that the countries of the former Eastern Bloc show little empathy toward current migration, despite their own Cold War Exiles having been accepted with understanding and sympathy in the West. One reason for it

---

[1] Finding Ovid and Ovidian motifs in exile poetry is evidence of this belonging. For at least an introductory idea about them see the book by T. Ziolkowski: *Ovid and the moderns*, although the treatment is far from exhausting.

may be that these countries lack any colonial history comparable to a number of Western countries, and were often in subjugated positions, albeit not colonized in the sense we mean when talking about some 'Third-world countries'. Poland was long-divided between other countries, the Czech Lands, Slovakia and Hungary were part of the Austrian monarchy, and they lack any prolonged experience of immigrants. Cultural alignment has been the litmus test for Eastern Exiles – although we speak of Eastern or Central Europe, their cultural foundations are largely shared with the West. Ovid, pre-dating Charles Baudelaire, as well as Alexander Pushkin or Milada Součková;[2] and Baudelaire himself are part of the history that 20th century European and Western poetry have in common. Poets from the Eastern Bloc were coming into a different environment, but could follow-on from a substantially shared culture, or rather, had no reason to define themselves in opposition to it, since it was also their own. In that respect, they were not the same foreigners as the poets of the 'third world'. An extreme case of such a 'homecoming' are the refugees from East Germany finding asylum in West Germany.

After the end of the Cold War, the so-called 'Second world' joined the West and gradually ceased to be a major topic, although relations between poetry on one and the other side of the Iron Curtain are an interesting chapter in themselves, in terms of influence and common tradition. Some studies work directly or indirectly with the thesis of mutual mirroring between Eastern and Western Bloc literature.[3] This does in essence capture some of the nature of communication between the two sides. Another important moment comes into play here: the countries of the Eastern Bloc were mostly on the periphery of Western literature, in literary terms. The influences of Romanticism and other movements, including the Avant-garde, came to Central and Eastern Europe largely from the West, and where they returned or were reflected back, this was largely down to individual authors (such as Kafka, Hašek or Kundera) rather than movements and tendencies. The Czech romantic poet Karel Hynek Mácha is a writer of European format, but his work has never achieved Europe-wide influence. Joseph Brodsky recalls that modern exile differs from Ovid's exile on

---

2   A poem by Jiří Kárnet with the emblematic name *Podle Ovidia* [According to Ovid] was published in the very first issue of *Svědectví* [Testimony] probably the most well-known Czech exile journal (no. 1, 1956, p. 42).

3   Two important monographs make the point, C. Cavanagh: *Lyric Poetry and Modern Politics* and J. Quinn: *Between Two Fires*.

the edge of an empire, and typically means a move to better conditions, so that *"taking this route is for an exiled writer, in many ways, like going home – because he gets closer to the seat of the ideals which inspired him all along".*[4]

The thesis about mirroring makes the point that in some cases the authors of the Eastern Bloc were returning to the West something they had originally accepted from it, but at the same time these themes, forms or approaches had undergone some transformation, thus bringing scope for a new understanding. In that sense, the East (the Second world) is not just a delayed image of the West, but also its reflection in the sense of a reflection upon it, considered awareness. On that basis, Justin Quinn reads Miroslav Holub's poems as a transformation of Beat Generation poetics, translated back into an Anglophone environment.[5] In her book, Claire Cavanagh compares the social importance of poets in Poland and the former Soviet Union with the limited social influence of poets elsewhere, especially in the United States – whilst the poet as a 'bard' is a legacy shared by both sides. Specifically, she uses the example of Czesław Miłosz to remind us how he himself was influenced by Anglophone poets and returned that influence within his poetry to the West.[6]

Exile poets are a special case when it comes to these movements back and forth, because they fall outside the simple model of two mutually reflecting sides – in a sense, they do not belong to either of them. Poets from the Eastern Bloc were coming to the West into a cultural environment identical or closely similar, often to the very countries where that culture had taken shape. Yet most of the time they continued to write in a language foreign to their host country. Their poetry could turn homeward, or to the exiled diaspora, or toward the new reality and readers of their new country. At this point, however, we begin to see quite significant differences between the various countries. While Polish exile, say, was still keeping touch with their home environment, in the Czech case, especially in the 1950s, the two sides were very much apart. This resulted in a number of writers, not just poets, disappearing from public awareness for quite some time.[7] This is not confined to Exiles, but also poets at home who were not allowed to publish and whose works came out greatly delayed,

---

4   J. Brodsky: The Condition We Call Exile, p. 21.

5   J. Quinn: *Between Two Fires: Transnationalism and Cold War Poetry*, p. 113ff.

6   C. Cavanagh: *Lyric Poetry and Modern Politics*, p. 248.

7   J. Brodsky openly admits that exile turns a writer into someone *"socially insignificant"*, J. Brodsky: The Condition We Call Exile, p. 22.

after 1989 – we can take Jiří Kolář as an illustrative example – this key poet of the 1950s and 1960s is known in the West almost exclusively for his collage artwork. In the cases of authors such as Vladimír Vokolek or Zbyněk Havlíček and others, we could speak of a period of internal emigration, as a result partly of their own decision not to compromise themselves by collaborating with the totalitarian regime, and partly because being officially published was denied to them. There was a certain alternative, with samizdat publications and unofficial cultural circles, especially after 1968, creating a kind of in-country diaspora, especially the *"underground"* of that name.[8]

Exiles from the East had to overcome setbacks to assert themselves in the West and reach out to any group of readers. Politically or culturally speaking, being Exiles, they had no great reason to speak critically towards the host country with some form of protest- or minority literature. Some degree of acclaim was won by poets who, like Miłosz, brought something familiar, yet new. The works of Czesław Miłosz or Joseph Brodsky, at this time probably the best known of the Eastern poets, show how distinctly rare such a resonance was – though a certain degree of exceptionality was necessary, or else conveying poetry from the East to the West would lose its meaning. The case of Miroslav Holub also tells of how this was not necessarily about Exiles and that these poets were perceived primarily as representatives of their part of Europe. Yet Holub can hardly be thought of as the voice of political opposition to the Czechoslovak regime, and a certain paradox of his work is that he remains a better-known poet in the Anglophone world than in the Czech Republic.

II

Czech exile poetry can also give the impression of being wrapped up in its own introspective themes, not caring for an audience. Such a view would be unwarranted, at least in part – poets like Kovtun, Brousek and Diviš wrote socially minded poems. Jiří Gruša (if we stay with the poets) and Petr Král entered German and French literature and their poetry achieved some acclaim,

---

8   cf. J. Bolton: *Worlds of Dissent* and M. Machovec: *Writing Underground. Reflections on Samizdat Literature in Totalitarian Czechoslovakia.*

and both of them also spoke out publicly. On the other hand, such a claim of isolationism has its merits, if we recall Ivan Blatný, or Milada Součková who deliberately kept herself apart throughout her exile and, to take an example, her poem on the very political theme of the occupation of Czechoslovakia in 1968 is hard to understand, for an uninitiated reader.[9]

As I have been saying, a lot of it was about prevailing times. The poetry of the 1950s was relatively confined to national languages and more prominently featured the nostalgic theme, while from the 1960s on, and especially after 1968, the literary scene becomes more widely open to transnational movements, more authors are switching their literary language or are active in a different environment, albeit in poetry to a lesser extent than in prose. The word exile is itself undergoing a transformation; growing stronger within it are tendencies opposed to nostalgia, sometimes referred to by the word nomadism.

Through all these shifts, the exile poet benefits from being able to give imagination free reign. Poetics and the poet's true situation begin correspondingly, though not unequivocally, to align. Joseph Brodsky points to the extreme case when he writes that exile situation accelerates the otherwise normal, 'professional' progression *"into isolation, into an absolute perspective: into the condition in which all one is left with is oneself and one's own language, with nobody or nothing in between"*.[10] In this state of 'isolation', there is no group the poem would address to begin with. Under the circumstances of Czech exile, no such thing happened, nor could it have, in all likelihood, namely that poetry would establish *the idea of a community (imagined society)* in Anderson's terms, or become the connector holding together an exile community. There were, as I have already said, several factors: the proximity to the cultures of the host countries did not foster the creation of a close-knit diaspora, nostalgia as the main theme of some poets

---

9   see p. 196. Milada Součková's life has paradoxical parallels with Czesław Miłosz: during the war she was in the resistance, after the war, she served much as he did in the diplomatic corps in the USA, resigned from her post; both poets later met at Berkeley. Yet her attitude to public affairs is nothing like that of Miłosz. In her letter to Jindřich Chalupecký dated 15 September 1981, she writes: 'But a bit of glory is a fine thing after all! Like just now, Miłosz getting the Nobelette. I know him, he taught at Berkeley when I did. Back then, at some centre of European Studies, he was quite out of his depth in debate. And today? Maybe he'll give a few lectures at Harvard now and get outrageous money and all the fame he can bear' (M. Součková: *Élenty*, p. 157).

10   J. Brodsky: The Condition We Call Exile, p. 28.

was not enough to provide such a function, and Czech exile never did find any other common theme, hard as it would have been to do so.

At such a moment, however, a poem can build an *imaginary* community, as is the case in Baudelaire's *Swan*, one of the prototypical poems of exile. Here, the community is not something defined through sharing common values, but by altruistic thinking of others and their fate. Ivan Blatný in his own way creates such an imaginary community, in this case an exceptionally private gathering, when in his poetry he evokes the dead alongside the living, though distant persons, as if exile and isolation were just the thing to make such encounters possible. Exile is a precondition here: the meeting of the living with the dead requires *a priori* the insurmountable distance created by exile.

Claire Cavanagh recalls in her book the well-known statements of J. S. Mill and T. S. Eliot about poetry being *overheard* and that the poet *speaks* to himself.[11] This does not apply to the majority of exile poets, in at least one respect. These poets don't usually recite or speak, but write – from Ovid's time on. In this case the orally-acoustic model is failing to capture anything of substance. If exile poems are evocative of voicing and speech, they do so mainly on the basis of a written text, in which it is remoteness from the reader that plays a key role, rather than soliloquy. For many of these poets, we could be excused for thinking about some elementary 'narcissism of writing'. When I write the word "I" on a blank page, it is a different thing than saying that word, howsoever in private, alone. The word on paper is visible and legible and creates a productive distinction between me and the written 'me', between the explicit speaker of the poem and the subjective author. This primary situation is underpinned by a bifurcated duality of the self and can take very different forms with different poets. It can be merely a formal duality, in which the depiction settles in some nostalgic stance; but it can also become a productive factor. Ivan Blatný's late poetry represents a never-ending process of mutual reflection between the described and the describing self, founded on the desire to get them synchronized in the present moment. Yet Blatný also makes use of differentiation to multiply identities – he writes about himself in the third person, identifying with himself as some Josef Kunstadt. Blatný develops the primary narcissistic set-up to a global scale, of a world which in all respects relates to Ivan Blatný. Everything coming into it from outside is filtered through the medium of his imagination. Con-

---

11   cf. Chapter 1, p. 44–45.

versely, for Milada Součková the essence is a denial of 'self' or distancing from it – by writing in the male gender, or in the non-identical, aestheticized alter-ego guise of Josefína Rykrová. Ivan Diviš constantly flicks between several positions: in some poems he sees himself as a poet whose mission is to critically evaluate the past history and present of Bohemia through his own person; in others he distances himself sharply from this role and concentrates on preserving his own separate existence, which Bohemia and everything associated with it threaten to destroy. The fundamental position of 'myself' as a significant poet is something he projects 'outward' toward his audience. Diviš's diction in this posture is distinctly rhetorical, but he never speaks to himself, his tone implies a 'grand' audience. The poem Soliloquy while the Foehn blows... sets up a paradoxical situation by its very title: the poet is seemingly speaking into the wind, in which his words are immediately lost, while indignantly castigating the whole nation as if it were his conscience: in so doing he creates an imaginary scene befitting his image of Bohemia. The poetry of Jiří Gruša, being much more based on the dialogue principle (unlike Petr Král or Věra Linhartová), amounts to a telling exception. German, as his new language of poetry, is something he deems substantially linked to conversation: 'A change of language was unthinkable without a close person firmly rooted in this new language.'[12]

Brodsky's 'isolation' also underscores the positive value of exile. The idea of the exiled poet in detached seclusion assumes the former, normative type of poet who is a spokesman for the group – but when it comes to modern poetry, the opposite poetic attitude is characteristic: the poet stands on the margins of society and is also an Exile within it. Such a life-stance is shared by modern poets, dating from Baudelaire at least. Physical exile, as a situation and position of being between two countries, languages and societies only intensifies this position. When Peter Král notes a 'sharpened and deepened sense of space' among exile poets, he refers to the lineage of poets who see better than others because they see differently, 'A poet makes himself a visionary through a long, boundless, and systematized disorganization of all the senses' to use Arthur Rimbaud's words.[13] And it is not all just about space: distance, separation, stepping back is what it takes to see things properly. The French poet Yves Bon-

---

12   R. Cornejo: Heimat im Wort, p. 468 (the author's interview with Jiří Gruša).
13   J. A. Rimbaud: Complete Works, p. 102.

nefoy uses the word exile when he characterizes a substantial aspect of poetic vision, the immediacy of the world, which suddenly turns into alienation:

> From the ravine a bird calls, invisible, we just know that it is there, this bird and not some other, and the mystery of this uniqueness, this absolute idiosyncrasy, tightens our throats; we recognize our own absolute uniqueness at this moment, transcending all other ways of being in the world. It is the experience of a world whose congruent indivisibility defies the fragmentation performed upon it by a linguistic analysis [...] yet the evidence for it does not last. The bird's calls have died away, and we are now aware of an unsettling silence. [...] All of this is very hard to describe, which is why I often attempt to do so. I would simply say that an instantaneous sense of existence was followed by a sense of exile.[14]

III

When thinking about exile, you can't avoid a storyline. The outcast departs from somewhere, arriving elsewhere, leaves something behind, and in their new situation achieves something, socially becomes someone else. In hindsight, reviewed and recounted, his journey becomes storytelling. Some of these stories have settled and remained associated with the names of well-known characters, whether mythical, as with Odysseus, Aeneas – or real, as with Ovid. Some of these stories also enter into the poetry of exile: sometimes in the form of comparisons with some given character, in the twentieth century typically as a cross-referencing quote or an allusion. Stories can't be avoided even when thinking about the topology of exile: Kafka or Hostovský, for example, help us understand something of Blatný; Goethe's journey to Italy, itself a poetic undertaking, stands in the background of Milada Součková's works. The story of the Exile, unjustly dragged out of an idyllic home, also establishes nostalgia as a figural motif conventionally to do with exile, and Exiles understandably

---

14   Y. Bonnefoy: Le carrefour dans l'image, pp. 13–14.

have the right to find solace in a story that connects them to other refugees of a similar fate.

Yet where exile poetry delivers its salient testimony, the story is only an underpinning, the material from which it is launched. Petr Král distinguishes exiled poets from prose writers in that the others – 'for the most part–, talk about their emigration experience in terms of their Czechism and their encounters with the morals and culture of the adoptive country', while 'poets spontaneously transpose the self-same experience to a more universal philosophical plane',[15] albeit, even for Král, this does not amount to an absolute difference between poets and novelists. The position of poetry, in the sense that all modern poetry at least is exile poetry, leads to this remoteness from just relaying experience, from telling what happened, toward something that constitutes an imaginary and universal antithesis to this state of exile. The first poet of exile in this sense is Charles Baudelaire – who, while remaining in his home town and *just* recalling a minor incident, *just* evokes other characters and *just* reminds us of a number of exile stories. But through the specific form of vision so true to modern poetry, this *just* duplicates the entire scene and shifts it to a position between entirety and exile, as pointed out much later by Yves Bonnefoy. The poet views his surroundings as if not part of them, and there is another side to things, a negatively felt antithesis that encompasses a whole culture just then being weighed-up against the present moment. Exile is not always nor in all respects just an existential experience, but at the heart of what exile poetry can convey is just this sense of expulsion, alternating with the experiencing of being.

---

15   P. Král: Exil v moderní české poesii, p. 557.

Bibliography

1. Bibliography, institutions and archive funds

There is a good bibliography of Czech exile publications in book form (Šeflová), but an indispensable source is Knopp's bibliography, provided in electronic form by the Institute for Czech Literature of the Czech Academy of Sciences, the "ÚČL AV" (https://clb.ucl.cas.cz/cs-cz/). That contains articles pertaining to literature. What is lacking, is any bibliography of magazine-published literary texts, including poems. In some cases, there are bibliographies of the individual exile magazines. Many of these magazines, including bibliographic references in electronic form, are available from http://scriptum.cz/. A register of the first 80 issues of *Svědectví* has been compiled (Kuneš).

Biographical information about most of these authors mentioned is provided by the *Slovník české literatury po roce 1945 ÚČL AV* [Lexicon of Czech Literature after 1945, from the Science Academy] (http://www.slovnikceskeliteratury.cz/). Biographical medallions of numerous lesser-known exile authors were published between 2005–2007 in the *Literární Noviny* newspaper by Viktor A. Debnár, and I mention some of them in the bibliography.

Knopp, František (ed.): *Česká literatura v exilu 1948–1989. Bibliografie*, Prague: Makropulos 1996.
Kuneš, Ilja (ed.): *Svědectví. Jmenný a věcný rejstřík: ročníky 1956–1987 (nos. 1–80)*, Paris: Svědectví 1988.
Šeflová, Ludmila (ed.): *České a slovenské knihy v exilu. Bibliografie 1948–1989*, Prague: Československé dokumentační středisko 2008.

My research was supported by funds from a number of institutions. Perhaps the most extensive collection of exile books and periodicals is managed by the *Libri prohibiti* library. In studying exile I have also made use of the literary funds of the National Library of the Czech Republic, the Library of the Institute for Czech Literature of the Academy of Sciences of the Czech Republic, the Library of the Philosophical Institute of the Academy of Sciences of the Czech Republic and the Museum of Czech Literature or "LA PNP" library.

I researched manuscripts in the LA PNP (Ivan Blatný, Milada Součková, Věra Stárková), and in the *Archives et Musée de la Littérature* in Brussels, where the works of Ivan Diviš are kept, among others. Thanks to the kindness of the owners, I was able to peruse the literary estates of Jiří Kovtun and Josef Lederer. Part of the Milada Součková estate which was not yet stored in the LA PNP at the time, was kindly made available by Kristián Suda. Research infrastructure sources of the Czech Literary Bibliography (http://clb.ucl.cas.cz) were used in the creation of this treatise.

2. Primary and secondary literature

Adorno, Theodor W.: *Minima Moralia. Reflections on a Damaged Life*, transl. from the German by E. F. N. Jephcott, London – New York: Verso 2005.

Adorno, Theodor W.: *Negative Dialektik. Jargon der Eigentlichkeit*, Frankfurt am Main: Suhrkamp 1997.

Almanach české zahraniční poezie 1979, ed. Daniel Strož, Munich: PmD 1979.

Ancient Greek lyrics [online], translated & annotated by Willis Barnstone, Bloomington: Indiana University Press 2010.

Anderson, Benedict: *Imagined Communities. Reflection on the Origin and Spread of Nationalism*, London: Verso 1991.

Anton, Herbert: *Der Raub der Proserpina. Literarische Traditionen eines erotischen Sinnbildes und mythischen Symbols*, Heidelberg: Winter 1967.

Attali, Jacques: *L'homme nomade*, Paris: Fayard 2003.

Bachelard, Gaston: *Water and Dreams. An Essay on the Imagination of Matter*, transl. from the French by Edith Farrel, Dallas: The Pegasus Foundation 1983.

Baker, Peter: Exile in Language, *Studies in 20th Century Literature* 14, no. 2 (1990), pp. 207–222.

Barfield, Raymond: *The Ancient Quarrel between Philosophy and Poetry*, Cambridge: Cambridge University Press 2011.

Bárta, Miroslav: *Sinuhe, the Bible, and the Patriarchs*, Prague: Set out 2003.

Baudelaire, Charles: *Correspondance*, I. (*Janvier 1832 – février 1860*), Paris: Gallimard 1973.

Baudelaire, Charles: *Œuvres complètes*, I, Paris: Gallimard 1975.

Baudelaire, Charles: *Œuvres complètes*, Paris: Robert Laffont 1980.

Baudelaire, Charles: *The Flowers of Evil*, transl. by William Aggeler, Fresno, CA: Academy Library Guild 1954.

Bělohradský, Václav: *Příchod doby cikánské aneb Evropou se jen potulovat...* (1989), in: V. Bělohradský: *Přirozený svět jako politický problém. Eseje o člověku pozdní doby*, Prague: Československý spisovatel 1991, pp. 209–221.

Benjamin, Walter: Some Motifs in Baudelaire. In: W. Benjamin: *Charles Baudelaire. A Lyric Poet in the Era of High Capitalism*, transl. by Harry Zohn, London: Verso Books 1985, p. 107–154.

Bethea, David M.: *Joseph Brodsky and the Creation of Exile*, Princeton: Princeton University Press 1994.

Biebl, Konstantin: *Dílo*, II. *1926–1929*, Prague: Československý spisovatel 1952.

Blanchot, Maurice: *L'espace littéraire*, Paris: Gallimard 1998.

Blanchot, Maurice: *L'indestructible* (1962), in: M. Blanchot: *L'entretien infini*, Paris: Gallimard 1992, pp. 181–200.

Blasing, Mutlu Konuk: *Lyric Poetry. The Pain and the Pleasure of Words*, Princeton: Princeton University Press 2006.

Blatný, Ivan: *Domovy*, Prague: Odeon 2007.

Blatný, Ivan: *Fragmenty a jiné verše z pozůstalosti*, Brno: Host 2003.

Blatný, Ivan: *Jde pražské dítě domů z bia ...*, Brno: Druhé město 2017.

Blatný, Ivan: *Pomocná škola Bixley*, Toronto: Sixty-Eight Publishers 1987.

Blatný, Ivan: *Pomocná škola Bixley*, Prague: Triáda 2011.

Blatný, Ivan: *Stará bydliště*, Brno: Petrov 1992.

Blatný, Ivan: *Texty a dokumenty 1930–1948*, Brno: Atlantis 1999.

Blatný, Ivan: *Verše 1933–1953*, Brno: Atlantis 1995.

Bolton, Jonathan: *Worlds of Dissent. Charter 77, The Plastic People of the Universe, and Czech Culture under Communism*, Cambridge, MA: Harvard University Press 2012.

Bonnefoy, Yves: *Le carrefour dans l'image. Un rapport au surréalisme*, in: A. Buchs: *Yves Bonnefoy à l'horizon du surréalisme. La réalité à l'épreuve du langage et de l'image*, Paris: Galilée 2005, pp. 11–25.

Bonnefoy, Yves: *Lieux et destins de l'image. Un cours de poétique au Collège de France (1981–1993)*, Paris: Seuil 1999.

Bowie, Ewen L.: Early Expatriates. Displacement and Exile in Archaic Poetry, in: *Writing Exile. The Discourse of Displacement in Greco-Roman Antiquity and Beyond*, ed. Jan Felix Gaertner, Leiden: Brill 2007, pp. 21–50.

Brehm, Christiane: *Der Raub der Proserpina. Studien zur Ikonographie und Ikonologie eines Ovidmythos von der Antike bis zur frühen Neuzeit*, Münster: Hochschulschrift 1996. Online.

Brodsky, Joseph: *The Condition We Call Exile*, in: J. Brodsky: *On Grief and Reason*, London: Penguin Books 2011, pp. 20–30.

Bronfen, Elisabeth: *Over Her Dead Body. Death, Femininity and the Aesthetic*, Manchester: Manchester University Press 1992.

Brousek, Antonín: *Doslov*, in: P. Javor: *Plamen a píseň. Výbor veršů*, Toronto: Sixty-Eight Publishers 1981, pp. 133–142.

Brousek, Antonín: *Návrat ztraceného básníka*, in: A. Brousek: *Podřezávání větve*, Prague: Torst 1999, pp. 463–481.

Brousek, Antonín: *Vteřinové smrti*, Prague: Český spisovatel 1994.

Čas stavění. Anthologie: Básně čes. exulantů, Vienna: Bohemica Viennensia 1956.

Cavanagh, Clare: *Lyric Poetry and Modern Politics. Russia, Poland, and the West*, New Haven: Yale University Press 2009.

Celan, Paul: *Gesammelte Werke*, I–III, Frankfurt am Main: Suhrkamp 2000.

Čep, Jan: Rodný úžas, in: J. Čep: *Poutník na zemi*, Brno: Proglas 1998, pp. 10–23.

Čep, Jan: Tajemství Kláry Bendové, in: J. Čep: *Polní tráva*, Prague: Vyšehrad 1999, pp. 335–344.

Chambers, Ross: *Baudelaire's Paris*, in: *The Cambridge Companion to Baudelaire*, ed. Rosemary Lloyd, Cambridge: Cambridge University Press 2005, pp. 101–116.

Chambers, Ross: *Mélancolie et opposition. Les débuts du modernisme en France*, Paris: José Corti 1987.

Charypar, Michal: *Máchovské interpretace*, Prague: FF UK 2011.

Chrétien, Jean Louis: *L'Espace intérieur*, Paris: Minuit 2014.

Claasen, Jo-Marie: *Displaced Persons. The Literature of Exile from Cicero to Boethius*, Wisconsin: The University of Wisconsin Press 1999.

Claudon, Francis: Exil et création littéraire: Hölderlin et Rousseau, in: *Exil et littérature*, ed. Jacques Mounier, Grenoble: ELLUG 1986, pp. 251–265.

Cornejo, Renata: Der Fall Jiří Gruša und sein ›Fallen‹ in die deutsche Sprache, *Zeitschrift für interkulturelle Germanistik* 6, no. 2 (2015), pp. 105–117.

Cornejo, Renata: *Heimat im Wort. Zum Sprachwechsel der deutsch schreibenden tschechischen Autorinnen und Autoren nach 1968: eine Bestandsaufnahme*, Vienna: Praesens 2010.

Cornejo, Renata: Jiří Gruša als Sprach- und Kulturvermittler zwischen der „alten" und „neuen" Heimat am Beispiel seiner Gedichte, *Germanoslavica* 20, no. 1–2 (2010), pp. 157–170.

Culler, Jonathan: *Theory of the Lyric*, Cambridge – London: Harvard University Press 2015.

Curtius, Ernst Robert: *European Literature and the Latin Middle Ages*, Princeton: Princeton University Press 1953.

Czaplińska, Joanna: Experimenty Lubomíra Martínka s textem a vlastní identitou, in: J. Czaplińska: *Přidaná hodnota exilu. Úvahy o české exilové literatuře po roce 1968*, Prague: Academia 2014, pp. 109–120.

Debnár, Viktor A.: Ani ta nejstrašnější zkušenost nestačí k básni, *Literární noviny* 17, no. 9 (2006), p. 10.

Debnár, Viktor A.: Čas boření, čas stavění, *Literární noviny* 17, no. 14 (2006), p. 10.

Debnár, Viktor A.: František Kovárna – zapálený vyslanec své vlasti, *Literární noviny* 16, no. 21 (2005), p. 11.

Debnár, Viktor A.: Jihočeský lyrik. Básník a esejista Jaromír Měšťan (1916–1965), *Literární noviny* 16, no. 25 (2005), p. 11.

Debnár, Viktor A.: Křesťanská existencialistka [Věra Stárková], *Literární noviny* 16, no. 23 (2005), p. 10.

Debnár, Viktor A.: Všestranný exulant. Básník, prozaik, publicista, překladatel a ekonom Jan Tumlíř (1926–1985), *Literární noviny* 16, no. 36 (2005), p. 11.

Deleuze, Gilles – Guattari, Félix: *A Thousand Plateaus. Capitalism and Schizophrenia*, transl. by Brian Massumi, Minneapolis: University of Minnesota Press 1987.

Den, Petr: *Slovo na cestu*, in: P. Javor: *Kouř z Ithaky*, New York: Universum Press Co 1960, pp. 5–7.

Denham, Scott D., McCulloh, Mark Richard (eds.): *W. G. Sebald. History, memory, trauma*, Berlin: de Gruyter 2006.

Diviš, Ivan: *Moje oči musely vidět*, Prague: Torst 2014.

Diviš, Ivan: *Návrat do Čech. Dopisy z let 1990–1999*, ed. Zdeněk Potužil, Prague: Torst 2011.

Diviš, Ivan: *Obelst; Přece jen...; Průvan*, Prague: Cherm 2006.

Diviš, Ivan: *Obrať koně!*, Munich: Monachia 1987.

Diviš, Ivan: *Odchod z Čech*, Prague: Evropský kulturní klub 1990.

Diviš, Ivan: *Poslední básně*, Prague: Paseka 2003.

Diviš, Ivan: *Slovem do prostoru*, Bratislava: Fragment 1993.

Diviš, Ivan: *Teorie spolehlivosti*, Prague: Torst 2002.

Diviš, Ivan: *Tři knihy. Beránek na sněhu. Odchod z Čech. Thanatea*, Brno: Petrov 1994.

Diviš, Ivan: *Uzlové písmo*, Prague: Československý spisovatel 1960.

Diviš, Ivan: *Uzlové písmo*, 2., updated edition, Prague: Československý spisovatel 1969.

Diviš, Ivan: *Teorie spolehlivosti*, Munich: CCC Books 1972.

Diviš, Ivan: *Žalmy*, Prague: Odeon 1991.

Dneska bych se omluvil a trochu bych toho už nechal (rozhovor režiséra Lubo Mauera s básníkem Ivanem Blatným), *Souvislosti* 24, no. 2 (2013), pp. 52–77.

Doblhofer, Ernst: *Exil und Emigration. Zur Erlebnis der Heimatferne in der römischen Literatur*, Darmstadt: Wissenschaftliche Buchgesellschaft 1987.

Ehlen, Thomas: Bilder des Exils – das Exil als Bild. Aesthetik und Bewältigung in lyrischen texten, in: *Exil, Fremdheit und Ausgrenzung in Mittelalter und früher Neuzei*, ed. Andreas Bihrer, Sven Limbeck, Paul Gerhard Schmidt, Würzburg: Ergon Verlag 2000, pp. 151–232.

Eliot, T. S.: The Three Voices of Poetry, in: Eliot: *On Poetry and Poets*, London: Faber and Faber 1965, p. 89–102.

Emerson, Ralph Waldo: History, in: R. W. Emerson: *Essays and Lectures*, New York: The Library of America 1983, pp. 235–256.

Evelein, Johannes F.: Traveling Exiles, Exilic Travel – Conceptual Encounters, in: J. F. Evelein: *Exiles traveling. Exploring displacement, crossing boundaries in German exile arts and writings 1933–1945*, Amsterdam: Rodopi 2009, pp. 11–31.

Fischl, Viktor: *Krása šedin*, Prague: Mladá fronta 1992.

Flusser, Vilém: *Bodenlos. Eine philosophische Autobiographie*, Düsseldorf: Bollmann 1992.

Flusser, Vilém: The Challenge of the Migrant, in: V. Flusser: *The Freedom of the Migrant. Objections to Nationalism*, ed. Anke K. Finger, transl. by Kenneth Kronenberg, Urbana, IL: University of Chicago Press 2003, pp. 1–15.

Flusser, Vilém: *Von der Freiheit des Migranten. Einsprüche gegen den Nationalismus*, Bensheim: Bollmann 1994.

Flusser, Vilém: Wohnung beziehen in der Heimatlosigkeit, in: V. Flusser: *Bodenlos. Eine philosophische Autobiographie*, Düsseldorf: Bollmann 1992, pp. 247–264.

Forsdyke, Sara: *Exile, Ostracism, and Democracy. The Politics of Expulsion in Ancient Greece*, Princeton: Princeton University Press 2005.

Gaertner, Jan Felix: The Discourse of Displacement in Greco-Roman Antiquity, in: *Writing Exile. The Discourse of Displacement in Greco-Roman Antiquity and Beyond*, ed. J. F. Gaertner, Leiden: Brill 2007, pp. 1–20.

Gaertner, Jan Felix: How exilic is Ovid's exile poetry?, in: *Writing Exile. The Discourse of Displacement in Greco-Roman Antiquity and Beyond*, ed. J. F. Gaertner, Leiden: Brill 2007, pp. 155–172.

Goethe, Johann Wolfgang: *Goethes Gespräche*, IV, herausgegeben von Woldemar Freiherr von Biedermann, Leipzig 1889; online: http://www.zeno.org/nid/2000486736X.

Goethe, Johann Wolfgang: *Italian Journey*, transl. by Robert R. Heitner, New York: Suhrkamp Publishers New York 1989.

Goethe, Johann Wolfgang: *Italienische Reise*, I–II, ed. Christoph Michel a Hans-Georg Dewitz, Franfurt am Main: Deutscher Klassiker Verlag 2011.

Goldhill, Simon: Whose Antiquity? Whose Modernity? The "Rainbow Bridges" of Exile, *Antike und Abendland* 2000, 46, pp. 1–20.

Gray, Benjamin D.: *Stasis and Stability. Exile, The Polis, and Political Thought, c. 404–146 bc.*, Oxford: Oxford University Press 2015.

Greek Elegiac Poetry. From the Seventh to the Fifth Centuries BC, ed. a transl. by Douglas E. Gerber, The Loeb Classical Library, Cambridge, Massachusetts: Harvard University Press 1999.

Gruša, Jiří: *Dílo Jiřího Gruši*, II. *Eseje a studie o literatuře a kultuře* I, Brno: Barrister & Principal 2015.

Gruša, Jiří: *Dílo Jiřího Gruši*, IV. *Eseje a studie o literatuře a kultuře* II, Brno: Barrister & Principal 2016.

Gruša, Jiří: *Dílo Jiřího Gruši*, VI. *Básně*, Brno: Barrister & Principal 2018.

Gruša, Jiří: *Grušas Wacht am Rhein aneb Putovní ghetto. České texty 1973–1989*, Prague – Litomyšl: Paseka 2001.

Günther, Hans-Christian: The Book of Iambi, in: *Brill's Companion to Horace*, ed. H.-Ch. Günther, Leiden – Boston: Brill 2013, pp. 169–210.

Hadot, Pierre: *N'oublie pas de vivre. Goethe et la tradition des exercices spirituels*, Paris: Albin Michel 2008.

Hadžagić, Sandra: *Paměť v exilu*, [dissertation], Prague: FF UK 2009.

Hahn, Sylvia: Ausweisung und Vertreibung in Europa, 1500–2000, in: *Exil und Literatur*, ed. Veronika Coroleu Oberperleiter, Gerhard Petersmann, Salzburg: Horn 2010, pp. 1–18.

Hardie, Philip: *Ovid's Poetics of Illusion*, Cambridge: Cambridge University Press 2002.

Havelock, Eric: *Preface to Plato*, Cambridge, Massachusets: The Belknap Press of Harvard University Press 1982.

Havlíček, Zbyněk: Metoda Monte Carlo, in: Z. Havlíček: *Skutečnost snu*, Prague: Torst 2003, pp. 30–33.

Havlíček, Zbyněk: *Veškerá poezie*, Prague: Dybbuk 2016.

Havlíček Borovský, Karel: *Stokrát plivni do moře*, Prague: Československý spisovatel 1990.

Hejda, Zbyněk: *Čteme jakýsi deník, svědectví o jeho životě*. O literární pozůstalosti Ivana Blatného, in: Z. Hejda: *Kritiky a glosy*, Prague: Triáda 2012, pp. 86–93.

Hexter, Ralph J.: Ovid and the Medieval Exilic Imaginary, in: *Writing Exile. The Discourse of Displacement in Greco-Roman Antiquity and Beyond*, ed. J. F. Gaertner, Leiden: Brill 2007, pp. 209–236.

Hokův, Václav: *Curych. Trojrozměrná mandala: básně, traktáty, mytologemy 1973–1976*, Zürich – Prague: Consultation 1989 (1990).

Hokův, Václav: *Lebka k líbání a jiné básně*, Prague: Klub přátel Tvaru 1994 (magazine supplement).

Hokův, Václav: *Masopustní nokturno*, Munich: PmD 1980.

Hölderlin, Friedrich: *Sämtliche Gedichte*, Frankfurt am Main: Deutscher Klassiker Verlag 2005.

Holub, Josef – Lyer, Stanislav: *Stručný etymologický slovník jazyka českého*, Prague: SPN 1992.

The Homeric hymns [online]. *A Translation, with Introduction and Notes* by Diane J. Rayor. Updated edition. Berkeley: University of California Press 2014.

Hostovský, Egon: *Cizinec hledá byt: román*, Prague: Melantrich 1947.

Hostovský, Egon: *The Hideout*, transl. by Fern Long, New York: Random House 1945.

Hostovský, Egon: *Listy z vyhnanství; Úkryt*, Prague: Akropolis 1998.

Hrdlička, Josef: *Poezie a kosmos. Studie o poezii a poetice*, 1. edition, Prague: Malvern 2017.

Hroch, Miroslav: *Na prahu národní existence*, Prague: Mladá fronta 1999.

Hugo, Jan, ed.: *Slovník nespisovné češtiny*, Praha: Maxdorf 2009.

Ingleheart, Jennifer (ed.): *Two Thousand Years of Solitude. Exile after Ovid*, Oxford: Oxford University Press 2011.

Iser, Wolfgang: *The Fictive and the Imaginary. Charting Literary Anthropology*, Baltimore: Johns Hopkins University Press 1993.

Jakobson, Roman: Doslov, in: Milada Součková: *Sešity Josefíny Rykrové*, Prague: Prostor 1993, pp. 214–215.

Jedlička, Josef (-jed-): Stanislav Mareš, Báje z Nového světa, *Svědectví* 13, no. 50 (1975/1976), pp. 359–360.

Jelínek, Ivan: Pomocník na farmě, in: Ivan Blatný: *Texty a dokumenty*, Brno: Atlantis 1999, pp. 384–386.

Jonák, Zdeněk: *Václav Hokův, imaginární portrét básníka a esejisty*, Prague: Z. Jonák 2010.

Kaiser, Gert: *Vénus et la mort*, Paris: Maison des sciences de l'homme 1999.

Kannisto, Päivi: *Global Nomads and Extreme Mobilities*, Farnham, Surrey, England: Ashgate 2016.

Klement Žebrácký, Václav: *Vzdech exulantův*, publ. with commentary by Milič Čapek, poem transl. by Jan Fišer, *Proměny* 16, no. 4 (1979), pp. 87–88.

Kliems, Alfrun: *Im Stummland. Zum Exilwerk von Libuše Moníková, Jiří Gruša und Ota Filip*, Frankfurt am Main: Peter Lang 2002.

Kollár, Jan: *Básně*, Prague: Československý spisovatel 1952.

Komenský, Jan Amos: *Duchovní písně*, ed. Antonín Škarka, Praha: Vyšehrad 1952.

Košnarová, Veronika: Jinde. Francouzská tvorba Věry Linhartové, *Česká literatura* 57, no. 5 (2009), pp. 623–650.

Košnarová, Veronika: *Ztracen v dějinách. Spisovatel Jan M. Kolár*, Prague: Academia 2013.

Kovtun, Jiří: *Blahoslavení*, Munich: Kulturní sekce Československého uprchlického výboru v Německu 1953.

Kovtun, Jiří: *Hřbet velryby*, Prague: Torst 1995.

Král, Petr: Certifikát pro Ivana Blatného, in: P. Král: *Vlastizrady*, Prague: Torst 2015, pp. 563–571.

Král, Petr: Exil v moderní české poesii, in: P. Král: *Vlastizrady*, Prague: Torst 2015, pp. 553–562.

Král, Petr: *Konec imaginárna. Modernost za hranicemi avantgardních programů*, Brno: Centrum pro studium demokracie a kultury 2017.

Král, Petr: *Prázdno světa*, Munich: PmD 1986.

Král, Petr: *Sebrané básně*, I, II, Brno: Větrné mlýny 2013, 2018.

Král, Petr: *Úniky a návraty. Rozhovor*, Prague: Akropolis 2006.

Kratochvil, Antonín: Tečka za jednou antologií, *Demokracie v exilu* (Munich) 1, no. 1 (1955), p. 5.

Lederer, Josef: *Básnické dílo*, Prague: Rozmluvy 1993.

Lederer, Josef: *Sopka islandská a jiné verše. 1969–1972*, Köln: Index 1973.

Leibniz, Gottfried Wilhelm: Principes de la philosophie [Monadologie], in G. W. Leibniz: *Principes de la nature et de la grâce. Monadologie*, Prague: Flammarion 1996.

Levin, Harry: Literature and exile, in: H. Levin: *Refractions. Essays in Comparative Literature*, New York: Oxford University Press 1966, pp. 62–81.

Lexa, František: *Beletristická literatura staroegyptská*, Kladno: J. Šnajdr 1923.

Lexa, František (ed.): *Výbor ze starší literatury egyptské*, Prague: Šolc a Šimáček 1947.

Linhartová, Věra: *Intervalles / Mezidobí*, transl. by Anna Fárová, Prague: Inverze 1994.

Linhartová, Věra: *Mes oubliettes*, Montolieu: Deyrolle 1996.

Linhartová, Věra: *Portraits carnivores / Masožravé portréty*, transl. by Jitka Hamzová a Miloslav Topinka, Prague: Akropolis 2015.

Linhartová, Věra: Pour une ontologie de l'exil / Za ontologii exilu, in: *Paříž – Praha, Intelektuálové v Evropě / Paris – Prague, Intellectuels en Europe*, Prague: Institut français de Prague 1994, pp. 65–69 / 71–75.

Linhartová, Věra: *Twor*, transl. by Anna Fárová, Prague: Inverze 1992.

Linhartová, Věra: Za ontologii exilu, in: V. Linhartová: *Soustředné kruhy*, Prague: Torst 2010, pp. 342–347.

Listopad, František: *Básně*, I, Prague: Dauphin 2011.

Mácha, Karel Hynek: *Básně a dramatické zlomky*, Prague: SNKLHU 1959.

Mácha, Karel Hynek: *Literární zápisníky, deníky, dopisy*, Prague: Odeon 1972.

Machek, Václav: *Etymologický slovník jazyka českého*, Prague: NLN 2010.

Machovec, Martin: *Writing underground: reflections on samizdat literature in totalitarian Czechoslovakia*, transl. by Kip Bauersfeld, Melvyn Clarke, Vanda Krutsky, Markéta Pokorná, Marek Tomin, Gerald Turner, Prague: Karolinum 2019.

Malura, Jan: Duchovní píseň v tvorbě pobělohorských exulantů ze Slezska, in: *Čistý plamen lásky. Výbor z písní pobělohorských exulantů ze Slezska*, ed. Jan Malura – Pavel Kosek, Brno: Host 2004, pp. 5–62.

Malura, Jan: *Písně pobělohorských exulantů (1670–1750)*, Prague: Academia 2010.

Mareš, Stanislav: *Báje z Nového světa*, Prague: Český spisovatel 1996.

Martínek, Lubomír: *Nomad's Land*, Prague: Prostor 1994.

Martínek, Lubomír: *Palimpsest*, Prague: Prostor 1996.

McGowan, Matthew M.: *Ovid in Exile. Power and Poetic Redress in the Tristia and Epistulae ex Ponto*, Leiden: Brill 2009.

Melmuková-Šašecí, Eva: *Patent zvaný toleranční*, Neratovice: Verbum 2013, pp. 74–81.

Měšťan, Jaromír: *Sladká jako med. Poesie z exilu*, Munich: J. Měšťan 1955.

Měšťan, Jaromír: *Potměchuť svoboda. Poesie z exilu*, Munich: Zvěrokruh 1962.

Měšťan, Jaromír: *Útěk do Egypta. Poesie z exilu*, Munich: J. Měšťan 1957.

Mill, John Stuart: Thoughts on Poetry and its Varieties, in: J. S. Mill: *Dissertations and Discussions*, London: John W. Parker and Son 1859, pp. 63–94.

Miłosz, Czesław: *Wiersze*, III, Krakow: Wydawnictwo Znak 1993.

Minkowski, Eugène: *Vers une cosmologie. Fragments philosophiques*, Paris: Éditions Payot & Rivages 1999.

Morava, Jiří: *C. k. disident Karel Havlíček*, Prague: Panorama 1991.

Musil, Robert : *Drei Frauen*, Reinbek bei Hamburg: Rowohlt 1979.

Nejstarší řecká lyrika, ed. Radislav Hošek, Prague: Svoboda 1981.

Němcová Banerjee, Maria: Sešity Josefíny Rykrové. The Poet as Reader, in: *Neznámý člověk Milada Součková*, ed. Michal Bauer, Prague: Ústav pro českou literaturu AV ČR 2001, pp. 34–43.

Němeček, Zdeněk: Verše exulantů. *Československý přehled* (New York) 1, no. 8 (1954), pp. 22–23.

Nešpor, Zdeněk R.: *Víra bez církve? Východočeské toleranční sektářství v 18. a 19. století*, Ústí nad Labem: Albis international 2004.

Neviditelný domov. Verše exulantů 1948–1953, ed. Peter Demetz, Paris: Editions Sokolova 1954.

Nezdařil, Ladislav: O autorovi, in: Peter Demetz: *René. Pražská léta Rainera Marii Rilka*, Prague: Aula 1998, pp. 141–159.

Nezval, Vítězslav et al.: *Bojím se jít domů, že uvidím kožené kabáty na schodech. Vítězslav Nezval – Konstantin Biebl: zápisky Vítězslava Nezvala a jiné dokumenty k smrti Konstantina Biebla*, Olomouc: Burian a Tichák 2011.

Norberg-Schulz, Christian: *Genius Loci. Towards a Phenomenology of Architecture*, New York: Rizzoli 1980.

Nováková, Teréza: *Děti čistého živého*, Prague: Odeon 1966.

Odložilík, Otakar: The Poet's Way, in: *Zahrada v zemi nikoho*, ed. Robert Vlach – Peeter Arumaa, Stockholm: Conseil National de la Culture tchèque à l'Etranger 1955, pp. 12–16.

Oras, Ants: Literature in Exile, in: *Zahrada v zemi nikoho*, ed. Robert Vlach – Peeter Arumaa, Stockholm: Conseil National de la Culture tchèque à l'Etranger 1955, pp. 7–11.

Ovid: *Tristia. Ex Ponto*, transl. by Arthur Leslie Wheeler; second edition revised by G. P. Goold. Loeb classical library. Cambridge: Harvard University Press 1996.

Pánek, Jaroslav: Exile from the Bohemian Lands in the Early Modern Era motivated by Religious and Political Reasons, in: Zlatica Zudová-Lešková: *Undaunted by exile! To the Victims of Religious, Political, National and Racial Persecutions in Central Europe between the 16th and 20th Century with an Accent on the Czech Lands*, Prague: Historický ústav 2015, pp. 31–58.

Panofsky, Erwin: *Et in Arcadia Ego.* Poussin and the Elegiac Tradition, in: Panofsky, Erwin: *Meaning in the Visual Arts. Papers in and on Art History*, New York: Doubleday 1955, pp. 295–320.

Papoušek, Vladimír: *Egon Hostovský. Člověk v uzavřeném prostoru*, Prague: H & H 1996.

Petruželkovi, Adéla a Antonín: Ediční poznámka, in: Blatný, Ivan: *Pomocná škola Bixley*, Prague: Triáda 2011, pp. 311–317.

Poe, Edgar Allan: The Philosophy of Composition, in: Poe, Edgar Allan: *Essays and Reviews*, New York: Library of America 1984, p. 13–25.

Preisner, Rio: *Až na konec Česka*, Purley: Rozmluvy 1987.

Preisner, Rio: *Česká existence*, London: Rozmluvy 1984.

Preisner, Rio: *Kritika totalitarismu. Fragmenty*, I, *Sázka o člověka*, Rome: Křesťanská akademie 1973.

Preisner, Rio: Na obranu německé „vnitřní emigrace" v letech 1933–45, in: R. Preisner: *Když myslím na Evropu*, I, Prague: Torst 2003, pp. 304–334.

Preisner, Rio: *Speculum exilii Bohemici, neboli, Exil a naše nynější politická filosofie*, 1. edition, Prague: Triáda 2017.

Procházka, Martin: Childe Haroldovo Dobrou noc a Budoucí vlasť. On the issue of the self in Byron's a Mácha's poetry, *Česká literatura* 30, no. 4 (1982), pp. 289–301.

Propertius, Sextus: *Elegies*, ed. G. P. Goold, Loeb Classical Library, Cambridge, Massachusetts: Harvard University Press 1999.

Přibáň, Michal: Kdo byla Reli Bernkopfová, *Host* 17, no. 2 (2001), pp. 40–43.

Přibáň, Michal: *Prvních dvacet let. Kulturní rada a další kapitoly z dějin literárního exilu 1948–1968*, Brno: Host 2008.

Přibáň, Michal – Morávková, Alena (ed.): *Poštovní schránka domov. Malá antologie exilové povídky padesátých let*, Prague: Společnost pro vědu a umění 2005.

Putna, Martin C.: *Česká katolická literatura. V kontextech 1945–1989*, Prague: Torst 2017.

Putna, Martin C.: *Řecké nebe nad námi. Aneb antický košík. Studie k druhému životu antiky v evropské kultuře*, Prague: Academia 2006.

Putna, Martin C. – Zadražilová, Miluše (ed.): *U řek babylonských. Antologie ruské emigrační poezie*, Prague: Torst 1996.

Pytasz, Marek: *Wygnanie – emigracja – diaspora. Poeta w poszukiwaniu czytelnika*, Katowice: Wydawnictwo Uniwersytetu Śląskiego 1998.

Quinn, Justin: *Between Two Fires. Transnationalism and Cold War Poetry*, Oxford: Oxford University Press 2015.

Quintilian, Marcus Fabius: *The Orator's Education*, transl. by D. A. Russell, Cambridge, Massuchusetts: Harvard University Press 2001.

Rabaté, Dominique: *Gestes Lyriques*, Paris: Corti 2013.

Reiner, Martin: *Básník. Román o Ivanu Blatném*, Prague: Torst 2014.

Reiner, Martin: Předmluva, in: I. Blatný: *Jde pražské dítě domů z bia …*, Brno: Druhé město 2017, pp. 7–13.

Rejzek, Jiří: *Český etymologický slovník*, Voznice: Leda 2001.

Rilke, Rainer Maria: *Die Gedichte*, Frankfurt – Leipzig: Insel Verlag 2006.

Rimbaud, Jean Arthur: *Complete Works*, transl. by Paul Schmidt, New York: Harper & Row 1975.

Rössel, H.: Der „Schwanengesang" des Martin Kopecký, in: *Deutsch-slawische Wechselseitigkeit in sieben Jahrhunderten*, Berlin: Akademie Verlag 1956, pp. 299–323.

Rousseau, Jean-Jacques: *Les Rêveries du promeneur solitaire*, [introduction and chronological overview] Jacques Voisine, Paris: Garnier – Flammarion 1964.

Rubeš, Jan: *Ivan Diviš. Catalogue des Archives littéraires déposées aux Archives et Musée de la littérature. Fonds des écrivains en exil*, Bruxelles: Archives et Musée de la littérature 1989–1990.

Rushdie, Salman: Imaginary Homelands, in: S. Rushdie: *Imaginary Homelands. Essays and Criticism 1981–1991*, London: Vintage Books 2010, pp. 9–21.

Said, Edward W.: Reflections on Exile, in: E. W. Said: *Reflections on Exile and Other Essays*, Cambridge, Mass.: Harvard University Press 2000, pp. 173–186.

Saint-John Perse: *Éloges*, Paris: Gallimard 1967.

Šajtar, Drahomír: Neviditelný domov, in: *Česká a polská emigrační literatura*, ed. Libor Martínek – Martin Tichý, Opava: Slezská univerzita v Opavě, Filozoficko-přírodovědecká fakulta, Ústav bohemiky a knihovnictví 2002, pp. 46–49.

Schneedorfer, Ivan: *Básně*, Prague: Torst 2002.

Schneedorfer, Ivan: *Básně z poloostrova*, Munich: PmD 1987.

Sebald, W. G.: *Die Ausgewanderten*, Frankfurt am Main: Fischer 1994.

Sebald, W. G.: *The Emigrants*, New York: New Directions 1997.

Segal, Charles Paul: "Tamen Cantabitis, Arcades". Exile and Arcadia in Eclogues One and Nine, *Arion. A Journal of Humanities and the Classics* 4, no. 2 (1965), pp. 237–266.

Seidel, Michael: *Exile and the Narrative Imagination*, New Haven and London: Yale University Press 1986.

Serke, Jürgen: Ivan Blatný. Flucht ins Irrennhaus, in: J. Serke: *Die verbannten Dichter. Berichte und Bilder von einer neuen Vertreibung*, Hamburg: Knaus 1982, pp. 155–165.

Sílová, Soňa: Dílo Terézy Novákové jako pramen poznání náboženského života východních Čech, in: *Po vzoru Berojských. Život i víra českých a moravských evangelíků v předtoleranční a toleranční době*, ed. Ondřej Macek, Prague: Kalich 2008, pp. 47–65.

Simpson, John (ed.): *The Oxford Book of Exile*, Oxford: Oxford University Press 1995.

Šmarda, Jan: Doslov. Zanedbaný zbytek literární pozůstalosti, in: I. Blatný: *Fragmenty a jiné verše z pozůstalosti*, Brno: Host 2003, pp. 116–120.

Šmarda, Jan: *Ivan Blatný v mých vzpomínkách*, Prague: Galén 2013.

Snell, Bruno: Arcadia. The Discovery of a Spiritual Landscape, in: *The discovery of the mind. In Greek philosophy and literature*, New York: Dover Publications 1982, pp. 281–309.

Součková, Milada: *Baroque in Bohemia*, Ann Arbor: University of Michigan Press 1980.

Součková, Milada: *Élenty. Dopisy přátelům 1942–1982*, eds. Zuzana Říhová, Kristián Suda, Richard Štencl, Prague: Prostor 2018.

Součková, Milada: In memoriam Vladislava Vančury, *Sklizeň* 5, no. 6 (1957), pp. 3–5.

Součková, Milada: *Kaladý, aneb, Útočiště řeči; Svědectví. Deník z roku 1939; Mluvící pásmo. (1938–1940)*, Prague: Prostor 1998.

Součková, Milada: Nezval nebo Blatný?, *Tribuna* 7, (July-August 1955), p. 12.

Součková, Milada: *The Parnassian Jaroslav Vrchlický*, Hague: Mouton & Co 1964.

Součková, Milada: The Prague Linguistic Circle. A Collage, in: *Sound, Sign and Meaning. Quinquagenary of the Prague Linguistic Circle*, ed. Ladislav Matějka, Ann Arbor: University of Michigan 1976, pp. 1–5.

Součková, Milada: *Případ poezie*, Prague: Prostor 1999.

Součková, Milada: „Říkám, že každý verš je hoden básně!", *Proměny* 16, no. 2 (1979), pp. 53–57.

Součková, Milada: *Sešity Josefíny Rykrové*, Prague: Prostor 1993.

Součková, Milada: *Sešity Josefíny Rykrové*, Prague: Prostor 2009.

Součková, Milada: Whitmanovi, *Sklizeň* 5, no. 7 (1957), p. 1.

Stabler, Jane: *The Artistry of Exile. Romantic and Victorian Writers in Italy*, Oxford: Oxford University Press 2013.

Starobinski, Jean: L'invention d'une maladie, in: J. Starobinski: *L'encre de la mélancolie*, Paris: Seuil 2012, pp. 257–281.

Starobinski, Jean: *La mélancolie au miroir. Trois lectures de Baudelaire*, Paris: Julliard 1990.

Starobinski, Jean: Mémoire de Troie, *Critique*, no. 687–688 (2004), pp. 169–182.

Starobinski, Jean: La nuit de Troie, in: J. Starobinski: *L'encre de la mélancolie*, Paris: Seuil 2012, pp. 307–337.

Starobinski, Jean: Saint-John Perse. Le jour dans *Exil*, in: J. Starobinski: *La beauté du monde*, Paris: Gallimard 2016, pp. 650–658.

Stašková, Alice: Die Geschichte begehen. Zur Poetik Petr Králs, in: *Migrationsliteratur. Schreibweisen einer interkulturellen Moderne*, ed. Klaus Schenk, Almut Todorow, Milan Tvrdík, Tübingen: Francke Verlag 2004, pp. 165–180.

Šťastná, Zuzana: *České překlady Johna Donna v kontextech širší překladatelské poetiky svých autorů*, [dissertation], Prague: FF UK 2016.

Štěříková, Edita: *Stručně o pobělohorských exulantech*, Prague: Kalich 2005.

Steiner, George: Extraterritorial, in: G. Steiner: *Extraterritorial. Papers on Literature and the Language Revolution*, London: Faber 1972, pp. 3–11.

Stephan, Alexander: Introduction, in: *Exile and Otherness. New Approaches to the Experience of the Nazi Refugees*, ed. Alexander Stephan, Bern: Peter Lang 2005, pp. 9–17.

Stich, Alexandr: Básník Havlíček, in: *Karel Havlíček Borovský: Stokrát plivni do moře*, pp. 255–282.

Stolz-Hladká, Zuzana: Human Existence as Strangeness and Writing as Estrangement – Aspects of Exile in the Texts of Vera Linhartová, *Canadian-American Slavic Studies* 33, no. 2–4 (1999), pp. 153–177.

Suda, Kristián: Exil a svět v poválečné tvorbě Milady Součkové, in: Kubíková, Pavlína, ed.: *Jak reflektujeme českou literaturu vzniklou v zahraničí*, Prague: Obec spisovatelů 2000, s. 67–73.

Suda, Kristián: Krátká „povídka" 39 básní, in: *Neznámý člověk Milada Součková*, ed. Michal Bauer, Prague: Ústav pro českou literaturu AV ČR 2001, pp. 44–52.

Švec, Michal: *Symbolika labutě ve finské poezii od lidové slovesnosti k symbolizmu* [online]. 2012; https://is.cuni.cz/webapps/zzp/detail/110427.

Tabori, Paul: *The Anatomy of Exile. A Semantic and Historical Study*, London: Harrap 1972.

Tally, Robert T. Jr.: Mundus totus exilium est. Reflections on the Critic of Exile, *Transnational Literature* 3, no. 2 (2011), pp. 1–10.

Taylor, Charles: *Modern Social Imaginaries*, Durham – London: Duke University Press 2004.

Taylor, Charles: *A Secular Age*, Cambridge, Mass.: Belknap Press of Harvard University Press 2007.

Trávníček, Jiří: Pod sankcí paměti, in: *Poezie poslední možnosti*, Prague: Torst 1996, pp. 166–184.

Tucker, Martin (ed.): *Literary Exile in the Twentieth Century. An Analysis and Biographical Dictionary*, New York – Westport – London: Greenwood Press 1991.

Tumlíř, Jan: Básničky z Ameriky, *Skutečnost* 4, no. 3/4 (1952), p. 75.

Tumlíř, Jan: *Hořká voda. Básně 1947–1950*, New York: Fund for intellectual freedom 1951.

Tumlíř, Jan: Hořká vodo poesie, *Skutečnost* 3, no. 3/4 (1951), pp. 68–70.

Tumlíř, Jan: Malá noční hudba budoucnosti, *Svědectví* 1, no. 1 (1956), p. 42.

Tumlíř, Jan: Namísto nákupu, *Svědectví* 1, no. 3–4 (1956), p. 229.

Vejvoda, Jaroslav: O sladkém neštěstí Václava Hokůva. (4. 1. 1932 – 20. 12. 1986), *Obrys* 7, no. 1 (1987), pp. 14–15.

Vladislav, Jan: Opustíš-li mne..., *Západ* 11, no. 1 (1989), pp. 27–28.

Vojvodík, Josef: *Povrch, skrytost, ambivalence. Manýrismus, baroko a (česká) avantgarda*, Prague: Argo 2008.

Vrchlický, Jaroslav: *Já nechal svět jít kolem*, Prague: Otto 1902; citation from *Česká elektronická knihovna – Poezie 19. a počátku 20. století*; http://www.ceska-poezie.cz.

„*V současnosti nevykazuje žádné psychiatrické symptomy*" [Lubo Mauer's interview with Ivan Blatný's doctor at St Clement's Hospital], *Souvislosti* 24, no. 2 (2013), pp. 92–95.

Waters, Willliam: *Poetry's Touch. On Lyric Address*, Ithaca: Cornell University Press 2003.

Weiner, Richard: *Básně*, Prague: Torst 1997.

White, Kenneth: Esquisse du nomade intellectuel, in: K. White: *L'Esprit nomade*, Paris: Grasset 2008 (1986), pp. 15–103.

White, Kenneth: *Open World. The Collected Poems. 1960–2000*, Edinburgh: Polygon Books 2003.

Williams, Gareth D.: *Banished Voices. Readings in Ovid's exile poetry*, Cambridge: Cambridge University Press 1994.

Williams, Gareth D.: *The Curse of Exile. A Study of Ovid's* Ibis, Cambridge: The Cambridge Philological Society 1996.

Wögerbauer, Michael et al.: *V obecném zájmu. Cenzura a sociální regulace literatury v moderní české kultuře 1749–2014*, II, Prague: Academia 2015.

Zahrada v zemi nikoho – Rohtaed ei kellegi-maal, ed. Robert Vlach – Peeter Arumaa, Stockholm: Conseil National de la Culture tchèque à l'Etranger 1955.

Zambon, Efrem: Life and Poetry. Differences and Resemblences between Ovid and Dante, in: *Two Thousand Years of Solitude. Exile after Ovid*, ed. Jennifer Ingleheart, Oxford: Oxford University Press 2011, pp. 23–40.

Zatloukal, Jan: *L'exil de Jan Čep*, Paris: Institut d'études slaves 2014.

Ziolkowski, Theodore: *Ovid and the moderns*, Ithaca: Cornell University Press 2005.

Zizler, Jiří: *Ivan Diviš. Výstup na horu poezie*, Brno: Host 2013.

Zlín, Karel: *Poesie*, Prague: Torst 1996.

Index